I0887520

REREADING ARISTOTLE'S *RHETORIC*

REREADING ARISTOTLE'S *RHETORIC*

Edited by
Alan G. Gross & Arthur E. Walzer

Southern Illinois University Press
Carbondale

Copyright © 2000 by the Board of Trustees,
Southern Illinois University
Paperback edition 2008
All rights reserved
Printed in the United States of America
11 10 09 08 4 3 2 1

Library of Congress Cataloging-in-Publication Data
Rereading Aristotle's Rhetoric / edited by Alan G. Gross and Arthur E. Walzer.
p. cm.
Includes bibliographical references (p.) and index.
1. Aristotle. Rhetoric. 2. Rhetoric, Ancient. I. Gross, Alan G. II. Walzer, Arthur E., 1944– .
PN173.A7R47 1999
808.5—dc21 99-30460
ISBN 0-8093-2267-6 (cl. : alk. paper) CIP
ISBN-13: 978-0-8093-2847-5 (pbk. : alk. paper)
ISBN-10: 0-8093-2847-X (pbk. : alk. paper)

The paper used in this publication meets the minimum requirements of American National Standard for Information Sciences—Permanence of Paper for Printed Library Materials, ANSI Z39.48-1992. ♾

Alan Gross would like to dedicate his portion of the volume to his three children: Jessica, Joshua, and Sarah.

Arthur Walzer dedicates his portion to his wife, Ginny.

Contents

Preface

Whitehead's observation that the history of philosophy is one long footnote to Plato can for us be transferred to the *Rhetoric:* All subsequent rhetorical theory is but a series of responses to issues raised by that central work. But the link between philosophy and rhetoric represents more than the appropriation of a convenient trope. This volume appears at a time when philosophers are beginning to show a genuine interest in the *Rhetoric.* This attention is both new and welcome. Half a century ago, David Ross saw the *Rhetoric* as "a curious jumble of literary criticism with second-rate logic, ethics, politics, and jurisprudence, mixed with the cunning of one who knows well how the weaknesses of the human heart are to be played upon" (1949, 275). The verdict at century's end could be just as dismissive. In 1995, Jonathan Barnes affirms that "modern philosophy does not greatly occupy itself with rhetoric" and justifies this neglect by affirming that despite all contention to the contrary, rhetoric is not an Aristotelian art (Barnes, 1995a, 259, 264).

Two recent collections within philosophy, one edited by David J. Furley and Alexander Nehamas, the other by Amélie Oksenberg Rorty, are far more sympathetic. But their perspective remains, no doubt appropriately, philosophical. Amélie Rorty describes the motive behind her volume in terms that speak for both collections: "to reclaim the *Rhetoric* as a philosophical work, to analyze its relation to Aristotle's ethics, politics, and poetics; his psychology and logic; his account of practical reasoning; his views on how styles of language affect persuasive arguments" (1996, ix). The essays in both collections reflect this emphasis. For these scholars, the *Rhetoric* is a minor work in the Aristotelian corpus. Though no longer an embarrassment, it is not regarded as particularly significant. Their interest lies largely in showing how the *Rhetoric* illuminates the corpus as a whole. Their method is systematically to interpret the more philosophically oriented passages in the *Rhetoric* in ways that cohere best with Aristotle's philosophy. Doctrines Aristotle advances in the *Rhetoric* are contrasted with those in the *Ethics* and *Politics,* or they are treasured for the light they cast on other works, such as the *Topics.* Where there are inconsistencies between what Aristotle says in the *Rhetoric* and ideas he advances in other treatises (and there are many), these latter works are given priority, and the apparent discrepancies in the *Rhetoric* are explained as resulting from its earlier composition or its having been written for a popular audience.

The perspective of the contributors to *Rereading Aristotle's "Rhetoric,"* for the most part scholars in speech communication, rhetoric, and composition, contrasts markedly with those of the philosophers featured in the other two collections. Our theme is not that the ancient quarrel between philosophy and rhetoric has been renewed but that a healthy division of labor must be assumed: Purely rhetorical issues are genuine and must be explored. For such explorations, the *Rhetoric* is central. Because Aristotle situates his reflection in opposition to Platonic and Sophistic versions of rhetoric, even those who might have preferred a different starting point have tended to frame their views with reference to his positions. There is no comparable situation in any other discipline: No other discipline would claim that a single ancient text so usefully informs current deliberations on practice and theory.

The essays in *Rereading Aristotle's "Rhetoric"* reflect on questions basic to rhetoric as a humanistic discipline while simultaneously interpreting the meaning of its central concepts. Some essays explore how the *Rhetoric* can help us understand the nature of the art. On this issue, the tensions within the *Rhetoric* often provide a direct passageway into our own conflicts. What does it mean to say that rhetoric is generative or epistemic as distinguished from instrumental or managerial? Should we think of rhetoric as the basis for an art of civic deliberation? Within this volume, Miller's exploration on topical invention within the Aristotelian tradition has implications for the first question; Gross's exploration of the meaning of *tekhnê* for the second. What does it mean to say that rhetoric is a contextualized, culturally situated art in contrast with arts such as logic and dialectic that have made more universalistic claims? Walzer's exploration of the special topics and Warnick's comparison of Aristotelian topical system to Perelman and Olbrechts-Tyteca's are informed by this question and contribute to answering it. Other essays show how a rhetorical perspective is distinguished from others. When Walker finds that Aristotle's account of the passions in the *Rhetoric* is not completely compatible with some typical Aristotelian attitudes, his impulse is not to explain away the inconsistency but to reflect on what this distinctive account suggests about rhetoric. In a similar vein, Farrell's probing of the enthymeme does not privilege logic's syllogism; rather, it attempts to understand what "validity" might mean in a rhetorical context. The influence the *Rhetoric*'s treatment of style had on subsequent understandings of rhetoric, the concern of Fahnestock's essay, is, or ought to be, near the center of our disciplinary concerns. This is equally true of John Kirby's essay on metaphor, originally meant for this volume but now readily available (see Literature Cited). As do philosophers, then, we probe the *Rhetoric* to understand our own discipline. Nevertheless our concerns are as distinctive as the disciplines themselves are.

Our commitment to the *Rhetoric* as a document of continuing relevance to our work as teachers and scholars does not imply a consensus on its meaning and use. Our differences may perhaps be best understood by means of Edward Schiappa's distinction between historical reconstruction—the attempt to capture the concepts and details of a work in its own terms—and contemporary appropriation—the attempt to infer contemporary applications (Schiappa, 1990, 193–94). Within this volume, Gaines faces the issue directly, warning us of the dangers of irresponsible appropriation, while Garver's essay demonstrates that even responsible appropriation is problematic. For his part, Green puts the issue into historical perspective by demonstrating how it was contested even in the interpretative practices of the Renaissance.

It is probably true that none of the contributors to this volume would embrace historical reconstruction for its own sake; nor would those interested in extending or applying the *Rhetoric* deny the necessity of grounding their interpretations in Aristotle's words or concepts. This volume, we hope, contributes to the progress of the discipline not by implying an unreasonable consensus but by raising the standards of what constitutes responsible disagreement.

We hope that scholars in philosophy and classics who have an interest in Aristotle will read and review this volume. We think that we have something to say to those two communities of scholars to whom we are, and will remain, heavily indebted. We also hope that our audience will include the rising numbers of scholars in other disciplines—history, philosophy, anthropology, and law, to name a few—who have found a rhetorical perspective useful in their own work. Our primary audiences are, nevertheless, scholars in rhetorical studies, including most prominently scholars in speech communication and composition, two disciplines that together embody a tradition characterized by a concern with rhetorical performance that stretches back unbroken to the Sophists, the first teachers of rhetoric. In these disciplines—two traditions of practice separated in American universities by historical accident rather than by a divergence in fundamental aims—everyone has meditated on the *Rhetoric* in search of a firmer disciplinary identity. Within this tradition, the *Rhetoric* is by consensus the *chef d'oeuvre*, the fountainhead, of such meditations.

Unless otherwise indicated, all quotations from the *Rhetoric* are from *Aristotle on Rhetoric: A Theory of Civic Discourse*, translated by George A. Kennedy (New York and Oxford: Oxford University Press, 1991). Quotations from other Greek and Latin texts are from the Loeb editions unless otherwise noted.

ON BOOK 1
OF THE *RHETORIC*

1

Aristotle's *Rhetoric* and the Contemporary Arts of Practical Discourse

Robert N. Gaines

Although the contemporary reception of Aristotle's *Rhetoric* has been the focus of substantial scholarly attention in Europe and America, there has been little consideration of what is arguably the most significant influence of the work in the twentieth century—namely, its application in the theory, criticism, and pedagogy of the practical arts of discourse. Accordingly, the present essay describes and provisionally assesses the principal ways that contemporary thinkers have used the *Rhetoric* in this connection. Within the essay, special attention is paid to applications of the *Rhetoric* in the disciplines of communication and English composition.

Introduction

The place of Aristotle's *Rhetoric* in twentieth-century thought has recently received treatment in two surveys, Natali (1994) and Leff (1993). Natali surveys European scholarship since 1950, focusing on the relation of Aristotle to "philosophical aspects of the modern revaluation of rhetoric." On Natali's account (367–70), the recent reconsideration of rhetoric originates in the works of Perelman and Gadamer, both of whom see Aristotle as offering a rhetorical mode of practical deliberation, one which may replace the scientific mode of formal reasoning associated with Descartes.[1] But whatever these theorists might share, Natali observes, they differ in their conceptions of rhetorical deliberation, for Perelman understands it as a means of inward reflection and preparation for reasoning to good decision, while Gadamer considers it a form of power and a means of shaping civic conscience (369). Natali argues that much European research on rhetoric after Perelman and Gadamer has developed in response to their views. He points, for instance, to Gadamerian proposals that as a model of practical rationality, rhetoric is essentially democratic (370–71, 377–78).[2] He also discusses positions more consistent with Perelman's stance, where rhetoric is conceived as a generative art that enriches common sense in discovering matters and arguments (371–72).[3] Ultimately, Natali shows how elements of Perelman and Gadamer's Aristotelianism have been turned back upon Aristotle to produce new readings of the *Rhetoric*—especially in relation to ethics and politics (374–75).[4]

Leff locates his study in America, with an emphasis upon scholarship "since the coming of the postmodern revolution." Leff describes contemporary rhetoricians as using Aristotle's *Rhetoric* as a locus of controversy over "different visions of what rhetoric is or should be" (314). Accordingly, he treats positions on three issues that frequently animate the dispute: Aristotle's relation to Plato, truth and ethics in Aristotelian rhetoric, and the status of rhetoric in Aristotle's system of arts. In connection with the first issue, Leff notes that some studies stress the distance of Aristotle's conception of rhetoric from that of Plato, particularly insofar as Aristotle recognizes probability as a legitimate interest of the rhetorician (315).[5] By contrast, other studies emphasize the association of Aristotelian and Platonic rhetoric, this either to aggrandize the *Rhetoric* for its insistence on knowledge and truth[6] or to discredit it for its "metaphysically tainted conception" of the rhetorical art (315–16).[7] As regards the second issue, Leff identifies three positions. One asserts that the relations between Aristotle's conceptions of rhetoric, knowledge, and ethics are "intimate and fundamental," since they exhibit basic consistency,[8] another that they are nonexistent because of Aristotle's very practical outlook on rhetoric,[9] and the last that they are moderate on account of the similarities between Aristotle's descriptions of rhetorical processes and the operation of practical wisdom (315–18).[10] Finally, on the third issue, Leff notes that every possible position on the artistic status of Aristotelian rhetoric is represented in the literature; scholars have argued respectively that rhetoric is a productive art, a theoretical art, a practical art, or some combination (318–23).[11]

These two surveys are extremely valuable, because they plot the latest trajectory of theoretical reaction to the *Rhetoric*. Yet despite their accomplishments, Natali and Leff leave essentially untouched what is arguably the most significant influence of Aristotle's *Rhetoric* in the contemporary era—namely, its application in the theory, criticism, and pedagogy of the practical arts of discourse, especially in the United States.[12] As a first step to remedy this omission, in the present essay I describe and provisionally assess the principal ways in which contemporary thinkers have used the *Rhetoric* in attempts to solve the problems of practical discourse.

In pursuit of these objectives, my discussion will observe certain disciplinary distinctions. As an artifact of the organization of American educational institutions, the arts of discourse have been divided for most of the century into two contingents, one concerned largely with oral discourse and located in departments of communication, the other concerned largely with written discourse and located in departments of English (cf. Berlin, 1990, 183; Murphy, 1982, 3–5). This division has given rise to two discernible traditions of Aristotelian influence; accordingly, in what follows I shall distribute my discussion between these traditions.

Another feature of the discussion will be its focus. Aristotle's *Rhetoric* has been applied to the criticism, pedagogy, and theory of the practical arts of discourse, but this application has not been symmetrical across the disciplines of communication and English. Therefore, while each venue of application will be inspected in both disciplines, the discussion will be shaped by disciplinary developments, ultimately stressing four ways in which Aristotle's *Rhetoric* has actually been used—for critical and theoretical purposes in communication and for pedagogical and theoretical purposes in English. However, in connection with three of the foregoing uses (namely all but critical applications in communication), the corpus of Aristotelian research is too broad to examine in its entirety.[13] Therefore, in treating these uses, the discussion will focus on a representative segment of the corpus, specifically, investigations exploring the value of the enthymeme in practical discourse. There are several considerations that commend this focus. First, enthymeme is the most intensively studied of all Aristotelian subjects among communication and English scholars. Second, enthymeme scholarship has significantly influenced the understanding of practical discourse in both communication and English. Finally, enthymeme studies provide numerous instances of theoretical research in communication and pedagogical as well as theoretical research in English. Accordingly, studies of the enthymeme will figure significantly in much of what follows.

The Speaker's *Rhetoric*

From its beginnings early this century, the discipline of communication has devoted considerable energy to the traditional object of rhetorical education, namely, the production of persuasive speakers; however, as a practical matter, Aristotle's *Rhetoric* has played a relatively minor role in this enterprise.[14] Where Aristotle has been more influential is within two lines of disciplinary scholarship—one concerned with the criticism of the arts of discourse, the other concerned with the advancement of rhetorical theory. In connection with the former, the way in which Aristotle's *Rhetoric* affected the field may be described briefly as follows. During the first quarter of the century, critical discussion of rhetorical discourse was a largely undisciplinized activity—frequently literary in its aims and methods (cf. Stewart, 1973, 2; Arnold, 1959, 3–5). However, in 1925 Wichelns published an essay in which he recommended basic principles for distinctively rhetorical criticism:

> The scheme of a rhetorical study includes the element of the speaker's personality as a conditioning factor; it includes also the public character of the man—not what he was, but what he was thought to be. It requires a description of the speaker's audience, and of the leading ideas with which he plied his hearers—his topics, the motives to which he appealed, the nature of the proofs he offered. . . . Attention must be paid, too, to the relation of the surviving texts to what was actually uttered. . . . Nor can rhetorical criticism omit the speaker's mode of arrangement and his mode of expression, nor his habit of preparation and his manner of delivery from the platform. . . . "Style"—

> in the sense which corresponds to diction and sentence movement—must receive attention. . . . Finally, the effect of the discourse on its immediate hearers is not to be ignored, either in the testimony of witnesses, nor in the record of events. (Wichelns, 1925, 212–13)

Wichelns's recommendations were immediately adopted in criticism of rhetoric.[15] As early as 1927, some critics, recognizing correspondences to Aristotle's *Rhetoric* in Wichelns's principles, cited Aristotle as the authority for their critical approach (see, e.g., Bauer, 1927; Simrell, 1927). By 1934, the approach—now called "Aristotelian"—had become dominant in the discipline,[16] so much so, that it served generally as the paradigm for a comprehensive critical project on American speaking, edited by Brigance in 1943.[17]

"Aristotelian criticism" achieved its ultimate statement in Thonssen and Baird (1948), where conceptions in the *Rhetoric* were characterized as "safe points of departure" for any criticism of rhetorical discourse (15).[18] Still, as early as the mid-1940s, some critics questioned the focus of "Aristotelian criticism" on discourse effects (e.g., Aly, 1946, 254). And during the early 1950s, it became fashionable to scorn the *Rhetoric* as well as "Aristotelian criticism" for lack of straightforward application to contemporary discourse (e.g., Wallace, 1953, 69–74; cf. Parrish, 1954, 11). This turn away from "Aristotelian criticism" was all but completed in Black (1965). Black insisted that—in his terminology—"neo-Aristotelian" criticism ignored "the impact of the discourse on rhetorical conventions" and "the influence of the discourse on its author" (35). He likewise argued that "neo-Aristotelian criticism" ruled out considerations of "an effect of the discourse on the critic" (76) and "the question of what value [the rhetor's] ends themselves possess" (78). Black's critique, along with the works of others in the late 1960s and early 1970s, reduced "neo-Aristotelian criticism" to a minor, "old-fashioned" approach within a broad spectrum of approved critical methods. And although there have been attempts to revive its influence (Hill, 1972; Leff and Mohrmann, 1974; Mohrmann and Leff, 1974), it remains in disrepute.

In assessment of this line of research, the crucial point is that throughout the rise and fall of "Aristotelian criticism," its proponents and opponents did very little that related to Aristotle and his *Rhetoric*. Of course, "Aristotelian critics" often referred to sources of persuasion, parts of rhetoric, and kinds of speeches. But such references were rarely tied to Aristotle's *Rhetoric* and never pursued beyond a superficial level—not even in explications of the "Aristotelian" approach (see, e.g., Baird and Thonssen, 1947, 136–37; Thonssen and Baird, 1948; Parrish, 1954; Hendrix, 1968; cf. Arnold, 1971, 105–6; Black, 1965, 32–33, 91–92). Moreover, opponents of "Aristotelian criticism" frequently quarreled with features that were thoroughly un-Aristotelian in their origin, for example, Wichelns's focus on rhetorical effects. And when opponents did fasten upon a feature with an Aristotelian correlate, for instance, the moral neutrality of rhetoric (*Rhet.* 1.1.13–14; on which, see Wisse, 1989, 72–74), they were generally loath to confront the doctrine in the *Rhetoric*, preferring merely to complain that the approach did not accommodate their critical aims (see, e.g., Black, 1965, 48–49, 78; 1970, 109–13; Campbell, 1972, 451–52, 454).[19] In all, both camps relied on an understanding of the *Rhetoric* so simple and bereft of detail that the theory was reduced to a handlist of terms and Aristotle to an empty authority.

Within the other line of research, namely that concerned with the advancement of rhetorical theory, a different though analogous development of Aristotle's influence may be noted. This much is clear from a look at scholarship that applies Aristotle's enthymeme to the theory of rhetorical argumentation. On account of the historical importance of Aristotle and the place of enthymeme in his *Rhetoric*, the enthymeme was of keen interest to American rhetoricians from the early 1920s onwards (see, e.g., Hunt, 1920; cf. Poster, 1992, 5). However, the first pragmatic study of the enthymeme was probably McBurney (1936).[20] McBurney opposed the standard view of the enthymeme as "truncated syllogism" and argued for its place in Aristotle's general theory of the syllogism (67). At the same time, he argued against the "usual interpretation" that the enthymeme was strictly a logical appeal, this to be contrasted with appeals to the speaker's character and the audience's emotions; in opposition he insisted that for Aristotle, "ethical, pathetical, and logical persuasion will be projected through . . . enthymemes" (64). McBurney's account initiated two strands of thinking.

In one the form of the enthymeme was at issue. McBurney's view was criticized by Bitzer (1959). Bitzer considered McBurney's syllogistic account of enthymeme inadequate because it did not distinguish between dialectical and rhetorical syllogisms (402–4). As a remedy, Bitzer returned to the notion that Aristotle's enthymeme was an "incomplete syllogism," that is, "a syllogism having one or more suppressed premises" wherein "the speaker does not *lay down* his premises but lets his audience supply them" (407). According to Bitzer, a speaker might or might not verbalize all the premises of an enthymeme, but that was "of no logical importance"; what was important was that completion of rhetorical argument required that the audience provide "missing materials" in a kind of "cooperative interaction" with the speaker (407–8). By 1974, McBurney's view was again under fire, this time from Lanigan, who insisted not only that the enthymeme was "an incomplete syllogistic form" (209) but also that "any proposition could be added by a listener to complete the enthymeme of a speaker" (221). Lanigan's conclusions found both support and extension in 1977, when Holmberg argued that for Aristotle "the enthymeme did not clearly reveal the terms of connection of a premise and its supposed logical conclusion" (233); rather, "the grounds of the connections of meaning are left undefined or ambiguous . . . and open for various and equally correct interpretations" (238). This general position was developed in relation to interactional argumentation by Jackson and Jacobs in 1980. Insisting that conversational arguers leave unsupported whatever gets immediate assent, they concluded that enthymemes achieve agreement, "not because the audience 'supplies' the unstated premises for a claim, but because the audience doesn't object to the claim" (262). Working along different lines, Aden described Aristotle's enthymeme as a postmodern argument form. Regarding enthymemes as incomplete insofar as that they lack a part—either observation, generalization, or inference (cf. Harper, 1973)—Aden proposed the suitability of enthymemes for postmodern discourse, because they encourage individual interpretation and their abbreviation facilitates transmission through mediated channels (1994, 55–56).

The second strand of rhetorical thought concerned itself with the sources of persuasion that Aristotle contemplated in connection with enthymemes. McBurney's view that enthymemes embodied logical, ethical, and pathetic appeals was followed without question by Wiley (1956, 21–22), whose chief concern was to elevate enthymeme from its "lowly place" in rhetorical theory and criticism (24; cf. Mudd, 1959). The nature of logical persuasion through enthymemes was also explored by Delia (1970), who argued that the enthymeme should be seen as "the employment of the deductive form in accordance with the operation of the natural rational process of consistency maintenance" (147). Emotional and ethical persuasion through enthymemes were explored by Fisher (1964) and Miller and Bee (1972). Fisher reasoned that since the enthymeme is "a rhetorical form of argument whose function is to convince or persuade," and since to convince or persuade, rhetoric must "address the whole man," it followed that the enthymeme achieves its end, "in part at least, by its appeal to man's emotional commitments" (201). Fisher's account was substantially enlarged by Miller and Bee, who argued as follows: Because the stem of *enthymêma* is *thumos* and *thumos* has as one of its meanings "soul, as shown by the feelings and passions" (201), it follows that "enthymemes inherently involve an affective component that operates from a base of feelings and emotions" (202). But since *êthos* and *pathos* both involve feelings and emotions (210–11), then there is an "inherent involvement of *êthos* and *pathos* with enthymemes" (211). This is where the matter stands at present.

In assessment of the application of Aristotle's enthymeme to advance rhetorical theory of argumentation, perhaps it suffices to say that most of the studies depart in significant ways from doctrines explicit in the *Rhetoric*. As regards the form question, Aristotle nowhere says that coproduction or elision of premises is essential to the enthymeme; rather, he is openly committed to contrary views. Specifically, he seems quite clear on the point that enthymemes always arise as the product of the speaker (cf. Cronkhite, 1966). One indication is his characterization of enthymemes within artistic sources of persuasion; for he says these are "prepared by method and by 'us'" (*Rhet.* 1.2.2, Kennedy, 1991). More explicitly, Aristotle features the speaker's exclusive responsibility for creation of enthymemes at 1.2.8 ("all [speakers] make proofs through 'showing' by expressing either examples or enthymemes"; my translation). Likewise, Aristotle makes perfectly transparent that enthymemes without elision occur. At *Rhetoric* 1.2.13 Aristotle says the enthymeme "[arises] from few [premises], often from fewer [premises] than from which the first form of syllogism [arises]" (my translation). Crucial here is Aristotle's use of the word *often (pollakis)*; for it unambiguously implies there are circumstances in which enthymemes do not arise from fewer premises than pertain to the complete syllogism (see Gaines, 1986, 196–97; Kennedy, 1991, 42; cf. Burnyeat, 1994, 22–23).[21]

In the matter of sources of persuasion, it is quite plausible that Aristotle thought enthymemes could be employed to display the speaker's character or arouse the audience's emotions.[22] However, the persuasive effect of character and emotion—once they are displayed or aroused[23]—is never described by Aristotle as enthymematic; rather, in multiple passages of the *Rhetoric*, Aristotle erects an impenetrable barrier between persuasion through enthymeme and persuasion through character and emotion.[24] This barrier is obvious at the beginning of *Rhetoric*, Book 2. Having summarized the accomplishment of Book 1, namely treatment of the special topics of enthymemes, Aristotle proceeds as follows: "But since rhetoric is for the sake of a judgment . . . , it is necessary not only [for the speaker] to perceive in reference to the speech, how it will be demonstrative and persuasive, but also to represent himself as a certain kind [of person] and to dispose the judge" (2.1.2, my translation; cf. Cope, 1877, 2:2, Kennedy, 1991, 120). In explanation of this comment, Aristotle makes two crucial observations. The first relates chiefly to the disposition of the audience: "For the speaker to seem to have certain qualities is more useful in deliberation; for the audience to be disposed in a certain way [is more useful] in lawsuits; for things do not seem the same to those who are friendly and those who are hostile, nor [the same] to the angry and the calm but either altogether different or different in importance . . ." (2.1.4, Kennedy, 1991). Here Aristotle evidently explains the mechanism by which audience emotion, once aroused, serves as a source of persuasion. Audiences are inclined to different judgments, that is, reason to different conclusions, depending upon what emotions they are experiencing at the moment. But the way that emotions affect audience reasoning is not itself described as a reasoning process; quite the contrary, the emotions are explained simply as mental contexts wherein different arguments seem reasonable. Accordingly, even if Aristotle sees audience emotions as somehow cooperating with enthymemes in securing persuasion, he does not conceive the contribution of emotions as enthymematic.

Aristotle's second observation concerns persuasion through the speaker's character: "There are three reasons why speakers *themselves* are persuasive; for there are three things we trust *other than logical demonstrations*. These are practical wisdom and virtue and good will" (2.1.5, Kennedy, 1991; emphasis added). Here Aristotle evidently distinguishes the speaker's character from enthymemes as a way of securing persuasion. He describes the components of the speaker's character as things on account of which we come to believe but which are "separate from the demonstrations," and within this context, "the demonstrations" to which he refers can only be enthymeme and example (see, e.g., *Rhet.* 1.1.11; 2.20.9; cf. 1.2.8). Accordingly, Aristotle suggests that insofar as the speaker's character serves to persuade, it is to be conceived separately from enthymemes and examples. This suggestion is clinched at 2.1.6; having explained why speakers might be mistaken through their lack of wisdom, virtue, and good will, Aristotle stipulates that "it is necessary that the [one] seeming to possess all these things is trustworthy to his hearers" (my translation). Within this description, Aristotle attributes trustworthiness to the speaker, not to a conclusion derived from some inference about the speaker's qualifications or character (cf. 1.8.6). My point is that once a speaker's character is displayed, the hearers believe what the speaker says simply because the speaker says it (cf. Fortenbaugh, 1992, 210, 226). Therefore, insofar as the speaker's character constitutes a source of persuasion, any explanation of the audience's belief resides in its impression of the speaker, not in an enthymeme. In the end, far from an assumption that all sorts of persuasion are embodied in enthymemes, Aristotle discloses a belief that character, emotion, and enthymeme each relate to persuasion in different ways (cf. Fortenbaugh, 1992, 235–36).

In light of the foregoing, the use of Aristotle in attempts to advance the theory of rhetorical argumentation may be described as follows. All the studies are drawn to enthymeme because Aristotle commends its importance. Nonetheless, most of them exploit their chosen subject merely as the platform to launch a doctrine that is either foreign or antithetical to explicit doctrines in Aristotle's position. Of course, there is nothing inherently wrong in holding views that oppose Aristotle—about enthymemes or anything else. But insofar as argument theorists directly or indirectly attribute such views to Aristotle himself, a problem arises; for they put words in Aristotle's mouth that he would have refused to speak. The result is a misappropriation of Aristotle's authority and, ultimately, the demotion of the *Rhetoric* to a shallow heuristic, devoid of consistency or theoretical force.

The Composer's *Rhetoric*

I now turn to the second tradition of Aristotelian scholarship in the practical arts of discourse, namely that associated with written communication in the English discipline. Although the influence of Aristotle is notable in some literary criticism produced from the 1930s to the 1950s, it was the *Poetics* and not the *Rhetoric* that motivated such study.[25] In fact, within twentieth-century scholarship on written discourse, Aristotle's *Rhetoric* has had a significant impact only on the theory and pedagogy of English composition—and even here its influence is a relatively recent phenomenon. From the turn of the century to about 1950, thinking and teaching about writing was dominated by an approach concerned with the modes of discourse: narration, description, exposition, and argumentation (Kinneavy, 1990, 215; O'Rourke, 1996, 246–47). In relation to this approach, historical rhetoric was relegated to a minor, supporting role (see, e.g., Manchester, Scott, and Thomas, 1918). And despite the efforts of some members of the composition community before 1920 (e.g., Worthington, 1916; Baldwin, 1917; Leonard, 1917), classical rhetoric was not perceived as an important source of principles for writing instruction until the 1960s, when it emerged as the foundation for one of four new conceptual perspectives on composition, namely, the cognitive, expressive, epistemic, and classical (Berlin, 1990, 208–12; cf. Berlin, 1987, 139–79).

The impetus for a revival of classical rhetoric in the composition field may generally be traced to two works, Corbett (1965) and Kinneavy (1971). Within the present context, what is most interesting about these works is the degree to which they took their lead from Aristotle's *Rhetoric*. Corbett's book was intended for composition students and adopted a hearty eclecticism in connection with the classical tradition. Still, within a general framework devoted to the rhetorical canons of invention, arrangement, and style, Corbett aligned his account of invention almost exclusively with Aristotle, treating three modes of persuasion, rational, ethical, and emotional (38–94), and explaining development of appeals with reference to common and special topics (94–142). Further, within his treatment of rational appeals, Corbett was at pains to show that Aristotelian principles informed his notions of syllogism, enthymeme (i.e., "truncated syllogism"), and example (45–70).

Kinneavy's book was more theoretical. It provided an account of four types of discourse—expressive, referential, literary, and persuasive (58–68). Within this scheme, Kinneavy defined persuasive discourse essentially in classical terms, and as the general model for his account, he chose Aristotle's *Rhetoric* (224–25). Following this model, his treatment addressed invention, arrangement, and style. And for each of these theoretical elements, he grounded his discussion in the *Rhetoric*. Accordingly, invention was handled under the rubrics of ethical argument, pathetic argument, and logical argument, with the last including sections on topics, example, and enthymeme or elided syllogism (236–53). Likewise, arrangement was discussed in connection with introduction, narration, argument, and conclusion (263–72), while style was explained with reference to clarity, dignity, appropriateness, and correctness (275–93, esp. 285–93).

Corbett and Kinneavy fostered Aristotelian scholarship in two related lines of inquiry, one dealing with composition pedagogy and the other with composition theory. Following Corbett, one of the earliest pedagogical works to take an Aristotelian approach to composition was Brandt et al. (1969). Conceiving argument as a mode of structuring a composition (14–15, 16–17), the authors defined "adequate" reasoning with reference to the syllogism, posited the enthymeme as an abbreviated syllogism, and ultimately concluded that "a good thesis statement is necessarily a kind of enthymeme" (17–18).[26] By 1980, the theory incipient in this account was developed in some detail by Green. According to Green, enthymemes or rhetorical syllogisms could be conceived as having "local effects" in simple reasoning processes, but they could also be understood to structure an entire discourse (623). Green explained the workings of the structural enthymeme in the following way:

> In a simple argument the writer's main point is the conclusion of the enthymeme, and the rhetorical strategy which the writer adopts to lead to this conclusion is the minor premise, the "because clause." The relation between the writer's conclusion (the thesis) and the writer's basic strategy (the minor premise) is enthymematic in the Aristote-

> lian sense because it always implies the existence of a second premise that joins the two clauses. This second and implicit premise is the major premise of the enthymeme. It is usually elided because the writer (if he or she is conscious of the premise at all) assumes that it is acceptable to the reader, that it is so much a part of a shared communal perception that to mention it would insult the reader's intelligence, advertise the writer's ineptitude, and slow down the discourse. (624)

Green ultimately argued that different sorts of structural enthymemes produced different rhetorical structures and that such differences could be represented in an analysis of "enthymemic predication" related to "four related levels of enthymeme, differentiated by their kinds of verbal force," specifically, the policy, value, consequential, and definitional levels (624–25).

The theory of structural enthymemes developed by Green was quite influential on subsequent attempts to provide compositional precepts for the classroom. For example, in Gage (1983) we find an elaboration on the basic notion.[27] Yet, Gage departed from Green in two major respects; he posited the enthymeme as a truncated syllogism and insisted that the enthymeme operates in ethical and emotional persuasion as well as it does in logical persuasion (38–39). Gage's stance on the enthymeme was adopted without much change in separate pedagogical studies by Hairston (1986) and Jacobi (1987). Although Hairston was concerned largely with the sociology of invention and Jacobi with contemporary epistolography, both developed applications of the enthymeme stressing its architectural features (Hairston, 1986, 64–65, 73–74; Jacobi, 1987 43–44, 49–50) and both assumed, first, that the enthymeme is always abbreviated (Hairston, 1986, 60–61, 64; Jacobi, 1987, 43) and, second, that it incorporates each of Aristotle's three artistic sources of persuasion (Hairston, 1986, 59; Jacobi, 1987, 43). The doctrine of structural enthymemes, having become crystallized in this way, now regularly appears in discussions of composition pedagogy (see, e.g., Emmel, 1994; Bensel-Meyers, 1992; Booth and Gregory, 1991; Gage, 1991b; cf. Gage, 1996; Wu, 1997).

This brings me to the second line of scholarship concerned with the relation of Aristotle's enthymeme to written discourse, namely, studies that have attempted to advance composition theory. Despite the trail blazed by Kinneavy, research in composition theory was still uncommon even a decade after his book was published (Connors, Ede, and Lunsford, 1984, 13). And Aristotelian research was no exception to this general rule. Accordingly, we do not find significant attention to Aristotle's enthymeme in composition theory until Connors, Ede, and Lunsford (1984),[28] where studies by Lunsford and Ede, Gage, and Raymond were published.

Lunsford and Ede discussed the Aristotelian enthymeme as part of a response to modern rhetoricians who disparaged classical rhetoric as rationalistic, overly dependent on logic, unidirectional, and, ultimately, concerned only with persuasion, even at the cost of manipulation or coercion (37–40). Aristotle came up for discussion in this context, because Lunsford and Ede considered his theory an appropriate representative of classical rhetoric. In addition, they argued that many modernist misconceptions grew out of limited readings of the *Rhetoric*, especially where Aristotle's notions of sources of persuasion and enthymeme were at stake (40). Within Lunsford and Ede's response, Aristotle's conception of enthymeme figured in every stage of the argument. Aristotle was not rationalistic or overly dependent upon logic, they insisted, because his three sources of persuasion, *logos*, *êthos*, and *pathos*, were by no means independent in his theory; rather, all three interacted in and were integrated by the enthymeme (along with the example, 42–43). Likewise, Aristotle's rhetoric was neither unidirectional nor bent on persuasion at any cost, this because his theory of enthymemes relied on their joint production by speakers and audiences (44; cf. Brent, 1996, 77).

The aims of Gage's study were quite different; he concerned himself with the relations of rhetoric and knowledge. Nonetheless, his discussion eventually arrived at a characterization of the enthymeme that agreed on main points with Lunsford and Ede. According to Gage, the enthymeme was central in the *Rhetoric* on account of Aristotle's view of knowledge:

> Aristotle sought to analyze the process by which agreement comes about; he did not, therefore, toss aside as mere tricks the techniques advocated by the handbooks, as Plato had done. Rather, he attempted to view these techniques in relation to the causes that account for agreement. To do so, according to his methods of analyzing anything, he needed a term for the final cause of persuasion that would function teleologically in relation to those familiar techniques, viewed as formal causes. He adapted the enthymeme as an architectonic principle, one which embodied the dialectic of rhetorical discourse and allowed the techniques of the handbooks to be ordered according to this end. The enthymeme brings together the dialectical considerations necessitated by the rhetor's search of mutually agreeable grounds for probable knowledge. (156–57)

Consistent with this account, Gage asserted that "the enthymeme cannot be constructed in the absence of a dialectical relation with an audience, since it is only through what the audience contributes that the enthymeme exists as such" (157). Further, given his understanding that Aristotle viewed the enthymeme "as a sort of metonymy for the whole rhetorical activity of discovering a basis for mutual judgment," Gage concluded that in addition to being an element of *logos*, the enthymeme "must embody decisions in the realms of *ethos* and *pathos*" (157, 282 n. 13).[29]

Raymond explicated the enthymeme in relation to example. Regarding the enthymeme, he reviewed several scholarly accounts, then proposed a consensus view. According to this view, the enthymeme represented an attempt to deal with the sorts of issues that are not resolvable by ratiocination or empirical data and with the sorts of audiences who cannot follow complex chains of inference. Moreover, the enthymeme could be conceived as differing from the syllogism in two ways: "The major premise in an enthymeme may be implied rather than expressed because the audience is presumed to know it," and "the major premise in an enthymeme may be unproven (or even unprovable) if the audience believes it" (142). As an adjunct to this general account, Raymond also asserted that examples were enthymematic, insofar as they required the assumption of a general principle (146–47). But for our present purposes, it seems most important to note that in his account of the enthymeme, Raymond differed with Lunsford and Ede as well as Gage in two respects. He did not support the view that enthymemes *per se* require cooperative production between speakers and audiences; neither did he support the view that enthymemes operate outside logical proof.

The basic perspective on the enthymeme taken by Raymond was also represented by Wallace (1986). However, Wallace's principal focus was not on the structure and scope of enthymemes or their relations to examples. Rather, he was concerned with the larger problem of the relation of Aristotle's notion of causes to the practical processes of exposition and persuasion. Within his discussion, Wallace related causes to enthymemes in several ways. Specifically, he pointed out that the Aristotelian materials of enthymemes, probabilities and signs, are constituted in the former case by causes and in the latter case by their correlatives, effects (120–21). He likewise illustrated how Aristotelian topics or places of argument—both particular and common—instantiate causes of one sort or another (119–20, 123). Within this context, Wallace also explained why causes are so intimately related to the form and content of enthymemes. As a logical instrument, he argued, the enthymeme "invariably . . . induces assent through a causal inference" (131).

The sort of stance adopted by Raymond and Wallace was opposed by Walker in 1994. Aiming for a more adequate concept of enthymeme, Walker explored senses of the term prior to Aristotle's use, particularly in Anaximenes and Isocrates. What he derived from these authors was a sophistic, non-Aristotelian notion: "The enthymeme is a strategic, kairotic, argumentational turn that exploits a cluster of emotively charged, value-laden oppositions made available (usually) by an exetastic buildup, in order to generate in its audience a passional identification with or adherence to a particular stance, and that (ideally) will strike the audience as an 'abrupt' and decisive flash of insight" (53). Noting that Aristotle's appropriation of enthymeme must "presuppose" this notion (53) and considering that Aristotle included "pathos and ethos among the enthymematic sources of persuasion" (54), Walker reasoned that "the enthymeme, in sum, shares with the dialectical syllogism an underlying rationality . . . ; but it is also, and distinctively, what Anaximenes and Isocrates describe" (55).

In addition to the foregoing studies, I should also mention theoretical explorations by Quandahl in 1986, Hesse in 1992, and Neel in 1994. All of these studies defended the accessibility of Aristotle's *Rhetoric* to contemporary "readings" and then offered such readings in connection with the enthymeme. Quandahl examined common topics in the *Rhetoric*, concluding that Aristotle saw them as principles that could be introduced into a context "to make useful statements about that context" (132). Based on this conclusion, she inferred that rather than devices for invention, common topics were, for Aristotle, part of a method of interpretation. Combining this inference with the assertion that most of Aristotle's common topics are figures and tropes (133),[30] she arrived at the position that the enthymeme is a form (or instance) of "figured language" and that Aristotle studied topical relations in connection with the enthymeme "not only as a theory of interpretive strategies but as forms of performance and power in specific contexts" (135).

Hesse approached the *Rhetoric* from a narrative perspective. Consistent with this perspective, he conceptualized the movement of a rhetorical audience from its initial state to final judgment as requiring narrative emplotment by the rhetor—"for," he said, "conviction is hardly the product of single arguments isolated in time" (32). Based on this conceptualization, Hesse claimed that in the *Rhetoric*, "a narrative dimension underlies the entire text, even the structure at the very heart . . . , the enthymeme" (34). Hesse's argument for this claim was that "enthymeme shares the same epistemological ground as plot, both depending on the configuration of wholes from parts through causal connection in time. . . . Just as "plot mediates between individual events and a story taken as a whole," configuring heterogeneous factors through a chronological dimension . . . , the enthymeme connects present facts to a prior theoretical ground, enabling a conclusion (34). Working from this formulation, Hesse contended that enthymemes, as narrative elements in argument, "support a 'larger' narrative level" in their roles as events "towards the text's conclusion" (35).

Neel's interpretation of the enthymeme arose as part of a larger argument that Aristotle's *Rhetoric* was "the first full articulation of the metaphysics that degrades rhetoric" (40). Within this argument, Neel asserted that "Aristotle ranks intellectual endeavors according to their foundations and their methods" (53). Therefore, since Aristotle distinguished between demonstration, dialectic, and rhetoric, and since demonstration used necessary truths in syllogisms, while dialectic used opinions in syllogisms, rhetoric—which also used opinions—had necessarily to employ some method other than syllogism. Reasoning thus he concluded: "Of this one claim, . . . I am certain: whatever an enthymeme may be, it *is not* a syllogism" (63). Regrettably, Neel was not at pains to specify the non-syllogistic nature of enthymeme. Still, we may presumably infer his view from the Aristotelian passages he stresses, namely *Rhetoric* 3.18.4 and 2.22.3, wherein Aristotle advises that enthymemes should be compressed as much as possible (64). Accordingly, it would appear to be Neel's interpretation that Aristotle's enthymeme was a compact form of reasoning, perhaps similar to syllogism, but inherently distinct.

Having seen the kinds of studies that have arisen in composition pedagogy and theory on Aristotle's enthymeme, we are now in a position to assess the ways in which they have used the *Rhetoric*. At the outset, it may be observed that most of the studies represent Aristotle's enthymeme as a syllogism that is either truncated or reliant on coproduction by speaker and audience; likewise nearly half of the studies represent the enthymeme as essential to the operation of each of Aristotle's artistic sources of persuasion. Now, I have already argued that such representations conflict with clear passages in the *Rhetoric* and, therefore, misappropriate Aristotle's authority for doctrines alien to his view. Accordingly, I will not reiterate these arguments here. Besides, it might well be proposed that what is most interesting in nearly all of the studies—both pedagogical and theoretical—really has little to do with how they construe the basic form of scope of the enthymeme.

Within the pedagogical studies, for instance, the most important matter to consider is how they use Aristotle's *Rhetoric* to arrive at the structural enthymeme. Crucial in this movement, I would suggest, is that all the studies take as their starting point the following conception: "Aristotle's enthymeme is a deductive argument structure which depends for its persuasive force upon audience agreement with premises that are typically suppressed and frequently probable." Such a conception is certainly consistent with Aristotle's view. But, upon close inspection, it appears equally consistent with other views of practical deduction—not least those recently offered by Toulmin (1958; cf. Fulkerson, 1996, 57, 64) and Perelman and Olbrechts-Tyteca (1958).[31] The upshot is that what makes the enthymeme an especially Aristotelian device for arguing—its formal relation to special and common topics, its material relation to signs, necessary signs, and probabilities, and, more generally, the intellectual apparatus that Aristotle erects around the enthymeme to guide its potential user, all this—is bled out of the "enthymeme" that is the object of elaboration in these studies. Of course, it could be objected that some abstraction and modification of Aristotelian doctrine is necessary to make his theory relevant to the contemporary era. Granted, but surely at some point in the revising of any theory, the revision may be seen to constitute a different theory.[32] And on this ground I would argue that pedagogical applications of Aristotelian enthymeme have superseded the source of their inspiration—this by a process wherein the Aristotelian notion was first reduced to the point that its uniqueness was discarded, then reconceptualized roughly in the image of contemporary argumentation. The outcome of this process, the "structural enthymeme," is a concept of significant pedagogical value, but what is "Aristotelian" about this concept is more nominal than substantial.

In theoretical studies, what seems to be most important is the way in which they derive insights from the *Rhetoric* that are somehow germane to the problem of composition. Lunsford and Ede resort to Aristotle's *Rhetoric*—especially his account of enthymeme—as a kind of bulwark in their defense of classical rhetoric as a possible paradigm for contemporary writing theory. However, in their zeal to promote Aristotle's *Rhetoric*, they distort his views of the enthymeme and thereby undercut the very principle they wished to establish—the utility of Aristotle's thought in the modern era.

Gage's study identifies an architectonic function for enthymeme in Aristotle's general theory of rhetoric. However, as regards this function, there may be a difficulty. Gage apparently argues that the enthymeme is architectonic because it serves as the final cause of persuasion. Now, Aristotle says nothing like this in the *Rhetoric*, and I think there is good reason to believe he would not have said it anywhere else. The reason is that Aristotle held the final cause to be the end for which something else exists or is done (see, e.g., *Phys.* 2.3, 195a23–26; *Meta.* 1.7.5, 988b6–11; 2.2.9, 994b9–16). If Gage were right, then Aristotle's view would be that the enthymeme is the end for which persuasion exists or is done. But this cannot be correct, for in the *Rhetoric*, Aristotle frequently characterizes the situation as quite the other way around—enthymemes lead to persuasion, persuasion does not lead to enthymemes (most decisive is *Rhet.* 1.2.8; see also 1.1.11–12, 1.2.6, 1.2.10–11). Should we call this a misappropriation? I believe so, because Gage obviously claims Aristotelian authority for a position that Aristotle could not have accepted.

Raymond and Wallace both turn to the *Rhetoric* for concepts and principles that are immediately applicable to written composition. Given such an aim, Raymond's account is perhaps the less satisfactory of the two, since he presumes that practical applications of Aristotle's enthymeme will be obvious, provided only that the conception is correctly understood. His account, therefore, explicates the enthymeme with considerable felicity but does not really address the problem of composition. Wallace begins with Aristotle's notion of the enthymeme and uses the Aristotelian causes as a way of conceptualizing the thought processes involved in argument, including strategy formation, thesis analysis, and exploitation of topics. By these means, he operationalizes Aristotelian doctrines in ways that are consistent with the *Rhetoric* as well as the project to which he addresses himself. Accordingly, Wallace provides a good example of how Aristotelian doctrine may be appropriated to the ends of composition theory.

Walker resorts to the enthymeme as a means to understand effective argumentation in the modern era. But in order to account for contemporary (and even unintentional) "enthymeming," he requires a conception of enthymeme that is more robust than "prevailing" interpretations of Aristotle's enthymeme as a logical device. To meet this requirement, he merges Isocratean and Anaximenean notions of enthymeme into a "sophistic conception," then attributes this conception to Aristotle as a necessary component of his enthymematic theory. The result is a worthwhile critical and theoretical heuristic. But it is hardly what Aristotle would have recognized as his personal conception of enthymeme. For one thing, Walker's derived conception is not a single, coherent theory, but three distinct theories. Isocrates' striking thoughts bear no resemblance to Anaximenes' reflections on investigation (cf. Poster, 1992, 12–14; Conley, 1984, 172–74). And Aristotle's conception differs from Anaximenes' in a variety of ways, not least in its logical definition and conceptual classification (cf. Grimaldi, 1972, 75–82). Accordingly, in attempting to give Aristotle's enthymeme more theoretical reach, Walker's account reaches far beyond Aristotle's theory.

Within contemporary readings of the *Rhetoric*, each of our authors attempts to provide a fresh account of the enthymeme that might inform future thinking on the subject. Insofar as these studies aim only to speak to a problem, "the enthymeme," it would be difficult to deny their ingenuity. However, if we are to assess them as disciplinary undertakings to comment on the enthymeme in Aristotle, then it is equally difficult to escape the judgment that they are shot through with misappropriation. Quandahl's "interpretive" reading conflicts with Aristotle's sharp distinction between logical and expressive matters within the *Rhetoric* 2.26.5 and 3.1.1. Moreover, the assertion that discussion of common topics in the *Rhetoric* constitutes for Aristotle a method of interpretation seems inconsistent with his independent development of interpretive theory quite apart from the *Rhetoric* in *Categories* and *On Interpretation.*

Hesse's "narrative" reading conflicts with Aristotle's explanation of enthymeme as apodictic or syllogistic proof. This much seems clear from Aristotle's remarks in the *Rhetoric* and *Prior Analytics*. In the *Rhetoric*, Aristotle represents the persuasive force of the enthymeme as arising from its relation to demonstration and syllogism at 1.1.11. In the *Prior Analytics*, he asserts that demonstrative syllogisms, dialectical syllogisms, rhetorical syllogisms, and even every form of conviction are achieved through the syllogistic figures he has identified earlier in the work (2.23, 68b8–14). He likewise observes that all figures of the syllogism may be reduced to what he has identified as the first figure (*A. Pr.* 1.7, 29b1–25). Now, Aristotle characterizes the first figure in the following way: "When three terms are so related to one another that the last is wholly contained in the middle and the middle is wholly contained or excluded from the first, the extremes must admit of perfect syllogism" (*A. Pr.* 1.4, 25b32–35, Tredennick). This characterization explicates what it is about a syllogism that makes the necessity of its conclusion apparent (*A. Pr.* 1.1, 24b22–26), namely the relations of inclusion and exclusion existing among terms in its constituent premises and conclusion (*A. Pr.* 1.4, 25b35–39; cf. Green, 1995, 28–29). Consequently, Aristotle's conception of the operation of syllogisms depends on apprehension of inclusion/exclusion relations, not on experience of the temporal sequencing. And whether or not we take it that the conclusions of enthymemes follow necessarily from their premises, their operation must certainly depend on the same sort of apprehension.

Finally, Neel's "metaphysical" reading conflicts with Aristotle's explicit statements in the *Rhetoric*, *Prior Analytics*, *Posterior Analytics*, and *Topics* to the effect that the enthymeme is one of several sorts of syllogism. Specifically, Aristotle describes the enthymeme as a syllogism or sort of syllogism at *Rhetoric* 1.1.11, 1.2.8, 1.2.13, 1.3.7–8, 2.21.2, 2.22.2, 2.24.1, *Prior Analytics* 2.27, 70a10–11, and *Posterior Analytics* 1.1, 71a10–11. Likewise, he conceives the enthymeme as rhetorical syllogism alongside dialectical and demonstrative syllogisms at *Prior Analytics* 2.23, 68b9–14 and *Posterior Analytics* 1.1, 71a9–11.[33]

Conclusion

To the extent that the studies discussed above are representative, I believe that two conclusions may be drawn about the use of Aristotle's *Rhetoric* in the contemporary arts of practical discourse. One is that much of the scholarship that purports to be Aristotelian either obscures Aristotle's thought, by reducing it to an unrecognizable abstraction, or subverts it, by misappropriating Aristotle's authority for conceptions that are alien to his view (cf. Leff, 1993, 324; Natali, 1994, 378–82). For example, we have seen that critical studies in communication and pedagogical studies in English composition generally rely on reductions of Aristotelian theory as the foundation for their positions. Likewise, we have observed that theoretical studies in both fields typically depend upon misappropriations of Aristotelian authority to justify or aggrandize the stances they assume in regard to discoursive practice.

The other conclusion is that contemporary scholarship in the discoursive arts would appear to exploit Aristotle more for the "brute force" of his disciplinary authority than for the cogency of his contributions to the disciplinary corpus. Certainly, rhetorical critics thought there was a benefit to be gained from styling themselves "Aristotelians" as opposed to "Wichelnsians." And it is hardly to be doubted that a similar motivation is behind identification of Aristotle as a source for the structural enthymeme, when other sources would do just as well (and perhaps better). But the tendency to which I refer is most obvious in theoretical studies. In both the communication and English fields we find theoretical research that attempts to justify modern and postmodern predilections by appeal to Aristotelian "certification." It is precisely for this reason that within such research Aristotle becomes an unlikely participant in a wide range of positions—logical subjectivism, post-faculty psychology, and narratology, just to name a few. In fact, so great is the pressure to secure Aristotelian approval for contemporary theory, that the *Rhetoric* has even been described as containing the principal elements of modern rhetoric in its entirety.[34]

To my mind, all this suggests that despite the towering presence of Aristotle's *Rhetoric* in the contemporary era, the actual import of this work for the criticism, theory, and pedagogy of the discoursive arts has by no means been determined. Presuming that such a determination would be valuable, whatever its outcome, I would like to close with some tentative suggestions about how this might be done. In general what I believe is required is a fresh return to the text of the *Rhetoric*. Of the many problems that surround interpretation of Aristotle's *Rhetoric* in the twentieth century, perhaps the most pernicious are the artificial expectations that readers bring to the work about the talents and motives of the author and the meanings and implications of the text. If the *Rhetoric* is to be understood at all, I propose, readers must approach the text with enough openness to permit their independent estimations of its meaning, significance, and utility.

In arriving at such estimations, I believe, readers have recourse to a pair of interpretive approaches. On the one side, readers may attempt to ascertain and apply Aristotle's rhetorical theory as expressed in the *Rhetoric*. The object here is to understand and evaluate the meanings intended by Aristotle in composing the treatise.[35] Within this enterprise, readers should certainly consider that the *Rhetoric* is a work of the fourth century B.C.E., with doctrinal relations to the rest of Aristotle's works and contextual relations to the intellectual, social, political, and cultural forces of the day. But it is equally important, I think, to recognize that even Aristotle knew his *Rhetoric* would need some adaptation, if it was applied outside the narrow context for which it was especially designed (see, e.g., *Rhet.* 1.9.26, 1.9.30). Thus, while the *Rhetoric* is a work rich in connections that illuminate its contents, it is also a work that is meant to stand on its own as a practical—and flexible—guide for discoursive conduct. Accordingly, for readers who elect this approach, the task is to confront the *Rhetoric* as a specific disciplinary proposal, to cooperate with Aristotle's assumption that contextual particulars will be supplied, and ultimately to judge what seems useful and what does not.

On the other side, readers may attempt to comprehend and apply rhetorical theory that is accessible in Aristotle's *Rhetoric*. The object here is for the historically situated reader to understand the significance of the *Rhetoric*.[36] Consistent with this object, readers begin with the realization that, like any other text, the *Rhetoric* is subject to a multitude of legitimate interpretations. The reader then encounters the work, conceiving it as a reply to a question of relevance to the reader's time, place, and experiences. Ultimately, through a process that poses further questions and requires an openness to the responses provided, the reader arrives at an understanding of the significance of the work for the reader's situation. Thus, for the reader adopting this approach, the task is to understand how the *Rhetoric* responds to contemporary problems of practical discourse and to decide whether these responses are adequate or not.

Now, in proposing these approaches as alternatives, I do not mean to suggest that readers have the further choice of combining them. The sorts of claims that readers can make in virtue of the two approaches are quite different. Within the first approach, readers are trying to find out about Aristotle's rhetorical theory and interpret the *Rhetoric* as the linguistic expression of Aristotle's intended meanings about that subject. Such readers are bound to represent their findings as reports of Aristotle's views, this because, insofar as they are successful, the content of their understanding is simply what Aristotle meant. Within the second approach, things are quite different. Here readers are trying to find out about rhetorical theory and treat the *Rhetoric* simply as a work about rhetoric that is subject to individual interpretation (and with regard to which Aristotle would have no privileged access). These readers are bound not to represent their results as reports of Aristotle's views; for insofar as they are successful, their interpretations necessarily contain assumptions and implications relevant to their individual situations. When the approaches are combined, readers assign nondistinctive or personal views to the historical Aristotle. This is a serious mistake, and throughout this essay I have characterized instances of this mistake as reductions of Aristotle's views or misappropriations of his authority. Kept separate and distinct, each approach seems capable of uncovering practical uses of Aristotle's work. And it is only through a cumulation of readings performed in both approaches that we shall be placed in a good position to decide whether and how much the contemporary arts of discourse should be guided by Aristotle and his *Rhetoric*.

Notes

The author gratefully acknowledges many valuable comments on this essay by Jakob Wisse. Of course, deficiencies that remain are the author's responsibility. The essay represents research funded in part by an award from the General Research Board of the Graduate School, University of Maryland, College Park.

1. See Perelman and Olbrechts-Tyteca (1950; 1958) and Gadamer (1960; 1967).

2. See, for example, Berti (1984), Raimondi (1984), Vattimo (1984), Fenocchio (1986), and Mayer (1991).

3. See Eco (1986), Plebe (1988), and Barilli (1986).

4. See, for example, Papadimitriou (1979), Lossau (1981), and Wörner (1990).

5. See Hunt (1920), Kinneavy (1984), and Gage (1984).

6. See Grimaldi (1972).

7. See White (1987), Poulakos (1984), Vitanza (1987), and Sutton (1986; 1991).

8. See Baldwin (1928), Thonssen and Baird (1948), Arnhart (1981), and Grimaldi (1978).

9. See Hunt (1920), Olian (1968), and Hill (1972).

10. See Self (1979), Johnstone (1980), Beiner (1983), and Garver (1986; 1988; 1989b; 1990a).

11. Productive art, Warnick (1989) and Atwill (1992); theoretical art, Kennedy (1980); practical art, Garver (1990a); and combination, McKeon (1965; 1971).

12. Natali focuses generally on research *in Europe*; Leff focuses narrowly on *intellectual reception* in the United States.

13. See, for example, the bibliography in Neel (1994).

14. At the turn of the century, belletrism informed public speaking theories; but during 1915–1930, belletrism was replaced by psychology (Arnold, 1959, 3–4; Gray, 1954, 433–40; Carrino, 1959). As early as 1920, social analysis of speaking was merged with the psychological approach (see, e.g., Woolbert, 1920). By the 1930s, this merger became entrenched (see, e.g., Monroe, 1935; Weaver, 1942; cf. Wallace, 1954) and still dominates public speaking instruction (see, e.g., Braden, 1961; Borchers, 1967; and Miletich, 1981).

15. On Wichelns's influence, see, for example, Bryant (1958, 5; 1973, 27–29); Arnold (1959, 5); Stewart (1973, 3–6).

16. See, for example, Hudson (1929), Berry (1931), Bryant (1933), King (1933), Brigance (1933), and Hunt (1934).

17. See Brigance (1943, 1:x); cf. Black (1965, 27–28).

18. Cf. Baird and Thonssen (1947).

19. Campbell (1972) does at least refer to passages in the *Rhetoric* in her attack on Hill (1972); however, her point is not to critique Aristotelian doctrine but to argue that Aristotle supports evaluations of speaker morality and absolute truth in rhetorical criticism.

20. McBurney's research rationale is explicitly practical (see 50–51).

21. Compare *Prior Analytics* 2.27, 70a10–28 (on which, see Aristotle, 1965, 500; Burnyeat, 1994, 32).

22. Wisse (1989, 20–28) considers the various possible relations of enthymemes to persuasion through the speaker's character and the audience's emotions. He rejects views that ethos and pathos are separate but enthymematic (as in Barwick, 1922; cf. Conley, 1982; Wörner, 1981) and that enthymeme incorporates ethos and pathos (as in McBurney, 1936; Grimaldi, 1972, 1980a; and Lienhard, 1966), and generally following Braet (1988; 1992), he takes the view that "ethos and pathos may be expressed by enthymemes, but also by other means" (21).

23. Cf. Brinton (1988, 211; 1986, 246–47).

24. Braet (1988; 1992) and Wisse (1989) discuss how the audience comes to have a conception of the speaker's character and experience emotions; neither addresses the independent problem of how speaker's character and audience emotion operate to influence the audience's judgment.

25. The "Chicago Aristotelians" posited Aristotle's *Poetics* as the paradigm for criticism (see Wellek, 1986, 63–68).

26. The original application of the enthymeme to composition pedagogy preceded Brandt et al. (1969) and even Corbett (1965); see, for example, Hughes and Duhamel (1962, 235).

27. Gage describes this article (1983) as supplementing his earlier comments on the structural enthymeme (1982a; 1982b).

28. To illustrate, Hood (1984)—a bibliography of enthymeme research—contains only one representative of composition theory on enthymeme prior to 1984, specifically, Gage (1982a).

29. The themes developed in Gage (1984) are also addressed in Gage (1991a).

30. This reproduces elements of Conley (1984) (on which, see Schenkeveld, 1994, 5–6).

31. That Perelman and Olbrechts-Tyteca's theory of argument is influenced by Aristotle is a complication here, but the fact is that their theory of argumentation proceeds as a development of contemporary logic, not Aristotelian syllogistic (1958, 1:13).

32. That the structural enthymeme is not *strictly* Aristotelian was recognized by Green (1995, 20–21 n. 5) and entertained by Gage (1996, 8, 16).

33. Much the same arguments apply to Burnyeat's proposal that for Aristotle, the enthymeme is not "a kind of syllogism" (1994, 30; 1996, 105) but a "concept of degenerate deduction" (1994, 18; 1996, 99). However, it should be noted that Burnyeat's position turns on a very limited application of the term *syllogism* in Aristotle's thought (cf. Barnes, 1981).

34. See Lunsford and Ede (1984a, 91–97; 1984b, 44–49).

35. I refer to philological hermeneutic. For foundations, see, for example,

Schleiermacher (1977 [1838]) and Boeckh (1886). Recent defenders include Betti (1954; 1955; 1962), Hirsch (1967; 1976), and, indirectly, Searle (1969; 1983).

36. I refer to phenomenological hermeneutic. For foundations, see, for example, Heidegger (1927). Contemporary adherents include Gadamer (1960; 1967) and Ricoeur (1969; 1981).

2

What Aristotle Meant by Rhetoric

Alan G. Gross

What did Aristotle mean by rhetoric? If we want to find out what Aristotle meant, we need to establish the meaning of his key words by searching out their use in every Aristotelian context, by looking for commonalities in use, and by making linkages with the use of other key words in reciprocating networks of interaction. When we do so in the case of rhetoric, we find that it is a productive art, and only a productive art. Rhetoric is, in Aristotle's scheme of things, a narrowly circumscribed set of skills. These are easily abused; however, when they are well used, they serve the best interest of the city-state and its citizens. This thesis is not new: The credit for originality is entirely Barbara Warnick's. It is true that in his insightful review article, Michael Leff finds Warnick's thesis unconvincing in the face of strongly argued alternatives: Johnstone's case that rhetoric is a practical art, Kennedy's that it is theoretical, and Garver's that it combines practice and production. Still, Leff does not despair of the claim. He comments acutely that it is "possible that Aristotle's conception of productive art was sufficiently elastic to include the *Rhetoric*." In this essay, I have tried to strengthen Warnick's thesis. I hope that this additional evidential muscle will overcome Leff's objections.

> Whoever builds a house or a ship or forges a sacrificial chalice reveals what is to be brought forth, according to the perspectives of the four modes of occasioning *[aitia]*. This revealing gathers together in advance the aspect *[eidos]* and the matter *[hulê]* of a ship or house, with a view to the finished thing envisioned as completed, and from this gathering determines the manner of its construction.
>
> —Heidegger, "The Question Concerning Technology"

Studies of ancient rhetoric have benefited greatly from a renewed interest in the Greek text on the part of such speech communication and composition theory scholars as Robert Gaines, Michael Leff, Edward Schiappa, David Timmerman, Barbara Warnick, and Kathleen Welch. This continuing activity has been motivated by a concern for differentiating between "historical reconstruction" and "contemporary appropriation." A scholar interested in the first "attempts to understand the contributions of past theorists . . . to understand the cultural context in which these theories originally appear"; a scholar interested in the second "attempts to utilize the insights of past theorists . . . in order to inform current theory" (Schiappa, 1994, xi). Though these two activities are distinct and equally useful, historical reconstruction is logically prior: to know that we are deviating from past theorists, and in what ways, we must know what those theorists intended.

Without for a moment dismissing postmodernist doubts concerning the recovery of authorial intent, and without neglecting its essential contestability after recovery in a particular case, we must insist on the worth, indeed, the necessity of such historical projects. The just criticisms of Derrida and Foucault notwithstanding, we may still, I think, regard the attempt to reconstruct the original meaning of the *Rhetoric* as legitimate, a project that, moreover, conforms to the routine practice of these authors. In his well-known debate with Searle, for example, Derrida criticizes Austin, as he must, by reconstructing the intent of *How to Do Things with Words*, and Foucault is constantly in the business of the historical reconstruction of intent. The historical reconstruction of intent, then, is the foundation on which sound contemporary appropriations must be built.

Criticism of past practice in this area has sometimes been harsh. According to Robert Gaines (unpublished) and Michael Leff (1993) a half century of scholarship on the *Rhetoric* in speech communication and in composition theory constitutes a virtual museum of misappropriations. In Gaines's view, "throughout the rise and fall of 'Aristotelian criticism,' its proponents and opponents did very little that related to Aristotle and his *Rhetoric*." What references there were, "were rarely tied to Aristotle's *Rhetoric* and *never* pursued beyond the superficial level" (5). In the specific case of the enthymeme, "all of the studies are drawn to [it] because the authority of Aristotle commends its importance. Nonetheless, most of them exploit their chosen subject merely as a platform to launch a doctrine that is either foreign or antithetical to Aristotle's view" (9). Leff is more forgiving of studies of specific aspects of the *Rhetoric*, but agrees with Gaines's general condemnation: "Interpretation of Aristotle . . . functions as a vehicle for articulating different visions of what rhetoric is or should be" (314); in his conclusion, Leff asserts that "anyone who works through this literature and its conflicting pronouncements might well conclude . . . that the *Rhetoric* is like tofu: something [that] turns out to be completely different in each recipe" (324).

Such sweeping condemnations are, perhaps, excessive. It is important to recognize, I think, that readers of Aristotle can deviate from his text in at least two ways. At worst, of course, they can be mistaken. In an article comparing modern to ancient rhetoric, composition theorists Lunsford and Ede are mistaken when they assert that Aristotle identifies two forms of knowledge, *epistêmê* and *doxa* (1984b, 46–47); publishing in the same collection, Gage is mistaken when he asserts that "Aristotle was . . . motivated to describe an art of rhetoric which made knowledge its object" (1984, 154). In making these statements, these authors are relying not on Aristotle, whom they do not consult, but on Grimaldi. In a lengthy footnote, the usually scrupulous Grimaldi cites a passage from the *Posterior Ana-*

lytics in which, he asserts, the philosopher calls *doxa* a form of knowledge (88b–89b; Grimaldi, 1972, nn. 22–23); in fact the passage is a careful exposition of Aristotle's considered and opposing view. In this case Grimaldi is mistaken.

On the other hand, scholars can engage in useful contemporary appropriation with, perhaps, an insufficiently rigorous sense of its distinction from historical reconstruction. In an influential article, Lloyd Bitzer states his bold conclusion: "that enthymemes occur only when a speaker and audience jointly produce them. Because they are jointly produced, enthymemes intimately unite speaker and audience and provide the strongest possible proofs. The aim of rhetorical discourse is persuasion; since rhetorical arguments, or enthymemes, are formed out of premises supplied by the audience, they have the virtue of being self-persuasive. Owing to the skill of the speaker, *the audience itself helps construct the proofs by which it is persuaded*" (1959; Erickson, 1974, 151; Bitzer's emphasis).

In his fine book on the role of rhetoric in contemporary political life, Thomas Farrell accepts but modifies this claim: "My only qualification of Bitzer's analysis is a suggestion that the convictions of the audience *about attributable qualities of virtue* (as dynamis) are not always fully formed as premises in advance of their enactment within an enthymeme. When they are indexed in time through the volition of common assent, the utterance gives them a new facticity" (1993, 76).

There is a single overriding problem with this subtle chain of inference, a chain that begins, purportedly, with Aristotle's text: There is in that text not a scintilla of support for either Bitzer's thesis or Farrell's modification. These scholars are mistaken, but they are not just mistaken; Bitzer's and Farrell's remarks are also *interesting*. They are not interpreting Aristotle; they are developing their own theories within an Aristotelian framework; they are engaged in useful contemporary appropriation. It is unfortunate, however, that they do not so label their contribution.

One would hope that commentators on ancient Greek rhetoric would develop a firmer sense of the differences between Aristotle and themselves. They do say they possess such a sense. Lunsford and Ede say that "one of the most essential characteristics of Aristotle's philosophical system is its integration" (1984b, 40), and they castigate what they take to be misinterpretation as "symptomatic of the misunderstandings that can occur when commentators ignore the fundamental connections among Aristotle's writings" (41). Bitzer is meticulous in his destructive criticism of other scholars' mistaken views of the enthymeme. But Lunsford and Ede deviate from their principles in their constructive arguments, as does Bitzer in his.

Such errors can be avoided only by a hermeneutics of self-restraint, one that insists to the point of pedantry on the primacy of Aristotle's key words, Greek words central to Aristotle's philosophical system. To define what Aristotle meant by his key word *rhetoric* is to understand its sense (equivalent to its dictionary meaning), its range of reference, and, finally, its speech-act force, the "exact range of attitudes the term can standardly be used to express" (Skinner, 1988, 121–122; see also Welch, 1990, 73). In this endeavor, the *Rhetoric* offers us only limited help;

therefore we must, it seems to me, by indirection find direction out; we must start from the Aristotelian corpus as a whole and work inward, hoping that this circuitous and extended journey will provide us with the constraints we need to capture the meaning we are after. In following this path, I focus initially not on rhetoric itself but on a class of activities of which rhetoric is a member, the *technai*. Because Aristotle repeatedly identifies rhetoric as a *technê*, a key word he uses widely in his works, through its elucidation I hope to complete an intellectual task that he has left incomplete: to define rhetoric. To do so will involve me initially in the explicit articulation of two sets of relationships: those that constitute *technê* as an Aristotelian way to truth, and those that constitute *technê* as a human potential and activity, linked to the more encompassing networks of deliberation, decision, and action that constitute the Greek city-state.

What *Technê* Is

To define anything is, for Aristotle, to specify its *aitia:* "the conditions necessary but not separately sufficient to account for the existence of a thing" (Ross, 1949, 73; *Phys.* 198a). They are four in number: the *hulê* or material cause, the *hothen* ('from which') or efficient cause, the *eidos* or formal cause, and the *hou heneka* ('for the sake of which') or final cause. To define *technê*, therefore, is to specify its four "causes."

What is the *hulê* of the *technai*? For Aristotle *hulê* can be what it is for us, matter perceived by the senses. But Aristotle also recognizes a form of matter other than sensible; the objects of mathematics are, for him, also *hulê*, *intelligible* matter (*Meta.* 1036a). Aristotle means this literally: Just as craftsmen are supplied with suitable *hulê*, so are statesmen. Aristotle mentions population and territory as *hulê* of the art of politics (*Pol.* 1325b).

Accordingly, the *technai* may be classified by *hulê* as follows:

> a. *those having a product composed of sensible matter:* carpentry and clay modeling, flute-making, ship-building, costume-making, shoe-making, building, cookery, perfumery, tailoring, and weaving are *technê* in this sense.
>
> b. *those having a product composed of states of sensible matter:* architecture, dancing, flute and harp playing, any kind of music making, painting, gymnastics, medicine, strategy, navigation, athletic training, training choruses, statecraft, acquiring the goods necessary to a good life, and running a household are *technai* in this sense.
>
> c. *those having a product composed of intelligible matter:* soothsaying, poetry, play writing, rhetoric, the verbal arts generally, grammar, dialectic, arithmetic, geometry, and surveying are *technai* in this sense.

These categories are sufficiently definitional to be easily extended; for example, we can add printing to the category of *hulê* proper, physical therapy to the category of states of affairs of *hulê* and novel to the category in which *hulê* consists of intelligible matter.

To complete a definition of *technê* by *aitia*, we must also specify its *eidos*, its *hou hothen*, and its *heneka*. The *eidos* of a *technê* is the essential form of its products. As with *epistêmê*, the essence of *technê*, its *to ti ên einai*, is a potency resident in the *psuchê*; but only in the case of the *technai* is this potency the equivalent of *eidos*, the essential form that, when combined with matter, just *is* a product (*Meta.* 1044a; 1043a; see also *GA* 734b). In a real sense, then, the *technê is* the *eidos:* "the art is the form" (*Meta.* 1034a); for the artisan in bronze, for example, *eidos* or essential sphericity is actualized in the production of a particular object, a particular bronze sphere (1033b1).[1]

All *technai* must also have a *hothen* and a *hou heneka*. The *hothen* or efficient cause is easily grasped because it is closest to our notion of cause. It consists of "the principles of change in another thing, or in the artist himself *qua* other" (*Meta.* 1046b). It is "the source of the first beginning of change or rest; *e.g.* the man who plans is a cause, and the father is the cause of the child, and in general that which produces is the cause of that which is produced" (*Meta.* 1013a; see also 996b and 1033a).The most problematic of the *aitia* is the *hou heneka* or final cause, puzzling because of its relationship to two sibling key words, *ergon* and *telos*. All three terms direct us to what a *technê* is *for*; all three are therefore examples of a final cause *(hou heneka)*, but of progressively more inclusive scope. In one of its senses, *ergon*, the scope seems narrowest. This is the sense in which "the *ergon* of a harper is to play the harp" (*NE* 1098a). In the *Topics*, Aristotle is more expansive on this point: "We shall possess the method completely when we are in a position similar to that in which we are in regard to rhetoric and medicine and other such faculties; that is to say, when we carry out our purpose with every available means. For neither will the rhetorician seek to persuade nor the physician to heal by every expedient; but if he omits none of the available means, we shall say that he possesses the science to an adequate degree" (101b).[2]

In the *Eudemian Ethics*, Aristotle makes a more inclusive sense of *ergon* explicit: "For some things have an *ergon* that is different from the employment of them, for instance the work of architecture is a house, not the act of building, that of medicine health, not the process of healing or curing" (1219a). It is this more inclusive sense of *ergon* that is identified with a product indexed for excellence: "If there is such a thing as shoemaking goodness *(aretê skutikê)* and a good shoemaker, their *ergon* is a good shoe; and in the same way in the case of other arts also" (*EE* 1219a). The products of the arts of intelligible matter may be derived by analogy: The work of a good physical therapist is a client free from pain; the work of a good novelist is a prize-winning novel.[3]

Aristotle recognizes an even broader sense of purpose, that of *telos*, in effect the final final cause. *Telos* is at the top of an ascending hierarchy in which each superordinate *technê* includes subordinate others: "Bridle making and the other trades concerned with horses' harness are subordinate to horsemanship, and this and every other military pursuit to the science of strategy, and similarly other arts to different arts again—in all these cases, I say, the *telê* of the master arts are things more to be desired than those of the arts subordinate to them; since the latter ends are only pursued for the sake of the former (*NE* 1094a; see also *Phys.* 194b). At the top of this ascending hierarchy, Aristotle places the political faculty *(politikê dunamis):* "the most authoritative of all" (*Pol.* 1282b).

How *Technê* Works

To study how the *technai* work is to study two psychological processes: their acquisition as *dunameis* in the *psuchê* and their actualization in the world. All of the *technai* can be acquired on the basis of experience. Acquisition on this basis follows an inductive and intuitive path from the particulars of sensation to the universals of experience: "Sense-perception gives rise to memory . . . and repeated memories of the same thing give rise to experience; because the memories, though numerically many, constitute a single experience. And experience, that is the universal when established as a whole in the soul . . . provides the starting-point [or *archê*] of art and science: art in the world of process and science in the world of facts" (*A. Pst.* 100a; see also *A. Pr.* 46a). To these three stages—sense-perception, experience, and the universals of experience—a fourth must be added. Propositional knowledge must be the final stage if sense perception is to be transformed into the *technê* of the master craftsman or the teacher: "Art is produced when from many notions of experience a single universal judgment is formed with regard to like objects" (*Meta.* 980b).[4]

Although the arts can be acquired on the basis of experience, (the way of the ordinary artisan and, of course, of the first artisan), whatever can be formulated as a set of principles can be learned through study and practice (*Meta.* 1047b; 1046b). For the master craftsman and the master teacher, therefore, though not for the ordinary artisan, the *eidos* is also the *archê*, the essential form is also a starting point from which appropriate products are, in a sense, deduced. While the starting points of the theoretical sciences are their postulates, "in the productive sciences the End is the starting-point and [postulate] *(poiêtikais to telos archê kai hupothesis)*; [for example,] since it is required that so-and-so be in good health, if that is to be secured it is necessary for such-and-such a thing to be provided—just as in mathematics, if the angles of a triangle are together equal to two right angles, such-and-such a consequence necessarily follows" (*EE* 1227b).[5]

For the master craftsman, *technê* is an intellectual virtue that consists of a set of *archai* from which deductive reasoning may be initiated (*A. Pr.* 46a; *Meta.* 1.1; *NE* 1139b). For the master teacher these same *archai* consist of a set of principles to be taught; students can master the *technê* in question through cycles of study and practice that produce progressively more competent actualization. This is what Aristotle means when he says: "He who learns to play the harp learns by playing it" (*Meta.* 1049b; see also 981a; 1047b). It is by actualizing these potencies and forming these habits that artisans function, respectively, as master craftsmen and master teachers: "superior in wisdom, not because they can do things, but because they possess a theory and know its causes *(to logon hexein autous kai tas aitias gnôrizein)*" (*Meta.* 981b).

Whether achieved by experience or by learning, the *technai* are all *dunameis* resident in the *psuchê* as "principles of change in another thing or in the artist himself *qua* other" (*Meta.* 1046b). But these *technai* are also *hexeis, trained* potencies: "A thing is 'potent' in virtue of having a certain 'habit' *(hexin)*" (1019b). These habits are "lasting and stable. Comprised among [them] are . . . all kinds of knowledge. For knowledge is considered as lasting and hard to displace from the mind . . . [becoming] second nature through long lapse of time" (*Cat.* 8b).

In the *Generation of Animals*, Aristotle provides us with his best description of the actualization of a *technê*, of a *dunamis* that is also a *hexis:*

> Nothing passes from the carpenter into the pieces of timber, which are [his] material, and there is no part of the art of carpentry present in the object which is being fashioned: it is the shape and the form *(morphê kai to eidos)* which pass from the carpenter, and they come into being by means of the movement into the material *(kinêseôs en tê hulê)*. It is his soul, *(psuchê)*, wherein is the 'form' *(eidos)* and his knowledge *(epistêmê)*, which causes his hands (or some other part of his body) to move in a particular way (different ways for different products and always the same for any one product); his hands move his tools *(organa)* and his tools move the material (730b; see also *Meta.* 9.9; 1066a).[6]

In this actualization we have a shift from cogitation *(noêsis)* to production *(poiêsis):* "That which proceeds from the starting-point and the form *(archês kai tou eidous)* is cogitation, and that which proceeds from the conclusion of the cogitation is production" (*Meta.* 1032b). When this process is completed, we have, through the exercise of an *energeia*, a product: for example, a house.

It is a consequence of the essence of the *technai* that they deal directly only with classes, not with individuals. For example, it is the business of the art of medicine "to judge . . . all persons of a certain type, considered as a class, who suffer from this or that disease" (*Meta.* 981a). As a result, in practicing the art of medicine, Hippocrates does not cure Callias or Socrates *qua* individual, ill with burning fever; rather, the *technê* of medicine accidentally *[sumbebêkos]* resident in Hippocrates enables him to cure Callias or Socrates as one of a *class* of human beings ill as a consequence of the *class* of illness known as burning fever. Nevertheless, "effects produced all concern the particular. For it is not the man that the physician cures, except *sumbebêkos* but Callias or Socrates or some person similarly named, who is [accidentally] a man as well" (*Meta.* 981a; see also *Meta.* 1033a).

In the actualization of a *technê*, no deliberation is involved directly: "Art . . . does not deliberate" (*Phys.* 199b; see also *NE* 1140a). Without deliberation, a drug may be properly prescribed, or camp correctly pitched. But it also may happen that art alone is unequal to the demands of a particular situation. As a consequence, practitioners of a *technê* may question "at one moment what tools to use, and at another how to use them; and similarly in the other spheres, we have to consider sometimes what means to employ, and sometimes how exactly any given means are to be employed" (*NE* 1112b). Under these circumstances, "the doctor may deliberate whether he shall give a drug, and a general where he shall pitch his camp" (*EE* 1227a). If they do so, however, they must reason not by the light of *technê* but of *phronêsis*. Although *technê* and *phronêsis* are alike in that they both deal with things that admit of variation (*NE* 1141a), only *phronêsis* is "a truth-attaining rational quality, concerned with action in relation to things that are good or bad for human beings"; only *phronêsis* allows us to recognize *to kath' hekasta,* particulars as particulars, individuals as individuals, the elements of deliberation (*NE* 1141b; 1142a).

As a typical practitioner of an art, the physician will deliberate by means of a practical syllogism, itself an actualization of *phronêsis*. The physician will argue that "since health is so-and-so, if the subject is to be healthy, it must have such-and-such a quality, *e.g.* homogeneity; and if so it must have heat. And the physician will continue reasoning until he arrives at what he himself finally can do *(kinêsis poiêsis)*; then the process from this point onwards, *i.e.* the process toward health, is called 'production'" (*Meta.* 1032b). Having arrived at a possible means to a desirable end, the physician will stop deliberating and treat the patient with heat. He has reached the conclusion of his practical syllogism, an action. Action, however, is not a necessary consequence of deliberation for "the mark of practical reasoning . . . is not that it culminates in action, but that in the same sense in which theoretical reasoning seeks to pass from the true to the true, practical reasoning seeks to pass from the good to the good" (Kenny, 1979, 128).

If a practical syllogism is valid, it necessarily leads to a good, but not necessarily an ethical or a political good. As a result, practical reasoning is insufficient for the full realization of the good in man or in the city-state. In the realm of practical reasoning, for example, we can define "an 'orator' as 'he who can see what is a plausible argument on any occasion and omit nothing,' and . . . a 'thief' as 'he who takes something by stealth'; . . . obviously, if they each act thus, the former will be a good orator, the latter a good thief" (*Top.* 149b). A practical syllogism may begin, after all, "Since embezzlement is so and so . . ."

It is only by reasoning ethically and politically that we transcend this unacceptable indifference, the moral neutrality of practical reasoning. Ethics is the paradigm actualization of *phronêsis*, action undertaken for the sake of the good life (*NE* 1139a). Indeed, *phronêsis* is the essence of ethics: "For if a man have the one *aretê* of *phronêsis* he will also have all the Moral Virtues together" (*NE* 1144b). The ethical reasoner transcends the limitations of practical reasoning not by reasoning differently but by reasoning from a different starting point, always the same: "since the End or Supreme Good *(to telos kai to ariston)* is so and so" (*NE* 1144a).

The reasoner in politics deliberates analogously: The truths of politics are just the truths of ethics writ large in the context of the *polis*. Just as the moral philosopher determines "the End or Supreme Good," so the political philosopher "lays down the end which is the standard whereby we pronounce things good or bad in the absolute sense" (*NE* 1152b, 1–4). From the first starting point, Aristotle derives the science of the good and the practice of the good life; from the second, which includes the first, he derives the science and practice of politics.

The *technai* must be viewed from two very different but compatible perspectives. The weaving of the weaver, the dancing of the dancer, the writing of the poet are constituent movements whose *erga* are products: the rug, the dance, the poem. But in so far as these movements or their actualizations are also the consequence of deliberation, they are the constituents not of their *technai* but of decisions or actions that further or undermine the good of citizens or of the city-state. It is through the mediation of *phronêsis*, and through *phronêsis* alone, that the *technai* are linked to the networks of deliberation, decision, and action that constitute the city-state.

What Rhetoric Is and How It Works

Although the Aristotelian corpus as a whole sheds no light directly on rhetoric, additional to that shed by the *Rhetoric* itself, it does, as we have seen, define *technê*; it does employ this key word and exemplify its instances with some consistency. Moreover, since rhetoric is a species of *technê*, we may legitimately incorporate the definition of *technê* into the definition of *rhetoric*; in addition, we may argue by analogy from the characteristics of other arts to the characteristics of the art of rhetoric.[7] As a *technê*, then, rhetoric may be defined in terms of its four *aitia*.

Reasoning by analogy, we can identify the *hothen* or efficient cause of rhetoric as a *dunamis* and *hexis* in the *psuchê* of the rhetorician. As a *dunamis*, rhetoric is differentiated from all other *dunameis* the subject, to see "in each [particular] case *(peri hekaston)* . . . the available means of persuasion" (*Rhet.* 1355b).[8] As a *hexis*, rhetoric is knowledge in the form of *archai*, "lasting and hard to displace from the mind . . . [becoming] second nature through the lapse of time." The *hulê* or material cause of rhetoric is compound. In part it is thought and language: Rhetoric is the intelligible matter of thought and language shaped for a purpose. But rhetoric is also a modification of sensible matter, an alteration in the vocalic apparatus of the speaker, in the surrounding air and in the aural apparatus of the audience, consequences of the production and reception of speech. The *eidos* of rhetoric, its formal cause, is the source of this modification: Matter and form together constitute each particular instance of rhetoric.

The *hou heneka* of rhetoric is its *ergon* and its *telos*. In the narrowest sense of purpose, an orator is "he who can see what is a plausible argument on any occasion and omit nothing" (*Top.* 149b). In this sense, the *ergon* of rhetoric is "not to persuade but to see the available means of persuasion in each case" (*Rhet.* 1355b).

But in a broader sense of purpose, rhetoric includes persuasion: "The objective [*telos*] of the speech relates to the . . . judge *[kritês]*" (1358b) and "the judge is, so to speak, simply one who must be persuaded" (1391b; see also 1377b). There is an even broader sense of purpose. In the *Nicomachean Ethics*, Aristotle says that rhetoric, strategy, and domestic economy are three *technai* subordinate to the actualization of the city-state (1094a). The ultimate *hou heneka* of rhetoric, then, its ultimate *telos*, is the good of the *polis*. It is these ends of rhetoric that are the starting points for its production.

A rhetorical faculty can be acquired on the basis of experience, mediated by means of induction and intuition. This is the way of the ordinary rhetorician (and, of course, of the first rhetorician). But whatever can be formulated as a set of principles can be learned through study and practice. For the master rhetorician and the master teacher, though not for his ordinary counterpart, the *eidos* of rhetoric is also its *archê*, the essential form is also a set of rhetorical principles. For example, "the first principle of *lexis* is to speak [good] Greek" (1407a). It is the mastery of these *archai* that characterizes master rhetoricians and master teachers of rhetoric: "superior in wisdom, not because they can do things, but because they possess a theory and know its causes" (*Meta.* 981b). For the master rhetorician, rhetoric is an intellectual virtue that consists of a set of starting points from which he may derive, through deductive reasoning, the guidance he needs to realize his ends; for the master teacher of rhetoric, this same *aretê* is a set of principles that guide students through cycles of study and practice as they produce progressively more competent actualizations.

Because rhetoric is *technê*, not *phronêsis*, it can deal with individuals only in so far as they are members of a class: "No art examines the particular—for example, the art of medicine does not specify what is healthful for Socrates or Callias but for persons of a certain sort (this is artistic, while the particulars are limitless and not knowable)—neither does rhetoric theorize about each opinion—what may seem so to Socrates or Hippias—but about what seems true to people of a certain sort" (1356b).

Because rhetoric cannot deal with individuals as individuals, by definition rhetoric cannot be identified with deliberation. Deliberation is not the activation of a productive faculty, though it may lead to such activation; it is rather the working through of a practical syllogism toward a purposive choice, "the deliberate appetition of things within one's power" (*EE* 1226b). The rhetorician must deliberate, therefore, not by means of *technê* but by means of a practical syllogism, an actualization of *phronêsis*. For example, he might reason thus: "Since persuasion is so-and-so, if the audience is to be persuaded, it must be roused to anger; if so the conditions for arousing anger in audiences must be present." Having arrived at a starting point, the rhetorician will stop deliberating and apply the appropriate *archê*. Deliberative and forensic oratory may be a consequence of deliberation; they may lead to deliberation; but they are not deliberation.

The Role of Rhetoric in the *Polis*

In the first chapter of Book 1 of the *Rhetoric*, a theory is presented in which the emotions are excluded on the ethical and political grounds that they warp the judgment of the audience and rhetoric is vindicated on the grounds that the true and the just deserves the best defense. In the second chapter, an alternative theory is put forward in which the emotions (and the character of the speaker) are included among the proofs. But this change in the scope of rhetoric in no way alters its subordination to the good of the citizen and the city-state. In both theories, rhetoric is a *technê*, a tool; in both, however, it is a tool always to be used for the good of the citizen and the city-state. In both Aristotelian theories of rhetoric, ethical and political deliberation are presupposed. It is in this sense that rhetoric is "a certain kind of offshoot *[paraphues]* of dialectic and of ethical studies (which it is just to call politics)" (1356a).

Because in both theories the ethics of the speaker and the good of the city-state are guaranteed by limits placed on the practice of rhetoric, each is compatible also with Aristotle's considered view of human beings, a view in which reason is their defining capacity: "Other animals live chiefly by nature, though some in small degrees are guided by habits too; but man lives by reason also, for he alone of animals possesses reason; so that in him these three things must be in harmony with one another; for men often act contrary to their acquired habits and to their nature because of their reason, if they are convinced that some other course of action is preferable" (*Pol.* 1332b).[9] Since it is clear that reason alone is insufficient for such action (*De Anima* 433a), a choice between these two theories depends only on an assessment of whether it is legitimate for the rhetorician to incorporate the emotions and values of the audience into his inventional process.

Throughout the *Rhetoric*, however, there are hints of a third theory of rhetoric, wholly incompatible with the other two; scattered remarks advise speakers to persuade in any way they can, sophistry not excluded. In Book 1, we are advised, in praising someone, "always to take each of the attendant terms in the best sense; for example, [one should call] an irascible and excitable person 'straightforward' and an arrogant person 'high-minded' and 'imposing' and [speak of] those given to excess as actually in states of virtue, for example the rash one as 'courageous,' the spendthrift as 'liberal': for this will seem true to most people" (1367a). In Book 3, similar advice is given: "The proper *lexis* also makes the matter credible: the mind [of the listener] draws a false inference of the truth of what a speaker says because they [in the audience] feel the same about such things, so they think the facts to be so, even if they are not as the speaker represents them" (1408a).

In this third view, there are no ethical limits to rhetorical practice. There cannot be, since those limits presuppose that if they are observed, the truth will prevail. This sophistic view may, however, be compatible with the actual role of rhetoric in Aristotle's Athens, if Josiah Ober's analysis is correct. In Aristotle's Athens, according to Ober (1989), the integrity of the city-state was guaranteed not by the ethical high-mindedness of its leading citizens but by a set of shared values that created harmony between the divergent interests of the mass and the elite. But although Aristotle's remarks may be explained, and his position justified in this context, it is difficult to see his sympathies lying in the direction of Athenian democracy, given his philosophical system as a whole, and his elitist and cerebral views of government, expressed in the *Rhetoric* as a contempt for popular audiences (1404a; 1415b; 1419a) and an intolerance of sham: "Thus . . . rhetoric dresses itself up in the form of politics, as do those who pretend to a knowledge of it, sometimes through lack of education, sometimes through boastfulness and other human causes" (1356a).

The passages that hint at this third theory remain a serious obstacle to those like Eugene Garver (1994b) who would claim either that the *Rhetoric* is a coherent treatise or that it integrates easily into Aristotle's philosophical system. Garver claims that the central question in the *Rhetoric* is "whether there can be a civic art of rhetoric" (1994b, 1). For Garver the answer is yes: "The project of the *Rhetoric* is to construct a civic relation between *technê* and *phronêsis*" (77). Garver cheerfully admits that "there is one difficulty with my thesis. Aristotle never explicitly says anything resembling it in the *Rhetoric*" (45). Garver then proceeds to construct a rhetoric that Aristotle *might* have written, one that he certainly *would* have written had he wanted to integrate it fully with his philosophical views. But what might have happened is not what did happen. In the two *Ethics* and in the *Politics*, Aristotle explores alternate theories in order to expound his own considered ones; in contrast, the *Rhetoric* dramatizes his inability to decide among inconsistent alternatives. As a consequence of these tensions, the *Rhetoric* underlines Aristotle's failure to integrate rhetorical theory and practice into the broader concerns of his philosophy. Essentially, we learn from his work only *that*, not *how*, rhetoric must be subordinate to the good of a well-ordered city-state.

Conclusion

What did Aristotle mean by rhetoric? At this juncture, I can do little more than reiterate my claim that rhetoric is a productive art, and only a productive art. Rhetoric is, in Aristotle's scheme of things, a narrowly circumscribed set of skills. These are easily abused; when, however, they are well used, they serve the best interest of the city-state and its citizens. This thesis is not new (McKeon, 1965; Warnick, 1989). It is true that in his insightful review article Michael Leff (1993) finds this thesis unconvincing in the face of strongly argued alternatives that he cites: Johnstone's case that rhetoric is a practical art, Kennedy's that it is theoretical, and Garver's that it combines practice and production. Still, Leff does not despair of the claim. He comments acutely that it is "possible that Aristotle's conception of productive art was sufficiently elastic to include the *Rhetoric*" (321). I hope that the evidential and argumentative muscle provided by this chapter will overcome Leff's objections.

In addition to my substantive point concerning the nature of rhetoric in the *Rhetoric*, I also want to make a methodological point concerning the reading of that work. If scholars want to find out what Aristotle meant, they need to follow their own advice and their own best practice: They need to establish the meaning of his key words by searching out their use in every Aristotelian context, by looking for commonalities in use, and by forging links with the use of other Aristotelian key words in reciprocating networks of interaction.

Notes

1. Although *eidos* and *morphê* are often equated, they are sometimes usefully differentiated; when they are, *eidos* consists of the formal properties that constitute what it is to be a *kind* of thing; *morphê* consist of the formal properties of a *particular* thing. Each bronze sphere exemplifies its essential form, its *eidos*; each sphere also has its particular dimensions, its *morphê*; the same poem spoken and written have the same *eidos*, but differ in *morphê*.

2. In this passage, Aristotle speaks of *methodon*, rather than *ergon*, but the reference to "all available means" reveals the synonymy in this case (see *Rhet.* 1355b).

3. In Aristotle there is a clear division: The end of speculative knowledge is its contemplation, that of productive knowledge, a product (*EE* 1216b). It is as a productive capacity that *technê* is clearly differentiated from *epistêmê* and, indeed, from all other Aristotelian ways of truth, *nous, phronêsis,* and *sophia* (*Meta.* 1032b; 1025b).

4. There is no way that the reconstruction of this process from these crucial passages can be freed from contention. But legitimate differences among classical scholars affect none of my claims. For a survey of the problem, along with some proposed solutions, see Barnes, ed., *Posterior Analytics*, 248–60.

5. Translating *hupothesis* as postulate according to Kenny 132.

6. In a second passage, Aristotle supplements this description: "Now the products which are formed by human art are formed by means of instruments *(organôn)*, or rather it would be truer to say they are formed by means of the movement of instruments, and this movement is the activity, the actualization *(energeia)*, or the art, for by 'art' we mean the shape *(morphê)* of the products which are formed, though it is resident elsewhere than in the products themselves" (*GA* 740b).

7. The practice of rhetoric must be distinguished from its study. The practice is a productive art whose *telos* is *poiêtikê*; its study is an *epistêmê* whose *telos* is *theorêtikê*. Although rhetoric *per se* is not an *epistêmê*, like an *epistêmê* it consists of a set of *archai*. In the *Rhetoric*, although no such set is mentioned, individual principles are spoken of as *archai:* For example, "the first principle *[archê]* of *lexis* is to speak [good] Greek" (1407a). It is because it consists of principles that rhetoric may be taught.

8. This is enough to differentiate rhetoric from dialectic according to the criteria of the second chapter of the first book, because rhetoric there encompasses *êthos* and *pathos*. By the criterion of the first chapter, rhetoric can be differenti-

ated from dialectic in that the latter is, unlike the former, interrupted discourse, one-on-one, and educational or heuristic in purpose.

9. Only the first theory, however, is compatible with Aristotle's deep distrust of the emotions. In the *Politics*, for example, he asserts that those without self-restraint can serve neither their own or others' interest (1309b), and he justifies the place of music in the *polis* in part by its ability to purge the emotions (1341b). In the *Poetics*, purgation is elaborated into a theory of tragedy.

3

Aristotle on Speaking "Outside the Subject": The Special Topics and Rhetorical Forums

Arthur E. Walzer

In the first chapter of the *Rhetoric*, Aristotle distinguishes his treatment of the art of rhetoric from his predecessors' by claiming that previous work focused too much on what is not essential—"speaking outside the subject." Aristotle implies that we know that the tactics he includes under the rubric "speaking outside the subject" are not essential because they have been proscribed in some forums. This essay traces the implications of Aristotle's description of what is essential and the basis of that judgment for our understanding of the degree of autonomy rhetoric as an art has for Aristotle by focusing especially on Aristotle's conception of a rhetorical forum. The essay contests recent readings of the *Rhetoric* that claim that for Aristotle rhetoric is constitutive of politics by arguing that Aristotle understands rhetoric's autonomy as significantly attenuated by politics, which for him defines what speaking to the subject means in a particular forum.

Aristotle refers to speaking "outside the subject" *(exotou pragmatos)* throughout the first chapter of the *Rhetoric*, where the phrase (or a slight variation) occurs at least six times (at 1.1.3, 1.1.5, 1.1.9, twice at 1.1.10, 1.1.11). Interpreters have not much emphasized the phrase; yet attending to it can show us a way to heal the alleged conceptual fracture between the first chapter and the rest of Book 1. Indeed, speaking "outside the subject" signals Aristotle's effort to make conceptual relevancy essential to our understanding of what a genuine art of rhetoric is, an effort manifest throughout Book 1. Furthermore, attending to the phrase and focusing generally on the criterion of substantive relevancy illuminates the nature of rhetorical practice as Aristotle understood it. It helps us understand Aristotle's vision of a rhetorical forum and provides insight into the relationship between politics and rhetoric in the *Rhetoric*. Properly understood, this relationship (I will argue) is quite different from that supposed by recent commentators who claim to find in the *Rhetoric* the view that rhetoric is prior to and constitutive of politics.

Speaking Outside the Subject

The most significant instances of speaking "outside the subject" are at 1.1.3–6, where it and a variant occur:

> 3. As things are now, those who have composed *Arts of Speech* have worked on a small part of the subject; for only *pisteis* are artistic (other things are supplementary), and these writers say nothing about enthymemes, which is the "body" of persuasion, while they give most of their attention to matters external to the subject; 4. for verbal attack and pity and anger and such emotions of the soul do not relate to fact but are appeals to the juryman. As a result, if all trials were conducted as they are in some present-day states and especially in those well-governed [the handbook writers] would have nothing to say. 5. for everyone thinks the laws ought to require this, and some even adopt the practice and forbid speaking outside the subject as in the Areopagus too, rightly so providing; for it is wrong to warp the jury by leading them into anger or envy or pity: that is the same as if someone made a straightedge rule crooked before using it. And further, it is clear that the opponents have no function except to show that something is or is not true or has or has not happened; whether it is important or trivial or just or unjust, in so far as the lawmaker has not provided a definition, the juryman should somehow decide himself and not learn from the opponents. (1.1.3–6)

Commentators often find this passage problematic, judging it inconsistent with what follows: In the second chapter and subsequently in the treatise, Aristotle devotes much attention to the pathetic and ethotic elements that these interpreters understand him censuring in his remarks on competing "arts" that emphasize speaking "outside the subject." Jacqueline de Romilly (1975), for example, draws on Friedrich Solmsen's conclusion that the first chapter was written earlier than the second to excise the first chapter entirely as inconsistent with, and superseded by, the second.

The argument for a radical inconsistency tends to assume on the basis of the metaphor of "warping the straightedge" that the basis for Aristotle's distinction between his approach and his predecessors' is moral: These others advocate unethical tactics; he will not. But recent commentators have read Aristotle's intentions differently from those that base their readings in large part on Solmsen's theory of the *Rhetoric*'s composition. While not denying that the first chapter is more "austere" (Engberg-Pedersen, 1996, 131), "highminded" (Lord, 1981, 336), idealized (Most, 1994, 188), and "Platonic" (Schütrumpf, 1994, 102) than much of the rest, this more recent work finds the relationship between chapters 1 and 2 more subtle and complex than discordant. The way to reconciling chapters 1 and 2 begins with an understanding of the distinction Aristotle draws between his approach and his predecessors' as technical rather than moral. John M. Cooper (1994) and Eckart Schütrumpf (1994) argue that Aristotle is claiming that his approach is more comprehensive, more complete, than earlier ones. Schütrumpf hears in 1.1.3–5 an echo of the section in the *Phaedrus* (269b7) in which the orator Thrasymachos, known for arousing emotion in his audience, is faulted on the theoretical level for not meeting the criterion of a genuine art of rhetoric (1994, 102). Schütrumpf also points out that in the *Metaphysics*, Aristotle faults previous work on the same ground: that it was incomplete (1994, 104). The implication is that Aristotle's primary point in censuring earlier writers who have emphasized speaking "outside the subject" is not between the moral and the immoral but between what is most essential to the art of rhetoric (speaking to the subject) and what is less so (those tactics grouped under the rubric "speaking outside the subject"). Aristotle is thus claiming that if these unessential tactics were proscribed, as they are in "well-governed" states, then "these writers would have nothing to say" (1.1.4) about rhetoric.

The reference to "well-governed" states (1.1.4) calls attention to a second point the passage makes—how we know what is essential, what supplementary, to an art of rhetoric. We know that tactics that move outside the subject are not essential because they have been proscribed in the past. This, then, becomes for rhetoric the basis of essentiality: what has not been prohibited. How do we know that speaking "to the subject" and not, say, a tactic's effectiveness is the criterion of what is essential to an art of rhetoric? We know because effective tactics have sometimes been prohibited (in part) precisely because they were effective. This logic, Aristotle reminds the reader, led to the prohibitions against emotional appeals in the Areopagus. But no assembly or court has ever prohibited relevant argument. While "other writers describe as an art things outside the subject" (1.1.11), which are but a "small part" of the art of rhetoric (1.1.3), his treatise will emphasize those aspects of the art least likely to be proscribed, for these are for that reason essential. This, at least, is Aristotle's boast.[1]

The passage thus makes two points that taken together suggest a paradox that illuminates an important feature of Aristotle's view of rhetoric. First, it identifies what Aristotle regards as one of his contributions to rhetoric, his emphasis on speaking to the subject, that is, the criterion of substantive relevancy.[2] His focus on the enthymeme and the example and on deriving relevant arguments from the *endoxa* and topics germane to a particular forum is the heart of this program, though, of course, a complete art will include supplementary elements as well. Second, that the test of what is essential is what cannot reasonably be prohibited is evidence that Aristotle understands rhetoric as subject to external regulation. This indicates that rhetoric for Aristotle is not a completely autonomous, self-governing art. If it were, then Aristotle might argue that rhetoric should decide what is the basis for its best practice; he might even argue that the forums in which rhetoric operates should be subject to reform on rhetoric's principles. But Aristotle does not make such an argument. Indeed, he acknowledges that under the strictest regulations, rhetoric might be limited to establishing the facts of the case, without reference even to the implications of those facts (1.1.6). The two points in this passage, then, taken together, suggest that rhetoric is both an art with essential principles and a changing, contextual art shaped by politics through the creation of forums that regulate its practice.[3]

Identifying what Aristotle regards as essential and what supplementary to an art of rhetoric is a challenging task, for the *Rhetoric* views its subject from shifting, even if complementary, perspectives. While Aristotle conceives of rhetoric as in some sense plastic, it is so within limits. Rhetoric has a history; it is objectively something. Its nature and the history of its application lead Aristotle to examine rhetoric from three different perspectives—as an ability common to all humans, as an art that can be systematically taught, practiced, and learned, and as a civic instrument subject to regulation and control by the state.

At its highest level of generality, rhetoric is "a mental faculty" (1.4.6), a *dunamis*, that, with dialectic, is one of two "distinct abilities of supplying words" (1.2.8). It is this faculty that enables us to "see the available means of persuasion in a given case" (1.2.1), even if, as an undeveloped faculty, our seeing is less than complete. At this level, "all people, in some way, share" in rhetoric, for "all to some extent try . . . to defend themselves and attack others" by means of speech (1.1.1). From an ethical perspective, while rhetoric can be used for ill, Aristotle assures us that, as a human faculty, rhetoric is potentially and properly among the "good things," comparing it to other positive human potentialities such as strength and health (1.1.13).

But Aristotle also treats rhetoric as an art, that is, as "a reasoned habit of mind in making something" (*NE* 6.4.1); in the case of rhetoric, the "making" is of a speech. To conceive of something first as a human ability and then as an art capable of being systematically studied and consciously practiced, it may be helpful for us to reflect on the process by which an academic discipline is created. The two—an art and an academic discipline—are, of course, not the same. There are disciplines that do not eventuate in products, are not arts in Aristotle's sense; and there are arts that are not disciplines. But to identify something as art is to say that it can be taught, that it can give a rational account of itself, and the same criteria apply to academic disciplines. In trying to identify what is essential to the art of rhetoric and what is not, it is revealing to apply the features of disciplinary definitions to Aristotle's treatment of rhetoric as an art—to identify the characteristic concerns, materials, and methods that he would regard as either present within the art or historically associated with it, as we might identify the characteristic concerns of an established discipline. In the famous passage in which Aristotle discusses rhetoric's characteristic concern with the contingent and the probable, Aristotle (as I read him) is attempting to reveal the essential province of rhetoric as an art:

> Its [rhetoric's] function *[ergon]* is concerned with the sort of things we debate and for which we do not have [other] arts and among such

> listeners as are not able to see many things all together or to reason from a distant starting point. And we debate about things that seem to be capable of admitting two possibilities; for no one debates things incapable of being different either in past or future or present, at least not if they suppose that to be the case; for there is nothing more [to say.] 13. It is possible to form syllogisms and draw inductive conclusions either from previous syllogisms or from statements that are not reasoned out but require a syllogism [if they are to be accepted] because they are not commonly believed *[endoxa]*; but the former of these [i.e., a chain of syllogisms] is necessarily not easy to follow because of the length [of the argument] (the judge is assumed to be a simple person) and the latter is not persuasive because the premises are not agreed to or commonly believed. (1.2.12–13)

Rhetoric is necessarily concerned with those questions (1) about which people disagree, (2) for which there are at least two plausible views, (3) and for which there is no substantive art capable of arbitrating the debate. Its materials are, for the most part, the common cultural beliefs *(endoxa)*, from which proofs are created, the basis for its distinction from Aristotle's other disciplines that are concerned with first principles or, in the case of dialectic, arriving at first principles. In terms of its concerns and materials, rhetoric is most similar to dialectic, but in its method it contrasts with dialectic. One difference is rhetoric's reliance on the enthymeme and the example. Another is methodological: Whereas the method of dialectic involves two people who are engaged in an effort to explore a subject, to discover truth, or to convince the other, the method of rhetoric is debate. "Opponents" (Aristotle's usual word, e.g., 1.1.6) seek a victory measured by the persuasion of an audience of "simple" people who are nonparticipants. This is what rhetoric as an art or discipline is for Aristotle.

From an ethical perspective, rhetoric is still neutral, but without the bias toward the good that it had when Aristotle, thinking of rhetoric as a human ability, compared it to health and strength. When he thinks of rhetoric as an art, Aristotle is more likely to compare it to boxing or wrestling; rhetoric is understood as providing the protection in verbal combat that the martial arts do in physical combat (1.1.12). If, at the level of a human faculty, rhetoric is a "good" (though one capable of being ill-used), rhetoric at the level of developed skill is for Aristotle a temptation. Later in Book 1, Aristotle observes that those who are skilled in speaking and successful in disputes are more likely to think they can do wrong with impunity than those not so practiced (1.12.2). This is one of the reasons why rhetoric needs to come under the control of politics—to ensure its best practice—while not, of course, changing what it, by definition, is: a speaker (or speakers) controlling or manipulating the response of groups of nonparticipants to questions of contingency.

At still a higher level of generality, Aristotle considers rhetoric as an instrument of public policy. At this level, rhetoric is seen in respect not to dialectic but to politics, in Aristotle's terms, as "an offshoot *[paraphues]* of dialectic and ethical studies (which it is just to call politics)" (1.2.7). The metaphor suggests that the character of rhetoric, as an instrument of essential civic institutions, is shaped and sustained by the constitution and political tradition, as inextricable from them as branch is from stem and root. We can see that there is inevitably a tension between what rhetoric is by definition, what it is essentially, and what it can become as regulated by forums under the guidance of *phronêsis*.

Special Topics and the Subjects of the Forums

My argument is that Aristotelian rhetoric understands the rhetorical forums as mediating the tension between rhetoric as an autonomous art and rhetoric as an instrument of politics. I view the special topics *(idia)* not only or even primarily as aids to invention; nor do I understand them primarily as a compendium for rhetors. Rather the special topics function as generic constraints; they define what is relevant within the three rhetorical forums. Aristotle's discussion of the special topics, then, is his delineation of what "speaking to the subject" means within the context of the forums that he identifies as the province of rhetoric. The special topics show the rhetor how to transform the *pragmata*—the matter at hand—into relevant argument.

In its general outline, Aristotle's definitions of the species of rhetoric and the special topics of deliberative, forensic, and epideictic rhetoric are well known. A speech situation consists "of three things: a speaker and a subject on which he speaks and someone addressed" (1.3.1). The subject of a forum combines its end with its mode and time. The mode or formal cause of the species *(eidos)* of deliberative rhetoric within the political forum is either exhortation or dissuasion (1.3.3); its temporal orientation is toward an unknown future and its objective *(telos)* to persuade the audience that the proposed action is to the advantage *(to sumpheron)* or not to the city (1.3.5); the mode of judicial rhetoric within the courtroom is accusation or defense (1.3.3) with an objective of persuasion about the just *(to dikaion)* or the unjust (1.3.5); the mode of demonstrative rhetoric or the discourse emanating from the dais on ceremonial occasions is praise or blame (1.3.3) with an objective of persuasion about the honorable *(to kalon)* and dishonorable (1.3.5)

The objective *(telos)* of the forum is the basis for substantive relevancy within it. Aristotle's understanding of relevancy is appropriately narrow. While concerns other than that mandated as the end of a forum are sometimes mentioned—the honorable in the deliberative forum, for example—such themes are not strictly relevant; nor will arguments based on them count as much. In chapter 3, Aristotle emphasizes this point in summary fashion:

> Here is a sign that the end of each [species of rhetoric] is what has been said: sometimes one would not dispute other factors; for example, a judicial speaker [might not deny] that he has done something or done harm, but he would never agree that he has [intentionally] done

> wrong; for [if he admitted that,] there would be no need of a trial. Similarly, deliberative speakers often grant other factors, but they would never admit that they are advising things that are not advantageous [to the audience] or that they are dissuading [the audience] from what is beneficial; and often they do not insist that it is not unjust to enslave neighbors or those who have done no wrong. And similarly, those who praise or blame do not consider whether someone has done actions that are advantageous or harmful [to himself] [1359a] but often they include it even as a source of praise that he did what was honorable without regard to the cost to himself; for example, they praise Achilles because he went to the aid of his companion Patroclus knowing that he himself must die, though he could have lived. To him, such a death was more honorable; but life was advantageous. (1.3.6)

The objective of a forum, once established, is a basis for predicting winning arguments. "Speaking to the subject" means, in the context of a particular forum, that the appeal is relevant to this objective.

Chapters 3 through 15 demonstrate how the *telos* of a particular forum shapes substantive relevancy and determines rhetorical efficacy. The special topics are the lens through which the subjects at hand *(pragmata)* become rhetorically effective. The special topics, then, mediate between language and reality for Aristotle.

The power that this criterion of relevancy exercises over the way a particular idea is valued within the forum is considerable. Subject matter relevance is more predictive of success than any other criterion—including a truth that is not made to seem relevant. The extent to which Aristotle is willing to push the criterion of relevance is especially clear in his discussion of deliberative rhetoric. At 1.4, Aristotle observes that to advise appropriately on matters of war and peace, the rhetor should know the relative military power of his city. That speaking to the subject of the forum is the overriding rhetorical criterion becomes clear when Aristotle advises that the rhetor should know the power of neighboring cities as well "in order that there may be a policy of peace toward the stronger and that the decision of war with the weaker may be one's own" (1.4.9). Honor, a most important commitment of Aristotle, and justice, *the* most important one, are ignored as less germane than survival and advantage in the political forum. Advice of a similar nature follows a few lines later in the context of Aristotle's discussion of the rhetor's need for knowledge of food supplies available to the city: "(It is necessary to keep the citizens constantly free from complaints from two [foreign] groups: those that are stronger and those that are useful for commerce)" (1.4.11). Again, the measure of the rhetor's policy recommendation within the political forum is utility *(sumpheron).* From the perspective of the art of rhetoric, the subject of the forum supersedes all other values.

The emphasis on utility within the deliberative forum shapes chapters 5 and

6, which, just as chapter 4, contain advice that appears amoral and inconsistent with Aristotle's treatment of the good elsewhere, especially in the treatises on ethics. Kennedy presents the content of both chapters under the common rubric "Ethical Topics Useful in the Deliberative Forum" (56, 62). In these sections, Aristotle takes up the constituents of the good, the relationship between them, and their relative value—concerns also, of course, of the *Eudemian Ethics* and the *Nicomachean Ethics*. Kennedy summarizes the conclusions of others who have compared Aristotle's treatment of the good in the *Rhetoric* with his treatment elsewhere: "In his ethical treatises, and especially in the *Nicomachean Ethics*, Aristotle shows a greater sense of urgency toward knowing and doing what is morally right and gives higher priority to the contemplative than the active political life" than he does here (62). Commentators have sought an explanation for this inconsistency in the early composition of at least some sections of the *Rhetoric* and have used the inconsistency here as an occasion to lament that Aristotle did not always revise his earlier texts after he reformed his ideas. But this response is misguided. Rather than concern ourselves with an apparent inconsistency, we might better ask whether the treatment of the good in chapters 5 and 6 of the *Rhetoric* is appropriate to its purposes and coherent within the confines of this text. After all, commentators do not similarly lament that when Aristotle considers justice and wrongdoing in his section on forensic rhetoric in chapters 10 through 15 of Book 1, he limits his definition of justice to what is consistent with the law and his definition of wrongdoing to what contravenes it. Aristotle's consideration of the ethical topics here is similarly appropriate to the context. Chapters 5 and 6 treat the good from a utilitarian perspective, a perspective that is appropriate to a deliberative forum whose subject is the advantageous *(to sumpheron)* and disadvantageous.

Chapters 5 and 6 show the power of the deliberative forum to shape the matter at hand to its end. These chapters examine the good and happiness *(eudaimonia)* from two perspectives quite different from the discussion in the *Nicomachean Ethics* I.7–10: In the context of the *Rhetoric*'s consideration of the deliberative forum, the perspectives are communal and utilitarian. The communal perspective is obvious, as Aristotle asks what a particular value treated from an individual perspective in the *Nicomachean Ethics* would look like "in the case of a nation or city" (1.5.5) or "as applied to the community" (1.5.6). But the more profound difference is the utilitarianism of Aristotle's discussion of the constituents of happiness in these chapters. This perspective contrasts markedly with the hierarchical perspective that characterizes the *Nicomachean Ethics*. The constituents of happiness, ranked on the basis of the degree of autonomy that can be derived from their intrinsic value in the *Ethics*, are here merely listed, presumably to be subject to evaluation on the basis of the effects in a given context. The principle that equates wealth and honor for the purposes of measuring the happiness they confer is akin to that which, under Bentham's system, equates pushpin and poetry for the purposes of weighing the pleasure each brings. Aristotle even explains how honor can be subject to evaluation based on its effects. Honor is not only its own reward; it brings,

Aristotle tells us, tangible benefits to the ambitious that parallel the benefits of wealth to the avaricious (1. 5.9).

Nothing in chapters 7 and 8 contradicts what is explicit in chapters 5 and 6: that Aristotle presents the concerns of his ethical doctrines from the utilitarian perspective that he accepts as a given in the deliberative forum. This perspectives helps explain a problematic passage in chapter 7, a chapter concerned with measuring the comparative advantage of effects. At 1.7.16, Aristotle notes, "And something whose opposite is greater and whose loss is greater [is greater]. And virtue is a greater thing than nonvirtue, and vice a greater thing than nonvice; for the former are ends, the latter not." As Kennedy notes, many commentators have been exercised by the "implied moral ambivalence" (70) of this line. But the next line makes clear that the basis for Aristotle's judgment is not the intrinsic worth of virtue and vice but their efficacy, their relative impact: "And those things are greater whose effects are finer or more shameful" (1.7.17). It is a calculus of effects, not inherent value, that for Aristotle is germane to the deliberative forum.

Chapter 8, which describes the implications for persuasion of different constitutions, is a fitting conclusion to the utilitarian treatment of the good within these chapters on the special topics of the deliberative forum. "The end of democracy is freedom, of oligarchy wealth, of aristocracy things related to education and the traditions of law, of tyranny self-preservation" (1.8.5). In cases in which the impacts of different goods are by objective measure equal, arguments based on those particular values honored within a particular constitution will be more efficacious than similar utilitarian arguments based on competing values not so honored by that constitution.

In chapter 9, which presents the special topics of epideictic rhetoric, Aristotle similarly defines the relevant in the context of this forum, the end *(telos)* of which is the honorable *(kalon)* and shameful. The first part of the chapter parallels chapters 5 and 6. Aristotle examines aspects of the good—here virtue—within the context of a forum whose end is persuasion about the honorable and dishonorable. It is not the highest calling to practice virtue for the sake of honor, so the rhetor cannot assume that arguments on behalf of virtue will count as praise where honor is the criterion of relevance. One purpose of the chapter is to clarify this relationship in order to establish the conditions in which virtue is relevant in epideictic rhetoric. On examination, it turns out that virtue is generally relevant to the honorable, at least in these two senses: that actions productive of virtue are necessarily honorable and that actions brought about by virtue are honorable (1.9.14). Nevertheless, honor and virtue are not coextensive, as one of Aristotle's examples is intended to illustrate: It is virtuous to suffer just punishment, but doing so confers no honor (1.9.15).

The second part of chapter 9 illustrates that relevancy and not truth is the basis for authority within epideictic rhetoric. Aristotle allows the rhetor considerable interpretative latitude so that whether the rhetor presents a demonstrably simple person as amiable or fatuous or a high-minded person as an idealist or as arrogant is less a result of search for truth than it is a function of the rhetor's intent on a particular occasion (1.9.28–29). When, in his concluding example, Aristotle advises the rhetor to find what the audience honors within the subject praised, we see that relevance has priority over reality itself, for the search for what to say begins with what is relevant in the context of the forum and not with the facts at hand.

Aristotle's discussion of the judicial rhetoric in chapters 10 through 15 is an effort similarly to define the relevant, here in the courtroom. His discussion begins with definitions appropriately limited to the context. Wrongdoing *(to adikein)* is defined as "doing harm willingly in contravention of the law" (1.10.3). The just *(to dikaion)*, the end of the judicial forum, is seen only with reference to legality. Articulating the relevant within this forum, then, entails unpacking this definition—that is, defining what the law includes (specific and common), what constitutes voluntary action, what the plausible motives for wrongdoing are, and what the plausible claims of those with a grievance might be.

The most interesting and discriminating discussion within this section is that concerning the relevant and plausible motives for wrong doing in chapters 10 and 11. An example of the kind of distinction Aristotle makes between what counts as relevant and what does not occurs at 1.10.9 and following. Aristotle is addressing the question of what causal arguments are relevant to establishing motive for theft. Some conditions are, in themselves, irrelevant as causes and can be ruled out: skin color and height, for example. As he says, "nothing is ordained as consequent of such qualities" (1.10.11); that is, they are not predictors of wrongdoing. Some qualities are clearly relevant as motives for theft, such as a demonstrated longing or desire for money or a demonstrated indifference to justice (1.10.9). Some are not irrelevant but nevertheless insufficient to count in themselves as relevant. Poverty is an example: In itself, the relationship between poverty and crime does not justify a correlative conclusion, but when combined with evidence of a longing for wealth, it is a contributing cause (1.10.9). It follows that evidence of an awareness of one's poverty might be evidence of theft because that awareness could be symptomatic of a longing for money (1.10.11), which is relevant as a motive and therefore germane to the forum. In his discussion at the end of chapter 10, Aristotle reduces the relevant motives in the context of the courtroom to two: "In short, all things that people do of their own volition are either goods or apparent goods or pleasures or apparent pleasures" (1.10.18). These, then, are the sources and limits of relevant motives in judicial rhetoric.

My emphasis on subject matter relevance as essential to Aristotle's understanding of rhetoric and constitutive of the rhetorical forum does not conflict with Aristotle's statement that the objective or *telos* of the speech "relates . . . to the hearer" (1.3.1). Indeed it confirms it. Once seated within a forum, hearers are, for Aristotle, constructed by the forum's concerns. His divisions of hearers into judges and spectators defines them in terms of the civic functions of the forums, and his strict definition of what they witness and judge defines them in terms of the subjects appropriate to the forums. His discussion of the special topics limits what is relevant to the hearers' carrying out an assigned role. For contrast, we might compare Aristotle's view of hearers as conditioned by the civic concerns of carefully defined forums to the taxonomies of advertisers who classify viewers demographically for the purpose of constructing them as hormonal targets of verbal and graphic stimuli. Aristotle's is a contextualized, political formulation, not a general, psychological one.

Chapters 3 through 15, then, demonstrate the relationship among the *telos* of a forum, substantive relevancy, and rhetorical efficacy. The special topics are the means by which an Aristotelian art of rhetoric shapes *pragmata*.

What is the basis for the rules and conventions that structure the rhetorical forums? Aristotle is quite clear on this in a passage at the beginning of Chapter 6. "But since the objective of the deliberative speaker is the advantageous and since [people] do not deliberate about this objective but about the means that contribute to it and these [means] are things advantageous in terms of actions and since the advantageous is good, one should grasp the elements *[stoicheia]* of the good and advantageous in the abstract" (1.6.2). This passage is crucial to our understanding of both the limits of rhetoric's autonomy and the power of rhetoric to shape *pragmata*. It is also crucial to the rest of my argument in this essay. The source for defining the ends that shape substantive relevancy within the forums—whether that source is a product of intuition *(nous)* or a consequence of dialectical exchange under the auspices of philosophy or, most likely, established within a constitution—is less important than what is clear from the passage: that the ends of the rhetorical forums are not the result of, or subject to, rhetorical deliberation. They are prior to rhetoric.

Rhetoric Dressed Up as Politics

My reading of the *Rhetoric* is not consonant with recent interpretations offered by Robert Beiner, Eugene Garver, and Thomas Farrell. These competing readings are impelled not principally by a desire to interpret the *Rhetoric* but by an effort to recover Aristotle's notion of practical reason as a way to reform contemporary political discourse. In the ethical works, in his *Politics*, and in the *Metaphysics*, Aristotle offers a description of reason that is purposive and situational, thus holding out the possibility of an alternative to the Enlightenment's conceptualization of reason as unmotivating and universal. Examining the *Rhetoric* from this perspective, Beiner, Garver, and Farrell see its value in large part as an aid to our understanding of how Aristotle envisioned practical reasoning functioning in the context of the civic life of the *polis*, a reading that invests the *Rhetoric* with a philosophical significance that, these scholars imply, it otherwise lacks.

But while Beiner, Garver, and Farrell do not claim to be contributing to the exegetical tradition of Aristotelian scholarship or claim that the readings they advance are complete or comprehensive, they nevertheless hold that the interpretations they provide are tenable and coherent and consistent with Aristotle's general views. While the tenor of Garver's intentions in *Aristotle's "Rhetoric": An Art of Character* (1994b) is suggested by his ironic acknowledgment that he was tempted "to write this [book] as an inquiry into practical reason and eliminate all references to the *Rhetoric*" (16), the book also provides the most complete and detailed reading of Books 1 and 2 since the publication of Grimaldi's *Commentary* (1980a; 1988); his work is sure to serve as a commentary, whatever his intentions. Garver's insights into the *Rhetoric* are often original and sometimes striking and helpful, but as an historical reconstruction of what Aristotle meant, his reading is ultimately misleading. Farrell's similar motives in *Norms of Rhetorical Culture* (1993) are manifest when he writes that his "intent . . . is revisionistic; but I believe it to be faithful in spirit to Aristotle's original project for *practical reason*" (10; my italics), a remark that can only invite the question of the degree to which *Norms* remains faithful to the spirit of the *Rhetoric*. Beiner's intentions are suggested by the title of his book, *Political Judgment*, and revealed in his emphasis throughout on the nature and validity of judgment in its relationship to rational community (e.g., p. 10). Although it is clear that his reading of the *Rhetoric* is guided by the aims of his project, he nevertheless claims to identify a view of rhetoric that does not merely take inspiration from Aristotle but is in fact Aristotelian. While the interpretations of Beiner, Farrell, and Garver differ among themselves in emphasis, generally the effort to see the *Rhetoric* as a primary location for the study of Aristotelian practical reason commits these authors to claim that Aristotle understands rhetoric as in some sense a *praxis*, not only or primarily as a *technê*. The implications of this view are radical for our understanding of Aristotelian rhetoric. For Farrell, the implication is that Aristotle understands the relationship between the parties to a rhetorical transaction as dialogic, for Garver and Beiner that Aristotle views rhetorical discourse as prior to and constitutive of politics.[4]

Farrell explicitly attributes to Aristotle a dialogic view of rhetoric. Farrell moves from the argument that rhetoric for Aristotle is in part a *praxis* to the conclusion that as a *praxis*, rhetoric has internal standards of excellence and that these standards include most prominently the "mutual regard that speakers and audiences must have for one another" (62). Throughout *Norms*, Aristotelian rhetoric is presented as "reciprocal" and "collaborative." The implication is that influence between speaker and audience is mutual and that rhetoric is an activity, a doing, in which the measure of the art is the conduct of the parties to the transaction, not the result. Farrell intends to counter the view that Aristotelian rhetoric is a productive, speaker-centered, unilateral art. His remark at one point that "Aristotle nowhere explicitly says that the aim of rhetoric is to persuade" (94) seems intended to call into question that Aristotle equates rhetoric with persuasion.

It is not true that Aristotle nowhere states that rhetoric's aim is to persuade, since in the *Nicomachean Ethics* Aristotle says almost precisely this: "A doctor does not deliberate whether to cure his patient, nor a speaker whether to persuade his audience, nor a statesman whether to produce law and order" (112b13–15). For Aristotle it virtually goes without saying that the purpose of rhetoric is persuasion, and scholars have traditionally (and correctly) understood the prototypical rhetorical situation of the *Rhetoric* as opponents attempting to persuade a nonparticipatory audience of judges or spectators. Rather than a decision emerging from an audience empowered by rhetoric (Farrell's reading), the *Rhetoric* assumes that a speaker is attempting to control an audience's response. There is evidence for this view throughout the text. At 1.1.10, Aristotle remarks that it is "serviceable to gain over the hearers." Furthermore, Aristotle's many reversible premises, which can be used to create opposing arguments that promote whichever of two conflicting inferences serves the rhetor's ends, would not make sense if empowerment, and not control, were the purpose. Finally, there can be no question in the presentation of the emotions in Book 2 that Aristotle sees the rhetor as in control: Speakers are said to "create" the emotional response in the judges (2.1.8), to "instill" and "produce" it (2.3.17), to "bring those who . . . are on the other side . . . over to whatever feelings he [the speaker] chooses" (2.4.32). This is the staple of a speaker-centered, controlling rhetoric, not one intended to empower an audience to an independent judgment.[5]

Ronald Beiner is admirably direct in his claim that Aristotle understands rhetoric as constitutive of and prior to politics:

> This teleologically structured character of political life is exemplified in the deliberative process, as shaped by rhetoric. Deliberative oratory recommends possible ends to be pursued. Rhetorical speech sets the "target" at which we should "aim."
>
> But we must be careful not to misunderstand the place of rhetoric within this teleology. It is not an "external" teleology, where rhetoric merely serves as means to an independently posited end. The point is not that we *use* rhetoric to attain our ends, but that our ends are themselves inextricably situated in a rhetorical medium, and are constitutively shaped by this medium. Our ends are not merely pursued rhetorically, they are themselves constituted rhetorically. This is what it means to say that political ends are subject to deliberation (and not simply manipulation). (1983, 95)

On Beiner's reading, Aristotle understood constitutional principles and political policies to emerge in the process of debate and discussion, making politics not external to rhetoric but its product. On this view Aristotelian rhetoric is not, with respect to politics, belated and instrumental but simultaneous and constitutive.

Against the constitutive view of Aristotelian rhetoric is not only the well-known statement in Book 1, chapter 2, of *Nicomachean Ethics* (1975) in which Aristotle identifies politics as the "authoritative" science that directs rhetoric and the other arts (1094a) but more importantly evidence within the *Politics* itself. The fear that seems most to haunt Aristotle in the *Politics* is of a democratic assembly that rules by decree, a fear he expresses repeatedly. An assembly overriding, by majority fiat, constitutional principles, laws, and traditions (the subjects of forums) is an example of a system in which rhetoric—the deliberation of an unrestrained assembly—is constitutive of politics. It is "rhetoric dressed up in the form of politics" (1.2.7). Far from Aristotle's ideal, it is what he feared most.

Aristotle's program called for a rhetoric under the direction of politics, which would mean on an operational level that a constitution, itself the product of philosophical discussion under the auspices of dialectic, would set limits on who participates in a forum and what counts as an argument. Participation in a political assembly or court can be limited to citizens, a status defined by a constitution. For example, we know from the *Politics* that Aristotle favored a relatively large but hardly universal franchise, in large part because he judged an educated middle class as most able at deliberation, "the readiest to obey reason" (4.11.1295b). A limited franchise and a strong constitution produce a deliberative body capable of, and committed to, deliberating about the good for the *polis*, he thought. That in the *Rhetoric*, Aristotle's characterization of the rhetorical audience contrasts with his view of the citizen-deliberators of the *Politics* is not a contradiction from an Aristotelian perspective. While the general parameters of the rhetorical audience (numerous and not expert) are assumed within disciplinary rhetoric, the character of a particular audience is set by the rules of forums as established politically. The ideal deliberators of the *Politics* differ from the audience typically assumed in the *Rhetoric* as the citizens of Aristotle's ideal polity differ from the contemporary citizens (as Aristotle regarded them) of democratic Athens (Sprute, 1994, 126–27; Beiner, 1983, 177–78 n. 25). It is not difficult to imagine how similar external constraints would limit what counts as an argument by evidentiary rules. "In well-governed states," Aristotle writes, the laws forbid "speaking outside the subject," and the Areopagus is an example of a court in which such strictures are enforced (1.1.5). Rhetorical practice will properly take its character from the political system and culture of which it is a part.

One might view Beiner's attempts (and Farrell's and Garver's) to blur the distinction between *technê* and *praxis* as an appropriately subtle response to a complex text. Beiner's frank concession that Aristotle may not himself have held the constitutive view of rhetoric (96) that Beiner had claimed to have teased out of Aristotle's work further suggests that Beiner thinks that intertextual ambiguities and tensions license his method. If this is true, then the ground of our disagreement shifts to one of appropriate hermeneutic restraint. That Aristotle explicitly defines rhetoric as a *technê* and nowhere qualifies or contradicts that explicit statement would seem to set a hermeneutic boundary: We can argue that *technê* itself is a complex term and attempt to attribute anything said in definition of the class *(technê)* to the individual member (rhetoric), but we may not, in the absence of textual evidence, attribute to Aristotle the view that rhetoric is a hybrid. Recent efforts to find in Aristotle a dialogic or a radical epistemic view of rhetoric as a basis for an argument that rhetoric is constitutive of politics, even though in a good cause, seem to me instances of the interpretative practice that McKeon harshly faulted thirty years ago: "The enthusiastic reformulation of what he (Aristotle) thought and the construction of what he should have said frequently carry the defense of his doctrines far from the evidence of his text and even into contradiction of his statements. . . ." (1965, 202).

Attractive as the constitutive, epistemic view of rhetoric is, we pay too great a price when even with the best intentions, we attribute it to Aristotle, for it blinds us to what the genuine Aristotelian view is. This cost becomes clear with Beiner's argument that there is only one alternative to his constitutive view of rhetoric, a debased "traditional one": "The traditional model upon which rhetoric has tended to be construed is that first I discern what I want, what my ends are, and then I choose the most efficacious medium in which to pursue it, the most effective means to the end. It is this model that has, as it were, 'given rhetoric a bad name'" (1983, 95).

But Beiner's "traditional model" of rhetoric is no more Aristotle's than is the constitutive one he opposed to it. The assertive "I" of Beiner's "traditional model"—"first I discern what I want, what my ends are, and then I choose the most efficacious medium in which to pursue it, the most effective means to the end" (1983, 95)—is not Aristotle's idea of the relationship between the rhetor and society. Rather, for Aristotle, forums provide the only ends that a speaking "I" can sensibly pursue if that "I" expects to be heard. Those ends come under the regulation of forums that are directed by politics. Crucial to an understanding of those ends is Aristotle's notion of speaking to the subject.

Conclusion

In linking rhetoric to both reason and to survival instincts (to attack and defend), Aristotle implied that unilateral, persuasive discourse will always be part of the human, cultural equation. Nothing in history since Aristotle would offer grounds for doubting this. If we would take inspiration from Aristotle, we would, rather than lament human nature or deny or repress it, attempt to contain and direct it to socially useful ends. If the *Rhetoric* is to be our guide, we would turn our attention not to redefining rhetoric as dialogic or as a form of *praxis* but to developing forums that constrain and direct rhetorical practice within the limits of our own constitutional principles.

In the *Institutes* (3.8.1–3), Quintilian complained about the nature of one such constraint—that within the deliberative forum. No doubt Quintilian was offended by Aristotle's insistence on utility alone as relevant to hearers in a political assembly and with Aristotle's concomitant dismissal of justice and honor as secondary, if not altogether irrelevant, in this context. But Aristotle saw, as among his most important contributions to rhetoric as an art, his emphasis on speaking to the subject. So he stressed it—so much so that he produced some examples that many readers, including Quintilian, have found disturbing. And yet, I believe Aristotle advances speaking to the subject as an ethical constraint on rhetorical practice.

The criterion of relevancy, though in itself morally neutral, nonetheless serves as a constraint, one that is, in a general sense, grounded in what is essential to the art as Aristotle defined it and could provide a reasonable basis for evidentiary rules. Speaking to the subject thus checks rhetoric from becoming the unrestrained technology of Beiner's "traditional" theoretical model while granting rhetoric the degree of autonomy that, as a genuine art, it must have.

Notes

I thank Alan Gross for his suggestions and careful readings of three versions of this essay.

1. I am not denying that Aristotle regards *pathos* and *êthos* as legitimate aspects of rhetoric, only that he sees his contribution as an emphasis on *logos*. In a gloss at 1.1.3, Kennedy points out that Aristotle's use of *"pisteis"* at 1.2.2–3 is intended to include *êthos* and *pathos*, while at 3.17.5, *"pisteis"* is intended as subject-oriented argument as distinguished from *êthos*. We cannot, then, be certain of Aristotle's intention here (at 1.1.3), but he emphasizes the centrality to rhetoric of arguing to the subject.

2. Support for understanding *"pragmatos"* broadly, rather than as a legal term, is to be found in both Liddel, Scott, and Jones (1968) and Grimaldi (1980a). Providing a gloss at 1.1.11, Grimaldi writes that "perhaps the best explanation of the phrase is 'irrelevancies'" (I.24); see also his *Studies in the Philosophy of Aristotle's "Rhetoric"* (Grimaldi, 1972, 44). Speaking "outside the subject" can apply to all of the forums of rhetoric.

3. The point I am making here may seem similar to one Eugene Garver makes in *Aristotle's "Rhetoric": An Art of Character* (1994). But though our conclusions are similar, the bases for them contrast. We both agree that Aristotle recognizes his contribution to rhetoric as emphasizing the importance of argument. Garver sees Aristotle's emphasis on argument as an effort to identify an internal end that regulates an art that is also (because it has an internal end) a practice (22–34). My point is that as a *tekhnê*, rhetoric is necessarily internally neutral—can potentially persuade to any end—but is subject to regulation from without, from politics. Though what is proscribed would vary as policies differ, Aristotle's insists that no reasonable policy could prohibit argument.

4. The openness and frankness that characterizes Garver's argumentative style allows him seemingly to disclaim conclusions that he seems to have argued for. For example, after maintaining that rhetoric is, for Aristotle, a "civic art, rather than a professional one," Garver adds, "But there is one obvious difficulty with my thesis. Aristotle never explicitly says anything resembling it in the *Rhetoric*" (45). Or Garver offers an apology if readers end up where his argument seems clearly to have taken them: "The more intelligible and attractive Aristotle makes the art of rhetoric, the harder it is to keep it subordinate to politics, as he insists it is. Indeed, by redescribing the kinds of rhetoric as kinds of practical discourse

and practical reason I may have myself contributed to this insubordination by abstracting the kinds of rhetoric from the institutional setting in which they function" (74). Since this argumentative style forces readers to choose, I choose to ignore the disclaimers and focus on the implications of the arguments.

5. Although *Norms* is not the target of its critique, my "Aristotle's *Rhetoric,* Dialogism, and Contemporary Research in Composition" makes some of these same points.

ON BOOK 2 OF THE *RHETORIC*

4

The Contemporary Irrelevance of Aristotle's Practical Reason

Eugene Garver

This essay explores the interrelations among Aristotelian practical reason, Aristotelian emotion, and their political context by looking at three things. First, it outlines Aristotelian practical reason and its differences from the Humean variety that supposedly characterizes modern people and modern moral theory. Second, it highlights some of the features of Aristotelian emotion, as exhibited in the *Rhetoric*, that seem most alien to contemporary theory and practice and asks whether these features are an integral part of a conception of emotion coordinate with Aristotelian practical reason. Finally, this combination of attractive picture of practical reason with a dubious vision of emotion is used to suggest that there is no simple road back to Aristotle. It is, in fact, just those features of Aristotle's emotions that are least attractive that tell us the most about Aristotle's world and our own. The essay concludes that Aristotelian practical reason is not available for us to adopt as a way of addressing our own moral problems and that we would not want to pay the price of adoption anyway.

"Back to Aristotle!" is the very peculiar rallying cry for some of those dissatisfied with contemporary moral life and moral theory. Aristotelian practical reason seems more attractive than the standard modern picture, in which reason is famously the slave of the passions. For us, practical reasoning starts from some desire. Without the desire, reason could never begin and would never end in action. What Alasdair MacIntyre calls Humean and Bernard Williams calls "Sub-Humean" reason is by itself not only inert but amoral: "Reason cannot tell me that I may not prefer the destruction of the world to alleviating the pain in my little finger.[1]

In the contemporary account of practical reason, reason's job is to construct connections between means and ends that allow that initial desire to transfer motivating force along the means/end chain. Modern logic is supposed to transmit whatever truth there is in the premises to its conclusions. It does not generate truth itself. A practical reason parallel to that conception of logic starts from a desire itself not determined by reason and transmits motivation from the end to the actions that will achieve the end. It follows that practical reasoning cannot be about actions that are good in themselves, and if reason cannot be about such actions, still less can practical reason itself be its own end.

Aristotelian practical reason seems to offer itself up as an alternative to this ugly picture that fits modernity only too well. What has not been considered, though, is that Aristotelian practical reason is part of a larger package. It makes sense alongside a coordinate vision of the emotions, and both of them make sense within a quite specific moral and political context. I turn to the *Rhetoric* not only to see practical reason in action but also to see it operating for good and ill, unlike the perfected practical reason that we see exhibited in the *Ethics*. The *Rhetoric* displays the interconnections between Aristotelian practical reason and the emotions it requires, as well as the political context in which it is functional and intelligible.

I want to explore the interrelations among Aristotelian practical reason, Aristotelian emotion, and their political context by looking at three things. First, I want briefly to outline Aristotelian practical reason and its differences from the Humean variety that supposedly characterizes modern people and modern moral theory.[2] Second, I want to highlight some of the features of Aristotelian emotion, as exhibited in the *Rhetoric*, that seem most alien to contemporary theory and practice and ask whether these features are an integral part of a conception of emotion coordinate with Aristotelian practical reason. Finally, and very briefly, I want to use this combination of an attractive picture of practical reason with a dubious vision of emotion to suggest that there is no simple road back to Aristotle. I believe it is just those features of Aristotle's emotions that are least attractive that tell us the most about Aristotle's world and our own. My title, then, "The Contemporary Irrelevance of Aristotle's Practical Reason," indicates that Aristotelian practical reason is not available for us to adopt as a way of addressing our own moral problems and that we would not want to pay the price of adoption anyway.[3]

Aristotelian Practical Reason—A Quick Sketch

In contrast to modern practical reason, Aristotelian practical reason is intrinsically motivating and inherently moral. There is a quick move, for the Aristotelian, from the affirmation of goodness to desire. Once I recognize that something is good, I consequently and immediately desire it. "No one wishes for anything except when he thinks it good" (*Rhetoric* 1.10.8). There is no gap between knowing and choosing. The Aristotelian practical reasoner cannot say, "I know what is best, but I don't feel like doing it. Why should I be moral?" Practical reasoning, unlike theoretical reasoning, has motivating and persuading force, and so his frequently quoted claim that "thought by itself moves nothing" continues: "What moves us is thought aiming at some goal and concerned with action" (*NE* 6.2.1139a35–36); a few lines later he will say that choice is indifferently called desiderative reason or rational desire (b4). For Hume, the sentence "thought by itself moves nothing" is categorical; for Aristotle, practical reason is exempt. Aristotelian practical reason is a mode of rationality that is inherently moral. "Reason urges people in the right way and exhorts them for their good" (1.13.1102b14–17). If reason can initiate its own projects instead of waiting on desire, then it can reason about ends and not only about means. Reason can fully rule, and morality can have a secure foundation.[4]

Alasdair MacIntyre describes individual moral development as a progress from Humean to Aristotelian practical reason. We all begin, he says, by taking reason as the calculation of means to ends given by desire. But some of us develop a mode of practical rationality in which we reason about actions worth doing for their own sake, and so reason becomes its own end. "Progress in practical rationality consists precisely in the transition from Humean to Aristotelian practical reasoning, from entirely personal contexts to contexts of practice" (1982, 302). We are born Humeans, and some of us develop into Aristotelians. We are born individuals, and some of us become citizens. We are born consumers, and some of us become noble.

Aristotle himself exhibits that movement from Humean to Aristotelian practical rationality. The model for moral deliberation in the *Ethics* is solving a geometry problem, but instead of reducing all practical reason to instrumental calculation, Aristotle shows that all practical reason is moral reason, and so deliberation can extend to acts chosen for their own sake.[5] Moral reasoning is not one species of practical thinking among others, because morality is not one kind of practicality, alongside others such as expediency, want-satisfaction, or prudence. Aristotle offers the prospect of circumventing what Sidgwick called the "dualism of practical reason."

While moral education should take us from Hume to Aristotle, the grand narrative of the history of civilization MacIntyre offers goes in the other direction. Once there was a polis in which people could develop the kind of practical reason that Aristotle describes, but now we are rootless, cosmopolitan consumers for whom Hume's account of practical reason is unfortunately true. MacIntyre's Humeans are then not children but degenerate adults or adults living in degenerate moral and political worlds. The modern world holds us all as perpetual children using instrumental reason to satisfy private desires, the only kind we have. In an inversion of Hegel's philosophy of history, where the Greeks thought that some were free and others slaves, now all are slaves.

Aristotelian Practical Reason and the Emotions

None of this is new or very controversial. What has not been explored in recent examinations of practical reason and Aristotelian practical reason is the way Aristotelian practical reason must be coordinated to a specifically Aristotelian conception of the emotions. The development of Aristotelian practical reason requires a development of emotions coordinate with such reason. It is not clear to me that Aristotle will continue to seem so attractive or so relevant once the emotional dimension is laid out more fully. Aristotelian practical reason and emotion make sense for people whose primary external good is honor; Humean practical reason and emotion are appropriate when the central external good is money.

The feature of Aristotelian practical reason that moderns find appealing is that it infers immediately from good to desire. Coordinate to that, Aristotelian emotions infer immediately from desire to goodness. By practical reason, if I think that something is good, I want it and act to obtain it. By Aristotelian emotion, if I want something, I therefore think that it is good. Where reason is intrinsically motivating, emotions are intrinsically assertive. "As assertion and denial are to thought, so pursuit and avoidance are to desire" (*NE* 6.2.1139a20).

We today can see something as good, or see that we should do it, and still have no motivation to act. A reason to act by itself does not create a motive for acting. People therefore know what is right without feeling committed to acting on that knowledge. And so people have thought that Aristotelian practical reason might solve modern moral problems, because it creates an immediate inference from thinking something good to a desire to act. The corresponding emotions fortify the connection between what is best and what is done by creating immediate inferences in the opposite direction, from desiring something to thinking it good and thinking it is deserved. The good man makes those inferences, and vices and moral errors consist in failing to make them:

> The pusillanimous person is worthy of goods, but deprives himself of the goods he is worthy of and would seem to have something bad in him because he does not think he is worthy of the goods. Indeed he would seem not to know himself for if he did, he would aim at the things he is worthy of since they are goods. . . . Each sort of person seeks what he [thinks he] is worth; and these people hold back from fine actions and practices, and equally from external goods, because they think they are unworthy of them. (4.3.1125a10–27)

What is interesting, and troublesome, is what else has to be true of the emotions for them to be assertive in this way. First, Aristotle's man takes things personally. If something is good, he wants it. At the same time, he takes things morally. If he wants something and thinks it good, he thinks he deserves it. Both these inferences are defeasible. A friend could see that something is good but want me to have it. In the same way, because practical reason is immediately motivating does not mean that it immediately creates the decisive motive. If I suddenly in the heat of battle figure out that philosophy is the best activity, I will not immediately walk away from the trenches. As I will show later, part of virtue consists in blocking these inferences. But while defeasible, these inferences are immediate: if I want something, I think it good, and if something is good, I want it.

Therefore Aristotle's man has a personal orientation to the world of value. No one can be good without taking things personally: The inirascible man is bad because he is not "the sort to defend himself and such willingness to accept insults to oneself and to overlook insults to one's family is slavish" (4.5.1126a7–9). "Men of great-souled nature are not fierce except towards wrongdoers, and their anger is still fiercer against their companions if they think that these are wronging them" (*Pol.* 7.6.1328a10–12). The enemy of virtue is not egoism. Many vices come from failing to take things personally enough, or to take things personally in the right way.

The account of *stasis* in *Politics* 5 shows in a particularly compact and striking way the difference that this personal orientation to the world of value makes, and how different Aristotelian practical reason and emotion are from the modern picture. The authors of the *Federalist* are perfect Humeans. They see rich and poor fighting over measures that will benefit one side or the other. In the past two hundred years, we have become increasingly able to see how easily I can rationalize my desires: Whatever I see advancing my interests I will call just. Of course, men engage in factional conflict over wealth and honor, but the primary cause is the desire for inequality and equality. In the *Politics*, by contrast, there is nothing special about money and honor. True, men fight over them, but people equally fight over "arrogance, fear, preeminence, contempt, disproportionate growth, electioneering, underestimation, [neglect of] small things, and dissimilarity" (5.2.1301a38–1302b4). Nevertheless, conflict and *stasis* are always motivated by and constituted by the desire for justice. Where we today might think that clashing claims about justice were euphemistic covers for the desire for money or public office, Aristotle sees it the other way around. We might both want the same goods, but conflicting desire only causes faction when we each think we deserve it.

Having Aristotelian emotions seems as attractive as Aristotelian practical reason—to those of us with neither. If I cannot move from desiring something to thinking that it is good, then my desire wanes. In that way, goodness is a test of whether I really desire something. I take responsibility for my emotions and desires. They are not whims. They are coordinate to assertions about what I think is good. The emotions are subject to moral assessment.

The emotions in the *Rhetoric* are indispensable to Aristotelian practical reason. Aristotle's treatment of the emotions in the *Rhetoric* has had a bad press because he shows how manipulable they are. But their manipulability is a sign of their rationality. Aristotle calls "'in accordance with reason' [things] that people long for on the basis of persuasion; for their desire to see and possess many things after hearing about them and being persuaded" (1.10.5). Manipulability is a property that exists along the boundary between the causal and the rational and allows border crossings. The emotions are not fully rational because they involve desire but are rational enough to be created and destroyed by argument.

Precisely this degree of rationality creates a space for responsibility and praxis between two domains in which, for different reasons, necessity makes praxis and responsibility impossible. I am not responsible for being purely affected; that is the domain of the involuntary. I am not responsible for the truth of my opinions. It is not that truths are involuntary, but they have a compulsive power and necessity of their own. Between these two lies praxis. As much trouble as the manipulability of the emotions causes, without it the rationality of the practical would be impossible.

Taking things personally makes the emotions rational enough to be open to persuasion. Aristotle's man not only infers from the fact that he wants something to the conclusion that it is good, but to the conclusion that he deserves it. To have one's desires thwarted is to feel wronged. If I act and succeed, I think I have earned and deserve what I get, and if I do not succeed, it is not only a personal failure but an injustice.[6] "People become calm if they think they themselves have done wrong and suffered justly; for anger does not arise against justice nor against what people think they have appropriately suffered" (2.3.15). Emotions become rational as they become moral. We today might think that taking things personally and taking them morally are different, even at odds. MacIntyre's account of moral development as moving away from personal contexts is only a half truth. We move away from one kind of personal context into another. For Aristotle, the personal and the moral are interdependent; we want to be friends with "those who are morally good and respected" (2.4.11). What is unjust "becomes more unjust as it is practiced on closer friends" (*NE* 8.9.1160a3; see *Rhetoric* 2.2.15). "There are two things above all which make human beings cherish *(philein)* and feel affection *(agapeton)*, what is one's own and what is dear" (*Pol.* 2.4.1262b21–23).[7] The more personally Aristotle's man takes things, the more morally. This is the paradox that makes a return to the detailed descriptions of the emotions in Aristotle's *Rhetoric* so rewarding.[8]

Aristotelian Emotions: Taking Things Personally and Taking Them Morally

Not just any emotions will be coordinate with Aristotelian practical reason, but the emotions in the *Rhetoric* fit the requirements perfectly. They are the emotions involved in deliberation and judicial decisions, the emotions we must feel in order to decide to act. "Fear makes men deliberate" (2.5.14). There are no objectless emotions, such as a generalized anxiety, or, as I will show later, the powerful emotions people today attach to ideological abstractions. Not only do the *Rhetoric*'s emotions always have objects, those objects are always other people. In other contexts we might be said to fear all kinds of dangers, but in the *Rhetoric* the object of fear is another person, not our own possible loss and not a fear *that* something will happen. Aristotle carefully distinguishes these emotional responses from reactions to actual pleasures and pains, losses, and gains. The more personal identity is social, the less emotional concern is invested in the private and the somatic pleasures and pains. The emotions of the *Rhetoric* are emotions of someone ready to decide and ready to act. These are emotions that orient a person practically to the world, enabling him or her to see the world as a series of opportunities and dangers for praxis. These are the emotions subject to rational persuasion.[9]

These are the emotions of the citizen. As I will argue later, these emotions are determinate manifestations of the *thymos*, and it is the *thymos*, not reason, that the citizen has and the slave lacks. The citizen's civic and personal identity comes from just these moral and rational emotions. The effective civic moral agent is someone whose emotions have the rationality and practicality of the emotions of *Rheto-*

ric 2, not the effeminate, childish, or slavish type whose life is devoted to satisfying the pleasures of the flesh. The slave's psyche is dominated by pleasures and pains, and so the slave is a permanent child capable only of Humean reasoning.

People today could say that Aristotle could elevate these more rational emotions and denigrate those more closely connected to the body because he was operating with a primitive psychology that couldn't see that *all* people's desires, not just those of weak people, have roots in the body or in the experiences of early childhood. Aristotle, though, might reply that it is not that modern psychology has discovered this universal truth but instead that modern psychology has had to develop this connection between apparently rational desires and emotions and more irrational and somatic roots to make sense out of modern psyches in which reason is the slave of the passions.

The Definition of Anger

I want to flesh out this picture of Aristotelian emotion before returning, toward the end, to the comparison of ancient and modern emotion and practical reason. The description of emotions coordinate with Aristotelian practical reason starts with the first emotion in the *Rhetoric*, anger, the emotion most closely identified with the *thymos*. The definition of anger as "desire, accompanied by pain, for conspicuous retaliation because of a conspicuous slight that was directed, without justification, against oneself or those near to one," shows three things about the nature of Aristotelian emotion coordinate with Aristotelian practical reason. First, anger is a response to insults as opposed to injuries. If I am really harmed, I would have things other than revenge to worry about; I would have to think about protecting myself, preventing it from happening again, or at least minimizing the harm. To take things personally in the way the angry man does requires *not* taking them personally in the more direct and obvious sense of personal harms or dangers. "Those who are scared out of their wits do not feel pity because so taken up with their own suffering" (2.8.1385b32–34).

Next, anger is a feeling that has built into its definition a desire for corresponding action: I am insulted and, so, want to retaliate. Aristotle's emotions are incipient desires. While more primitive desires might have satisfactions connected to them, all these emotions have actions intrinsically connected to them. Painful as anger is, the pleasures of contemplating and planning revenge can make me put off its consummation, which shows that the emotion itself has intrinsic value to me. The emotions coordinate to Aristotelian practical reason are most fulfilled in complexes of desire and action that are analogous to actions that are their own end.

Finally, I was insulted publicly—a *conspicuous* slight—and so want public revenge. Not only is anger a response to insults rather than injuries, but we are angrier at someone who does something for spite than for gain, so the things we take most personally are the things that affect us, as Humean bundles of desires, the least. Our true self is a public self, a denial of a private self.

It is because our personal identity is civic identity that we take things personally by taking them morally. Anger is a response to *unjustified* slights and insults. As I mentioned earlier, two things characterize the moral emotions in Aristotle's descriptions, the inference from goodness to desire and from desire to desert. It is because I think your charges are unwarranted that I am insulted by them and want revenge. If I become convinced that I got what I deserved, my anger disappears. If I become convinced that you got what you deserved, my pity is at least lessened; the more I think you lovable, the more I will love you. As I noted before, "People become calm if they think they themselves have done wrong and suffered justly; for anger does not arise against justice nor against what people think they have appropriately suffered" (2.3.15). It is, therefore, because I take things morally that I take them personally.

Aristotle's emotions create moral connections between self and world. We need such emotions for Aristotelian practical reason to function. But the picture is not one of unmixed brightness and hope. This then is the first aspect of the picture of emotion that we might find objectionable. Aristotle's man takes things personally where other conceptions of morality might instead counsel minding one's own business. He makes moral judgments, judgments about goodness and desert, in circumstances where, once again, we might think such judgments were the interfering moralizing of a busybody. The energy we might direct toward needs and their satisfaction Aristotle's man instead directs at the actions, responses, and characters of others. To be a citizen, for Aristotle, is to care about one another's virtue. Aristotelian practical reason requires Aristotelian emotions that are potentially always on duty. Aristotle's man can never retreat into a valuable private sphere. The face-to-face community is emotionally demanding.

Ancient ethics was all encompassing, while modern morality is confined to a determinate sphere, our relations to others. For us, some situations might be moral, while others call for technical, prudential, or aesthetic judgment. But the ancients allowed no such distinctions. Ancient ethics had as its subject the good life and the human good, while the "peculiar institution" of modern morality concerns duties and most centrally duties toward others.[10] In the modern vision, most of what makes for a good life is independent of morality. As Mill puts it, "ninety-nine hundredths of all our actions are done from other [than moral] motives, and rightly so done if the rule of duty does not condemn them" (1957, 23).[11] For Aristotle's man, all practical situations are moral, and ethical judgment and response is always appropriate. Some actions might be beneath one's notice, and some might warrant excuse, not censure, but there is nothing different in kind from morality.

So much too is a commonplace of current discussion, and true enough as a first approximation. But that contrast between ancient and modern has an important and unnoticed consequence. When ethics is not confined to a single sphere, there is also no specifically moral emotion either. Pity, sympathy, love, respect, and shame have all been singled out more recently as the passion that elevates us above self-interest into a moral realm. But if in ancient ethics there is no special sphere of prudence or interest, there could be no purely personal motive like self-preservation or the desire for power that needs countering by a peculiarly moral motive. The emotions in Aristotle's *Rhetoric* are equally personal and ethical, and that they are personal and ethical makes them by themselves neither good nor bad. "We are neither praised nor blamed in so far as we have feelings" (*NE* 2.5.1105b31). We should not wish that we too could have Aristotle's emotions or be glad that we do not.

Aristotle's Problems with Aristotelian Practical Reason

When Aristotle's man, unlike people today, thinks that something is good, he wants it. While that conception of practical reason might seem to solve our moral problems, Aristotle sees that it *creates* the fundamental moral problem of *pleonexia* and injustice. To think that because something is good, it should therefore be the goal that directs our choices is the essence of injustice: "Since the unjust person is greedy, he will be concerned with goods—not with all goods, but only with those involved in good and bad fortune, goods which are, [considered] unconditionally, always good, but for this or that person not always good. Though human beings pray for these and pursue them, they are wrong; the [right] thing is to pray that what is good unconditionally will also be good for us, but to choose [only] what is good for us" (*NE* 1.1129b1–7).[12]

Problems of greed and injustice for Aristotle are not problems of egoism and a failure to infer from goodness to desire; they are problems that arise because we *do* infer from goodness to desire. Injustice for Aristotle is not primarily a matter of wronging other people; it is in the first place a moral vice in which we infer immediately from goodness to action. It is for that reason that in the *Politics,* while political factions contest over honor and money, what is really at stake is equality and inequality. It's not that we both want the money but that we both think we deserve it.

People today might look longingly at Aristotle's practical reason because of the smooth movement from seeing that something is good to acting on it, but Aristotle sees that ease of movement as the source of moral problems. Aristotelian practical reason is essential for virtue and practical wisdom, which depend on immediate connections between good and desire. But that same practical reason has characteristic vices. It would stack the deck in the comparison of ancient and modern to look only at the virtuous side of Aristotelian practical reason and its emotions.

The *Ethics* and *Politics* are devoted to showing how practical reason in the good man and the statesman can *resist* the inference from the good to what I should do. In the *Politics,* thus, Aristotle says that problems of justice come from the fact that people judge badly in their own cause. They do so because they take a partial conception of justice and mistake it for true justice. It is not self-interest that precludes making a moral judgment but one moral judgment that precludes making a better moral judgment. The remedy, then, is not a moral restraint on self-interest but the more complex series of modifications of partial justice in *Politics* 4 through 6. And in the *Ethics*, as my quotation from Book 5 indicates, we do not refrain from injustice out of respect for others' rights or interests, but by seeing that there is a difference between what is good simply and what is good for me, that is, by slowing down the inference from what is best to what I should do.

The *Rhetoric* looks at the emotions through the same lens. When we turn from practical reason to the coordinate emotions, we find that the inferences from desire to good and desire to desert that are so attractive to us turn out to create new problems of their own. When I cannot move from desiring something to thinking that it is good, then my desire wanes. In this way goodness is a test of whether I really desire something. So much is in favor of Aristotelian emotion. But that same inference can make me more possessive of the things I do want, since now I see them not only as objects of my desires but also as things that I am right to desire, things that truly are good. "The cause of pleasure to those who give insult is that they think they themselves become more superior by ill-treating others." In the same way, the final four emotions in the *Rhetoric*, pity, indignation, envy, and emulation, depend on relations between desiring something and thinking that one deserves it—relations that do not in all cases make for better action, either in Aristotle's own eyes or in mine.

Pity, Indignation, Envy, and Emulation

As I said before, there are no specifically moral emotions for Aristotle. Since he has no distinction between self-interest and morality, there can be no specifically moral emotions. Being good is not a function of feeling some emotions rather than others, but of feeling the emotions in appropriate circumstances, directing them at appropriate objects, and responding with appropriate actions (*NE* 2.5.1105b29–1106a11). But in looking at the last four emotions in the *Rhetoric*, Aristotle does an unusual thing. Just as in the *Ethics* he tells us that there are some actions, such as adultery and murder, that are never appropriate and so have no "mean," so here we see that there are some feelings that the good man never has and others that are felt only or mostly by the good. Pity, indignation, and emulation are characteristic of good people, while envy is a mark of bad character.

Looking a little more carefully at these emotions will bring out even more how different Aristotle's moral psychology and consequently his conception of practical reason is from ours. These emotions will bring out more clearly the advantages and disadvantages of easy inference and transmission of motive power among the good, the desired, and the deserved. Most people today would agree with Aristotle that envy is characteristic of bad people and that pitying undeserved suffering is the mark of the good person. The difference between contemporary moral judgment and moral theory and Aristotle's comes to a head with indignation *(nemesis)*.

I would guess that most people today think that we can do quite well without getting indignant at undeserved good fortune. Most people I have asked confess to feeling indignation but resist Aristotle's suggestion that such feeling speaks well of them. And yet I do not think we can make this minor modification of Aristotle's moral psychology without abandoning the central ideas about practical reason and the emotions about the interconnectedness of desire, beliefs in goodness, and the sense of justice: "What is most opposed to pity is what people call being indignant; for it is in some way opposed to feeling pain at undeserved *misfortune* and, being pained at undeserved *good* fortune, arises from the same moral character [as does pity], and both emotions are characteristic of a good character, for it is right to sympathize with and pity those who suffer undeservedly and to feel indignation at those who [undeservedly] fare well; for what takes place contrary to desert is unjust, and thus we attribute being indignant to the gods" (2.9.1–2). (No one reading the *Rhetoric* alone could guess that *nemesis* was before Aristotle a cosmic force restoring justice in response to *hubris*. That last line is the only sign of such a connection, and Aristotle characteristically reads it backward, thinking that we project our emotions onto the cosmos, and so think that *nemesis* is a divine property. The presence of *nemesis* in Aristotle's psychology thus not only looks forward to the difference between a practical reason that centers on honor and one that focuses on money but also looks back to an archaic soul that Aristotle civilizes as he confines practical thought and emotion to the human world of the *polis*.)

"People are prone to indignation if they are worthy of great advantages and have acquired them; for [they think] it is not just for those unlike them to think themselves worthy of the advantages they have. [They are also prone to indignation] if they are virtuous and serious; for [then] they make sound judgments and hate unjust things. No good person would be distressed when parricides and bloodthirsty murderers meet punishment; for it is right to rejoice in such cases, as in the case of those who deservedly fare well" (2.9.12–14). Unless we are pained at violations of justice, at the undeserving succeeding as well as at undeserved suffering, we do not truly make the good our own and so are not good people. The emotional cost of being an Aristotelian practical reasoner should seem, to contemporary eyes, quite high. We can debate whether the fall begins with the destruction of the *polis*, the rise of Christianity, the birth of the nation-state, or the Enlightenment. Any of those is a plausible turning point in a narrative that traces the dissolution of Aristotle's interrelations among desire, beliefs in goodness, and the sense of justice.[13]

Whatever the history, we value pity but not indignation because we think it wrong to take everything morally. Moral response and judgment is one form of judgment among others. Sometimes it is right to look at events morally, and other times it is better to judge in terms of satisfactions, the workings of nature, luck, or the market, or by aesthetic criteria. Instead of feeling indignant that someone undeserving is promoted, we look at how happy the promotion makes the person and her family, or shrug it off as the way the world works. In any case, it's not my problem. Being moral is a part-time job for us, not for Aristotle. The idea of morality, as one category among others, is not so unattractive after all. To be capable of virtue, one must have moral emotions that are on duty all the time.[14]

How to Integrate Reason and Emotion: Back to Aristotle After All?

Aristotelian practical rationality and Aristotelian emotion need each other. Each without the other is atrophied. Practical rationality without the proper emotions is something close to the Humean: It is the ability to calculate, solve problems, achieve ends that are themselves given outside of reason. It is the ability to be a natural slave, whether to one's own passions or someone else's economic needs. When MacIntyre and others claim that we are all Humeans now, they show that those for whom reason is the slave of the passions are themselves slavish.

If the diagnosis that we are all Humeans now is correct, even if it is better to be an Aristotelian than a Humean, it of course does not follow that we either can or should become Aristotelians. Aristotle himself offers no pathway for natural slaves to become free members of political communities; the best they are capable of is becoming slaves to wise masters. Modern society, whether it starts from the destruction of the polis, the rise of Christianity, the birth of the nation-state or the Enlightenment, makes willingly becoming slavish attractive and rewarding.

To have the instrumental intelligence that makes one practically effective in the modern world requires that one *lack* the emotions Aristotle's man values. To see the world personally and morally is to disqualify oneself from the ability to weigh costs and benefits of proposed actions in a properly detached way, including the detachments of counting emotional costs and benefits as items to be weighed alongside external effects.

But there is another possibility too, one that complicates the narrative that would show the fall of man from Aristotle to Hume. It is possible to have the emotions that let us take things personally and so to affirm and deny, pursue and avoid, and yet have an imperfectly developed deliberative or practically rational ability. Without this rationality, those emotions are stunted as much as is rationality without the emotions that let us take things personally and morally.

Such a condition, in which we take things personally and morally but yet not practically, because we have not made the connections between the world and what we can deliberate about, choose, and do, accounts for the power, to which Aristotle could not be alive, of the motivating force of ideological abstractions that separate political passion from interest. Roman patriotism, Renaissance civic humanism, and Enlightenment nationalism all rely on motives that are alien to Aristotle. Aristotle's account of the emotions consequently looks ill suited for our contemporary psyches, which contain powerful irrational forces that split attention between the private and the ideological. We are persuaded of the power of those forces, while Aristotle is not. The more attention is directed to insults and status, the less one is likely to be concerned with either the purely private or the ideological, and conversely.[15]

I believe that Aristotle is aware of a primitive version of that same manifestation of spirit without intelligence that is so powerful today in the force of ideology. When he offers his racial psychology to show the superiority of the Greeks, he claims that Greeks have better reasoning powers than the wild Europeans of the North, but Greek superiority over the soft Asiatics is not in rationality but in *thymos* or spirit, a faculty that is closely related to the first of the emotions in the *Rhetoric*, anger.

"Spirit *(thymos)* is the faculty of our souls which issues in love and friendship and it is a proof of this that when we think ourselves slighted our spirit is stirred more deeply against acquaintances and friends than ever it is against strangers. . . . This faculty of our souls not only issues in love and friendship: it is also the source for us all of any power of commanding and any feeling for freedom" (*Pol.* 6.7.1327b37–1328a6). From this quotation we can see the connection between taking things personally and taking them morally. Asians make good slaves because they have intelligence but no *thymos*. Having an active *thymos* is the condition of personal identity, a condition that fully comes alive only in political communities through the agency of reason. To have a self is to have a sense of what is good for oneself and of what is just, and not simply a perception of pleasure and pain. But that sense of what is good for oneself and of what is just is what it means to be a political animal. On the other hand, the wild Europeans endowed with *thymos* and no reason cannot be enslaved but still are not fit to be citizens. Their freedom, like the power of ideology, is impractical because it is not tied to action as the more rational emotions are, and not tied to political context (see also *Metaphysics* 1.10.1075a11–25). Moral education consists in seeing oneself as a citizen. Personal identity is political identity.

Aristotle's Humeans: Deliberative Versus Judicial Rhetoric

I want to throw in one complication before ending. If there is any source of hope, this can be it. Aristotle recognizes the existence of Humean practical reasoners not only in children, women, and slaves but also in all of us in certain rhetorical situations. If Humean practical reasoners can exist within Aristotle's *polis*, maybe there are uncovered possibilities for Aristotelian practical reason today.

Aristotle distinguishes between deliberative and judicial rhetoric by saying that in deliberative rhetoric the speaker only has to prove the truth of his claims in order to make his case. The deliberative audience decides in its own interest and—the inference is implicit because it is so obvious—therefore they will be moved by the truth. They are not there to be entertained, or to give a prize to the most persuasive speaker. They are committed to deciding what is best for themselves. The earlier treatises on rhetoric, which tried to put "audiences in a certain frame of mind" without affecting their minds through reasoning, are, he says, consequently useless for deliberative rhetoric. The audience of deliberative rhetoric consists of Aristotelian practical reasoners, whose immediate inferences from what they think best to what they choose to do are the basis for the speaker's arguments. "In deliberative situations the judge judges about matters that affect himself so that nothing is needed except to show that the circumstances are as the speaker says" (1.1.10).

Aristotle thinks, though, that those who listen to judicial rhetoric are moved by factors other than argument, because the connection between truth and judgment is not so immediate. And so the passage I just quoted continues: "But in judicial speeches this [i.e., what is sufficient for deliberative rhetoric] is not enough; rather, it is serviceable to gain over the hearer; for the judgment is about other people's business and the judges, considering the matter in relation to their own affairs and listening with partiality, lend themselves to [the needs of] the litigants but do not judge. Thus . . . in many places the law prohibits speaking outside the subject [in court cases]; in deliberative assemblies the judges themselves adequately guard against this" (1.1.1354b35–1355a3).

In judicial rhetoric the speaker cannot presuppose the connection between truth and motivation of the Aristotelian practical reasoner, and so the speaker must create the motivation. He or she does so by stimulating emotions that make people take an argument personally and morally. Where deliberative audiences are Aristotelian practical reasoners, judicial audiences are Humeans. Thus Aristotle brings back in 2.1 the emotions that he excludes in *Rhetoric* 1.1, with the difference that now they are created in the audience via an argument. Aristotle's judicial orator will create for the particular case circumstances in which judges can make intelligent decisions by engaging in Aristotelian practical reason. That is, juries begin as Humean practical reasoners and are made, through the art of rhetoric, into Aristotelian practical reasoners. Of course they are only Aristotelian practical reasoners for that case; Aristotle makes no claims about any morally improving facets of the experience of rhetoric. But that they are temporarily Aristotelian practical reasoners is enough for Aristotle to be able to say, just before the lines last quoted, that "the method of deliberative and judicial speaking is the same."

While contemporary students of practical reasoning rarely think about rhetoric, judicial reasoning is the model for modern practical reason. We typically assume that practical reasoning has to proceed from rule to case and that the point of practical reasoning is to justify our actions. Motivation and justification are as distinct as discovery and justification are in the conception of scientific reasoning parallel to the modern picture of practical reason.[16] For Aristotle deliberation is the model for practical reason because there the Aristotelian combination of the personal and the moral is real and fundamental, while in judicial rhetoric that combination is only created by the speaker. But the fact that even in judicial situations audiences can act as Aristotelian practical reasoners is a huge achievement on the part of Aristotle's *Rhetoric*. He thinks that to make judicial rhetoric the central kind will treat people as Humean practical reasoners and that no art of rhetoric is possible on such a basis. But he also shows how judicial rhetoric can be incorporated within an art whose center is in deliberative rhetoric and that in the right circumstances people, and not only virtuous people either, can engage in Aristotelian practical reason. The current popularity of "virtue ethics" could use some reflection on deliberative rhetoric.

The contrast of Aristotelian to Humean reason is very great. If taking things morally and taking them personally were at odds, as they are in modern conceptions, then judicial rhetoric must be the paradigm for practical reason. Only in judicial reasoning do we take things morally because only there, and not in deliberation, are we judging impersonally and therefore morally. We act more justly and morally in judicial rhetoric because of the lack of a personal stake, while in deliberation selfishness is inevitable, and even appropriate. But Aristotle says that judicial rhetoric is *more* open to abuse because of this lack of personal interest. We want to get things right in deliberative rhetoric because they affect us. If judicial rhetoric is characteristically less ethical than deliberative reasoning, then selfishness is not the prime enemy of morality. Failing to take things personally disables us from taking them morally. The judicial audience can ask, "Why should I be moral?"

We might look longingly at Aristotle's practical reason because of the smooth movement from seeing that something is good to acting on it; Aristotle sees that ease of movement as the source of moral problems. The *Ethics* and *Politics* show how practical reason in the good man and the statesman can resist the inference from the good to what I should do.

Summary

The difference between ancient and modern practical reason is a difference between a kind of practical reason that is itself motivating and one that can only be the slave of the passions. Aristotle's practical reason permitted immediate inference from good to desire. Coordinate to that, Aristotelian emotions infer immediately from desire to goodness, and from desire to thinking that one deserves something. Aristotelian practical reason is attractive to us just because of this quick inference.

But for Aristotle himself, the immediacy of the inference does not solve a moral problem but creates one, that of injustice. Similarly, we find Aristotle's emotions attractive because when desires are connected to taking things personally and morally, we have a personal orientation to the world of value. But Aristotle here too sees these quick connections as creating problems as much as solving them. Aristotelian practical reason is a significant moral vision, but it makes sense only with a specific moral psychology of the emotions and a specific political context. Aristotelian practical reason, and Aristotle's man, are less desirable and less possible for us than the grand narrative of modernity's fall would suggest. To long after Aristotelian practical reason while rejecting his emotions or his political context is itself a kind of injustice: thinking that because something is good, I should have it.

Notes

Thanks for useful suggestions on an earlier draft of this paper from the editors and John Kirby.

1. The term *sub-Humean* is Bernard Williams's (1979, 17–28). The difference between Hume and the "sub-Humean" conception of practical reason is that

for Hume desires cannot become *reasons* for action, while for the "sub-Humean" reasons become reasons for action by being connected to antecedent desires, and those desires are reasons to act. Whether Hume should be taken as the paradigm of modern practical reason is a question I will not investigate here. The two conceptions share the crucial feature that makes them different from Aristotle, though: In neither is reason intrinsically motivating.

2. I want to understand Aristotelian practical reason. I am assuming for the sake of this argument that others have depicted Hume and modernity correctly. I think it is safe to say that ancient versus modern comparisons always oversimplify both sides of the comparison. There is no such thing as either "ancient" or "modern" practical reason as such. Neither the ancient nor the modern world can be that monolithic, and the idea of taking Aristotle as a typical ancient is as silly as it sounds. Toward the end, I will use the *Rhetoric* to point to a complication in Aristotle's picture and suggest that we might derive from that a clue to finding needed complications in its modern counterpart.

3. In addition to the correlations I make among kinds of practical rationality, kinds of emotions, and ethical and political context, there are also correlations between all those and conceptions of the human good. For correlation between kinds of practical rationality and conceptions of the good, see Warren Quinn (1992, 81–95).

4. See John M. Cooper (1988): "Aristotle's distinction between rational and non-rational parts of the soul has nothing to do with the modern distinction between reason (regarded as *the* faculty of concept-formation and the manipulation of concepts), on the one hand, and desire (regarded on its own as a concept-free faculty of urges), on the other hand. There are both conceptual thoughts and (if you like) 'urges' on both sides of Aristotle's distinction between *logos* and the *alogon*." For just one sign of how different Aristotle's conception of the rational and the irrational is from ours, see *NE* 8.6.1149b16, where *epithumia*, desire, is called "crafty," and *epiboulos*, in opposition to *thymos*, is straightforward.

5. I have explored these questions for the *Ethics* in detail in "Aristotle's Genealogy of Morals" and in "The Moral Virtues and the Two Sides of *Energeia*." I fill in the details of this sketch of Aristotelian practical reason in *Aristotle's "Rhetoric": An Art of Character.*

6. In the argument for natural slavery, for example, Aristotle argues that might does not make right, but might is a sign of right (*Pol.* 1.2.1254b25–37).

7. Cf. *NE* 9.7.1167b32–1168a9, 9.9.1169b30–1170a4; *EE* 7.12.1244b28–34; *Rhetoric* 1.11.21–23.

8. The term *Aristotle's man* is Stephen Clark's. I use it because it is less cumbersome than "the person (or man) with Aristotelian practical reason and Aristotelian emotion" (Clark, 1975).

9. Stocker (1983) makes a similar argument characterizing the emotions in the *Ethics*. The list of emotions in *Rhetoric* 2.1 is almost the same as the list in *NE* 2.4.1105b21–23.

10. I take the phrase from "Morality, the Peculiar Institution," the title of the final chapter of Williams (1985).

11. As Harry Frankfurt puts it, ethics orders "our relations with *other people*," while "*what to care about* [and] what to do with *ourselves*" lie outside ethics (1982, 257).

12. At another place Aristotle says that most men do just what he recommends here, choose the advantageous rather than the noble, but that this is not cause for praise. "Most people wish for what is fine but decide to do what is beneficial; and while it is fine to do someone a good turn without the aim of receiving one in return, it is beneficial to receive a good turn" (*NE* 8.14.1162b34–1163a1). See also "The benefactor's action is fine for him, so that he finds enjoyment in the person he acts on; but the person acted on finds nothing fine in the agent, but only, at most, some advantage, which is less pleasant and lovable" (9.7.1168a10–12). More complications can be found in the *Rhetoric*, where he tells us that young men choose the noble and disdain the useful, while the old aim only at the useful. It is those in the prime of life who are able to combine the two.

13. One grand narrative of the contrast of ancient and modern that looks specifically at the emotions is Shklar (1984).

14. Although this is obviously not the place to make such an argument, I think that this difference makes anachronistic and unfruitful projecting the idea of "moral luck" back onto Aristotle.

15. I believe that Hume is the first thinker to recognize the revolutionary power of ideological abstractions detached from interests.

16. The following quotation from Rawls seems to me a perfect example of the modern way of making judicial reasoning the fundamental kind of practical reason. It *is* especially telling because he calls it "deliberative rationality": "A rational individual is always to act so that he need never blame himself no matter how his plans finally work out. . . . This principle will certainly not prevent us from taking steps that lead to misadventure. Nothing can protect us from the ambiguities and limitations of our knowledge, or guarantee that we find the best alternative open to us. Acting with deliberative rationality can only insure that our conduct is above reproach, and that we are responsible to ourselves as one person over time" (1971, 422).

5

Pathos and *Katharsis* in "Aristotelian" Rhetoric: Some Implications

Jeffrey Walker

This essay considers the general account of *pathos* that appears not only in the *Rhetoric* and *Poetics* but also in Aristotle's political, ethical, psychological, and biological/ medical writings and reinterprets this account in light of recent theories of emotion and intentionality. Aristotle's account of *pathos* implies a rhetoric that is not quite "Aristotelian" in the usual sense and that sits uneasily with Aristotle's preferences. Nevertheless—and in the interest of *rereading* Aristotle's *Rhetoric*—it can be argued that the rhetorical implications of this account are at least partly recognized and reflected in the *Rhetoric* and in later Peripatetic thought.

"It is not right," as Aristotle says at the outset of the *Rhetoric*, "to twist the juryman into pandered anger or envy or pity; this would be the same as if someone intending to use a ruler should make it crooked," or *streblon*, meaning twisted, wrenched, distorted, warped out of shape (1.1.5). Aristotle is much concerned with what is required for "well-governed" assemblies, such as the Areopagus, in which appeals that go "outside of the facts" are forbidden or deemed irrelevant; his discussion of this point occupies most of *Rhetoric* 1.1. Moreover, one detects a vehement moral judgment in the philosopher's words: The verb "twist," *diastrephein*, can also mean "pervert"; and the idea that the rhetor is "pandering" to envy or pity, *proagontas*, portrays the pandering rhetor as a *proagôgos*, a pimp. A version of this attitude appears again at *Rhetoric* 3.1.5, in Aristotle's passing declaration that it is preferable and just to argue simply by means of "the facts" so that (as he says) anything other than apodictic demonstration is beside the point.

Such statements seem to reflect a settled, serious conviction; they suggest an ethics of persuasion. At the beginning of *Rhetoric* 2, however, Aristotle declares the necessity of "preparing" (*kataskeuazein*, 2.1.7) the "judger" (*kritês*, 2.1.2) by shaping the different *pathê* that will cause his "judgments" *(kriseis)* to "change" (*metaballein*, 2.1.8)—and then he proceeds to offer ten extraordinary chapters on several key *pathê* (2.2–11), starting with anger and including both pity and jealousy, the very ones he has proscribed as "perverters" of judgment. This account is followed, in turn, by six brief chapters on the emotional predispositions of several types of character: the old, the young, those in their prime, the wellborn, the rich, and the powerful (2.12–17, 1388b–1391b). All these chapters are, as many have noted, the first systematic account of emotional psychology ever provided. But what are they doing in the *Rhetoric*? Not only does the account of the *pathê* in Book 2 seem inconsistent with the expressed ethico-political convictions of *Rhetoric* 1.1 (and 3.1), but that account also seems, as George Kennedy has remarked, to have been imported into the text from somewhere else, as a late addition, and with only minimal adaptation to a discussion of rhetoric (Kennedy, 1991, 122, 164).

The apparent inconsistency between the moral attitude of *Rhetoric* 1.1 and the account of the *pathê* in Book 2 has typically been explained in one of several ways: Aristotle is opposed only to irrelevant appeals to emotion while leaving room for those emotions that are reasonable within the given case; Aristotle's psychology provides emotion with a rationality similar to (and part of) that of the enthymeme, and thus he brings *pathos* under the rule of reason; Aristotle's statements have been composed at different times and reflect earlier and later opinions, as he is moving away from Plato's influence; or, in Book 2, as again in *Rhetoric* 3's account of style and delivery, Aristotle is recognizing the rhetor's practical necessity to accommodate the "depravity" *(mochthêria)* of the audience of common citizens, the crowd of *hoi polloi* ("the many") that does the judging in the jury-courts and public assemblies. (Grimaldi, 1972 and 1980a; Fortenbaugh, 1975; and Wisse, 1989, are the major sources for these rationales; see also Conley, 1982; and Garver, 1994b, 104–38. On the compositional history of the *Rhetoric,* see Brandes, 1989, 1–9; and Kennedy, 1991, 5–7, 299–309.)

None of these explanations are completely satisfactory, partly because they undercut each other and partly because the seemingly contradictory statements about *pathos*, and the chapters on *pathos* themselves, may *all* be later additions composed around the same time (Kennedy, 1991, 304). Moreover, Aristotle's talk about audience "depravity" is especially troubling and significant: The word "depravity," *mochthêria*, derives from *mochtheô*, "to labor" or "be weary with toil," and suggests a vulgar sensibility blunted by hard work and limited education. Aristotle seldom manifests a high opinion of "the many," and in *Nicomachean Ethics* 10.9 he says that "the many" are "obedient" to fear but not to a sense of honor, that they avoid doing evil only because they fear the penalties, that their choices are driven by the wish for pleasure though they have never known what pleasure truly is, that in general their lives are ruled by *pathos*, and that their *pathos* is amenable not to *logos,* reason or discourse, but only to *bia,* force or coercion (1179b).

Aristotle's *Rhetoric* has long been read as a reply to Plato's critique of sophistic rhetoric as an irrational, epistemologically untrustworthy and ethically dubious *technê psuchagôgia*. Let us admit, however, that it has never been especially clear what role the famous account of *pathos* in Book 2 is meant to play in that reply.

Has Aristotle decided to embrace, after all, a version of sophistic *psuchagôgia*, and decided that the rhetor must apply to "the many" a rhetoric of psychagogic, pathological force? Well, maybe. In what follows, I mean to approach that question by considering the place of *pathos* in Aristotelian rhetoric in two main ways: on the one hand, by considering the fuller account of *pathos* that appears not only in the *Rhetoric* and *Poetics* but also in Aristotle's political, ethical, psychological, and biological/medical writings; and, on the other hand, by reading this expanded account in the light of recent theories of emotion and intentionality. My argument will be that the Aristotelian account of *pathos* implies a rhetoric that is not quite "Aristotelian," at least not in the usual neo-Aristotelian sense, and that is quite probably at odds with what Aristotle himself preferred. Nevertheless—and in the interest of *rereading* Aristotle's *Rhetoric*—my argument will also be that the implications of this account of *pathos* are at least partly recognized and reflected in the *Rhetoric*, and in later Peripatetic thought.

I propose to set sail in a leaky boat, as my vehicle will be the notorious concept of *katharsis* and my point of departure the frustratingly brief account of musical *katharsis* offered in *Politics* 8.7. Aristotle is considering musical education, and what types of music are appropriate for young men to learn to play, or only to listen to. Invoking a division of song-types into "the ethical" *(ta êthika)*, "the active" *(ta praktika)*, and "the inspirational" *(ta enthousiastika)*, Aristotle offers the following proposition: Music "serves the purpose both of education and of *katharsis*—and what we are calling *katharsis* is not now plain, but we shall speak of it again more clearly in the [treatise] on poetics *(en tois peri poiêtikês)*—and thirdly [music is] suitable to amusement, to relaxation, and also to giving rest from tense exertion" (1341b). Famously, the parenthetical phrase with its seeming reference to the *Poetics* leads nowhere: All that we find there is the single line, in chapter 6, that tragedy is "the *mimesis* of an action that is serious and complete and having magnitude . . . through pity and fear accomplishing the *katharsis* of such *pathêmata*" (1449b), a line that has itself been the subject of endless interpretive controversy. *Pathêmata* can mean "experiences" or "sufferings," or "emotional things," and thus can refer to the tragic events portrayed on stage; but it can also mean "emotional conditions" or states of mind and thus can refer to the pity and fear felt by the audience, and this variance makes elusive the specific meaning of *katharsis* in the *Poetics*. (For a recent discussion of this issue, see Nehamas 1994.) Thus, all we really can gain from the line in the *Poetics* is what we know already from the discussion in the *Politics:* that Aristotle is thinking of emotional *katharsis* in some way.

As it is often observed, the standard meanings of *katharsis* in ancient Greek are medical and religious. In the medical sense, *katharsis* is "purgation" of unhealthful substances from the body, usually through the application of some drug, a *pharmakon*; this is the usual sense that appears, for example, in the Hippocratic writings (see Hippocrates, *Aphorisms* 4; and Galen, *On the Natural Faculties* 1.13.40 and 3.13.188). In the older, religious sense (from which the medical meaning seems to have derived), *katharsis* is "purification," the removal of spiritual pollution, by means of some ritual (Langholf, 1990, 242–43). But, as Aristotle's parenthetical gesture in *Politics* 8.7 does make clear, he is using the term *katharsis* in a special, unusual way: What he means is "not now plain," and he recognizes that an explanation is required. The nearest we get to such an explanation in *Politics* 8.7 occurs almost immediately: Aristotle says that any *pathos* that can occur "strongly" in some "souls" or psyches occurs in all, in greater or lesser degree, and can be "roused" by the appropriate kind of music, and that those who experience this musically induced emotion are "put into a state (*kathistamenous*, cf. *kathistêmi*) just as if receiving a medical treatment and *katharsis*" (1342a).

In sum, and as the rest of Aristotle's discussion in *Politics* 8 makes clear, different kinds of music will produce different kinds of emotional states, and different kinds of souls have different emotional predispositions, making them more or less responsive to one or another kind of music. As Aristotle says, for example, "mechanics" and "laborers" (*banausoi* and *thêtoi*) have souls "distorted from their natural dispositions" *(parestrammenai tês kata phusin hexeôs)* and are thus responsive to music that "deviates" from the normal modes with high-strung, chromatically irregular melodies and discordant harmonies (1342a)—so that, as he believes, the young should not be trained to be professional musical performers. Such persons have to play the kinds of music their audiences require, including audiences of banausics and thetes, and in doing so they become habituated to the moods such music enacts, thus distorting their own souls into banausic and thetic vulgarity (1341b). For this reason, Aristotle holds that only the "ethical" types of music, *ta êthika*, are suitable for the young to learn to perform, in particular the Dorian mode, which is "most steady" and has a "manly character" (*êthos andreion;* 1342a–b).

All of this clearly resonates with Plato's *Republic*; and it is quite possible, as Andrew Barker has argued, that both Aristotle and Plato have built upon the theories of the fifth-century musicologist Damon, who apparently held that "music influences character" and that "melody is generated by movement of the soul, and . . . movements of different moral types create music of corresponding moral types"—and vice versa (Barker, 1985, 316–17). But, as regards emotional *katharsis*, Aristotle appears to be much closer to a different source, namely Gorgias of Leontini. The passage is familiar but worth quoting in full:

> There holds the same relation in the power of speech *(logos)* upon the soul's disposition, as in the disposition of drugs *(pharmakoi)* upon the body's condition. For just as with drugs different ones draw different juices from the body, and some put an end to sickness and some to life, likewise with speeches some cause distress, and some delight, and some put the listeners into a state of courage, and some with evil persuasions drug and bewitch the soul. (*Helen* 14; Diels and Kranz 1964, 292–93)

Here, of course, the analogy is with *logos*, not with music, but otherwise Gorgias's comparison throws useful light on just what Aristotle could mean by the *katharsis* of emotions. It is worth noting that the analogy with medicine is not complete: Emotional *katharsis* does not correspond precisely to medical *katharsis* but is a sort of counterpart. While in medicine the application of a *pharmakon* causes the secretion of "juices" from the body, resulting in a pleasurable feeling of well-being, in the case of *logos* or music, the *pharmakon* is a particular *technê*—such as the application of a particular rhythm or melodic mode—that causes the soul of the hearer to be "put into a state" (both Aristotle and Gorgias use the verb *kathistanai*) or to have its "disposition" *(taxis)* rearranged according to the "disposition" (*taxis* again) of the *pharmakon* or *technê* applied, and this "state" is expressed behaviorally and physically as a particular type of *pathos:* "fearful shuddering" *(phrikê periphobos)*, "much-weeping pity" *(eleos poludakrus)*, "lament-loving longing" *(pothos philopenthês)*, and so forth (*Helen* 8). The expressed *pathos* is caused to "come out of" the soul by the *pharmakon/technê*, just as "juices" are caused to come out of the body. But the different *pathê* that *logos* or music may draw from the soul are not necessarily bad or harmful "juices," for the listeners may be "put into a state" of courage or delight, as well as any other mood, and the *katharsis* of a *pathos* from the soul does not involve its being "purged away" but rather its becoming manifest. As Aristotle's account of musical *katharsis* in *Politics* 8.7 suggests, different emotional potentialities are latent in the ethical dispositions *(hexeis)* and physical "natures" *(phuseis)* of different types of character, and the process of *katharsis*—in the special and rather Gorgianic sense that he seems to intend—involves the application of a *technê* to produce from this latent potential an actual, particular, and physically embodied *pathos*. The *katharsis* is a forcing-out.

It is apparent in these passages that Aristotle is thinking of the *pathê*, and of the musical *technai* that produce *katharsis* of those *pathê*, as largely irrational forces grounded in bodily processes and predispositions. As Aristotle says in *On the Soul*, "all the *pathê* of the soul" *(ta tês psuchês pathê panta)*—including anger, gentleness, fear, pity, courage, joy, and loving and hating—belong to the body and are inseparable from it, for whenever they appear they are accompanied by bodily effects. Anger is not only a craving for revenge but also a "boiling of blood and heat around the heart" (403a–b). As Stephen Everson has argued, this account implies that "there is a material state which is sufficient for" the occurrence of any particular type of *pathos*, and that inducing the material state alone—such as blood boiling around the heart—would be sufficient to make a person feel, say, anger, even if there were no perceivable reason for that emotion (Everson, 1995, 186). As Aristotle points out in *Problems* 30, persons sometimes take on "melancholic" moods when they drink large quantities of wine, or become "merciful" or "savage" or "silent" or "affectionate," even to kiss on the mouth "someone whom noone would ever kiss if he were sober" (953a–b); and people of naturally "melancholic" dispositions are especially prone to such mood swings because they have an excess of black bile (955a). Thus, on this account, "angry" music would create a corresponding "motion" in the soul of the hearer and in consequence would "stir up" the bodily state of anger, especially in a person whose bodily nature was inclined already to greater than average "heat around the heart"; and at that point, the hearer would in fact be angry, albeit groundlessly.

Well, not quite. Anger is, after all, also a craving for revenge. As *Rhetoric* 2.2 amply points out, this craving is the result of a perception that one has been wronged, a perception mediated by *logos*. For how does one know when one has been wronged? And how does one know what counts as suitable revenge? Aristotle's chief contribution to the psychology of the *pathê* is his argument that a state of *pathos* consists simultaneously of its characteristic physical condition and the perceptions or cognitions that both motivate and define it. Blood boiling around the heart without any accompanying perception of "insult" is not yet "anger" but only a diffuse state, a choleric temper perhaps, a readiness to be provoked to anger by the first plausible (or even implausible) provocation that comes along. The amorous drunk starts kissing ugly people on the mouth not simply because the wine has triggered his urge-to-kiss but also because he has fallen into a state in which his wine-distorted perceptions (and his interpretations of those perceptions) define all sorts of people as erotically lovable; the perceptions and cognitions that define his *pathê* are askew. *Katharsis* of a specific emotion requires both physical arousal and the active presence within the soul of an appropriate conceptual frame.

In the *Nicomachean* and *Eudemian Ethics*, in the *Movement of Animals*, and in the *Problems*, there is a consistent recognition that the *pathê* are part of a psychological economy that humans share with animals (or at least the higher ones). For Aristotle, an emotion is a will-to-act in a specific way—a mode of intentionality—which is prompted, quasi-syllogistically, by sensations and perceptions that are mediated by cognition or (in humans) by *logos*. In *Movement of Animals*, Aristotle gives this example: "Desire says, 'I must drink'" while sensation, imagination or cognition says, of a particular object, "this is drink," so that "straightway one drinks" (701a). In the *Nicomachean Ethics*, Aristotle describes "practical reasoning" as the combination of a "general" opinion *(katholou doxa)* with "another" that pertains to particulars in the realm of sensation; his example is, "all sweet things are pleasant . . . that thing is sweet" (1147a). The combination of such "premises" compels the psyche to affirm the "conclusion," which takes the form of wanting to eat the sweet thing or, in the realm of practical action, picking it up and eating it. These parallel accounts suggest that a *pathos* is an urge-to-act produced as a "conclusion" from the complex "premises" available or present to the psyche, an urge that arouses and prepares the body for physical action and impels that action in a particular direction. As Aristotle says, "the *pathê* fittingly prepare the organic parts, and desire *(orexis)* the *pathê*, and imagination *(phantasia)* the desire; and [imagination] arises either from cognition *(noêsis)* or sensation *(aisthêsis)*" (*MA* 702a).

As William Fortenbaugh has observed, Aristotle's innovation was "a syllogistic explanation" of *pathos*, one that moved beyond the more common, older view that emotion is in essence a bodily phenomenon subject to manipulation simply by means of such *pharmaka/technai* as melodies, rhythms, and drugs. As Fortenbaugh notes, Aristotle says in *Eudemian Ethics* 2.1 that the "spirited" or passionate part of the soul, the *thumos*, "partakes of *logos*" in the sense that it has a "hearkening and obeying" capacity for appreciation and response (1219b). In *Problems* 28, similarly, he says that although *logos* cannot "command" a passion into existence, it can reveal to consciousness the cause or grounds for an emotional response (949b). Thus, it appears that Aristotle construes emotional response as "intelligent behavior open to reasoned persuasion" (Fortenbaugh, 1975, 12–14, 17–18, 26–32, 57). Later in this essay we will be considering whether or in what degree Aristotle really does consider the *pathê* "open to reasoned deliberation"; but here let us note some limitations to this view.

The key one is that we can take "syllogism," in the sense of the formal structure(s) of propositional reasoning described in the *Topics* and *Analytics*, only as an approximate analogy—a sort of "counterpart," again, to the psychological dynamics of emotional response—and indeed we probably should take "syllogism" only in its nontechnical, everyday sense in ancient Greek as inference-making or "adding things up" (Quandahl, 1986, 133; Walker, 1994, 47). While Aristotle describes the materials afforded by *phantasia, aisthêsis*, and *noêsis* as "premises" in an inferential process and describes the outcome of that process as a "conclusion" *(sumperasma)* (*MA* 701a, *NE* 1147a), it is clear that none of these materials need be strictly propositional. Further, the "syllogistic" operation of such diverse "premises" is, as Aristotle says, "simultaneous and quick" (*hama kai tachu; MA* 702b) and need not be given any conscious formulation. As Aristotle says in *Nicomachean Ethics* 7.3 (1147a), undisciplined persons in the throes of *pathos* declare *(legousin)* "proofs and verses of Empedocles" like actors speaking a part, without any real knowledge of either the true grounds of their state of mind or the subject whose propositions their mood has prompted them to spout. The "proofs and verses" are simply after-the-fact rationalizations, or notions and phrases the *pathêtikos* has seized on because of his *pathos*.

Most importantly, as Aristotle notes in both *Movement of Animals* and *Nicomachean Ethics*, the multiple, diverse, simultaneous, and not necessarily conscious "premises" operating in the "syllogistic" process of emotion may also be *conflicted*. An intentionality may be blocked or complicated by some counter-compulsion—an animal's wish to drink may be countered by fear of exposing itself to predators, or a perception that the water is out of reach—or, in human "practical reasoning," one *doxa* may be countered by another: A person confronted with a sweet cake may believe that "all sweet things are pleasant" but also that "sweet things are bad for health" (*MA* 701a, *NE* 1147a). In such cases, the contradiction is resolved not by refuting or rejecting any competing "premises" but simply by giving greater weight to those that have more "energy" in consciousness—or what a Perelmanian rhetoric would call "presence"—at the moment of decision (*NE* 1147a). All the conflicting "premises" still count as "true," but some count more than others. As is clear in *Rhetoric* 1.1, Aristotle is quite aware that the psychological dynamics of *pathos* may "warp" an audience of judges, forcing important and relevant *doxa,* and even "facts" that are acknowledged to be true, completely out of the process of deliberation.

In all of this, as we may note once more, Aristotle is not so far from Gorgias as one might think. As Gorgias says in *Helen* 15–19, desires derived from seeing beautiful or frightful things can "drive out thought" and momentarily (or even permanently) drive out habits of obedience to the laws, or to what is judged good and true. Sight *(opsis)* can "engrave in thought" *(enegrapsen en tôi phronêmati)* the "images of things seen" *(eikonas tên horomenên pragmatên)* so that, in effect, such images—and the pleasure/pain/desire that they arouse—operate in consciousness exactly as do the "premises" in Aristotle's "logic" of emotion, and, as with Aristotle, such "premises" tend to operate with greater force and presence to determine *praxis* than laws, scenarios of punishment for transgression (insofar as these are older, less vivid images in memory), or *katholou doxa* concerning the good and true. The chief difference between Aristotle and Gorgias on the subject of emotion is that Aristotle's analysis is more sophisticated, more detailed, more complete.

Aristotle, in sum, considers *pathos* as a physically embodied, psychologically compulsive will-to-act—a state that has a sort of rationality, or a dynamic that is loosely describable as a counterpart to the "syllogistic" process of inference and response in propositional reasoning. But it is neither wholly propositional nor strictly "syllogistic," nor is it wholly under the rule of *logos*, reason. For though *logos* mediates the perceptions (and interpretations of perceptions) that disclose to consciousness the cause for an emotional response, *logos* cannot "command" or compel emotions—and further, a state of emotion once aroused will tend to "warp" the mind and thence will strongly determine how it perceives and interprets any "premises" presented to it, which it attends to, which it allows to count most powerfully, and which it ignores. *Pathos* can extinguish thought or force it into certain channels. But because the process is describable, one can still contrive a *technê/pharmakon* that can, at least in principle, produce a *katharsis* of *pathos*—not of any *pathos* whatsoever at any time but of the specific *pathos* or the *pathê* latent in the emotional potentialities of a given person at a given moment.

Let us now bring our boat to another port. Aristotle's account of *pathos* resonates with recent philosophical and neurobiological accounts of emotional psychology—accounts that have, unavoidably, been present already in the background of my discussion to this point. Here I wish to bring these into the foreground, if only briefly in a condensed, summative form, partly to suggest the continued viability of Aristotelian *pathos* theory and to provide that theory with a "translation" into contemporary terms, but, more importantly, to suggest its implications for an understanding of the *Rhetoric*.

Perhaps the simplest way to sum up recent theorizing about emotion is to say that emotion tends to be portrayed as an intentional state—a set toward a particular mode of action or behavior, or a particular mode of attention—that fuses primitive (i.e., mammalian) psycho-physiological arousal-states with heterogeneous cognitive frameworks that may include conscious/subconscious beliefs and values (i.e., "discursive formations," ideologies, etc.), imageries, memories, behavioral scenarios, bodily routines, and so forth, as well as information, ideas, or perceptions immediately present to the mind. On the one hand, for example, neurobiological theories tend to grant the role of cognition in shaping emotional response, though the theories focus chiefly on the primitive arousal-states—aggression/escape, appetite, eros, and so forth—that are mediated by the lower, "mammalian" portions of the brain (the limbic system and the hypothalamus). Philosophical theories, on the other hand, tend to grant that emotions have an innate and irreducible physiological component that indeed gives them their urgency, their motive-ness, and even compulsiveness, though these theories place greater emphasis on "emotion" as the cognitive elaboration and constitution of a primitive arousal-state as a particular mode of intentionality. In the larger view that such perspectives adumbrate, a full-fledged "emotion" or "affect complex" is an acquired behavioral scenario—a "script"—that includes the presuppositional frameworks that define the range of possible causes for a given emotion and its possible range of expressions in actual behavior. (On intentionality, see Rorty, 1980, 103–5, 117–18; and Searle, 1983, 1–36; and 1992, 175–96. For neurobiological theories of emotion, see MacLean, 1980; McNaughton, 1989; Vincent, 1990; and Gray, 1991. For philosophical theories, see Solomon, 1976; Rorty, 1980; Calhoun, 1984; de Sousa, 1987; Greenspan, 1988; and Tomkins, 1995).

Thus, according to this general line of thought, the primitive and more or less diffuse arousal-state for (say) "fight/flight" may be differentiated into such conceptually and culturally constituted emotions as "anger," "hate," "derision," "disapproval," "suspicion," "shame," "fear," "terror," "anxiety," and so on, each with its own characteristic "script" or mode of intentionality. The arousal-state prepares the body for action, and the "script" for an emotion/intentionality gives the body an action to perform; depending on which "premises" are operative in consciousness, the "script"/emotion may shift or change, while the underlying state of arousal may stay the same. Indeed, a primitive arousal-state may not become intelligible or actionable until it achieves definitive resolution as one specific kind of emotion/intentionality—a specific *pathos*—permitting the deep, physiological compulsions of the primitive motives/affects to be channeled into, and "acted out" as, particular modes of passional attention, interpretation, and behavior. Moreover, if the general arousal-state cannot be given such resolution, if it cannot be channeled into definite attitudes and/or behavior, the result is likely to be mere distress, an unpleasant state of emotional turmoil and paralysis, in which the person is emotively "worked up" but cannot settle on a particular state of mind and so cannot respond or act.

In addition to providing a general "confirmation" of Aristotelian *pathos* theory (in its basic outlines), such thought also extends and clarifies it in certain ways. For example, the modern accounts make more explicit the cultural production of the cognitive/ presuppositional frameworks that constitute particular emotions or "affect complexes," whereas Aristotle tends to presuppose a "natural" norm from which the vulgar deviate. Further, the modern account not only provides more adequate descriptions of emotional physiology but also suggests an additional reading of Aristotle's *katharsis* metaphor. For if the cognitive construction of primitive arousal-states as specific emotions gives them clarification and actionability as modes of intentionality, then it is possible to understand emotional *katharsis* in a further sense as "purification" of an otherwise diffuse emotional turmoil, and also to understand how Aristotle might attribute "relief and pleasure" to the *katharsis* of even such painful emotions as "much-weeping pity" or "fearful shuddering" (as Gorgias describes them).

It is worth noting that, according to the Hippocratic *Aphorisms* (4.3), "If matters be purged such as should be purged *(hên men hoia dei kathairesthai kathairôntai)*, it benefits and [things] turn out well *(sumpherei te kai euphorôs pherousi)*, but in the opposite [cases] vexatiously *(ta de enantia duscherôs)*." The adverb *duscherôs*, "vexatiously," derives from the noun *cheir*, "hand," and suggests things getting unmanageable, "out of hand": The noun *duschereia* means "annoyance, disgust, peevishness, ill temper, loathing, nausea," and the adjective *duscherês* means "hard to manage, annoying, vexatious, uncomfortable, contradictory, captious, ill-tempered, unfriendly, hateful." It seems quite likely that Aristotle's notion of emotional *katharsis* does imply that a failed *katharsis* (resulting from an improper *technê/pharmakon*) would produce a state of *duschereia*, an unresolved, contradictory/vexatious and physically/psychologically unpleasant emotional confusion or dissonance—and will make a listener "hard to manage"—while a successful *katharsis* will produce the opposite effect.

A modern reinterpretation of Aristotelian *pathos* theory on the lines that I am suggesting has important implications for Aristotelian rhetoric—some of which do not seem "Aristotelian" at all and indeed are probably against the grain of Aristotle's own preferences. Nevertheless, as we will see, they may be reflected in the *Rhetoric* and in subsequent Peripatetic thought. But let us take the implications first. Perhaps the most important one is that *all* intentional or attitudinal states, including the states of *believing* and *doubting*, or the moods of rational assent and dissent, are types of *pathê* and emerge from within existing affects. (Searle lists the following as examples of "intentional states": "belief, fear, hope, desire, love, hate, aversion, liking, disliking, doubting, wondering whether, joy, elation, depression, anxiety, pride, remorse, sorrow, grief, guilt, rejoicing, irritation, puzzlement, acceptance, forgiveness, hostility, affection, expectation, anger, admiration, contempt, respect, indignation, intention, wishing, wanting, imagining, fantasy, shame, lust, disgust, animosity, terror, pleasure, abhorrence, aspiration, amusement, and disappointment" [1983, 4].) Recall that *pathos*, in its general sense in Greek, and in Aristotle, is something that cannot be consciously willed or "commanded" into existence but is something a person experiences or suffers—and that the *pathê* are thought to rise from the part of the psyche that is closely linked to the more physical, nonrational compulsions of desire and appetite but that "has reason" or *logos* in the sense of being able to appreciate and "obey" the "causes" for emotion presented to it. Believing and doubting, in this view, are not consciously willed attitudes but are experienced as *pathê* that arise from the affective/appetitive psyche's powers of interpretation and response.

As Kenneth Burke once pointed out, *peithein*, "persuade" or "persuasion," is cognate with "faith" (1969, 51–52). In Greek, to say that someone is "persuaded," *peithesthai*, is to say that he or she believes/trusts the "assurances" or *pisteis* presented to him or her, in the sense of "having faith" or being "faithicized." *Pistis*, though typically translated as "proof" or "appeal," more literally means "assurance, guarantee, trustworthiness, faith"; the cognate verb *pisteuein* means "trust, rely on, put faith in, believe in." Being-persuaded, then, *peithesthai*, is *trusting* or a form of trusting, and in that sense it is a specific type of *pathos*. Simply *to be able* to become persuaded, moreover, one must already be in a state of affect that impels one to attend to the rhetor's presented *pisteis*, to endow them with salience and relevance to some developing and exigent concern, and to draw inferences and to form evaluative judgments and responses. A person truly in a state of "no-affect," meaning in essence someone whose limbic system has been damaged, disconnected, or anesthetized, would have difficulty forming any motive or intention whatsoever, would be in a state of profound indifference, would be unlikely to take an interest in, interpret, or respond to anything at all, and thus could neither believe nor doubt, nor be persuaded nor not-persuaded by anything that a rhetor said, nor even make sense of it. (Persons with injured or disabled limbic systems are, in fact, likely to suffer a state of psychological and physical immobility, a profound *apathy*, in which they remain "conscious" but cannot speak or initiate voluntary movement [Brown, 1982, 453–54; and Walker, 1990, 309–10].) A similar though non-pathological effect occurs, of course, for the person who simply has no interest in an issue under discussion, cannot perceive any exigence or reason for concern, and is just bored stiff; under such conditions, the rhetor's arguments seemingly dissolve into mere babble and become, for the numbed listener, a featureless cognitive blur.

A second implication, closely related to the first, is that Aristotle's account of emotional psychology provides a basic model of "practical reasoning" generally, and—since that is the very realm with which rhetoric is concerned, as Aristotle conceives it (*Rhetoric* 1.2.12)—one may argue too that the process by which emotion/intentionality and willed action (*pathos* and *praxis*) arise as the "conclusion" from a conjunction of heterogeneous "premises" is also the process on which enthymematic argument (and rhetorical persuasion generally) depends. It is indeed its rootedness in *thumos* and the *pathê* that gives an *enthumêma*, or indeed any argument whatsoever, its value and its relevance for the audience the rhetor wishes to persuade; and it is the enthymeme's simultaneous embodiment of a heterogeneous set of *pisteis*, combining the "assurances" of *logos* (as apodictic propositional reasoning) with those of *pathos* and *êthos*, that makes it a powerful "encouragement" to belief and action. "Encouragement" may actually be the best translation of *enthumêma*, insofar as *thumos* means "heart" as the seat of affect. In such a view, it begins to appear that all enthymemes are enthymemes of *pathos* and that if we grant as well the Aristotelian view of enthymematic skill as the heart of skill in rhetoric, the art of rhetoric is at heart a *technê/pharmakon* for the *katharsis* by means of *logos*, discourse, of the *pathê* involved in practical judgment, choice and action. This comes close to saying, with Socrates in the *Phaedrus*, that rhetoric is a *technê psuchagôgia*, an "art of guiding the soul" by means of words (261a).

Finally, and especially if we begin to think of rhetoric as an art of shaping and guiding an audience's *pathê* toward a *katharsis* of particular moods/intentionalities in practical judgments/actions, a third implication is that rhetoric as *technê* must consist largely of what Chaim Perelman has called "techniques of presence," that is, techniques of emphasis that lend psychological prominence and memorability—or what Aristotle calls *energeia*—to particular sets of "premises" while shifting others into the background or margins of attention. These techniques include the various methods of amplification/iteration (or "dwelling on" a topic), as well as "imagery," rhythm and intonation, figures of speech, and methods of delivery, or in other words the aspects of rhetorical art that Aristotle turns to in *Rhetoric* 3 (Perelman, 1982, 33–40). This is not to say that rhetoric as a *technê* of emotional *katharsis* is an art merely of irrational emotion-mongering via stylistic manipulation. Rather, it is to say that, insofar as enthymematic argumentation in rhetoric (or perhaps any argumentation whatsoever) is necessarily always engaged with the shaping and guiding of an audience's *pathê*, and insofar as the structure of emotion is itself "enthymematic" or "syllogistic," and insofar as the *pathê* rise from cognitive frameworks that typically (and in a debate necessarily) will include *competing premises*, it will never be sufficient for the rhetor merely to declare the "premises" that should conduce to one or another mode of emotion-intention-judgment-action in the practical reasoning of an audience. It will always be the cognitive frames endowed with greatest "presence" or *energeia* in the audience's psyche that determine *which enthymemes* most effectively, persuasively guide its practical reasoning toward a specific *pathos/praxis*, or indeed which enthymemes are even perceived as enthymemes. And thus it will always be techniques of presence that largely condition, or determine, which enthymemes an audience attends to and responds to in its heartfelt thought.

Back to Aristotle. Lest the neo-Aristotelian reader feel that violence has been done to Aristotle, let me emphasize, again, that I am not at all claiming that the implications outlined in the preceding pages are the considered opinions of the Stagirite himself. Clearly, they proceed from a late-twentieth-century confirmation and extension of Aristotelian *pathos* theory's general outlines; and clearly they do not sit easily with what we take to be the usual Aristotelian preference for the life of reason. It is, however, arguable that Aristotle's account of *pathos* did in fact commit him to such implications, whether or not he liked them—and that we do indeed find some recognition of them in the *Rhetoric*, and in later Peripatetic thought.

It seems reasonably clear, by the time of Aristotle's composition of the notes that constitute his discussion of the *pathê* in *Rhetoric* 2.1–17—and again in *Rhetoric* 3, when he turns to matters of style, arrangement and delivery—that he has come to recognize not only that a demonstrative proof based strictly on the facts is insufficient in actual rhetorical practice but also that the *pathê* are a necessary, inescapable part of enthymematic reasoning, and that the *pathê* are themselves the products of a complex, pseudo-syllogistic or pseudo-enthymematic process with physiological as well as cognitive dimensions, a process in which techniques of presence may play a decisive role. Thus, in *Rhetoric* 2.1.2–3, Aristotle recognizes that "since rhetoric is for the sake of judgment . . . it is necessary not only to see that the discourse *(logos)* is demonstrative *(apodeiktikos)* and convincing *(pistikos)*, but to construct for both oneself and the judge a certain quality [of character], for it makes a great difference with respect to assurance *(pros pistin)* . . . that the speaker appear to have a certain quality [of character] and that [the listeners] suppose him to be disposed some way toward them, and in addition that they happen to be disposed some way as well." From this he passes to general observations on the roles of *pathos* and *êthos* in rhetoric and then proposes to "delineate" the *protaseis* or "premises" that constitute the *pathê* (2.1.8), just as he has already delineated the *protaseis* for symbouleutic, epideictic, and dikanic argument in *Rhetoric* 1.

This reference to *protaseis* suggests that Aristotle is thinking of the *pathê* as themselves enthymematic or quasi-enthymematic (Grimaldi, 1972, 147–51; Conley, 1982; and Kennedy, 1991, 123–24) and that, moreover, he is attempting to provide the *pathê* with something like the analysis of enthymematic "formal topics" that occurs later in *Rhetoric* 2. But—to return to the question from which we started—why is Aristotle providing this analysis at all? As William Fortenbaugh has noted, Aristotle's chief disciple, Theophrastus, said that "men of practical wisdom" *(hoi phronimoi)* should not do anything at all in anger *(orgê)*, "for passion *(thumos)* is most unreasonable *(alogiston)* and will never do anything with forethought, but . . . is subject to impulses." Theophrastus does allow, as Fortenbaugh points out, for the *phronimos* to become angry when anger is justified; but the *phronimos* is to desist from "uncontrolled, impetuous action" and must take thought before permitting himself to act upon emotion (Fortenbaugh, 1985, 210–11; see also Stobaeus, *Anthology* 3.19.12; and Seneca, *De Ira* 1.12.3, in Fortenbaugh et al., 1992, 272–73 and 344–45). It seems unlikely that Theophrastus's views on this point differ much from Aristotle's. The *Rhetoric*'s inventory of *protaseis* for the major judgment-warping *pathê* is probably meant to provide a basis for taking thought: The *protaseis* furnish lines of argument that can intervene and prevent (or at least slow down) impulsive choice and action and so induce a clarification and *katharsis* of the *pathos* proper to thoughtful understanding of the circumstances.

This line of explanation might account for Aristotle's arrangement of the *pathê* in *Rhetoric* 2.2–11 as paired opposites, and possibly also for his chiastic alternation of negative and positive emotions: anger and gentleness *(orgê/praotês)*; friendliness and hatred *(philia/echthra)*; fear and boldness *(phobos/tharsos)*; shame and shamelessness *(aischunê/anaischuntia)*; kindliness and unkindliness *(charis/acharistia)*; pity and indignation *(eleos/to nemesan)*; envy and emulation *(phthonos/zêlos)*. (It is worth noting here that "shame" is a positive emotion insofar as it embodies an ethical awareness of the shameful, whereas "shamelessness" involves a flouting and insulting of ethical standards.) In Aristotle's understanding of medicine, the causes of disease are "great excesses" or *megalai huperbolai* of heat, cold, moisture, and the like within the body, and the treatment of diseases typically requires an application of an opposite excess because "each brings the other to the mean" (*Problems* 859a). Drugs or *pharmaka*, likewise, produce *katharsis* and restore the body to a more equable disposition (when successful) because they introduce an "excess" *(huperbolê)* of heat, cold, or the like into the body (864a). If we step from medical *katharsis* to the looser notion of emotional *katharsis*, it would seem that Aristotle's inventory of *protaseis* for opposed emotions is meant as a kind of recipe book or *technê* for the concoction of rhetorical *pharmaka* that will serve to balance one emotion with its opposite, or to modulate one emotion with another, in order to bring the audience toward a thoughtful, appropriate, and justified emotional *katharsis* and response to the facts under consideration.

But we are forgetting something. As we have noted already, Aristotle's rhetor speaks not only to *hoi phronimoi*, "men of practical wisdom," but also to *hoi polloi*, "the many," whose lives are ruled by *pathos* and whose *pathos* is amenable not to *logos* but to *bia*, force. Nor does Aristotle believe that logos can "command" *pathos* into existence; it can only disclose the *aitia* or "cause" for emotion that an auditor's *thumos* will respond to. Nor will a disclosing by the rhetor necessarily take effect, since an existing state of *pathos* will condition which *protaseis* the *pathetikos* is willing to attend to, as he goes about spouting "proofs and verses" prompted by his mood. Further, a person's state of character determines which emotions he or she is likely to be capable of feeling. Aristotle's account of ethical virtues, in both the *Eudemian* and *Nicomachean Ethics*, treats a "virtue" as an acquired predisposition or *hexis* ("habit") with respect to both actions and feelings, *praxeis kai pathê*. The person of good ethics is a person who has acquired through training a cultivated set of emotional predispositions to respond to certain *aitiai* in certain ways, with certain feelings; the person of bad ethics has acquired a different set of *hexeis* and a different emotional responsiveness, or lack thereof (Kosman, 1980). Moreover, as suggested by Aristotle's account of types of *ethê* in *Rhetoric* 2.12–17—the young, the old, those in their prime, and the wellborn, the rich and the powerful—people's emotional predispositions vary not only according to the habits they have acquired through education and practice but also according to their age and social status. What all this implies, in sum, is that different people will not be equally responsive to the same *protaseis* for emotion, or will not respond in the same way, or simply may have little or no capacity for the particular *pathos* that a rhetor wishes to invoke.

Clearly, a *pharmakon* for the shaping and *katharsis* of appropriate, considered emotional response cannot consist of *protaseis* or *logos* only. The rhetor needs *bia* too. This is provided by techniques of presence, in particular by techniques of style and delivery, as well as the various figural means of creating distinctiveness, memorability, and *energeia*. As Aristotle notes at the beginning of *Rhetoric* 3, delivery (*hupokrisis*, "acting") is a matter of "voice" *(phônê)* and of how it should be used "for each emotion" by modulating "volume, harmony, rhythm." Moreover, he continues, "these things nearly always carry off the prizes in contests, and just as now the actors *(hupokritai)* have greater power than the poets there, so it is likewise in political contests, owing to the depravity of polities *(dia tên mochtherian tôn politeiôn)*" (3.1.4). From this observation, Aristotle proceeds almost immediately to the famous remark that "owing to the depravity *(mochtheria)* of the listener" the rhetor must pay attention to style and delivery, although it would be preferable to argue by means of the facts alone (3.1.5). Later in *Rhetoric* 3, Aristotle says that if a speaker's style and delivery successfully embody the "volume, harmony, rhythm" of, say, anger, the listener will experience a kindred feeling, even if the speaker in fact says nothing at all, and insofar as the speaker's *hupokrisis* of "anger" rings true, the typical listener will credit what he says as grounds for that emotion (3.7.1–5; this passage is discussed also by Wisse, 1989, 71–72). (There will be limits, of course: If what the speaker says seems radically inconsistent with his expressed emotion, the audience may be unpersuaded to join his feeling, just as if the voiced prosody of his style failed to match the listener's sense of what "anger" sounds like.)

We are now back in the realm of emotional *katharsis* by means of music, or a closely related realm. But again, it seems unlikely that Aristotle intends for the rhetor merely to "strike up" judgment-warping emotion by means of a quasi-musical, irrational *pharmakon* composed of emotive style/delivery. Just as Aristotle in *Politics* 8 prescribes the "steady" and "manly" Dorian modes for the musical training of the young, in the next two chapters of the *Rhetoric* (3.8–9) he prescribes for the rhetor paeonic rhythm in periodic sentences—a rhythmic structure that is both "dignified" *(semnotêta)* and "impressive" *(ekstêsai)*, and that conveys an aesthetic pleasure, memorability, and balance comparable to that of poetry while yet retaining the feel of natural speech. And, of course, the effect of such prosody may be further enhanced by the figural devices of "urbanity" *(asteia)* and *energeia*, including "bringing-before-the-eyes" and metaphor and simile, as well as such schemes as parisosis, isocolon, and antithesis, and so forth, which Aristotle goes on to discuss (3.10–12).

Significantly, the chief example of this stately and urbane style, aside from the various poets Aristotle cites, is Isocrates (3.9.7). In this connection we must note that, according to Dionysius of Halicarnassus, "whenever I read the speeches of Isocrates, whether written for the courts or assemblies or . . . [lacuna; epideictic occasions?], I become serious *(spoudaios)* in character *(en êthei)* and have a great stability of thought *(polu to eustathês echô tês gnômês)*, like those listening to libation music played on reedpipes or to Dorian or enharmonic melodies" (*Demos-*

thenes 22). As Fortenbaugh suggests (1994, 190), this statement seems to reflect a development in Peripatetic theory, in which "ethical" moods are distinguished from the *pathê*, a distinction that surfaces in Quintilian as "mild" versus "vehement" affects or "motions" of the soul. In the *Rhetoric*, Aristotle himself distinguishes between "ethical" and "pathetic" styles of delivery (3.12.2). Dionysius contrasts the *spoudaios êthos* that Isocrates' style produces in him with the effects of Demosthenes' style, which "transports" him *(enthousiaein)* and makes him feel "one *pathos* after another . . . disbelief, agony, dread, contempt, hatred, pity, goodwill, anger, envy, all the *pathê*. . . that master human minds" (*Demosthenes*, 22). Earlier in the same essay, Dionysius compares the styles of Lysias and Thucydides with "the lowest and highest" modes in music, noting that one has the power to astonish thought, induce tension and strain, and conduce *(proagôgein)* to *pathos*, while the other gives pleasure, induces relaxation and relief, and puts the listener into a state of *êthos* (*eis de êthos hautê katastêsai*; 2), and he observes as well that Isocrates' style is "ethical and also persuasive and pleasing" (*êthikê te kai pithanê kai hêdeia*; 4). It seems that in the example of Isocrates, we are close to Aristotle's ideal rhetor.

Probably the most distinctive rhetor-politician produced by the Peripatetic school was Theophrastus's student, Demetrius of Phaleron. Demetrius was governor of Athens under the Macedonian king Cassander, 318–307 B.C.E., and subsequently went to Alexandria as an advisor to king Ptolemy I, where he seems to have been involved in founding the Library of Alexandria (Walbank, 1981, 176; and Smith, 1974, 10). According to the list of titles reported by the somewhat unreliable Diogenes Laertius (*Lives* 5.5), Demetrius himself was the author of numerous treatises on politics, law, rhetoric, literary criticism, and other philosophical topics, as well as letters, biographies, what appear to be published "speeches" in an Isocratean mode—such as *Exhortation, Concerning the Ten Years, Concerning the Ionians*, and *Denunciation of the Athenians*—and other literary exercises, including *Aesop's Fables* and *Anecdotes*. Diogenes describes his character as "philosophical, blended with rhetorical vigor and power," and says that he ruled the Athenians by means of speeches in public assemblies *(dêmêgoriai)* and that he instituted "many fine things" for the city (1958, 82, 75), though he later became unpopular.

Cicero describes Demetrius of Phaleron as the successor to the great Attic orators of the earlier fourth century and says that he may have been "the most accomplished *(eruditissimus)* of them all," although his training was more for the parade-ground *(palaestra)* than for battle *(armis)*—meaning that his speech was characterized more by an epideictic *suavitas* than by the forceful *gravitas* required to overwhelm a listener's soul in the verbal combats of the forum (*Brutus* 9.37–38). This description is fairly close to Cicero's usual descriptions of Isocrates, and of the epideictic style generally (e.g., *Orator* 37–42). In Demetrius of Phaleron, in sum, we find a version of the philosophical dialectician-rhetor that Aristotelian-Peripatetic rhetoric seems to have intended: one who aims not at a Demosthenic art of *pathos* but at a more Isocratean, "ethical" rhetoric that by the *pharmakon* of style and delivery would promote a mood of *spoudaios êthos* in the listener and thence by the building and deployment of fitting enthymemes would guide that mood toward a thoughtfully balanced, responsible consideration of the case in hand, and finally toward a *katharsis* of appropriate emotions/intentionalities in judgments/actions that accord with genuine *phronêsis*.

At this point, we—and Aristotle—encounter another problem. For as we have seen already in Aristotle's account of musical *katharsis* in *Politics* 8, he considers different kinds of souls to have different degrees of responsiveness to the mood-inducing powers of any given type of music, just as different kinds of souls have variable responsiveness to the *protaseis* of a given type of *pathos*. Moreover, he believes that performance of the high-strung, irregular/discordant melodies that most effectively rouse the "distorted" *pathê* of banausics and thetes will morally corrupt the performer. Thus, in Aristotle's *paideia* (and much as in Plato's), the well-educated young man is not to learn to perform any but the "ethical" modes of music, though he may listen to the other kinds (and appreciate them with a fine analytic understanding). It seems that Aristotle's rhetor, in order to guard his moral integrity, would likewise have to refrain from using the stylistic modes that would enable him to be most effective with "the many" and would instead address himself primarily to those most capable of becoming *spoudaios,* "serious," in speech that is the prosodic equivalent of the "manly" and "steady" Dorian mode—although, of course, all people are responsive in some degree to every mood that music or rhythmic prosody can induce. This limitation on the rhetor is, of course, the essence of the problem with both Isocrates and Demetrius of Phaleron, or their difference from a rhetor of Demosthenic power, according to both Dionysius and Cicero. It also seems to be what Aristotle has in mind.

But if Isocrates and Demetrius of Phaleron exemplify Aristotle's ideal rhetor, he may have had another kind of practice in mind as well, namely the panegyric discourse that was Isocrates' forte and that would later be associated chiefly with sophistic practice. By means of an Isocratean panegyric, the Aristotelian rhetor might yet address "the many," applying to them a *pharmakon/technê* that would paideutically attune and accustom their souls to be responsive to the moods (and arguments) of a *spoudaios ethos*. We know that Theophrastus believed in and may have practiced a musical form of psychosomatic therapy. According to Apollonius's *Amazing Stories* (49.1–3), Theophrastus declared in a work called *On Inspiration (Peri Enthousiasmôn)* that music could cure "many of the *pathê* that occur to both the soul and the body," including "fainting, fright and long-occurring disturbances of thought," as well as sciatica and epilepsy (Fortenbaugh et al., 1992, 580–81; see also Barker, 1985, 316–17). Considering what Aristotle says about musical *katharsis* in *Politics* 8 and about the responsiveness of all souls in some degree to the emotive force of any type of music, it seems possible to imagine a Peripatetic version of panegyric, in stately, serious rhythms and in urbane, distinctive style, meant to serve as ethico-pathetic therapy for *hoi polloi.* Such a practice would certainly be consistent with the soul-improving psychagogy Plato seems to call for in the *Phaedrus*.

Again, we may see such a practice exemplified in Demetrius of Phaleron. As Philodemus of Gadara notes, with Epicurean disapproval, Demetrius considered the rhetor's art to include "the sophistic genus" *(to sophistikon genos)* as well as "the demegoric and dikanic" *(to dêmêgorikon kai dikanikon)*, and added a fourth genre called *enteuktikon hapasin*, which translates roughly as "meeting-with-all" or "interceding-with-all"—*enteuxis* means "meeting-with, converse, petition, intercession," and *enteuktikos* means "affable"—and this fourth genre Philodemus takes to include both "the intercessive with multitudes" *(to tois plêthesin enteuktikon)* and "the ambassadorial to potentates" *(to kata presbeian tois dunastais Philodemus, Rhetorica* I col. XLIa 6ff p. 222 Sudhaus, in Wehrli, 1968, fr. 157; an approximate English translation is available in Hubbell, 1920, 304). A Peripatetic version of sophistic/Isocratean *enteuktikon* before the multitudes may be what Cicero has in mind, when he says Demetrius "charmed" *(delectabat)* rather than "inflamed" *(inflammabat)* the Athenians (*Brutus* 9.37), and it may be what Diogenes Laertius describes when he says that Demetrius ruled by means of speeches *(dêmêgoriai)* in public assemblies. Certainly *enteuktikon* before a potentate was what Demetrius practiced as an advisor to Ptolemy I, if we do not call it *sumbouleutikon*, and in his relations with Cassander.

Let us now dock our boat. My argument has been that by attempting to include an account of *pathos* in his theory of rhetoric, Aristotle implicitly if unintentionally commits that theory to a recognition that all practical reasoning is pathetic reasoning, that all enthymemes are enthymemes of *pathos*, and that an art of enthymematic rhetoric meant to guide such reasoning is inescapably a psychagogic art or *pharmakon* for emotional *katharsis.* In such an art the various techniques of presence, matters mainly of style and delivery, will be indispensable for success. Aristotle does appear to recognize these implications, if only partially and reluctantly, and indeed the *Rhetoric*'s whole attitude toward persuasion of and by the *pathê* seems to be conflicted. The rhetor's art must be an art of *pathos*, and thus of style and delivery, but Aristotle seems to wish that it were not so. In consequence, he seems to prefer, on the one hand, an ideal of relatively small, well-regulated deliberative bodies composed of serious-minded men of power, *hoi spoudaioi dunamenoi*, as in a council of magistrates—or the Areopagus—where there will be less scope for grand-style eloquence and greater opportunity for reasoned discussion. For public addresses to "the many," on the other hand, Aristotle seems to contemplate an art of edifying, soul-improving psychagogy as an intervention into their emotional economies, as in Isocratean panegyric or the *dêmêgoriai* of Demetrius of Phaleron. The rhetorical *pharmakon* that Aristotle seems to have in mind is not meant to warp the judgment of the judger by means of anger, pity, and the like, but it would be an antidote to unconsidered, *pathos*-driven judgment, and would promote *katharsis* of more reasonable, "ethical" moods more suitable to prudent choice and action.

The rhetorical implications of Aristotle's account of *pathos* seem to have been more fully recognized by his successors. As is well known, from Theophrastus onward the major developments in Peripatetic rhetoric were in stylistic theory and delivery. Theophrastus himself was famous for his speaking voice—his name, which Aristotle gave to him in recognition of this quality, means "divine voice" (his original name was Tyrtamus)—and he was famous as well for the dramatic delivery of his lectures, in which "he avoided no motion or gesture" (Fortenbaugh, 1985, 274). As the late commentator Athanasius reports, Theophrastus said that *hupokrisis* was "for the rhetor the greatest [thing] with respect to persuasion, referring to the principles and *pathê* of the soul and the understanding of such things, so that the movement of the body and the pitch of the voice are in agreement with the whole science" (Fortenbaugh, 1985, 270; see also Fortenbaugh et al., 1992, 558–59). We know too that Theophrastus took great interest in prose rhythm and probably initiated the categorization of types of style, such as we see in *On Style*, the later Peripatetic treatise by Demetrius. Stylistic preoccupation was to be, of course, a central feature of "classical" rhetoric for all of later antiquity. Aristotle's account of *pathos* explains why so.

Aristotle's preferences could not contain the implications of his own account of *pathos*. It is significant not only that his successors would make their greatest contributions, in rhetoric, to the theories of style and delivery but also that succeeding centuries would find their image of the perfect orator not in Isocrates or Demetrius of Phaleron but in Demosthenes, the recognized master of *pathos* and pathetic style, the *pharmakon* whose principles the *Rhetoric* uneasily describes. Demetrius of Phaleron appears to have recorded how Demosthenes trained himself to be a master of delivery by studying with the actor Andronicus—and how Demosthenes declared the three most important things in rhetoric to be delivery, delivery, and delivery. But Demetrius also judged Demosthenes' theatrics too vulgar for persons of refinement, though they pleased the many (see Plutarch, *Demosthenes* 9, 11; Philodemus, *Rhetorica* I col. XVa p. 197; Photius, *Bibliotheca* 493a.41Be; Dionysius of Halicarnassus, *Demosthenes* 53; Cicero, *De Petitione Consulatis* 1.3—all in Wehrli, 1968, 161–67). Demetrius's ambivalent attitude toward Demosthenes, combined with his recognition of the power of Demosthenic practice, is Aristotelian through and through.

6

Aristotle's Enthymeme as Tacit Reference

Thomas B. Farrell

This speculative essay reexamines the problem of "validity" in Aristotle's enthymeme. On strictly formal criteria, the enthymeme's validity may always be called into question. Nonetheless, anyone who takes the *Rhetoric* seriously must puzzle over the distinction between real and "sham" enthymemes. In the body of the essay, two working criteria of enthymematic "reference" are introduced: first, of complicity with proper audience and, second, of compliance with facts, circumstances, and conventions proper to the argumentative form in question. With contemporary examples, an attempt is made to discriminate between sound and unsound enthymemes using the aforementioned criteria. The essay concludes by suggesting temporal "limit conditions" to enthymematic reference.

This essay is, in part at least, the result of a mistake. No, I am not implying that I was mistaken in agreeing to contribute something for this book. Rather, something "funny" happened on the way to a conference where a version of this essay was presented. My original title for this essay was "Aristotle's Enthymeme as Tacit Inference." But by the time the mistake-riddled program copy appeared, my title had mysteriously mutated into "Aristotle's Enthymeme as Tacit Reference." I suppose, given the possibilities, I should have been grateful; and so, in a somewhat playful spirit of gratitude, I decided to address Aristotle's Enthymeme as Tacit—Reference.

My point, then and now, was to press forward a little thought experiment in order to see to what degree judgments about enthymemes turn upon what I am calling their "referentiality." What I did not anticipate (but should have) is the sense in which *any* conceptual twist or "perspective by incongruity" on Aristotle's magnum opus unavoidably opens a Pandora's box of related issues. For any admirer of Aristotle's *Rhetoric*, there is something, well, "inspiring" in such a discovery. As with the Greek language, or perhaps Mozart's muse, there is something curiously bracing in the realization that we will never quite get "to the bottom" of all the mysteries in Aristotle's *Rhetoric*. It is simply too densely layered, with far-reaching, albeit elusive, tributaries to other aspects of his thought, Greek culture, and unknowable circumstance. So be it.

This much having been acknowledged, it is never less than illuminating to wrestle with this angel regardless of the stakes. And so, I propose to consider what I am calling the "referentiality" of Aristotle's enthymeme, over and against a broader problematic concerning the place and influence of Aristotle's philosophy within the much-contested parameters of his *Rhetoric*. First off, I propose a decidedly non-technical understanding of "referencing." I do not intend to suggest by this concept that there is some fixed, knowable, or determinate relationship between the terms of an enthymeme and the "objects" of the world. My meaning is, in fact, much closer to the first meaning suggested by the *Oxford English Dictionary* definition: "Reference: The act or expedient of referring or submitting a matter, especially a dispute or controversy, to some person or authority for consideration, decision, or settlement" (*OED* 1995). Were we to consider the person or authority in question to be acting in the capacity of an audience, then the dictionary meaning and my own would be very nearly exact. Of course, a great deal remains unsaid about this tacit "referring," not the least of which is the mystery of what is referred and how this referring is made to take place in practice. I will address these concerns in the body of my essay.

Secondly, I wish to make clear what I am not saying about the enthymeme. I am not saying that the enthymeme is tacit reference and nothing more. With my little moniker, "as," I am suggesting a simile and only alluding to certain aspects of an elusive larger whole. The enthymeme is, for Aristotle, the "substance" of persuasion itself. But since Aristotle never really defined fully either persuasion or its substance (the enthymeme), it follows that no statement as simplistic as mine could exhaust its attributes. All I mean to suggest is that we can appreciate some little-noticed aspects of the enthymeme by thinking of it this way.

My final and perhaps most controversial preliminary is that I want to position this understanding in an ongoing discussion about the place of *Rhetoric* within the overall constellation of Aristotle's philosophy. Doing this should allow us better to appreciate the "stakes" involved in my deceptively simple query about the enthymeme as tacit reference. We begin on this note.

By most accountings, the *Rhetoric* stands as a relatively minor work within the overall corpus of Aristotle's writings. And while influential for recurring generations of neoclassical rhetoricians, it has been all but neglected—until recently—by the canonical figures of philosophy. For all that, there is still a quite lively difference of opinion as to how the *Rhetoric* actually "fits in" with Aristotle's own philosophical convictions. Of course, we would need to have some agreement as to exactly what those philosophical convictions were in the first place, in order to offer clear demarcations across positions. And here the water muddies.

The pure "method" position, memorably articulated by Richard McKeon (1971), presents rhetoric as architectonic art, a system of invention that requires no epistemological and metaphysical presuppositions. Now from one point of view, that of more traditional philosophy, such a pluralistic vision of the *Rhetoric* essentially separates it from the philosophical doctrines of Aristotle by emptying the *Rhetoric* of any substantive foundational pronouncements. However, McKeon complicated this understanding by viewing Aristotle's own philosophical method as that of a pluralist, without (as he once put it) "hidden agendas." McKeon's decidedly unorthodox rendering of Aristotle had quite a bit to do with his own (i.e., McKeon's) eventual exile from the academic orthodoxy of the University of Chicago.

A second, somewhat more moderate position would acknowledge the indebtedness of the *Rhetoric* to the more basic presuppositions of the Aristotelian "worldview." There is (in addition to identity and noncontradiction) a dogged conviction that human nature is susceptible to persuasion, that the overall "ends" of deliberation are "settled," that informed civic culture makes better decisions than, say, tyranny. The debate then revolves around just how encompassing, and how restrictive, these more doctrinaire assumptions might be for the recovery of a rhetoric based upon Aristotle's conception. There is here a more conservative, neoclassical position, echoed by MacIntyre (1981) and, to some extent, John M. Cooper (1975), that suggests the *Rhetoric* is just not made for these times. There is a more liberal and (I like to think) egalitarian position that argues an Aristotelian-based rhetoric, with a little touching up and a little paint, might be made more relevant to whatever remains of late modernity (Farrell, 1993).

Finally (for my sketchy purposes here), there is a recent position that I would have to say is the 180 degree inversion of McKeon's stance, at least as I understand it. Its most articulate spokesperson is Eugene Garver, ironically enough a McKeon student. Garver (1994b) argues, over and against the positions of rhetoric as inventional method and as being indebted to Aristotle's philosophy, that Aristotle's *Rhetoric* essentially is a philosophy, or at least a fully encompassing ethic, a set of instructions on crafting character amid the contingencies of civic life.

Obviously, these are very different (perhaps irresolvably different) construals of the place of the *Rhetoric* in Aristotle's overall philosophy and worldview. What I now wish to suggest is that any attempt to take the enthymeme seriously as a mode of reflective argument admitting to discriminations of quality must, for better or worse (probably worse), fall headlong into the attendant philosophical concerns implied by the above positions.

A couple of "for instances" should be enough to help make my point. If, for instance, we maintain that enthymemes may be tested reflectively by judging the truth of their premises, it is rather difficult not to be lured back to what Bitzer (1968) has called Aristotle's empirical realism; for him, some things just are true, some not, and that's that. We end up, I believe, with the paradox of an art about the "probable" that ultimately turns upon a sedimented domain of the certain. But now suppose we were to turn the enthymeme another way and consider its validity as resting entirely upon formal distribution of terms within propositions. It then becomes a subset of propositional logic. Read this way, the enthymeme seems to fold in upon the *Organon:* that inventional method for all science, logic itself. Is this paradoxical? I think so, primarily because it takes what Bitzer (1959) has rightly called a variation of dialectical reason and makes it a variation of formal analytic. If we were to read Aristotle's "enthymeme" in the aforementioned way, then I think it becomes difficult, if not impossible, to distinguish valid from invalid or "sham" enthymemes. Is this a problem? Only if we wish to retain Aristotle's faith that qualitative discriminations about rhetorical reflection is possible.

Interestingly enough, the reading I described above is very close to the way Eugene Garver reads Aristotle's "enthymeme." In his important recent work, *Aristotle's "Rhetoric": An Art of Character*, Garver (1994b) is on record as stating that the Aristotelian distinction between sham and "valid" enthymemes simply does not hold up. He writes of Aristotle, "When he says that 'another [fallacy] is from a [non-necessary] sign; for this, too, is non-syllogistic [asyllogiston]' [2.24.1401b11], he seems to be condemning all of rhetoric. Considered purely logically, all rhetorical arguments are invalid; among invalid arguments it is hard to find a further distinction between real and apparent enthymemes" (163). He goes on to add, "I do not think this lack of a logical criterion of demarcation between real and apparent enthymemes is a flaw on Aristotle's part" (163). Notice that we do have the qualifiers "purely logically" and "logical," but Garver still seems to disregard criteria Aristotle employs, substituting his own rather slippery notion of good faith. I would just put it this way. If Aristotle claims to be offering grounds of discrimination between real and apparent enthymemes but then does not, then it is some sort of failing, even by Garver's elusive criteria. The most important lesson from the above interpretation is that it does turn upon a paradigm of demonstrative logic. Read exclusively from within the world of the universal "barbara syllogism," Garver must be regarded as correct. But I am not at all sure that this is what Aristotle had in mind.

When you have a question admitting to more than one answer, Aristotle says, you have a problem. I believe the differences of opinion sketched above are sufficiently befuddling to be termed problematic, and to provide an opening for my own more speculative approach. Here is my overall line of thought. Even though Aristotle was neither an idealist (in the Platonic sense) nor a relativist (in the skeptical Sextus Empiricus sense), he nonetheless believed that substantive, grounded discriminations could be made concerning questions of contingency and degree of "truth." I believe that this sense at least informs Aristotle's treatment of the enthymeme. Put another way, at least some comparable sense of the relative "worth," integrity, quality in rhetorical reasoning derives from a certain referencing by the enthymeme. Indeed, without some such sense, the only remaining competency conditions for enthymematic thinking would be completely interior to the form. An enthymeme would be, as some of our contemporary political discourse seems to suggest, sort of an "in-joke": You either get it or you don't. Actually, as I write, it strikes me that this too is a form of reference, but an extremely weak one. I wish to argue for a stronger sense.

To develop this little feature or aspect of the enthymeme, I need to do two things. First, I need to at least acknowledge the pitfalls my own approach implies.

And second, I need to provide at least intuitive grounds for believing that the referential and the formal, at least for Aristotle's *Rhetoric*, are not radically disjoined. First, since it at least appears to be close to the "empirical realism" part of the dichotomy I sketched above, how do we inscribe a sense of the enthymeme's reference that avoids falling into simplistic and disturbing disjunctions of "truth" and error? It is easy enough to take propositional logic into the world of reference. It is rather more difficult to come back. Put another way (a way recently put to me), once we treat the enthymeme as inhabiting a world of "predicative logic," it will be very difficult to recapture any "propositional logic" sense of validity.

Even though I am trying to steer a wide berth around strict predication, I agree that we enter dangerous territory whenever we try to attach reference to what is argumentative. Things change, and so do our interpretations of them. It would seem at least disturbing, and at most, non-Aristotelian, to have logic itself parasitic on a historically fluctuating lifeworld. The other option, Bitzer's, has drawbacks as well: a lifeworld preserver of rock-solid empirical reality.

But even in granting the danger, I must remind concerned parties that rhetoric is not "logic itself." It is, as McKeon pointed out, about plausible inference over things, thoughts, actions: items that are rather difficult to restrict to the purely formal. Nor is rhetoric restricted to the world of the "rock-solid." It inhabits all that is circumstantial, uncertain, fluctuating, problematic. This is why I believe that the inventor of "logic itself" placed rhetoric where it could be assimilated neither to predicative nor to propositional logic.

This is a rather bold claim. Obviously Aristotle never made the above distinction in the first place. But that is, in part, my point. If one were to crawl all the way back to the very beginning of Aristotle's *Organon*, one would find that the basic particulars with which inquiry must deal are in the mode of "categories." This seems, at first blush, to suggest Aristotle is headed in the direction of formal logic (as he is, but not quite yet). Categories are "predicables," aspects that may be attributed to something else. This something else is never exactly defined, other than to say it is whatever is neither predicated of nor present in something—so much for a logic of pure form and so much for a rock-solid empirical reality. The demonstration is too complex for these few pages. But I believe that once we allow for a branch of dialectical reason that solicits propositional arrangements of conventionally accepted predicables from audiences, it would be unfathomable to have a rhetorical argument of pure form.

This much having been hazarded, my second duty comes to the fore. I need to foreground an assumption that not everyone will accept, namely, that Aristotle's famous distinction between "valid" and "sham" enthymemes is worth preserving. Does it hold up under careful scrutiny? I believe that it withstands at least the somewhat dismissive treatment afforded in the previous discussion.

I will reintroduce an example from an unjustly neglected little essay by Fisher (1964) called "The Uses of the Enthymeme." To try and make the compacted reasoning of enthymemes clear to students, he would use the following example:

> *Student:* You have no right to flunk me.
> *Professor:* Why?
> *Student:* I came to every class.

I think the example shows one very important way, a way of reference, in which a would-be enthymeme invalidates itself. In the institutionally defined context of a graded course, class attendance is not a sufficient condition for a passing grade. The student has made a background assumption that is simply false to the "social facts" at hand, before a referenced authority-audience who "knows." In fact, what is particularly interesting about the example, for present purposes, is the way it seems to "bridge" the propositional and the predicative. One could simply say that one of the premises is false to the "facts" at hand. But one could also allow that the USC student was guilty of a false distribution, a formal error, in taking what may have been a necessary condition for a passing grade and treating it as a sufficient condition. Now, of course, this is not Aristotle's example. But Aristotle offers a great many examples not only of false premises in enthymemes but also of enthymemes with invalid form: the assumption of a fallible sign as an infallible sign, false predication of effect for cause, and so forth. If this were not at least some evidence of grounds for such a distinction, we have Aristotle's painstaking discussion of controversion. There he shows, in stupefying detail, how we might show apparent enthymemes to be invalid. So, it may be a minor point, but I think that Aristotle does offer a serviceable way of making grounded discriminations between enthymemes that are—as I said long ago—"rhetorically valid" (Farrell, 1977), and those that aren't.

My central point, which I would like to illustrate with an example or two, is that at least one sense of the "rhetorical validity" of an enthymeme comes from its "tacit reference." In fact, the way Fisher discredited the enthymeme illustrated above was by making the tacit part of the enthymeme referentiality explicit. This is what rhetorical critics do much of the time, whenever they are not indulging themselves with the pleasures of the text.

I turn now to what would seem the most immediately pertinent questions: What features of enthymemes allow such tacit referencing to occur, and to be judged? And, how do such provisional judgments emerge? The best I can really do with each question is sketch the outline of a direction for an answer. The features of enthymemes that admit to such referencing have not been much discussed in the literature. I suspect that this is because no one has been able to agree upon even a minimal definition of what an enthymeme is. This unfortunate fact notwithstanding, there does seem to be a loose, if inadvertent, consensus around certain features exhibited by enthymematic argument. It is thought to be uniquely rhetorical, implicated in the world of collective action or *praxis*, dependent in some participatory way upon how the hearer, as audience, thinks along with what is asserted and inferred. While there is no way of proving the point, I suspect that everyone from McBurney (1936) to Delia (1970) to Bitzer (1959) to Grimaldi (1980a) to Fisher (1964) to Burnyeat (1994) would concede these common features. What this suggests to me is that the enthymeme is partisan argument as collaborative utterance, an utterance whose well-foundedness would need to be confirmed or redeemed by the proper audience. Bitzer is really most helpful on this point, even though we must extend his discussion past its actual point of terminus.

In his landmark essay, Bitzer (1959) posits a fascinating "back and forth" movement of the enthymeme. Even though it does not lay premises down, as does demonstration, the enthymeme nonetheless works as assertion; here is its active moment of expression. Quite often, these assertions are transparent speech acts, as in his own example, "Let justice be done" (403). But, of course, enthymematic expression can never be self-validating; thus the necessary discursive move back to an audience who must subscribe to taken-for-granted background suppositions. The reader who recalls my initial definition of reference will recognize that we have already entered the process of reference simply by virtue of "calling" upon an audience to help complete our reasoning.

But this does not yet speak to the question of how provisional judgments are made about the "soundness" of enthymemes on other than strict formal criteria. My somewhat speculative answer is that more often than not these background conventions are not simply private intuitions but "social knowledge" that spills over into the common experience of many people. What is referenced by publicly articulated enthymemes is the mosaic of commonplaces, conventions, traditions, and provisional interests making up the *doxa* of rhetorical culture. It could be called "human truths," as Nussbaum would have it, public knowledge, as Bitzer would have it, social knowledge, as I would have it. But the specific moniker doesn't matter so much as the fact of knowing, suspecting, experiencing something of what is referred to. This is, I think, the primary rhetorical experience of what it means to be an audience. And it is why I agree with Garver at least on this one point: that the validity of an enthymeme could not be determined by formal logical criteria alone. Rhetorical arguments evoke and depend upon an outside experienced world, what the Frankfurt School called a "totality," which is all but irrelevant to logical demonstration.

In an essay from nearly a quarter of a century ago, this point is made with perhaps the most challenging counterexample in Aristotle's bestiary—the enthymeme from infallible sign:

> Aristotle states that only "necessary" propositions involve argument from infallible sign, and he provides two examples:
>
> 1. "The fact that he has fever is a sign that he is ill,
>
> 2. "The fact that she is giving milk is a sign that she has lately borne a child." These paradigms of argument from infallible sign reveal that such arguments are arguments from effect-to-cause and are therefore subject to empirical verification not to the powers of abstract intellect. The question here is not over formal validity of the reasoning process, but with the material truth of the propositions and their verifiability. (Miller and Bee, 1972)

Now if formal validation is not decisive, even with argument from infallible sign, it does raise the question of what we are to look for in this realm of reference that eludes purely formal constraint. In their concluding summary, Miller and Bee point the way toward a helpful answer to this question as well: "The first major point here is that hearers would have knowledge of the facts of the case. The second point, equally important, is that the context of an argument from infallible sign is always involved with the judgment of hearers, including implicitly the feelings and emotions. In short, an argument from infallible sign is necessarily rhetorical, not scientific, and effects *pistis* not *apodeiksis*."

The second section of this essay will attempt to unpack and generalize the above points, where judgments of enthymematic reference are concerned. But to summarize, the major reason that the enthymeme is the paradigmatic rhetorical form is that it captures a remarkably definitive sense of how we think when we are thinking rhetorically. Of course, we cannot attend to everything in our lifeworld at once. The enthymeme brings aspects of the experienced world, the array of our appearances, to the fore—hence rhetoric's particularity. The enthymeme calls upon its hearers to attend to these aspects it would, for now, highlight—hence rhetoric's special mode of attendance, described once by Henry Johnstone (1987) as the rhetorical "wedge." And the enthymeme, for better or worse, offers a provisional interpretative frame, a caption, that lends temporary stability to an otherwise unstable and ambiguous complex of appearances—hence rhetoric as thematizing, hermeneutic art.

From where we look at things, which is always some positioned place, enthymemes can only point us in a direction, well or ill founded, for now. I now want to broach the second question: How does the referencing of enthymemes contribute to judgments of their "soundness" or rhetorical validity (Farrell, 1977)? In expanding upon the overall direction of Miller and Bee's suggestion above, I also want to take a page from an earlier essay where I struggled with the extrinsic requirements for "soundness" in rhetorical argument. It does damage neither to that essay nor to our aforementioned treatment of the enthymeme to suggest at least the following criteria for soundness of reference:

1. The complicity of an audience proper to argumentative development of the enthymeme

2. The compliance of argument with facts and circumstances proper to its utterance type

The first criterion is a matter of proper initial reference. The second is a matter of meeting reference expectations proper to enthymeme type. Each is, like the materials of rhetoric themselves, contingent and probabilistic. The more important point is that neither is reducible to criteria of form alone. In the following examples, I sketch an illustration of what may be regarded as a sound enthymeme and then a case that rather conspicuously fails. I conclude with an example designed to show some limit conditions to enthymematic reference.

As an example of successful enthymematic reference, I am presenting an unusually artful, but highly controversial, statement made by President Clinton after the Oklahoma City bombing. The speech was given at a prayer vigil for victims of the April 19, 1995, bombing in Oklahoma City. The bombing site, as everyone knows, was a federal building, selected apparently because it symbolized the cold, sinister, ominous intrusiveness of state power.

Clinton wastes no time in restoring communal and nurturing qualities to the same symbol: "This terrible sin took the lives of our American family, innocent children in that building, only because their parents were trying to be good parents as well as good workers; citizens in that building going about their daily business; and many there who served the rest of us—who worked to help the elderly and the disabled, who worked to support our farmers and our veterans, who worked to enforce our laws and protect us. Let us say clearly, they served us well, and we are grateful" (April 1995).

Now this last line strikes me as an odd thing to say at a eulogy (unless there might be, in sinister quarters, some question about whether we are well served by such people). This is our first clue that Clinton is referring both to his immediate audience and to a world outside.

Proving, once again, that fanaticism is its own worst enemy, this grim occasion has given the president an opportunity to do something that all the public arguments in the world had not been able to do, that is, to recaption and thematize, to humanize the federal government: "But for so many of you they were also neighbors and friends. You saw them at church or the PTA meetings, at the civic clubs, at the ball park. You knew them in ways *that all the rest of America could not*" (emphasis added).

It is, I think, masterfully manipulative stuff; and we're not even at the controversial part yet. Here is our direct link to enthymematic reference:

> To all my fellow Americans beyond this hall, I say, one thing we owe those who have sacrificed is the duty to purge ourselves of the dark forces that gave rise to this evil [applause]. They are forces that threaten our common peace, our freedom, our way of life. . . . Let our own children know that we will stand against the forces of fear. When there is talk of hatred, let us stand up and talk against it. When there is talk of violence, let us stand up and talk against it. In the face of death, let us honor life. As St. Paul admonished us, let us not be overcome by evil, but overcome evil with good.

These do not seem, at first blush, to be remarks admitting to a controversial reception. But in the context of extremely volatile political discourse, hate speech, inflammatory personal attacks upon Clinton himself, this particular passage received a decidedly mixed (but, in my view, quite revealing) response. Some accused the president of trying to politicize the situation to his personal advantage. Others accused Clinton of trying to scapegoat forces of the Republican party's right wing as somehow implicated in the bombing itself. I think there are at least grounds for both accusations. But other than these meta-rhetorical challenges, it is very difficult to counter the referencing of the enthymeme itself. It runs something like—

> Premise assumed: Dark forces of fear/hate/violence/death create a climate for this evil.
> Premise asserted: These forces must be purged.
> (Stated conclusion) The best way to do that is to stand up for love/life/and good.

It names its negative clearly, it is cumulatively powerful, and it gives virtually all the high moral ground to Clinton. Moreover, as the president's more extreme political foes soon discovered, to attack the enthymeme was to validate it. If I were to say, as I used to do at airports, "Hey, hope you Nazis have a nice day," as I walked by my more extreme political opponents, the loudest response is the strongest vindication. So, Gordon Liddy, who had been instructing his listeners on the best places to shoot members of the Treasury Department, was fired the next day. The National Rifle Association, who had been recruiting lobby donations by referring to federal officials as "jackboot thugs," was finally—on May 17—forced to apologize for the tone of those remarks.

Now a great many contingencies entered into these more remote developments. The world of action, as Arendt memorably pronounced, is possessed of tributaries and implications that are potentially limitless. But that is exactly my point. The Clinton enthymeme, if cut off from its proper audience referencing, could seem to be so much hortatory emptiness. But this speech was an utterance of consolation with something more: an action step entirely appropriate to this audience of victims. So I infer that the enthymeme's validity is, at least in part, connected with its eventfulness. I would conclude by suggesting that episodes such as these actually had an additive effect of validating and legitimating the Oklahoma City enthymeme.

But, of course, in public life, much that is said, for whatever purpose, can implicate advocates in unexpected, unintended ways. Positions of public authority are particularly open to unsound referencing, since contexts can be made to shift in public, often without warning. Since we just examined President Clinton being what I would call rhetorically astute, it seems only fair to examine a case of the president being its opposite, rhetorically clueless (to use the technical term, first coined in Henry Peacham's "Garden of Compost").

The following excerpt of questionable competence could be subtitled "President Bill Tries to Ingratiate Himself with an Audience, Completely Forgetting That He Is President and Must Deal with Many Other Audiences." President Clinton is at a fund-raising dinner in Houston addressing well-heeled donors. He says, "Probably there are people in this room still mad at me at that budget because you think I raised your taxes too much. It might surprise you to know that I think I raised them too much too" (November 1995).

Now the point the president was trying to make was that he was forced to raise taxes because no Republican would support his 1993 budget. However, the remark quickly circulated throughout Washington. Republicans were giddy, and Democrats, predictably enough, were furious. Why? This is, I think, an interesting question, for, by trying to answer it, we can begin to appreciate how conventions and institutional "facts" are implicated by enthymemes. What the president was shooting for, of course, was chameleon-like identification with his audience, even to the perverse extent of being contrite over some of his own policies. But the anger of significant others in Congress is the far more plausible response, especially if we consider the taboo domain occupied by "taxes" in America. Saddled with the least progressive income tax in the Western Hemisphere, Americans support tax increases, as Walter Mondale learned in 1984, only as a last resort. As the grim joke about "death and taxes" indicates, dead certainties and absolute necessities go together. In suggesting that he had maybe raised taxes too much, the president was also referring to a process whereby Daniel Moynihan twisted Democratic arms and risked Democratic careers to stand behind the president. The same president now seemed to be suggesting that the very necessity to justify this risk might have been lacking all along.

Here we see both of our aforementioned criteria rather conspicuously violated. First, obviously, Clinton has picked the wrong audience for his alleged confession. If he has truly erred or "sinned," then he must go before those he has harmed most conspicuously, those whose "forgiveness" he will truly need. This would not be an audience of well-heeled potential contributors. Secondly, and even more obvious, there is no evidence available to anyone to suggest circumstances wherein this confession is appropriate. Let me be more blunt. There is no evidence to suggest that this "confession" is even sincere. While the outward "form" of confession is followed, it is the conspicuous failure of Clinton's enthymeme to reference itself properly before an audience knowledgeable in the relevant circumstances that renders this utterance unsound. Of course, the damage control brat-pack quickly swung into action. But the damage had been done. The unintended tacit reference of these presidential utterances was to a lethally costly battle that may not have been worth winning and a president more interested in being liked than in being right.

Earlier in this essay, I promised to conclude by exploring what I considered the "limit conditions" for tacit reference as a locus for provisional judgment about enthymemes. The kind of discourse I have in mind has always been controversial, on both ethical and aesthetic grounds. Moreover, many would dissociate it from the realm of the enthymeme entirely. It is a subspecies of exhortative discourse, a mutant offspring of apocalyptic discourse and the jeremiad. For want of a better term, I am calling this discourse premonitory. The term is designed to include rhetorical reflection dealing with still-unfolding future events. Both utopian rhetoric (say, the *Communist Manifesto*) and dystopian rhetoric (say, a good portion of the book of Revelation) make argumentative pronouncements about a world yet to come into existence. As noted above, it could be claimed that such discourse as this is not enthymematic at all. It would be, as Ed Black long ago argued, "exhortative." Certainly such discourse does have a declamatory quality, but so did Clinton's remarks in Oklahoma City. The tone of a discourse alone is not enough to dismiss its enthymematic properties. Further, it would take an unusually severe case of myopia not to notice certain unstated reflective allusions in both the *Communist Manifesto* and the book of Revelation. As the seals are broken, as the world historical class struggle reaches its apogee, well, you know.

This genre of rhetoric would seem to pose the greatest difficulties for my, or at least our copy editor's, thesis. For what can such discourse as this possibly be referencing? I think the answer is that such discourse is usually referencing certain arguable tendencies in a still-unfolding horizon of events, while reading these same tendencies as pointing in a radically upward or downward arc. Added to this is the fact that our rhetorical voice is usually far from being a disinterested onlooker in these events. Sometimes, as with Peter and Nikolai in Dostoevski's remarkably prophetic *The Possessed*, the apocalypse is an ongoing active invention. Sometimes we are called upon to repent, to step back from the brink. Sometimes we are called to arise, losing our chains, gaining the world.

So, premonitory reference is interested, unfinished reference. I would say that this sort of enthymeme comes closest to vindicating Garver's point about the indistinguishability of enthymemes real and apparent. By definition, there is no way of validating the prophetic voice, at the time. Some cases, like Chaplin's brilliant *Modern Times*, come incredibly close. Other cases, like the one I will briefly discuss, come considerably less so.

When I was a kid, one of the first songs I learned to play on guitar (because it was so easy) was the lurid apocalyptic protest song, Barry McGuire's "Eve of Destruction." It was number one for about five minutes in 1964. In it, the nearly hysterical singer warns of impending doom. Here is one of the better verses:

> Won't you understand what I'm trying to say?
> And can't you feel the fear that I'm feeling today?
> If the button is pushed, there's no runnin' away.
> There'll be no one to save with the world in a grave.

The chorus is, "You tell me, over and over, and over [this varies] again, my friend, that you don't believe we're on the eve of destruction." Kind of a nice little millennialist tune for its times. Much of the stuff about Red China; Selma, Alabama; and other dark prognostications dated themselves at the moment of utterance. Subsequent history has made the song more of a cold war novelty than anything else. I cited it, however, because its pattern is both prophetic and enthymematic, blatantly so. Here are the signs. And with all this evidence you still don't believe. It is a song of seemingly genuine exasperation, the first "You don't get it, do you?" song. Of all my cases, I find the role of premonition as rhetorical invention most interesting. Where the world of the "still to come" is involved, necessity must be suspended. Hope and premonition collide, with neither being disinterested bystanders. Reference is cloudy in such a sphere, but surely relevant. Whether there actually is a flood is the difference between a prophet and a huckster.

The uncertain reference in premonitory discourse also points us toward a mystery that is far too vast to be explored in these few pages. It is the mystery of time and the enthymeme. It is tempting to dismiss the aforementioned "Eve of Destruction" rant because, instead of offering a realm of tacit participation, it presents a polarized, forced choice. But such a dismissal would seem to miss the fact that Clinton's Oklahoma City enthymeme does exactly the same thing. The difference, I think, lies largely in the respective temporal positionings of each utterance. Clinton responds to an already known event (of admittedly mysterious origin). His speech of consolation and accompanying warning are validated by real-time eventfulness. Barry McGuire's authentic anguish notwithstanding, his discourse is largely nameless foreboding. This is nowhere near a satisfactory answer. But the limit conditions for reference as an indicator of enthymematic soundness are perhaps those lost moments of duration, deadened by history.

If the intuitions expressed here bear fruit (another uncertainty), there may be interesting blurred genres around the edges of the deliberative and the exhortative. It may also be the case that the exhortative genres of discourse move away from enthymematic reflection in direct proportion to their abandonment of temporal referentiality.

I hope to have shown something of the tacitly referential aspects in Aristotle's construal of the enthymeme, even if I have not arrived at a satisfactory theoretical account of its workings. Here are a few items on an unfinished agenda:

First, as I have tried to do here, we need to make explicit suppressed norms and background suppositions of enthymematic rhetoric. Sometimes, this practice will reveal forms and aspects of influence that would otherwise remain hidden. Sometimes, such a practice will help reveal why others think the way they do. But in either case, such a practice is a necessary component of an engaged rhetorical criticism.

Second, to help bridge, or at least perceive, the much-publicized gulf separating race, gender, religion, and class in our cultures, I think we need to try and unpack the conditions of affiliation that unite audiences with premises of commitment and conviction. Enthymemes that work usually find a communal home in the horizon of a broader cultural lifeworld than just one group, or just one interest. In finding even a single case of such a broad appeal, we uncover the possibility of inventing others.

Finally, the very fact that a discernible form of reference does occur in and through the enthymeme should remind us that rhetorical reflection has not disappeared entirely from the burned out landscape of political culture. While it takes on convoluted and hybrid forms, as befitting these political climes, it seems yet possible to make grounded discriminations about quality in controversial settings—maybe not all the time, but every now and again. As Habermas said recently about his own "norms," "That's not very much. But it's better than nothing."

7

Two Systems of Invention: The Topics in the *Rhetoric* and *The New Rhetoric*

Barbara Warnick

Comparison of two topical systems—the twenty-eight common topics in Aristotle's *Rhetoric* and the thirteen argument schemes in Perelman and Olbrechts-Tyteca's *The New Rhetoric*—reveals notable differences between inferences used by fourth century B.C.E. Greeks and argument forms in twentieth-century Western society. Unlike reasoning in Aristotle's day, post-Enlightenment argument emphasizes statistical probability and the rule of justice and distrusts argument from tradition. A comparison such as this of inferences in two cultures reveals a cultural embeddedness in rhetorical inference forms well suited to discourse adapted to an audience.

One of the *Rhetoric's* most widely recognized contributions is its system of common and special topics. For the most part, both classicists and rhetoricians concur that the *idia*, or special topics, provide the materials particular to a subject matter from which one can construct premises for enthymemes. William M. Grimaldi has noted that topics are "sources to which one has recourse to develop an understanding and thorough knowledge of the subject" (1974, 182). To speak intelligently on public policy, for example, a fourth century B.C.E. orator would need to know such things as the revenues and expenses of the city, the size of the city's defense force and its food supplies, and other facts. He would also need to know what his audience valued most highly, feared the most, and viewed as expeditious. Such statements of fact and basic value preferences make up the special topics in Book 1 of the *Rhetoric*.

About the twenty-eight common topics in Book 2, there is less concurrence among scholars. The topics are often referred to in spatial terms—as "seats" of argument, "regions" in which argument resides, containers, receptacles, and places where one can "find" an argument (Ochs, 1969, 420–21; Leff, 1983, 24). Few authors have speculated as to where these "places" might be.[1] When they do speculate, they seem inclined to locate that "place" in the speaker's mind, as does Carolyn R. Miller elsewhere in this volume when she concludes that we may think of the *topos* as a "place to which an arguer (or problem solver or thinker) may mentally go to find arguments." This view is corroborated by David L. Vancil, who noted that topics are "primarily descriptive of cognitive processes readily observable in any normally functioning human being" (1979, 30), and by Grimaldi, who maintained that "they are the ways in which the mind naturally and readily reasons" (1974, 185). On this view, the speaker engaged in invention of material would have recourse to those generic relations perceptible to the mind, such as identity, reciprocity, contradiction, equality, division, succession, and coexistence. From these, the speaker would relate one term or idea to another and thus build a proof.

The process of constructing *arguments* in a *rhetorical* relation with audiences may require an additional consideration, however. As the nature of the special topics indicates, the rhetor must also know the values, presumptions, predispositions, and expectations of the audience, and he must locate both his starting points (special topics) *and* forms of inference (common topics) with these in mind. In regard to the common topics of the *Rhetoric*, this meant making use of inference forms recognized and accepted in fourth-century B.C.E. Athenian society. Thus, in addition to the cognitive processes of the individual, one must look to another "space" to locate the reservoir of common topics available to a speaker. One must look to the habits of thought, value hierarchies, forms of knowledge, and cultural conventions of the host society.

I am not the first to make this observation. In his 1983 study of topical reasoning, Michael Leff observed that the connections made in the common topics "are relative to the audience addressed, and thus they arise from and are verified by social knowledge within a community" (25). Citing James Kinneavy on the point that topics enable one to formulate arguments that seem plausible to various audiences, David A. Jolliffe asked the question, "How are both the nature of arguments and the modes of reasoning used to produce support for them shaped by the community of writers and readers in which the discourse is intended to operate?" (1992, 262).

The aim of the present essay is to present a partial answer to this question. It so happens that contemporary readers have available to them for comparative study various topical systems from various time periods and cultures. This study will compare two of these—Aristotle's system of twenty-eight common topics in the *Rhetoric,* and Chaim Perelman and Lucie Olbrechts-Tyteca's topical schemes from *The New Rhetoric.* By laying these two topical systems alongside each other, we can achieve three aims. First, by considering contemporary uses of the special topics as described by Perelman and Olbrechts-Tyteca, we may better understand their uses in Aristotle's time. Second, by reading outward from the twenty-eight to the culturally embedded modes of thought they represent, we can appreciate some of the cultural mores and ways of speaking that gave rise to them. Third, the contrast between the two systems will improve our understanding of how topics themselves operate as "the available means of persuasion in each case" (1.1.14).[2]

The Function of the Common Topics

Before considering variations in the two topical systems, I should like to consider more specifically how a common topic functions. My thinking on this matter is influenced by work I have completed on *The New Rhetoric*'s topical system as used in contemporary discourses (Warnick and Kline, 1992; Warnick, 1996). Perelman and Olbrechts-Tyteca devised a system of thirteen argument schemes that seemed to them to represent the patterns of topical use in modern discourse—speeches, essays, tracts, literary works, and other sources. Two-thirds of *The New Rhetoric* (1969) was devoted to detailed description and exemplification of these schemes as represented in fig. 1.[3]

I. Quasi-logical	contradiction, incompatibility	01
	identity, definition, analyticity, tautology	02
	reciprocity, rule of justice	03
	transitivity, inclusion, division	04
	weights, measures, probabilities	05
II. Based on the Structure of Reality	liaisons of succession	06
	liaisons of coexistence	07
	symbolic liaisons double hierarchies differences of degree & order	08
III. Establishing the Structure of Reality$_1$	example	09
	illustration	10
	model and anti-model	11
IV. Establishing the Structure of Reality$_2$	analogy & metaphor	12
V. Dissociation		13

Fig. 1. Argument schemes in *The Realm of Rhetoric.* First published in "The New Rhetoric's Argument Schemes: A Rhetorical View of Practical Reasoning" by Barbara Warnick and Susan Kline in *Argumentation and Advocacy*, 29 (1992). Reprinted courtesy of *Argumentation and Advocacy.*

Perelman and Olbrechts-Tyteca identified these schemes as *loci* of argumentation that enable the arguer "to induce or increase the mind's adherence to the theses presented for its assent" (1969, 4). In studying argumentative discourse, they sought a system that would enable them to describe the workings of the inferences used by arguers, and they discovered it in Aristotle's topical system. "Without either knowing or wishing it," Perelman said, "we . . . discovered a part of Aristotelian logic that had long been forgotten or, at any rate, ignored and despised" (1990, 1083). The part they discovered included the common topics in the *Topics* and the *Rhetoric*, which were transformed into their schemes.

The common topics from the *Rhetoric* and *The New Rhetoric* function similarly. Each topic provides a frame or grid minimally connecting ideas or terms in a sketchy, to-be-filled-in manner. As Friedrich Solmsen pointed out, the common topic is "a 'type' or 'form' of argument of which you need to grasp only the basic structural idea to apply it forthwith to discussions about any and every subject" (1941, 40). This inference pattern or "form" is recursive and recognizable in the culture in which it is used; it may or may not occur in other cultural contexts. But once a topical pattern has developed into common use, it will be used over and over in various manifestations and will be effective by virtue of its recognizability.

As an example, one could consider reciprocity, a scheme present in both the *Rhetoric*'s and *The New Rhetoric*'s topical systems. This pattern grows out of the belief that two roles or situations that are symmetrical should be treated reciprocally (e.g., "You should treat your subordinates as you expect your superiors to treat you"). The idea is that relative opposites (lessor/lessee, father/son, buy/sell) require each other such that if *X* entails *Y*, to posit *X* is to posit *Y* (Grimaldi, 1988). Here is an example of a reciprocity argument based on relative opposites: If it is not shameful for you to sell them, neither is it for me to buy (2.23.3). Aristotle labeled this relation "from correlatives" (Topic 3), and of it he noted that "if to have done honorably or justly is predicated of one of a pair, to have experienced [it honestly or justly] belongs to the other. . . ." (2.23.3). This pattern repeatedly emerged, for example, in the writings of Isocrates:

> I had no patience with the perversity of men who take women in marriage and make them partners in all the relations of life, and then are not satisfied with the compacts which they have made but by their own lawless pleasures bring pain to those whom they expect never to cause *them* pain. (*Nicocles* 1:40)
>
> You should be such in your dealings with others as you expect me to be in my dealings with you. (*Nicocles* 1:49)
>
> Do not do to others that which angers you when they do it to you. (*Nicocles* 1:61)

The principle of reciprocal treatment and action is so widely prevalent and recognized that it has served as a framework for arguments concerning human action in both Aristotle's society and our own.

By contrast, the cultural embeddedness of certain other common topics is illustrated in Aristotle's twenty-eight by Topic 1, "From Opposites." This assumes that if opposites have opposite qualities and that if a quality can be predicated of one, its opposite can be predicated of the other; for example, if to be temperate is a good thing, then the lack of self control is harmful; or, since it is unjust to be angry at those who have done wrong unwillingly, it is also inappropriate to thank someone who has been coerced into doing good (2.23.1). Application of this pattern, which cannot be found among *The New Rhetoric*'s schemes, would seem odd to audiences today. An arguer in Aristotle's time might say, "If we ought to do good to our friends, then we ought not to do good to our enemies" (*Top.* 104a25); or, "Since false statements are persuasive, many truths turn out to be incredible" (paraphrase of 2.23.1). To a contemporary reasoner, such predication of opposites would seem strange. But arguments such as these were persuasive to the ancient Greeks. As Richard Garner has observed, "The Greeks imposed many different sorts of binary divisions on their world. Some were contrasting, competing oppositions; other [*sic*] were merely alternatives or doubles; but all were carefully matched and balanced" (1987, 75). Garner went on to note that even when the irregularities of human life posed situations in which there would seem to be no diametric opposition, "the artifice of sophistic rhetoric could almost always correct the effects of sublunary asymmetries" (78). Both Garner and K. J. Dover (1974) have noted the prevalence of symmetrical and oppositional reasoning forms in Greek discourse and observed that a good portion of their persuasiveness was due to their aesthetic appeal.

Topical systems can be viewed as catalogs of the habits of mind endemic to a given culture. While some common topics, such as reciprocity, may persist from one cultural setting to the next, others, such as the argument from opposites, may lose their appeal. This essay will show, for example, that the rule of justice, so central to *The New Rhetoric*'s system, is nowhere stated explicitly in Aristotle's topical system. Conversely, some of the topics important to Aristotle, such as "Looking at the Time" (Topic 5) and "Altered Choices" (Topic 18), seem unusual to us today. As will be shown through the examination and contrasting of the two systems, inference patterns are culturally dependent rather than formal or universal.

Because this essay will consider argument forms as recursive forms isolated from their contexts, I want to state at the outset a caveat also expressed by Perelman and Olbrechts-Tyteca. To the extent that an analyst strips away context to identify structure, that person strips away rhetorical meaning and makes an interpretation of the argument. In other words, one reads a logical frame or infrastructure into an argument stated in ordinary language. This is always a risky business, both because it is reductive and because it assigns a contestable meaning or interpretation. In anticipation of possible objections to this procedure, I will have recourse to what Perelman and Olbrechts-Tyteca say on the matter. They remind readers (1969, 187) that isolating an inferential link outside of the argument's context is always dangerous because of the importance of context in assigning meaning. Nonetheless, they say that describing logical schemes is often useful because "discourse is an act which, like every other act, can for the hearer, become an object of thought" (189), and they say that "only an attempt at clarification . . . would enable the speaker, and especially his hearers, to become aware of the mental schemes which they are using or which are acting upon them" (188).

General Comparison of the Two Systems

Both Aristotle's common topics and Perelman and Olbrechts-Tyteca's argument schemes are intended to catalog and conceptualize argument inferences in current use. That is, they are descriptive rather than normative, providing a catalog of warrants. Kennedy (1991, 320) defined a *topos* as "a form or strategy of argument usable in demonstrating propositions. . . ." Aristotle's twenty-eight probably described a set of strategies employed by the speakers he observed or present in the works he read.[4] That *The New Rhetoric*'s system was intended to be descriptive was made clear by Perelman when he described (1990, 1083) how he and Olbrechts-Tyteca analyzed a range of discourse from politics, law, ethics, and daily deliberations to develop their account of arguments in use. The emphasis in *The New Rhetoric* on the schemes, along with Perelman's own insistence on the importance of a contemporary topical system, led Kennedy to conclude (1991, x) that "among major theorists of rhetoric, Chaim Perelman is perhaps the one most indebted to [Aristotle]."

Nevertheless, there are at least three significant differences between the approaches to the topics in the two works. The first is that Aristotle reduces all forms of rhetorical reasoning to two—the enthymeme and the example (2.20.1)—while Perelman and Olbrechts-Tyteca are inclined to identify other inference patterns. That is, Aristotle assumes that all reasoning can be displayed either syllogistically or inductively. *The New Rhetoric*'s authors, recognizing the paucity of this system for describing *in vivo* argument, generated a wide range of descriptive mechanisms, including dissociation, model and anti-model, and symbolic liaison. Enthymematic arguments in their system were confined to the category "quasi-logical."

A second difference arises from the respective theorists' intended uses for their topical systems. Aristotle seemed concerned largely with providing a defense for the study of rhetoric and a description of the activity so that it could be taught and practiced. His twenty-eight topics were an important part of the logical resources that could be employed as "available means of persuasion," presumably by the students of the Academy. Perelman and Olbrechts-Tyteca, on the other hand, appeared more interested in developing a topical scheme to be used in studying argumentative discourse and understanding how it influences audiences. Their enthusiasm in the conclusion to their work is almost palpable when they promise that "many . . . questions just touched on here provide the study of argumentation with a field of research of incomparable wealth" (1969, 509).

The third difference is that while Perelman and Olbrechts-Tyteca studied largely written arguments, Aristotle seems to have intended his treatise for use in developing oral arguments for the courts, senate, and ceremonial occasions. He recognized the uniqueness of oral argument—the need for simplicity so that the audience could follow a speech's reasoning, for parsimony so that listeners would not be bored, and for clarity so that inference patterns would not confuse them. While admitting that "the technique of public speaking differs from that of written argumentation" (1969, 6), *The New Rhetoric*'s authors nonetheless focused pretty exclusively on the latter. Furthermore, they lifted their examples out of context and chose many esoteric and obscure passages. Their examples, removed from their oral and textual context, are often hard to understand. As a result, many argument theorists and rhetorical critics have been reluctant to make use of their topical system in analyzing texts or researching new forms of argument.

Specific Topical Comparison

A detailed comparison of the two topical systems can be found in the appendix at the end of this essay.[5] Of the set of nineteen schemes and subschemes from *The New Rhetoric*, thirteen can be found among Aristotle's twenty-eight. Furthermore, of the six that seem to be missing, two—sign and illustration—appear elsewhere in the *Rhetoric*. The absence of a Perelmanian scheme from Aristotle's system does not necessarily indicate the absence of that reasoning form in fourth-century B.C.E. Greece. For example, dissociation (an inference form newly identified by Perelman and Olbrechts-Tyteca) occurs frequently in the orators. Of the *Rhetoric*'s twenty-eight, six topics do not appear in *The New Rhetoric*. These are number 1 ("From Opposites"), number 5 ("Looking at the Time"), number 6 ("Opponent's Utterance"), number 17 ("Identical Results"), number 18 ("Altered Choices"), and number 23 ("Responses to Slander").

The differences between these systems are due partially to their nature and intended uses as discussed earlier in this essay. Some of Aristotle's topics, such as "Opponent's Utterance" and "Responses to Slander," seem particularly apt to speaking situations in Athenian law courts. It could be, too, that Aristotle's list was intended to be suggestive—a list of inventional resources for teachers and students—while Perelman and Olbrechts-Tyteca's list was intended to be exhaustive. Their typology was constructed through content analysis of hundreds of arguments over a ten-year period. Nevertheless, by moving outward from the two lists and considering other forms of supporting evidence, such as studies of the two cultures, arguments in use in the cultures, and Aristotle's own list of special topics, one can infer that certain of these differences are due to the recognizability and acceptability of various topical patterns in the two respective cultural settings. The remainder of this essay will consider three notable differences—weights, measures, and probabilities (absent in Aristotle's common topics), argument from tradition (absent in Perelman and Olbrechts-Tyteca), and the rule of justice (absent in Aristotle).

Weights, Measures, and Probabilities

Forms of argument represented in the *Rhetoric* do not include argument grounded in statistical probabilities, except in a rather minimalist sense. Policy analysis and decision theory of the kind currently used are artifacts of post-Enlightenment culture. Perelman and Olbrechts-Tyteca's account of these practices notes that certain factors, such as the likelihood of a given outcome and the magnitude of its effects, are given certain values and considered in combination. All elements are reduced to quantitative measurement; and the alternative producing the greatest (quantified) good for the largest number of people will be preferred. Noting that argument from probability "entails a reduction of the data . . . to elements which seem more easily comparable" (1969, 259), Perelman and Olbrechts-Tyteca imply that relying solely on this criterion essentially reduces the locus of quality to the locus of quantity.

The effect of this practice is to confine the stasis of argument to a single value dimension, setting aside competing values connected to what is unique, irreplaceable, irreparable, absolute, and so forth. In commenting on application of the locus of quantity in the sciences, Perelman and Olbrechts-Tyteca affirm:

> In contemporary natural sciences, facts are increasingly subordinated to the possibility of measurement, in the broad sense of that term. The natural sciences display a resistance to any observation which cannot be fitted into a system of measurement. . . . A scientist verifying the conclusions reached by another scientist, after certain experiments, will take into account all the facts that occur and that are relevant to the soundness of the proposed theory but does not feel he has the right, in the controversy, to introduce other facts that are not relevant within the set limits. (1969, 102)

The form of probability argument referred to here is *statistical* or *numerical* probability. In *The Uses of Argument*, Stephen Toulmin alludes to the contemporary inclination either to reduce all forms of probability argument to this single form, or to prioritize or valorize this form over other forms when he notes that "in the philosophy of probability . . . it causes only trouble if one thinks of the scientific applications of the term [probable] as the sole satisfactory ones. The everyday uses, though not numerical, are none-the-less perfectly definite" (1969, 89).

Various forms of these nonnumerical everyday uses are what play a role in Aristotle's *Rhetoric* and *Topics*, as opposed to statistical probability, which is nowhere to be found. (Here I want to clarify that I am alluding to "probability" in quantified form rather than to "probabilities" as what most people believe to be the case or "what happens for the most part" [1.2.15].) A simple nonstatistical version of the locus of quantity does play a role in fourth-century B.C.E. oratory, however, as shown in its appearance in the *idia* and its role in the discourse of the day. When it does occur, it appears in the simple form of enumeration as proof. For example, Demosthenes argued that some of the politicians supporting Philip "who were beggars are suddenly growing rich. . . . While you [citizens of Athens] . . . have passed . . . from affluence to destitution" (*On the Chersonese* 66). Isocrates observed that "when the Thirty [tyrants] took over the City . . . they put to death fifteen hundred Athenians without a trial and compelled more than five thousand to leave Athens and take refuge in the Piraeus . . ." (*Areopagiticus* 67). Also, Aristotle readily listed quantifiable *idia* such as city revenues and expenses, a person's wealth and number of children, and goods said to be scarce or plentiful.

A somewhat more sophisticated use of the locus of quantity is illustrated in Plato's *Phaedrus* by the pseudo-Lysias: "If you are to choose the best of a number of lovers, your choice will be only amongst a few; whereas a general choice of the person who most commends himself to you gives you a wide field so that in that wide field you have a much better prospect of finding someone worthy of your friendship" (1979, 28). The locus of quantity plays the primary role in this argument, and it is conceived in terms of the size of the pool of possible lovers as well as the likelihood of finding one that is suitable. The locus of quality is not excluded, however, since it enters into determining which individual "most commends himself to you" and is "worthy of your friendship."

Of the twenty-eight, one topic that may be taken to rely on a potentially quantifiable probability is Topic 25. The speaker using this topic has recourse to the issue of whether there is or has been a better plan of a different sort from what is advised or enacted. If the topic is concerned with what has already been done, its use would be applicable to forensic speaking to defend a client in a law court by arguing my client could not be guilty of this act because he could have acted much more successfully in some other way (Cope, 1877). Other commentators ascribe this topic to deliberative speaking when it is applied to future action, and Grimaldi concludes, "I can perceive no reason to exclude this topic from any of the three kinds of discourse" (1988, 331). If applied to future action, the topic involves weighing the comparative benefits and disadvantages of various courses of action: Which course might result in the least loss of life, the greatest profit to the state, and so on? Results such as these could be expressed in quantified terms.

Another potential use of quantifiable probability may be embedded in Topic 20, useful, Aristotle says, to "both litigants and deliberative speakers" (2.23.21). Here the speaker argues that a person is more likely to act or avoid action if those factors are present that impel or deter action. These include whether the action was possible, easy, and advantageous (or the reverse) and whether the punishment was less than the reward of the action. Although such factors could be nonquantifiable, they also could potentially be conceived in quantifiable terms—for example, if the rewards and punishments were monetary, in terms of profits and fines.

Argument from Tradition

Post-Enlightenment ideologies and the high regard in which scientific and technological advances are presently held disinclines contemporary audiences to accept unquestioningly arguments from tradition (e.g., We should undertake or continue to do what we have always done) or authority (e.g., We should do *X* because that is what authorities say we should do). *The New Rhetoric*'s treatments of presumption and argument from authority reflect that view. Perelman and Olbrechts-Tyteca conclude that "argument from authority no longer holds a legitimate place in our intellectual arsenal" (1969, 306). They disagree with this view, noting the importance of precedent in law and the generally acknowledged value of maintaining social order. Nevertheless, they note that policy analysts and scientists tend to dismiss authoritative argument as "pseudo-argument, intended to camouflage the irrationality of our beliefs and win for them the consent of everybody or of the majority by appeal to the authority of eminent persons" (306).

Disparagement of arguments from tradition and authority is nowhere more apparent than in contemporary theories of fallacy in which they have been marginalized as illegitimate. The stature of such arguments, however, is very culture dependent. In Athens in the fourth century B.C.E., such appeals were generally considered credible. Aristotle's inclusion of them in the twenty-eight common topics reflects the level of acceptance they enjoyed.

Appeal to past time appears to play a role in Topic 5, "Looking at the Time," in which present action is to be correlated to past action: "If before accomplishing anything, I asked to be honored with a statue if I succeeded, you would have granted it. Will you not grant it [now] when I have succeeded?" (2.23.6). This has everything to do with the appropriateness of matching present actions to what would have been done or anticipated in the past. As Grimaldi observes, "The argument has its force in an accepted inevitable relation between the accident of time and the object, e.g., if X is true at t [sub 1] in the past, then it is also true at t [sub 2]. In such an instance, time is viewed as an integral part of a larger whole which includes the object (X) argued for" (Grimaldi, 1988, 301). This differs from appeal to tradition, which implies that one *ought* to do *X* because *X* was what was done in the past. In "Looking at the Time," one considers rather the proportionate relation of past and present to a larger sense of what is appropriate. In the *Panegyricus*, for example, Isocrates argues: "It is disgraceful for us, when our fathers who engaged in the Trojan expedition because of the rape of one woman, all shared so deeply in the indignation of the wronged that they did not stop waging war until they had laid in ruins the city of him who had dared to commit the crime,—it is disgraceful for us, I say, now that all Hellas is being continually outraged, to take not a single step to wreak a common vengeance, although we have it in our power to accomplish deeds as lofty as our dreams" (*Panegyricus* 1: 181–82). The aspersions cast upon present inaction by contrast to past glory here make apparent Topic 5's effectiveness when it is appropriately deployed.

The veneration of tradition and appeal to past action are reflected, too, in the *idia* where Aristotle reminds the itinerant speaker to "speak of whatever is honored among each people as actually existing" (1.9.30). As Dover has observed, there was among the Greeks a "consciousness of continuity with forebears, a consciousness of particular importance when ancestral examples can serve as a stimulus to virtue" (1974, 245). In his own appeals to panhellenism, Isocrates did not hesitate to remind his readers of "a government whose character is hidden from no one, but evident to all—one which, as you all know, is a heritage from our fathers, which has been the source of numberless blessings both to Athens and to the other states of Hellas . . ." (*Areopagiticus* 2: 59). *Topoi* that had recourse to "how things used to be" evidently were expected to draw a favorable response among Aristotle's contemporaries.

The situation was similar in regard to appeals to authority. Topic 11, in which one has recourse to the judgment of all, or of "at least most people, or the wise (either all of them or most) or the good" (2.23.12), was often used to support a verdict or recommendation. Every one of the examples Aristotle provided of this *topos* involved an unquestioning acceptance of authority—judges, those whom judges approve, those whose judgment cannot be opposed, the gods, or particular individuals, such as a father, a teacher, Socrates, and others. Grimaldi noted that testimony based on authority may range from an actual past fact to a scientific or theoretical principle to a fact of religion, and the statement may be on the witness's own knowledge (immediate) or on that derived from others (mediate) (1988, 312).

Authority appeared to be vested in the individual by virtue of his status, which resulted from his station in life as well as his deeds and character. Only male citizens were eligible for the highest offices; aliens, women, freedmen, and slaves were not regarded as authorities. Thus power and decision making rested with the political leaders and adult males who served as public officials (MacDowell, 1978, 66–67, 170–71). Within this group, certain acts could confer prestige, and many of these are treated in the *idia*—courage, patriotic acts, works done by choice and not for one's sake, and successes gained for others (1.9.15–18). Thus, the testimony and observations of individuals in these positions who possessed such qualities of character would be regarded as reliable in Greek society.

The Rule of Justice

Contemporary Western legal systems are generally grounded in the principles of individual rights and equal treatment under the law. Many legal decisions are two-phased: First, they consider the class or category to which the individual should belong, and second, they determine the individual's rights in that category. Perelman observed that the whole art of casuistry consists in attributing characteristics to a group or individual that puts them in a certain class—for example, "All Ms possessing the quality A ought to be P" (Perelman, 1963, 46).

Determination of the class or category itself is a major function of legal deliberation. Perelman thus emphasized the importance of what he termed "the rule of justice," which holds that beings of one and the same essential category be treated in the same way (Perelman and Olbrechts-Tyteca, 1969, 218). Judges who decide upon the appropriate penalty or award in a given case invoke this principle:

> To each the same thing.
> To each according to his merits.
> To each according to his works.
> To each according to his need.
> To each according to his rank.
> To each according to his legal entitlement. (1963, 7)

Perelman expanded this principle to make it, along with reciprocity, a form of field independent argument in many situations in which fairness and equal treatment are in question.

In contemporary courts of law, the rule of justice regulates the application of precedent and constrains judges in their decisions. Perelman observed that within this system of jurisprudence, the judge "is bound to observe established rules, classification, division into essential categories—these are laid down for him, and he must, as a matter of obligation, take account of them" (1963, 24). Of course, the judge may emphasize certain characteristics or principles of application while setting others aside; the process is neither strictly formal nor deterministic. Nevertheless, the principle that persons who are similar should receive the same treatment is so ubiquitous as to prevent arbitrary outcomes and preserve individual rights.

The situation was quite different in the courts of law of classical Athens. In a situation where jurymen were the judges, juries numbered in the hundreds, and plaintiffs and defendants spoke for themselves, legal proceedings rested less on precedent than on the advocates' ability to persuade the judges that a decision in their favor was a decision in the public interest (Jones, 1956, 66–67). As Dover noted, "The question which a lawsuit or an indictment posed to a Greek jury was not necessarily or always, 'How can we be fair to this individual?' but 'What action in respect of this situation is likely to have the best consequences for the strength of the community?'" (1974, 158). This emphasis on community welfare rather than individual rights probably accounts for the absence of the rule of justice from Aristotle's twenty-eight topics. There are many senses in which the laws and the law courts of classical Athens were different from those of twentieth-century Western society.

In a note at 1.10.3, Kennedy points to these differences, reminding the reader that Greek common law (based on unwritten natural law) should be distinguished from the specific written laws of Greece and from "*common law* in the Anglo-American tradition, which is the law of precedent and equity as established by judicial decisions" (1991, 88). The importance of equilibrium in the *polis* meant that the Athenian juryman was primarily concerned with restoring the status quo when it had been unwarrantably disturbed. This often called for a different kind of judgment grounded in *phronêsis* rather than strict application of precedent. In restoring equilibrium, jurors who acted "now as legislators, now as judges" were often asked "to proceed as if they were called on to play the part of a legislature" (Jones, 1956, 66).

The outcome of their deliberations might be one in which strict justice based on equal treatment would be overridden by other, competing values of society. In the *idia*, Aristotle seemed to view "fairness" more in the context of taking the "larger picture" into account. That juror was viewed as fair who forgave human weakness and who looked not to the law but to the intent of the legislator, not to the part but to the whole, and not to what a person was but to what he or she had always been (1.13.17–18). Fairness was viewed as more likely to result from arbitration than from a court decision and constituted "justice" that went beyond the written law.

This view of the workings of the courts should not, however, lead the reader to conclude that the principle of equivalent treatment was absent from the Athenian legal system. Dover has noted that particular cases were often brought under a general rule by being represented as analogous to other cases that fell under that rule. Although jurors could not be called to account for their actions, they were nonetheless aware that their verdicts could be counted as precedents (Dover, 1974, 292). The absence of the rule of justice from the common topics and its virtual nonexistence in the special topics simply meant that it was less prominent and salient in Greek culture than it is today.

Conclusion

The New Rhetoric's and the *Rhetoric*'s topical systems have been criticized because, as systems of reasoning, they are neither universal nor formal. Instead, they seem to incorporate material elements that disqualify them as systems of logic. For example, Van Eemeren, Grootendorst, and Kruiger questioned whether, in regard to *The New Rhetoric*, one can even "speak of an argumentation *structure* or an argumentational *schema* in the sense in which the terms are used in logic" (1987, 255). They level this criticism because of the confusion between Perelman and Olbrechts-Tyteca's categories of quasi-logic, which are based on the form of the inference, and the other categories, which seem to be based on material elements. In regard to the *Rhetoric*, Ochs concluded his study of its topical system by lamenting that the system was not logical. "Before we could correctly designate Aristotle's rhetorical topics as a 'logical system,' we would need to posit the axioms on which the system is based. There is, however, nothing in the presentation of these topics which resembles the principles of non-identity, excluded middle, or non-contradiction that are the axioms of the syllogism" (1969, 425).

But the logical system put forward in the *Rhetoric* is not a *formal* logical system, nor is it intended to be so (Warnick, 1989). Its starting points are not intuited axioms but beliefs, values, and facts known to the audience; its reasoning forms are not complex but simple and accessible; and its structures are not explicit, precise, and exhaustive but implicit, approximate, and partial. It is for these reasons that Aristotle observed that "a well schooled man is one who searches for that degree of precision in each kind of study which the nature of the subject at hand admits: it is obviously just as foolish to accept arguments of probability from a mathematician as to demand strict demonstrations from an orator" (*NE* 1094b23–28).

To recognize that the common topics lack the precision and validity of scientific demonstration and formal logic is not to say that they are "illogical." Rather, they possess their own form of logic—a rhetorical logic entirely suited to discourse addressed to nonspecialized audiences in the law courts, the senate, and the public forum. Such audiences are more likely than philosophers or specialists to be convinced by forms of reasoning that draw upon accepted value hierarchies, act/person relationships, antithetical reversals of an opponent's utterance, and relations viewed as correlative or analogical. Rather than being abstracted from their context and stripped of ordinary language and life experience, the *Rhetoric*'s common topics emerge from structures in the discourse and life experience of a culture and reflect its ways of thinking and being. That is what makes them recognizable and uniquely well suited for use in discourses intended for the general audience.

Appendix: *The New Rhetoric*'s Schemes Compared to the *Rhetoric*'s Common Topics

***New Rhetoric*'s Scheme**	**Example**	**The *Rhetoric*'s Common Topic**	**Example**
1. Contradiction, Incompatibility —Show the conflict between two mutually exclusive alternatives. —Structurally similar to the disjunctive syllogism.	Wait, what I'm hearing is that if I want people to trust me, I've got to deceive them into thinking I'm something I'm not.	#14 "Criss Cross Consequences" One exhorts or dissuades on two contrasting matters where the matters are opposites.	A priestess did not allow her son to engage in public debate, saying "For if you say what is just, the people will hate you, but if what is unjust, the gods will."
		#15 "Between Thoughts and Actions" When people do not praise the same things openly that they do secretly.	They praise the just and the beautiful while privately wishing for what is to their advantage.
		#22 "Conflicting Facts" Looking at contradictions in dates, actions, and words as applied to	He says he loves you [Athenian people], but he took the oath with the thirty.

New Rhetoric's Scheme	Example	The *Rhetoric*'s Common Topic	Example
		the opponent or to speaker and opponent.	
		#26 "Actions Compared" When something is about to be done that is contrary to what has been done; look at them together.	People ask, "Should we sacrifice and sing dirges to Leucothea?" "Don't sing dirges if you regard her as a god, and if you regard her as a human, don't sacrifice."
2. Identity, Definition, Analyticity —Indicate normal or descriptive meanings, or point out essential elements. —Predicate is adjectival or descriptive. —Predicate stipulates characteristics or limits extension of a concept to elements that are spelled out. —Subject/predicate relationship is relatively stable.	This is a judgment call in that we don't know for certain; we don't have proof.	#7 "Definition" —Grasps the essence of a thing. —Draws syllogistic conclusions about the subject. —Shows *what* something is, not *that* it is [*A. Pst.* 92b].	"The divine is either a god or the work of a god." (X believes that Y is divine in origin. So, X must believe that gods exist.)
3. Reciprocity, Rule of Justice			
a. Reciprocity —Structurally similar to the conditional syllogism. —Two beings or situations treated equivalently. —Both are reduced	And if I did not publish the required number of articles, then I would not be promoted.	#3 "From Correlatives" —Agent or referent in both cases must be the same. —Equivalent treatment is applied to both.	One who shares in the misfortunes of a position should share in the benefits as well [Palmer 1932, 17].

New Rhetoric's Scheme	Example	The *Rhetoric*'s Common Topic	Example
so as to make them appear symmetrical. b. Rule of Justice —Based on the principle that beings in the same category should be treated in the same way. —Stresses characteristics that place both together.	Are we going to go after Gary Hart and not after the next Presidential candidate we get a tip about?		
4. Transitivity, Inclusion, Division a. Transitivity —Because a relation holds between a & b and between b & c, then it holds between a & c. —Structurally similar to the categorical syllogism. —Transfers claimed characteristic to conclusion through a middle term.	What we ought to do is to make our case. The research program is what's important. And I want to see us make our case through the research program.	#8 "Ambiguous Terms" —Varied meanings of a word. —Requires avoidance of equivocation in middle term. —Seems to assume the necessity of stability of terms across premises [*Top.* 106 a & b; 130a]. #2 "Inflections" A statement involving one form of a word changed so as to admit another form of the same word.	The *just* is not entirely good. For what is done *justly* would be good. But to be put to death *justly* is not desirable.
b. Inclusion —Whole is treated as similar to each one of its parts. —Makes transference from part of parts to whole. —Usually value of the whole greater than the parts it contains.	I'm not saying I hate the press. I think the press is wonderful. Freedom of the press is part of our basic freedoms in this country.	#12 "From the Parts" —Of all those things of which the genus is predicated. —One of its species must also be predicated [*Top.* 111a33].	X has knowledge (X possesses the genus). Therefore, X has grammatical knowledge or musical knowledge (X possesses the species).

New Rhetoric's Scheme	Example	The *Rhetoric*'s Common Topic	Example
c. Division —Enumerates, stipulates alternatives. —Assumes the sum of parts equals the whole. —Parts are exhaustively enumerable.	As a former mayor who has just been appointed to a corporate Board of Directors, I now have an institutional duty; I have a corporate duty; and I also have other interests as a citizen.	#9 "From Division" —Take at each stage only elements in the essence. —Divide consecutively. —Leave out nothing. —As in induction, the inference must be added [*A.Pst.* 91b].	All people do wrong from one of three reasons: For this, or this, or this. Now, two of these are impossible. Even [the accusers] themselves do not assert the third.
5. Weights, Measures, and Probabilities —Make use of a stable standard of judgment. —Make comparisons that can be checked. —Postulate a magnitude. —Reduce topic that can be evaluated in terms of frequency.	They should give all the subjects the experimental drug because if before 95% or 100% died in a month and now, with the drug, 20% or 40% died, it would be very clear.	Not in the common topics, unless one counts the more and the less.	
6. Liaisons of Succession —Unite a phenomenon to its causes or consequences. —Connect phenomena at the same level of reality.	I've learned never to lie to a reporter because everyone I've seen who's done it has gotten into a great deal of trouble.	#13 "Simple Consequences" Based on the idea that something good and bad follows from the same cause.	To acquit him will encourage wrongdoers. To condemn him will make others hesitate to do likewise [Palmer 1932, 46–47].
		# 19 "Attributed Motives" —The purpose for which something might exist or might happen. —Is attributed so as to put the better or worse construction	Someone gave someone something so that he could cause him pain after he took it away.

New Rhetoric's Scheme	Example	The *Rhetoric*'s Common Topic	Example
		on an opponent's action.	
		#20 "Incentives and Deterrents" —What turns the mind in favor of or against something. —Considers whether an action was possible, easy, advantageous, or harmful to enemies. —If punishable, whether the punishment is less than the reward of the action.	
		#24 Cause —If the cause exists, the effect does. —If it does not, there is no effect.	The Persian expedition came against Athens because Athens raided Sardis.
		#25 "Course of Action" Is there a better plan of a different sort that will be more advantageous?	
7. Liaisons of Coexistence —Unite two phenomena not on an equal level. —Seek to establish a relationship between an observable and what is not observable.	Any candidate who would go to the Cozy Condo Cottages with a woman who is not married is the biggest idiot who walked the earth and for that reason alone is unqualified to be President of the U.S.	Not in common topics. Included in treatment of sign at 1.2.16–18.	The woman has milk, so she has given birth. Socrates was wise and just. So, the wise are just.

New Rhetoric's Scheme	Example	The *Rhetoric*'s Common Topic	Example
8. Symbolic Liaisons, Double Hierarchies, Differences of Order			
a. Symbolic Liaisons —Characterized by a relation of participation between symbol and what it evokes. —Use recognized, concrete symbols. —Bring about transference between the symbol and the thing symbolized.	Persuading patients to take unproven treatments of unknown safety awakens memories in my mind of snake oil salesmen who used to go around saying, "Trust me, it will work. I know it will work. Just give me your money."	#28 "Meaning of Names" The person's name represents the person's character.	"Polus" as name in *Gorgias*, to represent the colt, or an impulsive person.
b. Double Hierarchies —Correlate a contested hierarchy with an accepted one.	There's something terrible about the downfall of a king, more so than about the downfall of a beggar.	#4 "More and Less" If the lesser thing is true, the greater is also.	If not even the gods know everything, human beings can never do so.
c. Differences of Degree and Order —Convert differences of degree into differences in kind and vice versa. —Used to minimize or maximize the significance of an act or phenomenon, converting kind to degrees and degrees to kind.	"Even though your program is full, I'd like you to make an extra slot for him." "Well, the end point of these protocols is not really that sharp. So we might take an extra case under those circum-stances."	No corresponding topic.	
9. Example —Designed to	[To enter an expensive protocol	#10 Induction —"Example is a	—When the orator at Mantias at

New Rhetoric's Scheme	Example	The *Rhetoric*'s Common Topic	Example
establish a rule or principle. —Is actual, concrete, succinct. —Presupposes existence of regularities. —Implies disagreement on the rule the example is invoked to establish.	for an AIDS cure] "I would not take all your money out of the bank; I wouldn't ask all your brothers and sisters to raise money; I wouldn't have a fund-raising drive, because the chances of this helping you in the near future are very small."	kind of induction" [*A.Pst.* 71a6]. —Use of multiple examples to establish a general principle.	Athens was disputing the parentage of his son, the boy's mother declared the truth. —The woman of Dodona identified the son of Ismenias. —[So], women everywhere discern the truth about who [is the father] of children.
10. Illustration —Seeks to clarify or show the import of a rule or principle. —Must strike the imagination. —Can be elaborate.	I think it's absolutely unreal to tell this patient, "You won't have a better chance if you get this new drug rather than the placebo." Of course, you suspect it's more useful than aspirin or you'd be giving everybody aspirin and placebos.	No common topic. The fable (2.20.5–8) probably fulfills this function.	
11. Model and Anti-model —Intended to encourage/ discourage imitation or behavior. —Presents person or group as model to be imitated or avoided. —Person or group must be recognized and admired or denigrated by the audience.	Why don't you order that everyone in the White House take a drug test, Mr. President? You and your spouse have spoken eloquently about drug control in this country. Let's be an example.	No common topic.	

New Rhetoric's Scheme	Example	The *Rhetoric's* Common Topic	Example
		#11 "Existing Decisions" —Argument from authority. —About the same or a similar matter. —Especially if all always so judge, or —At least most people, or the wise, or the good.	The gods spared one who protected his parents. . . . You should punish one who does not [Palmer 1932, 41].
		#21 "Incredible Occurrences" —What seems patently improbable is probable. (Palmer calls this "too poor a story to be a lie.")	Do not convict me of such madness that I would choose to discourse to you about statements so contrary to the accepted view, unless I had something true to say about them [Palmer 1932, 67].
		#27 "Previous Mistakes" To accuse and defend based on mistakes that have been made.	
12. Analogy and Metaphor —Must be interpreted as a proportion: A is to B as C is to D. —Unknown proportion is inferred from known. —Theme (unknown) comes from a different realm than phoros (known). —Foregrounds certain relationships; leaves others in background.	"I think that in the stock market you can't make a level playing field, and I think that these insider trading laws are basically high level lying." "What you are saying is that, because you can't stop all people from stealing, you should not have a law against stealing; you should permit everyone to steal."	# 16 "Proportional Results" —A version of "From Opposite." —If you would do X in Y case, then you should do its opposite in the opposite (similar) case.	They tried to force Iphicrates's underage son to perform public service because he was tall. He said: "If you deem large boys men, you should vote that small men are boys."

New Rhetoric's Scheme	Example	The *Rhetoric*'s Common Topic	Example
13. Dissociation —Distinguishes one term from another and sets up a hierarchy where one term is valued (Term II) and the other devalued (Term I). —Creates a distance from Term I. —Arises from widely accepted hierarchies, like appearance/reality. —Restores coherence when incompatibilites arise. —Reorganizes conceptions of reality.	Our job is not to simply spread the bottom line in a few nifty, well chosen paragraphs in the *Boston Globe*. Our job and our responsibility is to review the data very carefully, to have recognized experts and statisticians review it, and suggest changes prior to publication.	No common topic.	

Aristotelian Topics That Do Not Appear in *The New Rhetoric:*

#1 "From Opposites"—Like reciprocity, but from opposing rather than symmetrical conditions or situations, e.g., "If war is the cause of present evils, then things should be set right by making peace."
#5 "Time"—If an agreement was made in the past, it should be honored in the present, e.g., "If, before I accomplished anything, I asked to be honored with a statue if I succeeded, you would have granted it. Will you not grant it now when I have succeeded?"
#6 "Opponent's Utterance"—Turning what has been said against oneself upon the one who said it. The opponent should be the one who seems more likely to have done wrong. "If you, being Aristophon, would not play the traitor, would I, Iphicrates?"
#17 "Identical Results"—If some result is the same, the things from which it resulted are also, e.g., "Those who say the gods are born are as impious as those who say they die. In both cases, the result is at some time the gods did not exist" [and to hold that to be true is impious].
#18 "Altered Choices"—Not always choosing the same thing before and after an event, e.g., "It would be terrible if, when in exile, we fought to come home, but having come home we shall go into exile in order not to fight."
#23 "How to Meet Slander"—Pointing up act/person misinterpretations. A form of counter sign argument, perhaps?

Notes

1. Another sense in which the term *topos* was used in Aristotle's time was to refer to a "site" of discourse, or a ready-made argument then circulating in the discourse community. Solmsen noted that these commonplaces were available "for either enhancing or minimizing, say, the trustworthiness of the witnesses, the importance of oaths to be sworn in court, etc." (1941, 40). Solmsen further observed that Aristotle's innovation was to replace this "ready-made argument" system with the idea of a type or form of argument such as that discussed in this essay.

2. References to the *Rhetoric* in this essay will be to the Kennedy (1991) translation and ordered as Book, Chapter, and Section (e.g., 1.1.14). References to Kennedy's notes or commentary, however, will follow the standard author-date system (e.g., 1991, 21).

3. The breakdown of the scheme taxonomy represented here is a simplified version of *The New Rhetoric*'s system from *The Realm of Rhetoric* (Perelman, 1982).

4. In her conclusion to a detailed study of the use of topics in the orators, Palmer (1932, 80–84) considered whether Aristotle derived his system from the speeches and oral arguments of the day. She noted that as many of his illustrations were derived from poetry and philosophy as from oratory. Palmer found hundreds of examples of some topics (such as *a fortiori*) in the orators and none of other topics (Topic 2, Topic 8, and Topic 28). Nonetheless, Aristotle derived no more than seven of his examples from the orators. So, Palmer concluded, "however much Aristotle profited by listening to oratory, the only considerable section of Attic oratory studied in the producing of this chapter of the *Rhetoric* was the epideictic orations of Isocrates" (84).

5. Many of the labels for the twenty-eight topics in this chart are from D'Angelo (1984, 58). D'Angelo constructed his chart using the labels provided in marginal headings for 2.23 in Cooper (1932, 159–72).

8

The Aristotelian *Topos:* Hunting for Novelty

Carolyn R. Miller

Although the *topoi* have routinely been thought of as instruments of decorum, serving a managerial function in rhetoric, Richard McKeon noted that they can also be understood as sources of novelty, as having a generative function. To establish what the Aristotelian *topos* can contribute to contemporary interests in generative rhetoric, this essay examines the conceptual contexts from which Aristotle drew his use of the term and the framework from which he drew his thinking about invention. Sources examined include his earlier works, the *Physics* and *On Coming-to-Be and Passing-Away*, as well as aspects of pre-philosophical Greek thought that constitute what has been called the "venatic paradigm," in which metaphors of hunting are prominent. Topical theory may help us construct a postmodernist invention in which novelty is situated, relative, and accommodative—understood in dynamic tension with decorum.

Recent interest in the canon of invention raises new questions about Aristotle's *Rhetoric*. One development in particular that enables us to reexamine Aristotelian thought is the attribution of epistemic or generative powers to invention. Robert Scott introduced this notion explicitly in 1967 and a few years later led a committee of the National Developmental Project on Rhetoric to characterize invention as "a productive human thrust into the unknown" (Scott, 1967; Scott et al., 1971, 229). The committee called for a "generative theory of rhetoric" that would help explain "the coming-to-be of the novel, the new, the 'invented'" (230). Although this general approach to invention has been central to much subsequent thinking, the specific explanatory task identified by the committee has not been pursued, and the potential contribution of Aristotelian concepts to this question has not been explored in any detail.[1]

One effect of this interest in the generative powers of rhetoric has been to re-accentuate the distinction between invention and discovery. In both Latin and Greek, the verbs for "invent" *(heuriskein, invenire)* ambiguously include what are now two senses: that of coming upon what already exists (discovery) and that of contriving something that never existed before (invention). The English verb once included both senses as well, but the former is largely obsolete, and the latter is, according to the *OED*, the "chief current sense": to create, produce, devise, originate. Invention, especially outside the domain of rhetoric, has come to concern novelty.

In rhetoric, however, the former sense has traditionally been assumed: The rhetor examines a preexisting inventory of "stock arguments" and "commonplaces" to select those that are most appropriate to the situation at hand. The dissociation between invention and discovery developed during the sixteenth century and hardened with the modernist rise of science, industry, and nationalism, and it is a sign of rhetoric's long obsolescence that it has adhered to the older meaning of invention *as* discovery. The dissociation was further complicated by Francis Bacon, who declared that "Invention is of two kinds much differing: the one of arts and sciences, and the other of speech and arguments." He went on to explain the difference in memorable terms: "The invention of speech or argument is not properly an invention: for to invent is to discover that [which] we know not, and not to recover or resummon that which we already know. . . . Nevertheless, because we do account it a chase as well of deer in an inclosed park as in a forest at large, and that it hath already obtained the name, let it be called invention: so as it be perceived and discerned, that the scope and end of this invention is readiness and present use of our knowledge, and not addition or amplification thereof" (Bacon, 1952 [1605], 13.1.6). In this view, rhetoric neither discovers nor invents; it can only rediscover or recover. It is not generative or epistemic but "managerial," to use the term Douglas Ehninger applied to eighteenth-century rhetorics, because it selects and deploys proofs already created or discovered by means other than rhetoric. As a managerial art, rhetoric has been concerned primarily with accommodation to situation and audience, that is, with decorum; in contrast, the arts of science, technics, and poetics concern novelty, both that which is discovered and that which is invented.

Recent interest in the generative potential of rhetoric thus challenges a long tradition but also promises much for the revival of rhetoric as a cultural enterprise in an age that reveres technical invention and scientific discovery. One contemporary theorist whose work has promoted this connection is Richard McKeon. McKeon identified invention as the part of rhetoric that could be used to provide some system and guidance to the present-day fascination with creativity and innovation (McKeon, 1987, 14). Beyond that, he suggested that rhetorical invention can be "an art which is productive of things and arts or skills rather than of words and arguments or beliefs" (14). In a direct challenge to the Baconian bifurcation of invention, he claimed that a reconstituted invention can be used to "generalize" the art from presentation to discovery—from the use of words to constructions about experience, from creation in language to discovery of possibility and existence. "We need," he said, "a new art of invention and discovery in which *places* are used as means by which to light up modes and meanings of works of art and natural occurrences and to open up aspects and connections in *existence and possibility*" (14; emphasis added).[2]

Here McKeon is pointing specifically to Aristotle's concept of the *"topos"* and its subsequent manifestations in the "commonplace" tradition. Aristotle uses the metaphor of *place* in both rhetoric and dialectic to suggest how probable reasoning proceeds in open-ended, contingent situations about matters that do not admit of certainty. Although Aristotle never defines *topos* (according to Kennedy's editorial note to *Rhetoric* 1.2.21), it functions rhetorically as a conceptual place to which an arguer may mentally go to find arguments, like Bacon's hunter in the forest. Aristotle's statement that rhetoric is the "ability, in each particular case, to see the available means of persuasion" (*Rhet.* 1.2.1) does not suggest that he necessarily understands rhetoric as generative, but he does intimate in the *Topics* that reasoning leads to novelty, or at least to something we didn't begin with: "Reasoning is a discussion in which, certain things having been laid down, something *other than these things* necessarily results through them" (*Top.* 100a, emphasis added).[3]

Since Aristotle, topics have been conceived alternatively as pigeonholes for locating already existing ideas and as generative patterns of thought or methods of analysis. As Michael Leff notes, "The term 'topic' incorporates a bewildering diversity of meanings. Hence, among modern authors we find conceptions of the topics ranging from recurrent themes in literature, to heuristic devices that encourage the innovation of ideas, to regions of experience from which one draws the substance of an argument" (Leff, 1983, 23–24). He finds the "classical lore of topics . . . as confused as the modern efforts to revive it" (Leff, 1983, 23–24). That this concept has been so difficult to understand and yet so persistent suggests that further exploration may be useful, particularly at the point of ambiguity between invention and discovery.

In his essay "Creativity and the Commonplace," McKeon takes some pains to refute the tradition that made of the commonplaces an arid catalog of prior knowledge or fixed clichés, aids to memory more than to invention. Instead, he sees commonplaces as sources of novelty, as the "places for the perception, discovery, and explanation of the unknown" (1987, 31), "the sources of new perceptions operative in new directions in the thought and culture and philosophy of the twentieth century" (34). Apparently, this is possible because the commonplace serves literally as a place where the familiar can be "brought into contact with" the unfamiliar or with transformations of the familiar (35). Doctrines, terms, and lines of argument may be combined and recombined in an exploratory fashion under the aegis of, or within the realm of, a commonplace, with its accompanying concepts, doctrines, structures. McKeon thus locates a paradox: that *topoi* serve *both* managerial and generative functions—they can effect both novelty and decorum. It may be significant that the doctrine of the commonplaces reached its pinnacle during the Renaissance, a period both obsessed by novelty and consumed with concern for decorum.[4]

In this essay I aim not to resolve the centuries of debate about what Aristotle really meant; if this task is feasible, it is one for which I am not qualified. Rather, I hope to establish that the *topos* is still a useful concept, to pursue McKeon's notion that it has generative capacities, and to suggest some of the conceptual resources it provides for understanding invention. My claim is not that Aristotle was necessarily aware of these resources in any explicit way but rather that he had some powerful intuitions that we can elaborate and articulate in developing a neo-Aristotelian theory of invention. First, I will sketch some evidence that the spatial metaphor of the *topos* is still a powerful one for conceptualizing invention as generative and then suggest some dimensions of the concept that are implicated in Aristotle's use of it. Finally, I'll broaden the discussion beyond the *topos* to examine some related aspects of Aristotle's thought about invention and the background against which it may be understood.

Recent attempts to characterize technical invention provide some evidence for the continued utility of topical thinking in a field that has become identified with novel creation. For example, in his exploration of aeronautical design, Walter Vincenti describes "three hidden, mental activities" that engineers seem to use in producing designs: "search of past experience," examination of "new circumstances," and selection of options "most likely to work" (Vincenti, 1990, 245–46); these activities match very closely Aristotle's common topics of past fact or analogy, future fact or circumstance, and possibility/impossibility. Elsewhere, Vincenti suggests that "intellectual concepts" serve as important theoretical tools for the reasoning that engineers do (215) and that various kinds of performance specifications serve in specific ways to enable and constrain design work (98–100); these resemble closely what Aristotle called "special topics." Another example comes from an artificial intelligence project that attempts to model the software design process: One of the most important components in that process is, the authors note, "previous experience, in the form of knowledge of the commonly occurring structures . . . in the domain." They use the term *cliché* to describe these recurring structures, with a kind of apology for the "pejorative" connotation of "overuse and lack of creativity," explaining that "in the context of engineering problem solving, this kind of reuse is a positive feature" (Rich, Waters, and Reubenstein, 1987, 81). This formulation alerts us to the fact that the special topics of any domain can become commonplaces within that domain.

Cognitive research on discovery and invention has produced several spatial concepts. Herbert Simon's influential program of cognitive processing research has drawn heavily on the concept of the "problem space," represented as a tree diagram on its side, with an initial "problem state" at the left and increasing numbers of branches to the right, at least one of the branches being the solution (the end state or goal state) (Newell and Simon, 1972, 811). The space here is a bounded space (Bacon's "inclosed park") that is understood to include or contain the object of the search; the process is conceived of as discovery rather than invention.

In a set of historical case studies of inventors, psychologist Michael Gorman and historian Bernard Carlson focus on the mental representation that an inventor develops, in which the productive regions are the fuzzy or unspecifiable aspects, or "slots": "To test and refine their mental models, inventors insert all sorts of familiar objects in the slots" (Gorman and Carlson, 1992, 585). In fact, they suggest that the inventor's repertoire of mechanical representations serves the same function as rhetorical commonplaces, calling it a "mental set of stock solutions" from which an inventor draws in testing out a mental model (52). What this approach to invention emphasizes is the generative potential of the familiar, the possibility of novelty within the commonplace. New technology is created, in an important sense, from old technology.

Gorman and Carlson take the term *slot* from a retrospective study attempting to extract heuristic principles for technical invention from the historical development of hand tools (Weber and Perkins, 1989). Weber and Perkins use the psychological concept of the "frame," a representation of a possible object or concept, consisting of a series of "slots in which particular values, relations, procedures, or even other frames reside. . . . The slot is a generalization of the idea of a variable" (51). In their discussion of slots and frames, Weber and Perkins note the reliance of cognitive discussions of invention on spatial terminology, commenting that "it is natural to adopt a spatial metaphor in discussing frames and invention" (56). Whether or not it is natural, it is certainly common. While these examples reflect the commonly noted preference of Western culture and of Indo-European languages for using spatial metaphors to represent cognition, they also suggest that there might be a particular enduring explanatory power in spatialization as applied to the problem of novelty and thus a particular richness to Aristotle's metaphor.

Of the primary interpreters of Aristotle, Richard McKeon and William Grimaldi are the ones who have most emphasized the generative function of the *topos*. McKeon's discussion, quoted above, suggests that the *topos* serves as a "space" for combination and recombination. Grimaldi understands *topoi* as potentially "productive of knowledge" and as "sources for intelligent discussion and reasoning in dialectic and rhetoric," but he says little about how they may operate generatively (Grimaldi, 1972, 129, 119). In surveying pre-Aristotelian uses of the term *topos*, Grimaldi finds that while Aristotle probably did not originate the idea of *topoi* as sources of inference or argument, he seems, characteristically, to have formulated explicitly what was only latent in previous treatises or catalogs. Grimaldi also cites uses similar to Aristotle's in both Isocrates and Demosthenes, noting in addition some evidence that what Aristotle called special topics were sometimes called *kairous* rather than *topous*, a connection suggesting that heuristic discovery can become opportunity.[5]

But *topos* appears as well in other Aristotelian treatises, in the relatively early "logical" treatises *Categories* and *Topics*, as well as in the *Physics*, where it is a key problematic term; all of these probably predate the *Rhetoric* and so can help inform our understanding of what Aristotle could have meant there.[6] We can, in particular, draw some tentative conclusions about both the relationship between form and substance and the distinction between the common and the special *topoi*; in both cases, the distinctions are more sharply drawn in what seem to be the later works.

The problem that Aristotle was trying to solve in the *Physics*, according to

Henry Mendell, was the relationship of matter *(hylê)* to form, extension, and change (Mendell, 1987). Place is important to Aristotle here because it is through change of place that we understand motion. Aristotle's treatment of place in the earlier *Categories* did not distinguish matter and form and did not account for change; he used a Platonic notion of place as a prime substance that is coextensive with the object occupying the place. In the later *Physics*, he rejected this possibility because two bodies *(sômata)* cannot be coextensive (4.209a7). Thus, place cannot be matter *(hylê)* (*Phys.* 209a21), but it is not independent of matter, for Aristotle did not believe in the void; place contains, but is not, shape or form *(eidos)* (*Phys.* 209a22), because it is separable from that which is in the place (see also *Phys.* 209b18–25). Place is "a surface-continent that embraces its content after the fashion of a vessel" (*Phys.* 212a27), or, as Mendell puts it, it is the "inner limit of a containing body" (206).

The comparison of *topos* with a vessel or container *(aggeion)* is extended: Not only is a vessel a "movable place," a place is an "immovable vessel" (*Phys.* 212a15). Aristotle further notes that containers may themselves be contained. Thus, "you at this moment, are in the universe because you are in the air, which air is in the universe" (*Phys.* 209a34). Any object, therefore, has both "its special and exclusive place" and places that are "'common' to it and other things" (*Phys.* 209a32). It is striking that Aristotle here uses exactly the same terms, *idios* and *koinos*, that he uses in the *Rhetoric* to describe the particular and the common topics (1.2.21). Aristotle's thinking in the *Rhetoric* may, then, be related to that in the *Physics* and therefore at least partially glossed by it. In what follows, I will suggest the implications for rhetorical theory of Aristotle's treatment in the *Physics* of form and substance and of the *topos* as container-like.

Aristotle emphasizes that what makes *place* "appear so mysterious and hard to grasp is its illusive suggestion now of matter and now of form" (*Phys.* 212a8–10). Mendell suggests that in wrestling with this problem, Aristotle fails to maintain *topos* as a concept distinct from both matter and form. Subsequent commentators on the rhetorical *topos* have run into this same issue again and again.[7] Grimaldi, for example, noting that the *topoi* must concern "both the material and formal element" in dialectic and rhetoric (1972, 119), suggests that the *koinoi topoi* are forms of inference (131) and the *idia* are material propositions (124). Thomas Conley has taken issue, denying that Grimaldi presents a realistic process of reasoning and claiming that he misrepresents Aristotle by turning the *koinoi* into entire arguments, rather than the argumentative premises that Aristotle intended (Conley, 1978). Conley, like Otto Bird some time earlier (Bird, 1961), suggests that the *topos* functions like a Toulminian warrant, a suggestion that, while it does not account for the power of the spatial metaphor, does provide one way of resolving the form-substance conundrum. Within an argument, a warrant must both provide substance that connects evidence to claim and take a form (whether implicit or explicit) that allows an audience to make this connection.

However, treating the *topos* as a warrant forecloses another issue, that is, whether it should be thought of as a concept or a proposition. If it is a warrant, of course, the *topos* must be a complete proposition in order to function as an argumentative premise. Leff has suggested that dialectical and rhetorical topics differ in this regard: In dialectic, the topics must provide a way to relate the terms of propositions (that is, they must supply middle terms), while in rhetoric, the topics must provide relations between propositions and between propositions and audiences (Leff, 1983, 25). Cogan, however, suggests that the understanding of *topoi* as propositions was part of a medieval shift in topical theory away from the spatial metaphor to an abstract, logical understanding. Using Cicero's Latin term *sedes*, which originally carried a "spatial or architectural sense of 'residence,'" medieval discussions of topical invention, largely unrhetorical in their search for validation of universal propositions (180), treated the *sedes* as complete propositions, rather than as "empty 'residences'" (Cogan, 1984, 178). Thus, the *sedes* became a "seat," understood as a logical foundation (Cogan, 1984, 176). When a *topos* is thus conceptualized as a part of an argument, rather than as a source for an argument, the spatial metaphor begins to weaken and the generative use of the *topos* is traded for a structural one.

Aristotle's original metaphor, however, seems to require us to conceive of *topoi* not as propositions but as sources from which propositions (or terms, in dialectic) may be obtained. The *Physics* suggests that such sources can be thought of as containers, perhaps of not completely determinate shape with not completely determined contents. Within such a container, productive and not completely predictable or predetermined combinations of concepts may occur; within it, new (or old) connections between audiences, terms, and propositions may (or may not) be found (or created). The *topos* is like a cauldron in which form and substance are brought together, where *hylê* and *eidos* interact to create material shaped for argument and persuasion.[8]

Another implication of the *Physics*, however, is that the special topics cannot contain this kind of productive interaction, since only one determinate thing can be located in the place exclusive to it, like the place on the shelf for the seventeenth volume of an encyclopedia. Under such a strict interpretation, use of the special topics would be much like the way Aristotle conceives "atechnic" (or nonrhetorical) proof, serving only to locate a preexisting argument and not requiring much rhetorical artistry (*Rhet.* 1.2.2). And since Aristotle also notes that we make more use of the special than of the common topics (*Rhet.* 1.2.22), we can surmise that he didn't appreciate the generative potential of the container metaphor so much as he did its managerial potential. The examples given earlier of contemporary technical invention suggest, however, that topics may be specific to a particular field of argument without being so specific that they serve to identify only one preexisting proof. We may, then, more productively take "common" and "specific" as relative, not absolute, terms and thereby retain the generative potential of the container metaphor.

Returning to the context in which Aristotle brought the term *topos* to bear on both physics and rhetoric, the issue that was central to much of Greek philosophy at the time was the problem of change, or "becoming"—*genesis* (Peters, 1967, 69). After Parmenides, change was understood as paradoxical, and the Platonic commitment to an ontology of unchanging Forms, a metaphysics of Being, was one response to this problem.[9] Aristotle criticizes Plato's view as too narrow, and in his treatise *On Coming-to-Be and Passing-Away* (*genesis* and *phthora*)[10] he distinguishes several kinds of change. There are three kinds of ordinary change, or *metabolê*: alteration (change of quality), growth (change of size), and locomotion (change of place). In addition, there is change of substance (*GC* 318b–320a), *genesis* (or *phthora*) (his examples include the seed being converted to blood and water coming-to-be or passing-away into air).[11] This is the only kind of change that can involve the creation of something new. Heavenly bodies are in another realm, a realm of Being, beyond all kinds of change: Unalterable and indestructible, they consist of unchanging "primary substance"—there are no novelties in the heavens, as generations of Aristotle's followers maintained.[12] But for Aristotle, both physics and rhetoric belong to the sublunary realm of change, a world of Becoming.[13]

This brief glimpse at the philosophical context suggests how differently Plato and Aristotle must have thought about rhetoric and how each could have conceived invention. In the Platonic world of Being, invention can only be discovery, but in the Aristotelian world of Becoming, it can also be creation; novelty and innovation are possible. And further, only in a world of Becoming can decorum be important, for only in such a world could it be violated; and only in a world of change can *kairos* be a useful notion, for only there does one moment offer different possibilities from the next. In a world without change, on the other hand, representation is the only rhetorical challenge.

Intellectual virtues take radically different forms in these two sorts of worlds, and Aristotle's discussion of them in the *Nicomachean Ethics* reflects this division. In the world of Being, where any motion is continuous and cyclic and existence is necessary (*GC* 338a1–3), the appropriate intellectual virtues are *epistemê* (scientific knowledge), which provides demonstration of things that are universal and necessary; *nous* (intelligence or intuition), which gives knowledge of first principles; and *sophia* (wisdom), which combines scientific knowledge and intelligence (*NE* 1139b, 1140b–1141a). Quite another cluster of virtues is relevant to the sublunary realm of contingency and possibility, where things can be other than they are: These include *phronêsis* (prudence), *euboulia* (resourcefulness or good deliberation), *sunesis* (understanding), and *gnômê* (judgment or consideration) (*NE* 1140a–b; 1142b–1143a). These are the virtues important for choice, for political life, for rhetoric.

I want to suggest that these virtues for the world of change are elaborations and refinements of an older, less respectable set of intellectual skills, those concerned with finding means to a given end, regardless of whether Aristotle would find that end noble or not. He mentions *deinotês*, the faculty of "cleverness," which is related to *phronêsis*, but lacks moral scruple (*NE* 1144a). Cleverness, moreover, is related to the older *mêtis*, a quality frequently attributed to Odysseus, the polymetic, or many-skilled, the paragon of craftiness and cunning.[14] *Mêtis* is needed by the navigator, the physician, the hunter, the warrior, the weaver, the politician, the sophist; it is the *aretê* of the banausic, not of the aristocrat.[15] In their study of the role of *mêtis* in Greek culture, Detienne and Vernant note that although it is essential in a world of Becoming and central to the Greek system of values, operating in a wide and important domain, *mêtis* was submerged by the subsequent tradition that emphasized the world of Being, both in the philosophy of the Greeks themselves and in that of their successors. They suggest particularly that Aristotle's discussion of *phronêsis* retains the spirit of *mêtis* and that the sophists occupy a "crucial position in the area where traditional *mêtis* and the new intelligence of the philosophers meet" (Detienne and Vernant, 1978, 4).

The earlier mode of thinking that features *mêtis* has recently been characterized as a "paradigm" distinct from the philosophical, Platonic, scientific, or Galilean worldview in Western thought. It has been called by several authors the "venatic" paradigm, because it relies on the "epistemology of the hunt" (Eamon, 1994, 281–285; Ginzburg, 1989, 117).[16] The venatic, or conjectural, worldview concerns the individual case rather than universal knowledge, probability rather than certainty, qualitative rather than cumulative or quantifiable information, and inferential rather than deductive thought, since it depends upon the reading of signs. As Carlo Ginzberg puts it, behind the conjectural paradigm "we perceive what may be the oldest act in the intellectual history of the human race: the hunter squatting on the ground, studying the tracks of his quarry" (105). He notes that medicine became the most important conjectural enterprise, with the physician reading symptoms in the individual patient (this semiotic model of medicine is challenged, later, by the scientific, anatomical model) (118). But the politician is an equally instructive exemplar, as shown by Thucydides' description of Themistocles, the early fifth-century Athenian leader who defeated the Persians at Salamis and brought Athens to prominence in the Aegean:

> In immediate problems he excelled in forming the best opinion, thanks to the most rapid reflection, and where the future was concerned he also knew how to come to the most correct conclusion on the most distant perspectives. When dealing with any matter he also knew how to explain it clearly; even if he was not familiar with it he nevertheless formed a valuable opinion about it. Finally, even if the advantages and disadvantages were still indiscernible he was capable of foreseeing them as accurately as possible. In short, through his natural resources and facility this man was without equal when it came to improvising whatever was necessary. (Qtd. in Detienne and Vernant, 1978, 313–14)

The context provided by the conjectural worldview casts several features of Greek rhetoric in new relief. For example, the frequent comparisons, especially in Plato, between rhetoric (or sophistry) and medicine, hunting, navigation, and other crafts suggest the continuing presence of the venatic tradition.[17] Aristotle's term *êthos* also has a venatic source, its early sense being "haunts" or "the places where animals are usually found," according to Charles Chamberlain; Homer, for example, used it to refer to the wild pastureland of horses. By transference to humans, the term came to mean "the arena where someone is most truly at home" and then an essence that resists the influences of others, always with the strong implication of habituation (Chamberlain, 1984, 99). Chamberlain points out that these older senses of the term *êthos* were still quite present in the fourth century, noting such uses in the Aristotelian corpus and in Isocrates and arguing that Aristotle exploits the historical implications of the term in both his works on ethics.

Aristotle's discussion of arguing from signs also has some roots in this tradition. He draws upon medical examples: "There is a sign that someone is sick, for he has a fever"; "it is a sign of fever that someone breathes rapidly" (*Rhet.* 1.2.18). His term for necessary sign, *tekmêrion* (1.2.17),[18] is related to the root term *tekmar*, which Detienne and Vernant associate with the conjectural worldview, particularly as it applies to navigation and divination: A *tekmar* can be a journey's destination or a celestial sign by which one steers (148).[19] The verb *tekmairesthai* commonly meant to judge from signs, to estimate or conjecture. Even this most certain of Aristotle's sign-terms, then, is closely connected with the world of the hunter and the sailor, in which one lives by one's wits in the midst of uncertainty and change. And the term *topos* itself, of course, has a strongly geographic primary sense. While I can't support the claim that Aristotle consciously chose his rhetorical terms to make these connections to the world of the hunter, he does show a continuous awareness of and interest in the etymology of his conceptual vocabulary and so is likely to have been aware of the implications I point out.

Venatic imagery persists in Latin and humanist descriptions of invention. It is present in Cicero in a constrained form, in words like *odorari*, *(per)vestigare*, and *venari*, which essentially compare the rhetor to a hound, tracking down proofs or smelling out the situation, as in this example from Antonius's discussion of invention in *De Oratore:* "In art, in observation, and in practice alike, it is everything to be familiar with the ground over which you are to chase and track down your quarry" (2.147)[20] A more common set of images compares the *topoi* to the sources or fountainhead of a stream,[21] and a long passage in Quintilian's description of topical invention combines these two images:

> Let us now turn to consider the 'places' *(locos)* . . . in the sense of the secret places *(sedes)* where arguments reside, and from which they must be drawn forth. For just as all kinds of produce are not provided *(generantur)* by every country, and as you will not succeed in finding a particular bird or beast, if you are ignorant of the localities where it has its usual haunts or birthplace, as even the various kinds of fish flourish in different surroundings, some preferring a smooth and oth-

> ers a rocky bottom, and are found on different shores and in divers regions (you will for instance never catch a sturgeon or wrasse in Italian waters), so not every kind of argument can be derived from every circumstance. (Quintilian, 5.10.20–22)

Walter Ong has shown that hunting imagery was common in Renaissance treatments of topical invention, notably in Agricola and Thomas Wilson. The passage in Wilson is especially vivid:

> A place is, the restyng corner of an argumente, or els a marke whiche geveth warning to our memorie. . . . Those that bee good harefinders will soone finde the hare by her fourme. For when thei see the ground beaten flatte round about, and faire to the sighte: thei have a narrowe gesse by al likelihode that the hare was there a litle before. Likewise the Huntesman in huntyng the foxe, wil soone espie when he seeth a hole, whether it be a foxe borough, or not. So he that will take profeicte in this parte of Logique, must bee like a hunter, and learne by labour to knowe the boroughes. For these places bee nothing elles, but covertes or boroughes, wherein if any one searche diligently, he maie finde game at pleasure. (Qtd. in Ong, 1983, 120)

Ong attributes the Renaissance use of hunting imagery to the secondary use of the Latin term *sylva* (forest) to mean an abundance or collection of material and of the Greek cognate *hylê* to mean material or matter as well as its primary sense of felled trees or timber. Thus, Ben Jonson called his commonplace book *Timber, or Discoveries upon Men and Matter,* and Bacon titled his collected observations on natural history *Sylva sylvarum* (Ong, 1983 [1958], 118–19).[22]

These Renaissance uses of venatic imagery provided a vocabulary of invention for subsequent discussions of science and technology. As Paolo Rossi notes, in sixteenth- and seventeenth-century thinking about the mechanical arts, "there was continuous discussion, with an insistence that bordered on monotony, about a logic of invention conceived as a *venatio,* a hunt—as an attempt to penetrate territories never known or explored before" (Rossi, 1970, 42). Likewise, according to William Eamon, the same image appears "repeatedly in the scientific literature" of the same period, with science portrayed as a hunt for the secrets of nature. Eamon notes particularly that the hunt is a central figure for Bacon, appearing throughout his works as an emblem of his new scientific method, most prominently as Pan's hunt, after the god of hunting.[23] Nevertheless, even as science and technology borrowed this rhetorical imagery and used it to characterize discovery and invention, rhetoric declined, in part because of its inability to account systematically for novelty.[24] The imagery lost its cultural authority quickly, and accounts of technical-scientific invention turned methodological and philosophical in the later seventeenth century.

Can the venatic paradigm help us conceptualize invention, discovery, and novelty today? Is Aristotle's concept of the *topos* still useful? Modernist science and technology have a radical understanding of novelty that owes something to Plato's conception in the *Meno:* "But how will you look for something when you don't in the least know what it is? How on earth are you going to set up something you don't know as the object of your search? To put it another way, even if you come right up against it, how will you know that what you have found is the thing you didn't know?" (*Meno* 80d). Novelty under the Platonic worldview must be absolute, revolutionary, even unrecognizable; it must violate the expectations of decorum. The venatic worldview does not represent such radical novelty satisfactorily, since the imagery of both hunting and navigation presupposes the existence and recognition of that which is sought: Hunters may know what they track or may unexpectedly discover new game, but they do not, presumably, create their quarry.[25]

What novelty might be within the conjectural or venatic worldview has never been fully thought out, but topical invention may be the best working model we have to start with. Unlike philosophical or scientific (or Romantic) models, topical invention relativizes novelty by situating it. Scott Consigny's discussion is instructive here. He suggests that in an inventional art of rhetoric the *topos* must serve both as an *instrument* with its own capacities that apply in any situation and as a *realm*, a specific place where the rhetor thinks and acts (Consigny, 1974, 182). He connects the latter sense of *topos* to Bitzer's notion of the rhetorical situation (and we might also adduce the Burkean term *scene*).[26] As a realm, a *topos* implicates not only subject-matter but also rhetor and audience, reminding us that it is, after all, a *rhetorical* instrument.

To be rhetorically useful, then, as well as comprehensible, novelty must be situated. Rather than offering the radically new, it must occupy the border between the known and the unknown. It will be just that which cannot be defined or specified beforehand but which can be recognized and understood afterward. The metaphor of the *topos* captures this requirement by specifying a region of general conception without specifying its exact contents or connections. The Aristotelian *topos* of degree, or of ways and means, suggests a conceptual shape or realm where one may find—or create—a detail, a connection, a pattern that was not anticipated deductively by the *topos* itself. The *topos* is conceptual space without fully specified or specifiable contents; it is a region of productive uncertainty. It is a "problem space," but rather than circumscribing or delimiting the problem, rather than being a closed space or container *within* which one searches, it is a space, or a located perspective, *from* which one searches. I am thinking here of the linguistic notion of "semantic space."[27] Bird approaches this conception when he suggests that "Topical arguments . . . are those that depend for their validity upon a semantical relation between their significant terms" (Bird, 1962, 322).

Such semantic networks may be conditioned both by the peculiarities of community history and by apparently logical relationships (like opposition and inclusion); some linguists resort to "fuzzy logic" to describe them because they are never fully systematizable or predictable, and they vary from language to language and even from dialect to dialect. A *topos* might be thought of as such a point in semantic space that is particularly rich in connectivity to other significant or highly connected points. For a politician, the topic "ways and means" would have a complex set of such connections, and for an aeronautical engineer, concepts like "force," "boundary layer," and "moment-curve slope" are richly connected to other concepts (Vincenti, 1990, 216). They thus can serve as intellectual tools that yield new viewpoints. William Nothstine develops a similar approach, which he calls a hermeneutic ontology of place; he sees the *topos* as a situated perspective within a horizon of possibilities, a "vantage-point which allows what is hidden to become seen" (1988, 156). Viewing a problem from the vantage of a *topos,* so to speak, can reveal or make possible new combinations, patterns, relationships that could not be seen before. A concept operating as a *topos* locates the borderland between the familiar and the unfamiliar, the known and the unknown. When one hunts in this borderland, whatever one finds may *become* one's quarry.

Inventiveness is often associated with a rich store of prior knowledge. The utility and generativity of a *topos* as a source of patterns and relationships depends upon the richness and connectedness of the knowledge available for recombination. We can see the relevance of the assumption in Roman rhetoric that wide and deep knowledge of one's own culture and civilization is essential to effective rhetorical practice and therefore the most important part of the training of the orator. We may then think of the function of the *topos* in another way, as an aid to pattern recognition, specifically as a region that permits or invites the connection between the abstract and the concrete, between a pattern and the material in which it is instantiated, between *eidos* and *hylê.*

In trying to explain how the *topos* may function to produce novelty under a generative view of invention, I have also, necessarily, touched on how it functions as an instrument of decorum. For although under the philosophical-modernist worldview, novelty and decorum are opposed and incompatible qualities, under the conjectural worldview, they are closely complementary and mutually dependent. Leff has shown that in Cicero's conception, decorum functions as a connective force in rhetoric: connecting rhetor and audience, integrating form and content (Leff, 1990, 121). Decorum is not only accommodative, in Leff's view, but also moral and aesthetic. Aristotle's discussion of *to prepon* (*Rhet.* 3.7), although seemingly restricted to considerations of verbal style, similarly suggests that propriety is not a superficial or slavish matter but rather a force that must be highly attuned to situation and equally attuned to substance: "The *lexis* will be appropriate if it expresses emotion and character and is proportional to the subject matter." Propriety or decorum is thus related to both *pathos* and *êthos*, as well.[28] It has accommodative, aesthetic, and moral value.

Ciceronian decorum, according to Leff, is "a flexible principle that coordinates particular discourses as they simultaneously build internal coherence, refer to a context of facts and circumstances, and stretch outward to alter perception of that context" (118). He thus suggests that decorum is not only integrative and connective but also, at least potentially, innovative. Conversely, I have been suggesting a rhetorical conception of novelty that makes it situated, relative, and accommodative. A revived theory of topical invention should make novelty and decorum complementary and interactive, opposing impulses that can be implemented only in tension with each other.[29]

By de-radicalizing novelty, a revived topical theory may also help remove the wedge that modernism drove between discovery and invention, even as it rejected the *topoi*. Topical thinking may help us recover a world in which invention and discovery are not so different, a world in which what the hunter finds is never completely unexpected but may often be startling or surprising—and may be put to novel uses. The *topos*, perhaps a vestige of early Greek venatic thinking, is one of Aristotle's more important contributions to rhetorical theory. In rereading Aristotle, along with the subsequent history of rhetoric, we may find that it is a richer concept than he realized, one that may help us understand the generative potential of invention in an inevitably postmodernist rhetorical theory.

Notes

1. Richard Young's work is also important for reemphasizing the role of invention during this same period (Young, 1976; Young, Becker, and Pike, 1970).

2. Thomas Kuhn points out that in science the distinction between discovery and invention is "artificial," because discovery (factual novelty) and invention (theoretical novelty) are intertwined in the history of scientific work (1970, 52–53).

3. The irony here is that while Aristotle describes reasoning as thoroughly deductive, it is now widely agreed that strictly deductive reasoning does not produce new knowledge but rather reveals propositions tautologically implicit in the premises. Another way of seeing novelty in dialectic is in the middle terms rather than in the conclusions; novelty thus functions as a means, rather than an end. Zulick (1970), however, has recently proposed that rhetoric and dialectic differ specifically in their generativity: Dialectic proceeds by eliminating alternatives, while rhetoric creates a "wealth of arguments" (113). Zulick discusses the enthymeme as a generative device in Aristotelian rhetoric, but not the *topos*.

4. Similar approaches to the dynamic I am describing here have been made by Scott Consigny and James Jasinski. Consigny (1974) has suggested that rhetoric must be both a "heuristic" and a "managerial" art, that it must have the inventional resources both to engage in any situation at all (he calls this "integrity") and to engage with the material details of a particular situation ("receptivity"). James Jasinski (1995) has been developing an account of prudence that includes two dimensions, audacity and accommodation, a pair of concepts analogous to novelty and decorum, which he applies to republican rhetoric.

5. Liddell and Scott (1968) indicate the use of *topos* as commonplace in both Aristotle and Isocrates and also note a metaphorical use to mean opening, occasion, or opportunity, meanings essentially identical to *kairos*.

6. Standard opinion, including Rist's detailed study of the development of Aristotle's thought (Rist, 1989), holds that much of what became known as the *Organon*, which includes the *Categories* and the *Topics*, was written at an early stage in Aristotle's thinking, when he was still heavily influenced by Plato, possibly during his first residence in Athens, when he was at Plato's Academy (367–347) or in the period just afterward, when he was in Assos, Lesbos, and Macedonia (347–340). The *Physics* is usually dated in this second period (Ross, 1964 [1923], 18), and Mendell seems certain that it is later than the *Categories* (Mendell, 1987). Kennedy dates the *Rhetoric* to just after this, when Aristotle was back in his home city of Stagira (340–335), possibly beginning it "in anticipation of his return to Athens" (1991, 301), although an earlier tradition attributes it to his second residence in Athens, shortly after his return (335–332) (see Freese's "Introduction" to *The "Art" of Rhetoric*, 1975 [1926], xxvi; and Ross, 1964 [1923], 19). Rist concurs with this latter dating, with the exception of Book I, chapters 5 through 15, dated during Aristotle's first period in Athens, about 358–354 (1989, 6, 23). These speculations about chronology should be compared to Barnes's conviction that the evidence is too scant to permit a confident chronology of Aristotle's writings (Barnes, 1995b, 22).

7. Leff cites the major contemporary statements on this issue in his recent review of American scholarship on the *Rhetoric* (Leff, 1993, n. 4).

8. Lakoff and Johnson claim that container metaphors help to structure the way we think about argument when we focus on its content (even the term *content* is part of the metaphor); such metaphors, they claim, are grounded in everyday ontological experience (Lakoff and Johnson, 1980, 29, 92). My claim that the *topos* is a container may further be related to the "conduit metaphor" that Reddy has shown to underlie the way we think about language (words are packages that contain meanings) and communication (messages are sent in a channel to a receiver) (Reddy, 1979). Reddy and others have shown how misleading the conduit metaphor can be, but I think there's sufficient difference between claiming that words are containers for meanings and that *topoi* are containers for possible arguments that the criticisms do not vitiate the utility of the *topos*-as-container.

9. Parmenides had denied the possibility of any change (including motion) because he saw it as requiring an impossible transition from nonbeing to being (or the reverse). Zeno's paradox of Achilles and the hare is just one example of this more general denial of change. See Peters's discussion of *genesis* and *on* (being) and Poster's essay on the relationship between ontology and rhetoric.

10. This treatise is also called *On Generation and Corruption*, from the Latin terms (and abbreviated *GC*).

11. "Matter *[hylê]* . . . is the substratum *[to hypokeimenon]* which admits of coming-to-be and passing-away" (*GC* 320a2). Some of Aristotle's difficulties are reflected in the variety of terms he uses for substance, or whatever is contained by form: *ousia*, being *(Cat.)*, *sôma*, body, and *hylê*, matter *(Phys)*, *hypokeimenon*, substratum *(GC)*. See Peters (1967) on *hylê* and *ousia*.

12. Aristotle's reasoning on this point is interesting: Heavenly bodies have only circular motion, a perfect motion that has no contrary, and "it is in contraries that generation and decay subsist" (*On the Heavens* 270a22).

13. "Let us then start from the datum that things of Nature . . . do move and change" (*Phys.* 185a13); "most of the matters with which judgment and examination are concerned can be other than they are" (*Rhet.* 1.2.14).

14. The goddess Metis, the daughter of Ocean, was the first wife of Zeus, who swallowed her when she first became pregnant, fearing that she would produce a son who would exceed him in cunning. Instead of a son, the union of Zeus and Metis produced a daughter, Athena, who sprang from Zeus's head, fully armed in some versions, to become the goddess of prudence and the crafts, as well as the patron of Odysseus. See Kastely's discussion of the significance of Odysseus in fifth-century Athens as the "embodiment" of Rhetoric (1997, 87–91).

15. The paradox in the suggestion that *aretê* could apply to mechanical laborers highlights the dissonance that fourth-century aristocrats might have felt between the heroic age in which *mêtis* operated and their own social structure. It also reflects the transformation of *aretê* from excellence to virtue, moving from the practical to the moral world.

16. Ginzberg (1989), describing the roots and development of the methodology of the humanities, especially history, in the nineteenth century, also calls this paradigm presumptive, divinatory, conjectural, and semiotic (117). Eamon is describing the rise of science in the seventeenth century. Both cite Detienne and Vernant.

17. For the comparison with medicine, see especially *Gorgias* 459–60 and 464–65 and *Phaedrus* 270b; for hunting, see *Sophist* 219–22; for navigation, *Gorgias* 511d–e.

18. Aristotle distinguishes three degrees of relationship between signs and signates: probabilities *(eikota)*, signs *(sêmeia)*, and necessary signs *(tekmêria)*. Grimaldi's explanation of the differences is useful (Grimaldi, 1980b).

19. In one of the mythical traditions that Detienne and Vernant (1978) describe, Tekmôr is a primitive deity who provided differentiation within the darkness and who often appeared with Poros, the pathway (140); thus, when navigators attempt to plot courses, they *porous t'apetekmaironto* (149).

20. Other examples occur at *De Oratore* 1.223, 2.166, and 2.186 and *Topics* 2.7.

21. See, for example, *De Oratore* 2.117, 130, 141, and 162. Fantham notes that metaphors deriving from springs and streams already constituted a cliché in Cicero's time (1972, 161). I am grateful to Jakob Wisse for helping me locate Cicero's images of hunting and streams in discussions of invention.

22. *Hylê* may thus belong to the venatic tradition, although it doesn't appear in Aristotle's *Rhetoric* or *Topics* (Conley, 1978, 96).

23. Eamon cites several passages in *De Augmentis Scientiarum*, *De Sapientia Veterum*, and *Novum Organum*. He does not cite the passage from *Advancement of Learning* that I quoted at the beginning of this essay.

24. I have made this argument in more detail elsewhere (Miller, 1995).

25. Plato classifies both sophistry and hunting as acquisitive arts, in contrast to creative arts such as agriculture, animal husbandry, and pottery (*Sophist* 219, 223).

26. Consigny's account is similar to Leff's discussion of the tension between what he calls the "inferential" and the "materialist" perspectives on invention, a tension he sees exhibited throughout the history of rhetoric. The inferential perspective prefers simplicity, seeing rhetoric as a distinct faculty concerned with the forms that any argument can take; it emphasizes topics common to any field of argument and topical systems that are compact, memorable, and teachable. The materialist perspective prefers relevance, seeing rhetoric as necessarily engaged with its subject-matter; it emphasizes topics specific to a subject-matter, and its topical systems become detailed, complex, and not very systematic. Clearly, both perspectives are valuable; Leff claims that no one has succeeded in integrating the two (Leff, 1983, 42). See also my earlier discussion of this issue (Miller, 1987).

27. Linguists talk about "mapping semantic space" by describing shared features, entailments, and presuppositions of terms. One of the paradigm examples is the term *bachelor*, which is connected in specific ways to other terms such as *male, academic degree, fur seal,* and *marriage* (Bolinger, 1975, 209).

28. One of Kennedy's notes to this chapter indicates that Aristotle here introduces terminology used in his later writing on ethics (1991, 235 n. 80).

29. Isocrates makes a good case study of how novelty and familiarity serve as competing rhetorical impulses. Only Isocrates among the ancient Greeks saw novelty as a rhetorical virtue: "Oratory is good," he claimed in "Against the Sophists," "only if it has the qualities of fitness for the occasion *(kairos)*, propriety of style *(prepontos)* and originality of treatment *(kainos)*" (Isocrates, 1928, 13). He also claims in the opening of his "Antidosis" to be presenting something "novel and different in character," and Werner Jaeger notes that his "Panegyricus" was intended "to state, in a new language, new ideals—not only for the moral life of the individual, but for the entire nation of the Hellenes" (1944, 70). However, as the recent discussion by Yun Lee Too points out, his interest in novelty was opposed by his commitment to tradition and to the repetition of familiar themes *(ta archaia)*, including myths and passages of his own prior works (1995, 53–61).

ON BOOK 3 OF THE *RHETORIC*

9

Aristotelian *Lexis* and Renaissance *Elocutio*

Lawrence D. Green

This essay concerns the Renaissance reception of Aristotle's *Rhetoric*, a perspective influenced by a view of the work as an ancillary treatise on ethics and dialectic, a tradition of Greek intellectual work in which Aristotle did not necessarily play a major role, and an interest in classical rhetoric whose focus was more Cicero and Quintilian than Aristotle. These three strands do not form the context for a Renaissance understanding of *lexis*; rather, these strands form the starting points of their understanding of Book 3.

For many writers during the Renaissance, the defining characteristic of rhetoric was *elocutio*. Other aspects of rhetoric, such as invention or disposition, were also important, but they were caught up in larger arguments about whether they belonged to the discipline of rhetoric or more properly to some other discipline, such as logic or ethics. Hardly anyone, however, disagreed about the disciplinary status of *elocutio*. Indeed, without this fundamental agreement, the pedagogical realignments of Petrus Ramus would have made little sense, just as the earlier reshaping by Erasmus of traditional rhetoric in terms of *elocutio* would have fallen on deaf ears. Our own age has not been very sympathetic to this Renaissance fascination with *elocutio*, preferring instead to focus on the relations between rhetoric and logic or choosing to see *elocutio* in terms of its relations to formal poetics; and only recently have our critical sympathies begun to shift. But Renaissance sympathies meant that when writers began to think about the newly rediscovered text of Aristotle's *Rhetoric*, they would see Book 3 as being far more central to the entire rhetorical enterprise than we are apt to see it today. They tried in particular to make sense of Aristotelian *lexis* in terms of their own rhetorical and philosophical traditions. What they saw is not always what we see today.

The Renaissance tradition of *elocutio* was Latin, Roman, and, more specifically, Ciceronian (Green, 1994b). It was a tradition in which Aristotle's *Rhetoric* had played almost no part. The Greek text had dropped from sight during late antiquity, and what little we know of it for over a millennium is through occasional reference in other documents and by its appearance in semitic and Arab contexts.

When the *Rhetoric* finally does reappear in the West, it first does so in partial paraphrases from Arabic. In the thirteenth century, William of Moerbeke provides a complete Latin translation, and scholastic commentary based on that translation demonstrates that the *Rhetoric* was viewed almost exclusively in the context of Aristotelian ethics and dialectic. Not until the fifteenth century does this situation begin to change, with the exodus of scholars and manuscripts from Byzantium. Neither the Greeks in the East nor the Latins in the West thought that Aristotle's *Rhetoric* was a particularly important treatise, but for very different reasons. The Greeks viewed their philosophical and literary tradition as an unbroken continuity in which Aristotle played a significant but still minor role. Hermogenes was their major classical rhetorician, Plato their major classical philosopher, and both were primarily starting points for a lively tradition that continued to the present. The Greek East knew and cared very little about Cicero, while the Latin West knew and cared very little about Hermogenes. Both cared about Aristotle, but in different degrees and for very different reasons, and until the Renaissance, neither cared much about his *Rhetoric.*

These three traditions—Ciceronian, Byzantine, and Aristotelian—provide the contexts for Renaissance efforts to understand the complex materials of Book 3 of the *Rhetoric*, and all three are present at the rebirth of the *Rhetoric*. When the Greek scholar George of Trebizond emigrated to Italy, his first major project in rhetoric was an amalgamation of Hermogenes with Cicero; his second was a new Latin translation of Aristotle's Greek *Rhetoric*. The principal subjects of Book 3 were all of great interest to Renaissance writers: the constituent parts of good diction and grammar, the different kinds of styles, the metaphorical aspects of language, and the organization of parts of an oration. But the same rhetorical traditions and immediate social needs that made these subjects interesting to Renaissance writers also made it difficult to understand Aristotle's treatment of them. Then, as now, prior theoretical commitments and intentions led commentators to read Aristotle's text in particular ways, sometimes creating problems where we today see none, and sometimes answering questions that we today find unresolvable. In the following discussion, I will focus on some of the ways that Renaissance writers sought to accommodate Aristotelian *lexis* to prevailing Ciceronian and Hermogenean theories of *elocutio*. I will reserve for the next two sections my discussions of how larger Aristotelian theories of ethics and psychology were used to resolve problems in the *Rhetoric* and adjust Aristotelian *lexis* to Renaissance *elocutio*.

The Ciceronian and Byzantine Traditions

Many commentators seemed to approach Book 3 with the conviction that they already knew what Aristotle meant to say, even if Aristotle himself was clumsy in saying it. For these commentators, Aristotle meant to say what Cicero and Quintilian later said, and the task of commentary was to clarify the muddy correspondences. This effort at accommodation and assimilation starts with the very conception of what Aristotle had in mind in Book 3 by the word *lexis* (*Rhet.* 1403b8; my text is Kassel, 1976). In modern English translations, *lexis* is rendered variously as "style" (Freese, 1926, 345) or "language" (Roberts and Barnes, 1984, 2237) or "way of saying" (Kennedy, 1991, 3.1.1), and George Kennedy rightly points out the fluidity of this term (1991, 216). But in 1570, Johann Sturm was much more direct and certain of himself: "*Lexis* is nothing other than *elocutio*," and by *elocutio* Sturm meant the third of the Roman offices of rhetoric (*"lexis" nihil aliud est, quam elocutio*; Sturm, 1570a, fol. 309v). As Sturm explains, other writers have established five *officia*, and while Aristotle only discusses three of the five, Aristotle still shares the Roman view of rhetoric. Aristotle's *Rhetoric* addresses *inventio*, *elocutio*, and *collocatio; inventio* requires intellectual acumen; *elocutio* calls for clarity and for a love of ornamentation; and *collocatio* deals with judgment (Sturm, 1570a, fol. 429v). By *collocatio*, according to Sturm, Aristotle intends both *dispositio* and *pronuntiatio*, while *memoria* is ignored because it was not important in Aristotle's time; but if it had been, Aristotle presumably would have treated it (Sturm, 1570a, fol. 309v).

If Sturm is at all unusual, it is only in the details of his explanation, since the main lines of his argument are common in the Renaissance. In 1545 Daniele Barbaro offered a different kind of analysis, not to defend the Roman *officia* in Aristotle but rather to defend in Aristotle his own version of the three Roman rhetorical goals of teaching, pleasing, and moving (Barbaro and Barbaro, 1545, 546). By gathering bits and pieces out of Plato's *Phaedrus* and Aristotle's *De anima*, Barbaro concludes that Aristotelian rhetoric is based on a triad of psychological faculties and that "the speaker who wants to draw opinion must first excite those counselors whom nature placed in our souls, namely Intellect, Anger and Desire, and with these cords the orator draws us along" (Barbaro and Barbaro, 1545, 5; see Green, 1994a). The Intellect is for teaching, Anger for moving, and Desire for pleasing. Subtlety is needed to move the Intellect, while Anger and Desire are moved forcibly for excitation and gently for pleasing (Barbaro and Barbaro, 1545, 5). This tripartite distribution of functions explains why Aristotle's *Rhetoric* has three books: In the first is the theory of teaching, in the second the power of moving, and in the third the rules for pleasing men. Barbaro's account presents all sorts of problems, both Ciceronian and Aristotelian, and he struggles mightily to confine "teaching" and "moving" to their respective books, but Book 3 poses particular difficulties. In Barbaro's reading, Book 3 deals with the speech itself and is thus dedicated to the Ciceronian goal of "pleasing." Such pleasing rests upon the power of Desire, despite the fact that Aristotle deals with both pleasure and desire largely in Book 1, not Book 3.

Despite the different approaches adopted by Sturm and Barbaro, the details of exegesis prove very similar. It is assumed by both commentators that Aristotle and Cicero inhabit the same intellectual world, that their goals for rhetoric are the same, and that Aristotelian *lexis* aligns with Ciceronian *elocutio*. The more explicit and extensive rhetorical works of Cicero can be used to explain obscure or laconic passages in Aristotle, and Aristotle is best understood as the precursor of Cicero in an unbroken tradition. Thus even the differences among Cicero, Quintilian, and Aristotle are smoothed out, since, as Barbaro explains, they are all saying the same things (Barbaro and Barbaro, 1545, 597). Cicero tells us that metaphors are like clothing, born first of dire necessity, then become delightful past the needs of protection, and now they even glitter (*De Oratore* 3.155–56). Quintilian's metaphors substitute on a fourfold categorical basis: for example, an inanimate thing for an animate being, an animate for an inanimate, one inanimate for another, and one animate for another (*Inst.* 8.6.8–12). And Aristotle's metaphors substitute by relations among genus and species. The fact that metaphor is no longer an overarching category for Cicero or Quintilian seems not to bother Barbaro, much less the problem that different psychological processes are called into play. Equally untroubled is the commentator Cipriano Suarez, who offers a best-parts version of rhetoric that blends together Aristotle, Cicero, and Quintilian—at least, for the first two books. When Suarez gets to his own Book 3 on *elocutio*, he draws extensively on Cicero and Quintilian but has almost no reference whatsoever to Aristotle. He discusses a long list of figures and tropes, assuming again that Aristotle is merely saying the same as the two Romans whom he cites extensively (Suarez, 1569, 47–87). So also, the numerous prefaces that Petrus Ramus provided for the *Rhetorica* of Audomarus Talaeus casually group together Aristotle, Cicero, and Quintilian (Ramus and Talaeus, 1599, 3, 20, 23, etc.). Despite all this coordination between Greek and Roman rhetorical traditions, however, there remains throughout the Renaissance a pronounced asymmetry between the two. Cicero's treatises are used extensively to explicate Aristotle, and Cicero's speeches are used extensively to illustrate Aristotle, but Aristotle is hardly ever used to explicate or illustrate Cicero.

Roman rhetorical theory provided one way to approach Aristotelian *lexis* during the Renaissance. Another approach was in terms of the Hermogenean theory of *ideas*, which had only recently been introduced to the Latin West from Byzantium. In the early Quattrocento, the Greek émigré George of Trebizond had established himself as a leading rhetorician in the Latin West by combining the unfamiliar Greek Hermogenean theories of style with the familiar Latin rhetoric of Cicero (Monfasani, 1976, 318–27). For many decades George's *Rhetoricorum libri V* (1433/34, first printed 1472) provided the only Western access to the theories of Hermogenes so that even after Hermogenes's own treatises became available, it still seemed natural to think of Hermogenes in terms of Cicero. When we consider that it was already commonplace to understand Aristotle in terms of Cicero, the further connection between Aristotle and Hermogenes should not surprise us.

Daniele Barbaro provides an example of just such a connection when he starts to explicate Aristotle's discussion of the *lexeōs aretēs*, the "virtues of style." In Aristotle's discussion in Book 3, the two principal virtues are *perspicuitas* and *decorum*. Barbaro starts by discussing *perspicuitas*, which he divides into *elegantia* and *puritas*, which he could have done by relying only upon Cicero. But Barbaro then divides *decorum* into *amplitudo* and *dignitas*, and these in turn are broken down into *severitas, circumductio, asperitas, splendor, vigor,* and *vehementia* (Barbaro and Barbaro, 1545, 549). By now Barbaro is deep into a discussion of Hermogenean *idea* theory as he understands it, and it is a full twenty pages before he returns to Aristotle's treatise. When he finally does so, he explains that while *inventio* is best understood from Aristotle, *delectatio* is best achieved with Hermogenes (Barbaro and Barbaro, 1545, 569).

Barbaro was probably getting his Hermogenes from George of Trebizond's Ciceronian amalgam in *Rhetoricorum libri V,* although he claimed to be offering a fresh reading (Barbaro and Barbaro, 1545, 548). On the other hand, the Hermogenean credentials of Johann Sturm were impeccable. He produced Greek and Latin editions of Hermogenes with commentaries (Sturm, 1570a; 1570b; and 1571) and composed his own lengthy *De universa ratione elocutionis rhetoricae* (1574), which relies heavily on Hermogenes. Sturm's use of Hermogenean *idea* theory to explain Aristotelian *lexeōs aretēs* is very different from Barbaro's. Sturm understands Aristotle's two "virtues" of *perspicuitas* and *decorum* in terms of the later Roman *genera dicendi*, or "kinds of speaking." As Sturm puts it, "Aristotle establishes two general categories for expression; they are *perspicuitas* and *decorum*, and, as divisions go, this is very general indeed *[est valde generalis].* Cicero tells us that the Latins have three kinds of expression—impressive, humble, and intermediate. Hermogenes, however, has seven kinds, and these he calls *ideas. Perspicuitas* is what Hermogenes calls *saphēnein* [clarity], and he gives it the place of honor, which makes perfectly good sense to me" (*Perspicuitatem Hermogenes vocat "saphēnein," et ei primum locum dat: quae efficit, ut res ipsa facile intelligatur;* Sturm, 1570a, fol. 322v). Lest we misunderstand the kinds of equivalences that Sturm sees between Aristotle and Hermogenes, he later tells us explicitly that the words *aretē, idea,* and *virtus* all refer to what the Romans called *genera dicendi*, "for an *idea* is nothing other than a kind of speaking which is both excellent and appropriate" (*"hē tou logou phrasis," genus dicendi ipsius orationis: nunc oratorium dicendi genus vocat "aretōn," idean et virtutem. Nam idea nihil aliud est, quam laudabilis, et conveniens orationis forma;* Sturm, 1570a, fol. 322v).

While it is understandable that Renaissance writers should turn to Hermogenes to explain Aristotle, this does not mean there was anything necessary or inevitable in such a move, and it certainly was not universal. Piero Vettori, for example, in his massive commentary on Aristotle's *Rhetoric,* has endless recourse to Cicero and Quintilian, to Plutarch, to Demetrius of Phaleron, to Dionysius of Halicarnassus, but hardly any to Hermogenes, and Vettori does not bother to include Hermogenes in his extensive list of Greek and Latin authorities (Vettori, 1548, sigs. III 1r–III 2v; occasional references to Hermogenes are found in Book 3, e.g., on page 454). So also, Antonio Riccoboni knows the commentaries by Barbaro and Sturm very well, and yet he himself ignores Hermogenes (Riccoboni, 1606b). Equally suggestive is the stance of George of Trebizond, who started the Hermogenean craze in the Latin West. A few years after George completed his *Rhetoricorum libri V,* he produced the first new Latin translation of Aristotle's *Rhetoric* to appear since the medieval period, and later he explained that Aristotle's great virtue was in laying out clearly for the first time the significant precepts of the art of speaking (George of Trebizond, 1523a, A4v–A6). But having conceded so much, George apparently did not think that Aristotle was in the same league with Hermogenes, and he made no effort to coordinate what each had said about *lexis*. When George came to Book 3 of the *Rhetoric*, he translated Aristotle's *lexeōs aretē* very forthrightly as *elocutionis virtus* (George of Trebizond, 1523b, fol. 129r). If there was a link between Aristotelian stylistic virtue and Hermogenean *idea* theory, it was not readily apparent to the West's leading expert on Greek rhetoric.

When we look at Renaissance schemes and tropes, the strongest link is not between Aristotle and Hermogenes, or between Aristotle and Cicero, but between Hermogenes and Cicero. Tropes and figures are a staple of Ciceronian rhetoric, but they are alien to Aristotle. On the other hand, Hermogenean *ideas* were understood to have a rhetorical impact akin to that of various figures of speech. Thus it is not all that surprising that when Daniele Barbaro attempts to discuss tropes and figures in the context of Aristotle's *Rhetoric*, he does not do so in the context of Aristotle's discussion of metaphor but instead in the midst of his extended excursus on Hermogenean *idea* theory. So also, Johann Sturm's extensive analysis of schemes and tropes in *De elocutione* does not attempt to trace those figures back to Aristotle but instead places them in the context of Hermogenean theory (Sturm, 1574). However much Renaissance writers on *elocutio* wanted Aristotle to be their progenitor, when it came to the details of Ciceronian figures, they turned to Hermogenes and used Aristotle only for broader theoretical contexts.

Ethics and *Lexis*

Another approach to Aristotelian *lexis* has its roots in the medieval interest in the *Rhetoric* as an ethical treatise. Aristotle himself provided the opening for ethical considerations in Book 3 by his early references to *mochthēria,* a word which indicates a wretched state of affairs—generally due to some sort of inability or incapacity, and often there is a sense of corruption. The issue for Renaissance thinkers was whether Aristotle presents Book 3 as a grudging concession to the moral corruption of political institutions and human souls, or as a scientific recognition that institutions and souls respond to more than just the cold bare facts of the case at hand (*tois pragmasin*; *Rhet.* 1404a6). If Aristotle's use of *mochthēria* refers to moral degeneracy, then the Renaissance fascination with *elocutio* and *actio* amounts to little more than pandering to the degenerate. If, on the other hand, Aristotle's *mochthēria* refers to the complexity of human psychology, then Renaissance *elocutio* and *actio* may be noble enterprises. And in either case, it would be helpful to know whether Aristotle at this point was talking about *elocutio,* or *actio*, or both. Renaissance writers could not agree on which it was, and neither can modern writers.

Aristotle addresses two separate subjects at the start of Book 3: *lexis* and *hupokrisis*. I have already mentioned the variety of modern English translations for *lexis;* the modern consensus for *hupokrisis* is "delivery." In the first passage in which *mochthēria* is used, Aristotle mentions the lamentable *mochthēria* of contemporary political institutions (*tēn mochthērian tōn politeiōn; Rhet.* 1403b34–35), and he clearly has *hupokrisis* in mind—that is to say, Athenian institutions grant too much scope for the histrionics of delivery. But then Aristotle mentions the equally lamentable *mochthēria* of the hearer (*tēn tou akroātou mochthērian; Rhet.* 1404a8), and here the object of *mochthēria* is much less clear. Perhaps the human soul responds overly to *hupokrisis*, as Antonio Riccoboni thought when he read this second passage in terms of *actio*, thus linking together both instances of *mochthēria* (*in ciuilibus certaminib. plus tribueretur actioni, quam aliis rebus, vitio scilicet Rerump. et ob improbitatem auditorum; qui patiebantur se transuersos agi, cum spectare magis argumentationem deberent;* Riccoboni, 1606b, 284). On the other hand, perhaps the human soul responds overly to *lexis*, as both Carlo Sigonio and Marcantonio Maioragio thought when each read the passage in terms of *elocutio* (*loquitur Aristoteles de actione, non vt Sigonius cum Victorio, Marioragio & aliis, de elocutione*; Riccoboni, 1606b, 284). Or then again, perhaps the human soul responds overly to some combination of the two; Piero Vettori was willing to split the difference between *elocutio* and *actio*, but in such an equivocal manner that Riccoboni is convinced that Vettori is speaking exclusively about *elocutio*.[1] Such disagreement is not peculiar to the Renaissance. Modern readings show the same variety, ranging from "l'action" (Dufour and Wartelle, 1972, 40; Wartelle, 1982), to "the arts of language" (Robert and Barnes, 1984, 2238), to "the subject of expression" (Kennedy, 1991, 3.1.6), and finally to "style" and "everything else" (Freese 1926, 347).[2]

The object or objects of Aristotle's lamentable *mochthēria* are not the only difficulty here. The question of how to understand what Aristotle intends by the very word itself is equally problematic, but here the difficulty betrays more clearly the biases of the Renaissance. The dominant note in this tradition had been sounded as early as William of Moerbeke in the thirteenth century, when he translated *mochtherīa* as *malitia* (*propter malitiam civilitatum* and *propter auditoris malitiam;* Moerbeke, 1978, 282). This reading was confirmed in the ethically oriented commentary by Giles of Rome using almost the same words (*propter malitiam ciuitatum* and *propter auditorum malitiam;* Giles of Rome, 1515, fols. 91r and 91v). In Giles's view, the end of rhetoric is to show the ethical value of something and not its truth (*Magis est finis rhetoricae ostendere aliquid esse bonum vel malum quam esse verum vel non verum*; fols. 16r), but he does so by relying upon distinctions among rhetoric, dialectic, and logic that had particular force during the medieval period and did not survive into the Renaissance (O'Donnell, 1969; Murphy, 1969; Green, 1998).

It is perhaps more surprising that the Greek émigré George of Trebizond in 1445 accepts and goes beyond the medieval Latin reading of Moerbeke and Giles. For the first passage, George offers *propter civitatum depravationem,* and for the second, *propter auditorum pravitatem* (George of Trebizond, 1523b, fols. 128v), thus condemning the very same stylistic bravura on which George had earlier built his career with *Rhetoricorum libri V.* Ermolao Barbaro in 1479 sees the issue in clearly moral terms, and his translation of Book 3 goes freely beyond Aristotle's text or George's reading: The Athenian law courts and assemblies are morally corrupt *(corrupta iudicia civitatem et mores)*, as are Athenian auditors (*vitio audientium;* Barbaro and Barbaro, 1545, 142).

The tradition of moral condemnation does not go unchallenged, however difficult it might have been for Renaissance writers to break free of it. Antonio Riccoboni, for example, sees the inadequacies both of institutions and souls in more ambiguous terms—possibly incapacity, possibly depravity (*ita in civilibus certaminibus propter improbitatem Rerump.* and *Veruntamen multum valent, vt dictum est, propter auditoris improbitatem;* Riccoboni, 1606a, 218 *bis*). Piero Vettori sees the inadequacies of political institutions but more generally acknowledges the insufficiencies of humankind rather than the moral failings and venal sins of Athenians. Vettori tells us that "Unless I am mistaken, *mochthēria* does not refer to the depravity of souls ready for every kind of villainy but rather a defect of nature, which is made worse by long practice of habit" (*"mochthēria" valet hic (nisi fallor) non pravitatem animi ad omne facinus parati, sed vitium potius naturae, quae mala consuetudine deterior facta sit, ac sinat se a vero abduci*; Vettori, 1548, 455). It is not the fault of historical Athenians that they do not live in the perfection of Plato's ideal republic, and they hardly can be blamed on that score. Even Vettori's very measured response should remind us of the fact that the Renaissance in general had no very great sympathy for democracy, experimented only sporadically with republicanism, and had a deeply ingrained sense of the rightness of hierarchy (both political and theocratical) even as people chafed against the constraints of such hierarchy.

The range of Renaissance responses to the problem of *mochthēria* goes to the heart of Renaissance views of *elocutio*. Is *elocutio* a dangerous moral deception, or a necessary evil, or a useful corrective for the inherent failings of humankind? The Renaissance discussions of later chapters of Book 3 generally reflect the perspectives adopted for the early chapters. Metaphor, for example, can be seen as a search for better names or for deceitful names. Rhythm, to take another example, can be seen as a pleasant preparation for substance, or as a lulling of the mind to obscure vacuousness or venality. But here I will focus on just one example from later in Book 3, when Aristotle discusses the second principal *lexeōs aretē*, "propriety of style" (*to de prepon exei hē lexis; Rhet.* 3.7, 1408a10). When a speaker uses a style that matches his subject matter, it gives the appearance that his emotions, his character, and his intellect are all in accord with one another, and such accord makes his subject matter more credible to an audience. Aristotle's phrase is *paralogizetai te gar hē psukhē* (*Rhet.* 1408a20–21), which Freese reads amiably as "the mind of the hearer is imposed upon" (Freese, 1926, 379). Much closer to the Renaissance point of view is Kennedy's "the mind [of the listener] draws a false inference of the truth" (Kennedy, 1991, 3.7.4). Indeed, the more common Renaissance reading is *animum decepit*, that is, the hearer is cheated or defrauded by *decorum* itself. George of Trebizond provides an early Renaissance version of this reading as *decipiuntur* in his chapter "De decoro" (George of Trebizond, 1523, fol. 130v), and in Marcantonio Maioragio's chapter "De decoro in eloquutione," it is *decorum* itself that draws the listener into error (*nam animus auditoris in errorem trahitur, qui ea vere dici putat*; Maioragio, 1562, fol. 56r).

The accounts by other commentators are somewhat more sympathetic. Ermolao Barbaro sees the audience granting the speaker the kind of credence we grant to actors (*Ducitur enim & quasi rapitur audientium animus, ut se credant actori, et putent uera esse, quae ita dicuntur*; Barbaro and Barbaro, 1545, 616). Antonio Riccoboni thinks of *decorum* as character manifested through *elocutio* (*Persuadet autem rem etiam accommodata ad eius naturam elocutio: capitur enim animus, quasi ille vere dicat, quia in talibus sic se habent*; Riccoboni, 1606a, 237) and later comments that such *decorum* can induce a sense of character where it does not exist (*Quare arbitrantur rem ita se habere, etiamsi non se habeat ita, vt dicit orator;* Riccoboni, 1606b, 301; see also his "De elocutione decora," 300–303). Piero Vettori, however, advances an explanation for the fraud of *decorum* that nearly mimics Aristotle's own discussion in Book 2 of how a *skhēma tēs lexeōs* (*Rhet.* 2.18.1401a7) can create a fallacious enthymeme. Here in Book 3, *decorum* can so control the listener that he mistakes fiction and deception for truth. And the common experience of Vettori's own day confirms that a harmony of style, emotions, and intellect can lead mere mortals into error (*Animus enim eorum, qui audiunt, in errorem rapitur, qui putat dicentem, verè, & ut res se habet, loqui: nec cogitat totam illam orationem posse fictam, ac commenticiam esse: decipitur autem abductus fallaci quadam conclusione, quam ipse sibi struit: animaduertit enim saepe huiuscemodi temporib. mortales ita se habere: vulgo nanque, cum huiuscemodi quippiam ipsis contigit, ita affecti animo sunt: de captione autem hac, quae "para to hepomenon" est & uocatur, in .II. horum librorum egit, cum locos indicaret fallacium argumentorum*; Vettori, 1548, 505).

Given what we like to think we know about Renaissance celebrations of *elocutio* and of *decorum*, the commentary tradition clearly presents us with a problem at this juncture. In the seventeenth century these troubling ethical questions would be answered increasingly in the negative, and especially in England *elocutio* would come under an attack from which it never fully recovered. Those who wanted to attack *elocutio* would be helped in great part by the aftermath of Ramus's pedagogical innovations, which had the unintended effect of isolating *elocutio* from invention and disposition, and in time even these latter two offices would be attacked. But during the sixteenth century, these questions could still be answered positively, albeit in a guarded manner. Daniele Barbaro, for example, defends Aristotelian *lexis* and *hupokrisis* by arguing that every motion of the mind has its own face, and voice, and gesture, and it is important that these inevitable concomitants of expression not be at odds with what is expressed (Barbaro and Barbaro, 1545, 547–48). To put it differently, harmony may or may not enhance, but discord always threatens. This is the same kind of guarded defense that Cipriano Suarez offers, first for *elocutio* and then for *actio.* Inattention to *elocutio* is like "leaving a sharpened sword in its scabbard" (*similia gladio condito atque intra vaginam haerenti;* Suarez, 1569, fol. 47v). So also for *actio,* which is eloquence of the body. Voice appeals to the ears, gesture to the eyes, and only through the ears and eyes can emotion reach into an audience's soul (*Actio est quasi corporis quaedam eloquentia,* and *alter oculos, altera aures movet, per quos duos sensus omnis ad animum penetrat affectus;* Suarez, 1569, fol. 89r and 89v). Thus *elocutio* and *actio* must accord with emotion. If they diverge, the argument will suffer. If they converge, the argument will be clear, and appropriate, and may even be enhanced. Suarez thus manages to bring Aristotle into alignment with Cicero and Quintilian, but in doing so he underscores a Renaissance ambivalence about how to understand Aristotelian *lexis.* Is Renaissance *elocutio* truly a positive rhetorical force, or does it merely neutralize a potentially negative response? Does Aristotle's *lexis* actually do anything, or does it merely liberate the active elements of Books 1 and 2 of the *Rhetoric*?

Phantasia and *Elocutio*

Renaissance commentators settled their qualms about *elocutio* by focusing on the way that *phantasia* functions in the human soul. It is a notion that has dropped out of modern exegesis of the *Rhetoric.* Right after Aristotle speaks about the *mochthēria* of the hearers in Book 3, he says that "all these things" are *phantasia* and are directed toward the audience (*all' hapanta phantasia taut' esti kai pros ton akroātēn; Rhet.* 1404a11–12). Modern translations generally take both *lexis* and *hupokrisis* as the immediate referents for *hapanta* ("all these things"), but I cannot find a modern translation that takes the word *phantasia* seriously. Kennedy's translation is typical of modern approaches: "but all these things are *forms of outward show* and intended to affect the audience" (Kennedy, 1991, 3.1.6), an echo of Freese's earlier "*mere outward show* for pleasing the hearer" (Freese, 1926, 349). Both translations sharply diminish the force of *phantasia* in particular, and the ethical stature of *lexis* in general, but neither translation is as unsympathetic as Roberts and Barnes's "All such arts are *fanciful* and meant to charm the hearer" (Roberts and Barnes, 1984, 2238), itself an echo of the open hostility of Cope's nineteenth-century *"mere fancy,"* glossed further as "the mental presentation, a mere copy, without reality" (1877, 3:8). Somewhat more sympathetic is the reading by Dufour and Wartelle, *"car tout cela n'est qu'affair de sensibilité"* (Dufour and Wartelle, 1972, 40). All of these translations, to some degree, have the effect of acceding to the proposition that *lexis* is an ethical fraud and a cheat, in some way inimical to the respectable work of enthymematic persuasion.

But neither the modern notion of fantasy nor the late-Romantic notion of fancy accords very well with *phantasia* in Aristotle's other writings, or, for that matter, with *phantasia* in its few appearances elsewhere in the *Rhetoric.*[3] Renaissance writers, on the other hand, thought that *phantasia* could explain the psychology of *elocutio.* They were inclined to take Aristotle's *phantasia* here in Book 3 at face value, usually just transliterating the Greek into Latin, and then look for ways to make the word consistent with their understanding of Aristotelian psychology drawn from the *De Anima* and *Ethica Nicomachea* (Eden, 1986, 62–111). Such efforts effectively reconstitute *lexis* as an ethical enterprise for the Renaissance mind, an enterprise cheerfully sought out rather than grudgingly engaged in as a sad necessity, and ultimately it is an enterprise consistent with enthymematic proceeding as described in Books 1 and 2 of the *Rhetoric.*

Renaissance Aristotelians saw a continuity between body and soul and divided the soul into vegetative, sensitive, and intellective faculties (sometimes also called "souls"). The intellective faculty is itself unable to initiate or execute anything in isolation from the other two faculties, and nothing from the phenomenal world can reach the intellective faculty without first passing through the sensitive faculty. The sensitive faculty actively and passively acquires impressions *(species)* and uses subordinate faculties such as appetite, memory, and cogitation, to manipulate those impressions into *phantasmata* that are then passed on to the intellective faculty (Rist, 1971). It is *phantasia* that provides these *phantasmata.*

For many Renaissance commentators, rhetoric operates in the middle ground between the sensitive and intellective faculties (Green, 1998). The lower boundary for rhetoric is defined by the vegetative faculty, which involves no vice or virtue, no knowledge, and no opinion. Its upper boundary is roughly in the middle of the intellective faculty, which contains both perfect knowledge and human opinion. The higher part of the intellective faculty is the realm of philosophy and theology, while the lower part of the intellective faculty represents the highest reaches of rhetoric. Both parts of the intellective faculty require traffic with the sensitive soul, since "there is nothing in the intellect that was not first in the senses" (Parks, 1988, 470). Universal premises reside in the intellective faculty, unable to move themselves or move men. Particular premises and all the other *phantasmata* are provided by the sensitive faculty, and when they combine with universals, they can cause motion.

Thus the Renaissance understanding here in Book 3 of the *Rhetoric* is that everything in rhetoric is done to create *phantasia* and that *phantasia* will shape opinion. In the formulation by Daniele Barbaro, *Anima igitur prima est, in qua rectam opinionem inducit orator: deinde Res, quae animae partes excitant* (Barbaro and Barbaro, 1545, 548), and many other commentators follow this line of thinking.[4] Piero Vettori is even more explicit about the workings of *phantasia* in Book 3. Here Aristotle deals not so much with teaching as with *species*, a term that comes directly out of Renaissance understandings of *De anima.* As for the phase *phantasia estin*, Vettori explains that the stuff of rhetoric is unlike the stuff of geometry, which exists apart from opinion and language. Thus Aristotle's brief comment here in Book 3 that "no one teaches geometry this way" was not seen as a denigration of rhetoric in favor of geometry but as a clarification of Aristotle's own point that each subject has recourse to the *elocutio* that is appropriate to it and should be evaluated according to its own propriety. Antonio Riccoboni goes even further, citing Cicero's response when he was accused of rejecting Epicurus because of his inelegant style. Cicero replied that "it is not the style of your philosopher that offends me, for he expressed succinctly what he wanted and spoke plainly so that I understood" (*De finibus* 1.5.15). Eloquence is neither to be celebrated nor shunned; it is instead a simple fact of language, and it must be appropriate to the purpose at hand.

Renaissance commentators have physical and psychological processes in mind when they speak about *phantasia*, and in the *Rhetoric*, when they talk about setting something before the eyes *(ante oculos ponere)* of the audience, they are being more than simply colorful or emphatic. The sensitive faculty receives a physical *species*, and for Riccoboni, Aristotle must be taken literally at *Rhetoric* 3.11 when he says that a metaphor transfers a name from one *species* to another *species* (*Decimus locus est ex prouerbio, quod est translatio, cum quid à specie ad speciem transfertur;* Riccoboni, 1606b, 325). Riccoboni goes through each of the many *urbana* Aristotle discusses in chapters 10 and 11, observing that it is difficult to understand some of the particular urbanities—they are remote from Riccoboni's own time and he is not a member of Aristotle's *urbs.*[5] Some require careful explanation before the time-bound oddities of Aristotle's local quips can once again have any immediacy, before they can again function as physical *species.* Riccoboni takes a scholarly delight in correcting the misapprehensions of other commentators, and at the end of several of these revivifications of distant details, he triumphantly repeats his choric phrase "This is a metaphor and present to your eyes" (*Est translatio, & ante oculos;* Riccoboni, 1606b, 317 *bis,* 318, etc.), rather like an elocutionary version of the logical *quod est demonstratum.*[6]

Riccoboni's own proceeding here with Aristotelian *lexis* illustrates a typical Renaissance understanding that it is difficult for an auditor to convert material *species* into immaterial *phantasmata* if the phenomenal material is far off, distant, or obscure. This is the general psychological underpinning for Riccoboni's analysis of metaphors in *Rhetoric* 3.11.5, where Aristotle explains that metaphors should not be unusual and far fetched, nor evident and well known, but instead fairly close and yet not too obvious (*translationem non oportere esse alienam, & longe petitam, nec eminentem, & omnibus notam. Quod repetitur hoc in loco, illam nempe ducendam esse a propinquis, & minime apertis;* Riccoboni, 1606b, 319). Thus Renaissance commentators can talk about metaphors and enthymemes in almost the same language, and they hear echoes in Aristotle's discussions of the two subjects that we today do not always hear. At this same passage in Book 3, Aristotle adds the seemingly gratuitous comment that rhetoric differs from philosophy in that the philosopher must discern similarities among things that are far apart from one another *(Vt etiam in philosophia simile in longe distantibus cernere solertis est)* and that do not present themselves *ante oculos* (Riccoboni, 1606b, 319). The Latin phrasing here is much the same as that used in Book 1 to characterize enthymemes, where Aristotle says enthymemes are best used with auditors who cannot *logizesthai porrōthen* (*Rhet.* 1.2.1357a4). In our own age we have seized upon this Greek phrase as proof that Aristotle thought the audience was syllogistically handicapped; in Kennedy's translation, the audience cannot "reason from a distant starting point"

(Kennedy, 1991, 1.2.12), and in Freese's more caustic reading, they cannot "follow a lengthy chain of argument" (Freese, 1926, 23). But Renaissance commentators thought Aristotle was explaining enthymemes in Book 1 by drawing upon the same psychology used for *lexis* in Book 3: Auditors in public affairs are generally not able to grasp things unless they are *ante oculos,* that is to say, physically or geographically present, and by extension temporally present.

By definition, the subjects about which auditors commonly must deliberate are all distant—either physically or geographically or temporally—and none of them are *ante oculos.* Thus the orator uses enthymemes to make the distant seem immediate to auditors who cannot *longe distant ratiocinari* (*apud eiusmodi auditores, qui quae procul sita sunt videre, & ex ijs quae longe distant ratiocinari non queunt.*; Muret, 1585, 11), or *ratiocinari longius* (Riccoboni 1606b, 14), or *procul ratiocinari* (George of Trebizond, 1523b, fol. 110), and who cannot think about things that are *ab oculorum aspectu* (Vettori, 1548, 42). So also in Book 3, when Aristotle says that metaphors should not be far fetched, *ou porrōthen dei* (*Rhet.* 3.2.1405a35). Renaissance writers again read the phrase in terms of the sensitive faculty: *translationem non longe, sed ab iis, quae cognata & communia sunt* (Riccoboni, 1606b, 290–91). Vettori is more explicit: The words should not be far off, but close at hand (*Hoc etiam (inquit) animaduertere in transferendis uerbis oportet, ne longe ducantur, sed ex rebus, quae propinquae & affines inter se sint;* Vettori, 1548, 471). He glosses Aristotle by referring to similar phrases in Demetrius and Cicero. For Demetrius, metaphors should not be far off *(porrōthen)* but instead from the same general area (*autothen;* Demetrius, 1927, 78). And Cicero insists that the resemblance *ne longe simile sit ductum* so that the mind's eye is not strained and the similitude will strike the senses of the hearers (*De Oratore* 3.163).

The proper realm of the soul for rhetoric is in the unperfected movement between the sensitive and intellective faculties. The orator uses enthymemes of Book 1 to bring distant notions that are *ab oculorum aspectu* and uses *lexis* of Book 3 to place them *ante oculos,* before *phantasia* shapes them for their final journey to the higher intellective soul. The psychology of the orator thus stands in contrast to that of the philosopher. As Daniele Barbaro points out, the proper realm of the soul for philosophy is the higher intellective faculty: "The intellect is the name for that mental power which, if it perfects itself, is rewarded with wisdom, knowledge, and correct opinion" (*At uis animi, quae Mens nominatur, si suspicit, et attollit uim suam, uel sapientia, uel scientia, uel recta opinione decoratur, et insignitur;* Barbaro and Barbaro, 1545, 4), and in this realm the philosopher (or geometrician) has little further reliance upon *species* as he draws similarities among things *in longe distantibus* (*Rhet.* 3.11). Thus the ethical stature of rhetorical *elocutio* in the Renaissance is determined finally by an understanding of the proper functioning of human psychology.

Some Renaissance writers would take one further step in this ethical analysis, and in so doing they would inadvertently assure that subsequent writers would see in *mochthēria* human depravity rather than human psychology. John Rainolds in his Oxford lectures on the *Rhetoric* during the 1570s attributes many of mankind's intellectual failings to the fallen state of mankind after the loss of Eden, and in this he follows Juan Luis Vives (Rainolds, *Aristotelis rhetorica*, in Green 1986, 138–42, 140; Vives, 1531). John Milton illustrates a seventeenth-century version of the problem of human cognition and human psychology. We strive to know God, but "because our understanding cannot in this body found it selfe but on sensible things, nor arrive so cleerly to the knowledge of God and things invisible, as by orderly conning over the visible and inferior creature, the same method is necessarily to be follow'd in all discreet teaching" (1644, 2). Thus Aristotle's *mochtheriā* finds an analogue that stems from Original Sin, and the intellect must harness the sensitive faculty to serve it in both divine and secular learning.

Rereading Book 3

The effort to accommodate and assimilate Aristotelian *lexis* to contemporary *elocutio* was in no way restricted to just the authors I have discussed or, for that matter, restricted to the Renaissance. The effort continues throughout the eighteenth and nineteenth centuries and is having another resurgence in our own time. I have argued that the Renaissance effort to understand the *Rhetoric* in the prevailing contexts of Ciceronian, Hermogenean, and Aristotelian studies was fraught with difficulty and that while these contexts made the text comprehensible, it did so at some cost. All three of these prevailing contexts, however, seemed to require that commentators grapple with the text and that new translations be made. The towering stature of Aristotle throughout the middle ages and Renaissance, particularly in dialectic and ethics, meant that a treatise on rhetoric by him simply could not be ignored, whether to attack Aristotle, defend him, or simply to understand and extend the Aristotelian corpus. And in the humanist focus on Aristotle's *Rhetoric*, there can be felt a kind of delight in using an icon of scholasticism to undercut the perspectives of scholasticism.

To these imperatives we may add the authority of Cicero, who held that Aristotle was a river of eloquence and who tried to claim Aristotle as his progenitor in theories of rhetoric. With the expanding role of Ciceronian rhetoric in Renaissance pedagogy came an increasing need to substantiate the ancestry Cicero claimed, if for no other reason than to make long-suffering pedagogues feel better by letting them claim a better pedigree. With all the many vicissitudes of rhetoric over the centuries, the most enduring of the Latin *officia* had been *elocutio*, taught in one form or another in seemingly all ages, even when reduced to simple lists of figures devoid of supporting theories. When George of Trebizond blended Hermogenes with Cicero, he effectively elevated this pedagogical fact to an imperative, saying repeatedly that the primary task of the rhetorician was to teach *elocutio*, and he provided a theoretical justification that went beyond what even Cicero and Quintilian had claimed: "Wherefore, if speech is proper to man and by it he most especially differs from the other animals, I do not think anyone doubts that of all the things nature has given to mankind, the most eminent is *elocutio.*" (I use here Monfasani's translation of *Rhetoricorum libri V* based on MS Wien NB, lat. 2329: *Quare si loqui proprium hominis est eaque re a ceteris maxime animalibus differt, nemini dubium esse puto omnium rerum quas natura humano generi prebuit, elocutionem esse prestantissimam*; Monfasani, 1976, 282.) As John Monfasani observes, George takes *elocutio*, which had been merely one of the five offices of rhetoric, and here elevates it to being the chief characteristic of humankind. Teachers of composition thus moved from the periphery to the center of the humanist enterprise, and for struggling teachers, then as now, this would be a seductive theoretical claim.

The fact remained, however, that pedagogues had little need for Aristotle when they taught practical rhetoric. Renaissance writers had already embraced the more elaborate and preceptive stylistic discussions of Cicero and, more recently, of Hermogenes, and when they came to Book 3 of Aristotle's *Rhetoric*, some felt he added little of immediate use. Marc Antoine Muret, for example, translated only the first two books of the *Rhetoric*, and when his disciple Francesco Benci published that translation in 1585, Benci made no effort to adduce a translation of the missing book.[7] As for Benci's own lectures on Aristotle's *Rhetoric* in the 1580s, they were clearly meant to demonstrate the applicability of Aristotle's theories to immediate rhetorical situations in the Renaissance. The student notes we have of those lectures (dated 1586–87) suggest that when it came time to turn Aristotelian *lexis* to immediate account, Benci or his colleague simply bypassed Aristotle and substituted Book 4 of the *Ad Herennium* (Green, 1994a). I have so far found no arguments in the Renaissance to parallel those in our own time concerning the genuineness of Book 3, much less its relation to and order of composition with respect to the first two books, but we may suspect that something of the kind may have been going on. Antonio Riccoboni, for example, has a discussion of how Book 3 completes the design that Aristotle articulates in Book 2, but it is not clear whether he is responding to someone else's argument or whether he is offering a standard statement about the unity of the *Rhetoric* (1606b, 239–40, on *Rhet.* 2.18.1392a3).

If pedagogues had little immediate use for Aristotelian *lexis,* then scholars were interested in it, and in the course of the Renaissance, they sought increasingly to understand classical treatises in their own right. Piero Vettori, for example, makes no effort to appropriate Aristotle for contemporary use and instead puts his massive talents and industry into a philological and literary examination of Aristotle's exploration of language and composition in Book 3. For Vettori there was no question that the treatise was a whole of three books, and such confidence would only be enhanced during the succeeding decades as notions of method were embraced throughout Europe (Green, 1997). Raphael Cyllenius Angelus produces a massive book-length diagram of the entire *Rhetoric* in 1571, and Theodore Goulston produces numerous quasi-ramist diagrams of the *Rhetoric* in 1619. Both kinds of effort are based on a conviction that the Aristotle who generated Books 1 and

2 necessarily had Book 3 in mind from the start. Such an organic view of the *Rhetoric* was not dependent upon Renaissance theoretical innovations in method. On the contrary, it built upon earlier studies in Aristotelian ethics and psychology, and our exegetical faith in the place of *lexis* within the *Rhetoric* did not begin to falter until those larger theoretical understandings began to crumble.

Notes

1. Vettori, for example, rejects the reading of the concessive *homōs* at *Rhet.* 1404a9 (which he knows of from manuscripts associated with MS Parisinus 1741) and justifies omitting the concession (Vettori, 1548, 455–56): *"quod ad dicendum tamen pertinet, habet quiddam necessarium in qualibet disciplina: contra illos autem disserit, qui plebeio atque incondito sermone utebantur, & omnia ornamenta orationis contemnebant: poscit enim (inquit) non nihil diligentiae oratio, quamcunque artem tractes, ut quo sine aliquo incommodo praetermitti non queat."* In the Huntington Library copy of Riccoboni 1606b, a sixteenth-century marginal note objects to Riccoboni's polemical failure to credit Vettori's measured position: *"tamen Victorius de actione etiam explicat"* (284).

2. Manfred Lossau offers a plausible modern explanation as a way of correcting other modern interpreters (Lossau, 1971), but he has not convinced other translators, and I have found no such explanations as his in the Renaissance.

3. For modern discussions of *phantasia* elsewhere in Aristotle, see Watson (1982) and Rees (1971); for a brief discussion of *phantasia* in the *Rhetoric*, see Philippe (1971, 35–41).

4. Francesco Robortello offers a version of this account in his commentary on Aristotle's *Poetics*: *"In hominibus vis quaedam est, quam Graeci 'phantasian' vocant; eam nos cogitandi vim appellare possumus, haec imagines à sensibus ad se peruenientes recipit, retinétque; atque ad simplicem mentem, quam intellectum vocant, transmittit; quas cum simplex illa, ac pura mens receperit, ac distinxerit, vocantur 'ennoiai' se 'ennoēmata,' à nostris notiones"* (Robortello, 1548, 28–29). Baxter Hathaway discusses Robortello's commentary here in terms of Renaissance efforts to understand imagination in Aristotle (1962, 329–31), while Kathy Eden explores it in terms of Renaissance efforts to align the psychology of image and imagination with Christian ethics (1986, 149–53).

5. Kennedy follows the Renaissance lead in translating *ta asteia* (*Rhet.* 1410b7) as "urbanities" (1991, 3.10.1), but Freese's earlier "smart sayings" (1926, 395) still captures some of the sense of trying to be stylish and *au courant* in the big city. For an account of this concept after Aristotle, see Schenkeveld (1994).

6. For a study of the impact in Renaissance England of the related rhetorical concepts of *enargeia, energeia, evidentia,* and placing ideas *ante oculos*, see Plett (1975); for classical theories see McCall (1969).

7. Muret's own letter to Benci seems to put Book 3 to the side: *"Tertium, ut saepe ex me audijsti, latine reddi posse vix puto"* (Muret, 1585, sig. [4]). Muret did,

however, write about aspects of Book 3; see, for example, his several inaugural lectures of 1576, *"Cum Aristotelis libros de arte rhetorica interpretari inciperet"* (1751, 231–45) and also *"Conatus emendandi duos locos è tertio libro Aristotelis De arte dicenti"* (1580, 159–60).

10

Aristotle and Theories of Figuration

Jeanne Fahnestock

In Book 3, chapter 10, Aristotle identifies three verbal devices that produce effective expressions: metaphor, antithesis, and energeia. Aristotle presumably has no developed concept of figures of speech, but by distinguishing these three devices, he establishes prototypes for the three subsequent categories of the figures: the tropes, schemes, and figures of thought. By grouping these three, he also identifies the semantic, syntactic, and pragmatic sources of figuration, and, unlike his successors, he unites them with a strong view of the functional nature of the figures in rhetorical discourse, as a detailed examination of the figure antithesis demonstrates. The current fixation on metaphor and the obscurity of antithesis represent a loss of Aristotle's functional understanding of the figures.

Book 3 of the *Rhetoric* appears at first to be Aristotle's grudging concession to a demand that he produce a complete art, one that will include not only sources of support but also advice on *lexis* and taxis, "for it is not enough to have a supply of things to say, but it is also necessary to say it in the right way" (3.1.2). Aristotle apparently would have preferred that manner of saying count for nothing compared to the matter said, and that the facts of the case alone should suffice for a judge's decision. But given the usual "corruption" of audiences, he has to acknowledge that delivery is a factor and that therefore "expression . . . has some small necessary place in all teaching; for to speak in one way rather than another does make some difference in regard to clarity, though not a great difference" (3.1.6).

Yet despite this unenthusiastic start, Aristotle's treatment of *lexis* in Book 3 does make a substantial contribution to the linguistic art of rhetoric when judged against the fuller discussions of style in later classical and early modern treatises. Aristotle does, for example, stipulate the important categories of stylistic assessment taken up in later rhetorical commentaries, including word choice, prosody, perspicuity, appropriateness, correctness, and the nature of the "mean" for prose composition. Compared to later manuals, however, Aristotle's comments on these issues are perfunctory, and his cursory treatment is especially obvious in the scant attention he pays to the formal verbal devices that will later be called the figures of speech. By contrast, the first-century B.C.E. *Rhetorica Ad Herennium* catalogs some sixty-four such devices, and later manuals, notably the grand compilations of the sixteenth century, amplify the catalogs of the ancients, creating more intricate distinctions and divisions. Aristotle only mentions a handful of "figures" including asyndeton, metaphor, simile, hyperbole, antithesis, paronomasia, and devices like parison and homoioteleuton associated with producing balanced *cola*. As Kennedy points out, Aristotle has no word for figure of speech (Kennedy, 1991, 242), nor does he explicate a thoroughly worked out theory of figuration. Thus it often seems easier to discuss what Aristotle does not accomplish in Book 3.

It can be argued, however, that the treatment of *lexis* in Book 3 does illuminate the much more detailed attention to figures in the Hellenistic and Roman rhetorical tradition and that Aristotle does in fact establish a theory of figuration, at least by default. This theory of figuration results in part from the *de facto* categories of verbal device established in the *Rhetoric*, categories that in turn suggest the nature and uses of figuration. Furthermore, there is much in Aristotle's incidental remarks on verbal devices that not only anticipates but even goes beyond later commentary on what the figures of speech can accomplish. Thus Aristotle may actually have had a fuller understanding of the potential uses of verbal devices than later writers who focused exclusively on the figures as vehicles of ornamentation or literary expression. He may have specified fewer devices, but he seems to have held a more complex view of the effects that verbal devices could achieve.

Critical to a reassessment of Aristotle's implicit theory of figuration is the moment in chapter 10 when he specifies three devices that can help an arguer create distinctive, "urbane" expressions: metaphor, antithesis, and energeia at the service of "bringing before the eyes" (3.10.6). These three are the sources of "well-liked expressions" (3.10.1) that create "quick learning" (3.10.4). They are, in effect, keys to creating what we would call "sound bites," brief trenchant phrases that are more likely to fix themselves in listeners' minds and be repeated to others or perhaps even quoted on the evening news. These three sources of sophisticated and memorable *lexis* hardly receive equal attention in the discussion that precedes and follows their sudden specification. Indeed, Aristotle constantly circles back to metaphor in the chapters on *lexis,* he has little to say about energeia, and his attention to antithesis, though of crucial importance (see below), is brief and disjointed. Nevertheless, simply by listing and bracketing together these three devices for a memorable style, Aristotle creates three categories of figures of speech, and in his comments on how these and other devices work, he does establish a theory of figuration. Though Dirk Schenkeveld has argued that the *Rhetoric*'s notion of the *asteia*, the sources of urbane expression, disappears in subsequent rhetorical treatises (Schenkeveld, 1994), it is possible to find the seeds of the subsequent growth of the "figures" in this grouping. For Aristotle's three keys to a smart style can be seen as prototypes, in the sense of exemplary members, for what will become the three major categories of figures of speech: metaphor of the tropes, antithesis of the figures of diction, and energeia of the figures of thought.[1] Looking back at Aristotle's select three from the perspective of the later tradition, each can be seen as standing for one of these three great divisions of the figures of speech that will appear and persist in later rhetorical manuals for two thousand years. Thus for much of the rhetorical tradition, they represent what Aristotle would call a first division of the genus of psycholinguistically active verbal devices, and an examination of the key treatments of the figures in the *Rhetorica ad Herennium*, the *Institutio Oratoria*, and the *De Oratore* and other treatises by Cicero would confirm that they continue to inhabit separate divisions, divisions that in a sense grow up around them.

This paper will examine the nature of each of these three prototypical devices defined in Book 3 as a way of exposing Aristotle's implicit theory of figuration, pointing out that each concerns a different linguistic dimension. I will also argue that Aristotle has a special understanding of the "figures" as formal verbal epitomes of underlying rhetorical functions, a definition that can be illustrated by a detailed analysis of the figure antithesis. Though long ago eclipsed by metaphor, antithesis provides a key to how figuration and argumentation are intimately related in a uniquely rhetorical art. The final section of this paper will briefly address the question of why metaphor has monopolized scholarly attention and will recommend a return to Aristotle's more expanded understanding of the power of verbal devices suggested in Book 3 of the *Rhetoric*.

The Three Devices and the Three Sources of Figuration

In order to appreciate how Aristotle's three key devices resemble the later division of the figures into three categories, it is necessary to examine each according to its nature and effect. How does Aristotle characterize the three sources of *asteia*? How do they differ from each other so that it is necessary to distinguish them, and how are they alike so that it is reasonable to group them?

On a first pass, Aristotle's three special devices, and the three subsequent categories of figuration they represent, can be partitioned according to what are now familiar divisions of linguistic analysis: semantics, syntax, and pragmatics.[2] Thus recognizing a metaphor, and the other figures later grouped with metaphor in the category of tropes, requires an implicit semantics and, at a minimum, some notion of word classes. For tropes are the figures that tamper with the signifying function in a way that is noticeable only because words can be grouped into different types. Indeed the *Poetics* defines metaphor as an operation across semantic categories; it is a "movement *[epiphora]* of an alien *[allotrios]* name from either genus to species or from species to genus or from species to species or by analogy" (Kennedy, 1991, 295 [1457b]). The implication that semantic transference depends on types of words is carried on in the *Rhetoric*, where Aristotle consistently uses "metaphor" as a genus term; thus he speaks of "species" of metaphor (3.2.7), names four kinds of metaphor (3.10.7), and identifies the simile (3.4.1) and hyperbole (3.11.15) as types of metaphor, a practice that licenses the later naming of more precise varieties depending on where the transferred words come from (e.g., synecdoche from the name of a part). Though the Latin *Ad Herennium*, the first full treatment of the figures, does not employ "metaphor" as a genus term, it does semantically define ten similar devices, of which metaphor is the first, as instances where "the language departs from the ordinary meaning of the words and is, with a certain grace, applied in another sense" ([Cicero], 1954, 333). Two hundred years later in the omnibus *Institutio Oratoria,* Quintilian uses the then-established category name, tropes, of which metaphor becomes a species, and defines tropes in a way that also suggests their semantic nature: "By a *trope* is meant the artistic alteration of a word or phrase from its proper meaning to another" (3:301).

Aristotle's second source of memorable language, the antithesis, represents the second category of figures, the figures of diction (sometimes referred to by the generic and confusing name "figures of speech"). In this category the source of figuration is not semantic transfer, as in the case of the tropes, but rather some device of syntactic patterning imposed on the wording. Such patterning is a salient, though not the only, feature in the Aristotelian definition of antithesis, with its double *cola* of equal length (see below). Surely the many devices that specify the patterns created by strategic repetitions (e.g., anaphora and epistrophe) and the other devices for achieving an aural resemblance among *cola* (e.g., isocolon) are all identifiable syntactically and even to some extent prosodically by the cadences they produce. Aristotle refers to antithesis, the prototype of this family of devices, as deriving its virtue in part from "shaped language" (*schêmata,* Kennedy, 1991, 245). Thus in the rhetorical tradition this family of devices is also known as the schemes.

The third of the *asteia,* energeia, belongs to a once robust third division known by a very misleading label as the figures of thought.[3] This category is difficult to define, but we can begin to understand it from the perspective of pragmatics, the dimension of linguistic analysis concerned with what an utterance is supposed to accomplish for the speaker and with how it functions in a particular situation. Quintilian captures the pragmatic or situational nature of the figures of thought when he tries to distinguish them from the schemes. "For the former [the figures of thought] lies in the conception, the latter [the schemes] in the expression of our thought. The two are frequently combined, however, as in the following passage: "'Now, Dolabella, [I have no pity] either for you or for your children' *[Iam iam, Dolabella, neque me tui neque tuorum liberum]*: for the device by which he turns from the judges to Dolabella is a *figure of thought,* while *iam iam* ('now') and *liberum* ('your children') are *figures of speech*" (3:356–357). Thus Quintilian singles out the device that exploits the immediate circumstances of the utterance as a figure of thought or, in his expanded phrasing, a figure of "mind, feeling or conceptions" *[mentis vel sensus vel sententiarum]* (3:357). Cicero was using a figure of thought in the passage Quintilian quotes when he singled out Dolabella for direct address. Certainly Aristotle's energeia fits into a category of figures of thought defined by a pragmatic rationale as would many of the other figures typically grouped here, like frankness of speech (praising listeners by pretending to criticize them) or emphasis (defined in figure manuals as managing to communicate more than is actually said). None of these figures of thought, energeia included, can be pinned down syntactically or semantically; it is impossible to write a precise set of instructions and say, "Do this and you will achieve energeia," as one can with antithesis and metaphor. (Even the direct address to Dolabella could have been achieved by looking at him without using his name.) As Cicero observed in the *Orator*, the figures of thought are so free from a particular surface form that they persist even after the wording is changed (Cicero, 1988, 365), something that could not be said of either metaphor or antithesis. Therefore energeia and indeed most of the figures of thought can only be approximately specified by the effects they are supposed to achieve, the speech acts they are intended to accomplish. Hence the justness of placing them in the pragmatic dimension of language, since they are usually identified either by the speaker's illocutionary intent (to describe vividly in the case of energeia) or by their perlocutionary effect (again for energeia, to bring before the eyes).

That the figures of thought specify intended or accomplished speech acts has historically made this grouping the most extensible and open ended of categories. Gérard Genette describes the process by which rhetoric can produce such figures as follows: "It ascertains a *quality* in the text that might not have been there—the poet describes (instead of designating with a word), the dialogue is abrupt (instead of connected); then it substantializes this quality by naming it—the text is no longer descriptive or abrupt, it *contains* a description or an abruption" (Genette, 1982, 53). That is in fact how energeia, the presumed device, is constructed from "bringing before the eyes," the desired effect, in Book 3 of the *Rhetoric*. But by this rationale, there would be no end to the possible reification of effects. Any namable speech act could become a device, an openendedness that Quintilian tried to correct in the conclusion of his chapter on the figures of thought when he jettisoned devices like threats and exhortations, calling them straightforward methods of speaking that could, however, be combined with some other more easily identified figures (3:439). But the line between what is and what is not a figure of thought is ultimately impossible to draw.

Aristotle's original three sources of an urbane style, metaphor, antithesis, and energeia, can, then, expose an implicit theory of figuration by virtue of their distinctiveness. They map onto both the three separate categories of the figures in the rhetorical tradition and also onto current distinctions in linguistic analysis. Metaphor involves the transference of a word from its ostensible semantic class, antithesis requires specially "shaped" *lexis* in double *cola*, and energeia names the effect a speaker is trying to produce, a "bringing-before-the-eyes" of the audience. But, it must be admitted, the three categories that grow up around these three prototypical devices—tropes, figures of diction, and figures of thought—do not remain pure. The neat division between the tropes as semantic, the schemes as syntactic, and the figures of thought as pragmatic becomes strained when it is compared to the actual lists in some manuals. Thus the *Ad Herennium* places *hyperbaton (transgressio)*, which concerns inverted word order, among the "tropes" (337), and includes among the figures of diction schemes that affect only a single word by adding, deleting, or transposing letters or syllables (301–5). Later writers obviously struggled to purify the categories and make them consistently correspond to clear divisions. But by Quintilian's time, many alternate classifications had accumulated, and Quintilian records such problems, acknowledging for example that *hyperbaton* could also be a *figura verborum,* that is, a scheme, as well as a trope (3:339), or that irony could be either a trope or a figure of thought (3:401). These category confusions, however, reveal the prevailing theories about the figures, demonstrating that some consider term selection, others phrasing, and others intentions. It also remains true, as it was for Aristotle in Book 3, that most of the tropes and figures of diction can be defined semantically and/or syntactically and that most of the figures of thought can only be specified by the intent they betray or the effect they should achieve.

If Aristotle's original three devices can be distinguished from each other on the basis of the dimension of language affected, he nevertheless groups them in chapter 10 on the basis of what they all can accomplish. Thus the issue in trying to reconstruct Aristotle's implicit theory of figuration shifts from what these devices are to how they work. What are the sources of their effectiveness that led to their grouping? Metaphor, to begin with, may be defined as semantically based figuration, but what is its mechanism? The *Poetics* speaks of the movement of an alien name (1457b) and the *Rhetoric* of choices between "a word in its prevailing and native meaning and metaphor" as alone useful in prose (3.2.6). Though speakers commonly use both according to Aristotle, his last-quoted comment divides usage into two domains, the literal and the figurative. There is a proper word or phrase that can be replaced by another imported from an "alien" context. The principle of figuration implicit here is the well-known one of substitution. Any departure from the expected or ordinary choice of *lexis* is then an instance of figuration, though for prose Aristotle recommends a careful choice of metaphors or substitutions that are neither too banal nor too disconcertingly strange (3.10.6). This characterization of metaphor as the uncommon choice has always been problematic, even in Book 3. For metaphors are at once common in the language as a whole ("for all people carry on their conversations with metaphors"; 3.2.6), and yet they have to be an unexpected alternative, and as far as the *Rhetoric* is concerned an inconspicuous one, to the literal choice in any specific instance.[4]

There is, of course, no reason to limit the mechanism of substitution to metaphor (and by extension to all the tropes). It is possible to use substitution as the rationale for all three categories of the figures, as Pierre Fontanier did in *Les Figures du Discours,* the last of the "renaissance" figure manuals written early in the nineteenth century (Fontanier, 1977, 12). Thus while a trope replaces a "proper" word with some borrowed alternative, figures of thought were sometimes defined as substitutions as well. In the case of these pragmatic devices, the substitution involved replacing the usual communicative function of a locution with an insincere one. So Quintilian, again aware, as noted above, of the potential openendedness in the category of figures of thought, limits his discussion to those "which depart from the direct method of statement" (3:375), such as questions asked with the intent of making an assertion or denials of taking up a topic made with the express purpose of introducing it. Among the figures of diction, it is also possible to speak of substitution when presumably straightforward phrasing is replaced by specially "shaped" language; asyndeton, for example, the elimination of connectives (categorized in the *Ad Herennium* as a figure of diction), can be described as a substitution for the usual manner of using connectives.

Such a conception of the figures as substitutions for "ordinary" language persists in the rhetorical tradition. But is substitution a consistent principle in Aristotle's discussion of the *asteia*? The only clear invoking of substitution in Book 3 concerns metaphor. In the case of antithesis (and other devices for producing symmetrical *cola*), there is perhaps a recommendation of replacing paratactic with periodic phrasing, but in the case of energeia, there is no suggestion of substituting one effect with another. Thus substitution does not seem to be a unifying concept for the *asteia* in Book 3.

Nor is substitution, with its cognate notion of *écart*, a departure from the literal, a sufficient explanation of figuration in any case, because it leaves unanswered the question, What is the substitution for? The traditional answer, that the tropes and figures substitute extraordinary expressions for ordinary ones in order to "ornament" a text, begs the question of what it means to ornament a text and how a particular device performs this function. Even a useful correction of the notion of "ornament" that conflates it with "armament" still suggests that figures are removable and inherently unnecessary (Vickers, 1988, 314). A twentieth-century answer, that substitution serves defamiliarization, is not satisfactory either, first because it merely renames the effect and second because it assumes that defamiliarization is self-evidently a goal in itself at the service of "poetic" language. But that rhetorical language is specifically not poetic language (3.1.9) and that rhetorical *lexis* should not draw attention to itself (3.2.4) are surely two of the main claims of Book 3.

Though all later treatments of the figures, beginning with the *Ad Herennium*, describe them as ornaments to a text, and though Lausberg (1960) in his grand compendium of classical rhetoric places all the figures under "Ornatus," Book 3 says nothing about *lexis* serving ornamentation in the sense of adding value to what is already present in the text. Traditionally the fourth of the four virtues of style (perspicuity, correctness, appropriateness, and ornamentation), ornamentation may have been added by Aristotle's pupil Theophrastus to the first three virtues, which Aristotle does mention. But Aristotle himself does not offer "value added" rationales for verbal choices. Instead his comments suggest that certain devices are compelling because they are perfect formal embodiments of the speaker's meanings and intentions. They map function onto form by epitomizing certain patterns of thought or argument.

A case that illustrates this functional understanding is Aristotle's account of asyndeton and its "opposite" in chapter 12: "Furthermore, asyndeta have a special characteristic; many things seem to be said at the same time; for the connective makes many things seem one, so that if it is taken away, clearly the opposite results: one thing will be many" (3.12.4). In other words, a series without connectives seems to Aristotle to express the separateness and therefore the multiplicity of the items mentioned; as he says of his offered example, "'I came; I spoke; I besought' (these things seem many)" (3.12.4). The special verbal device here, the elimination of connectives or asyndeton, expresses a specific meaning, the idea of multiple distinct objects, actions, or notions. The form itself delivers this meaning regardless of the actual items in the series, and it is this general meaning or ideational function that distinguishes the device (see Blettner, 1983). Conversely, Aristotle suggests that adding connectives can unify the items of a series. Thus the phrasing "I came *and* I spoke *and* I besought" would emphasize the combination of these three separate actions. In other words, the version with asyndeton says "I did three different things," while the version with polysyndeton says "I did all three of these things," a subtle but potentially significant distinction. (Perhaps not accidentally, Aristotle describes these reverse effects using the syntactic reversal of the antimetabole—"many things seem one/one thing will be many"—in itself an example of the unifying of form and function that Aristotle claims here for asyndeton.)

In the same way that Aristotle explains the effect of asyndeton, he suggests the ideational work epitomized by several of the verbal forms he discusses in Book 3 (Vickers, 1988, 314). But of all these devices, he singles out the three sources of *asteia* as especially effective formal devices and tries to account for their effectiveness. By contrast, the *Ad Herennium* expeditiously names devices and provides examples, but it speaks only vaguely of general effects like force and charm; of asyndeton it says only that it "has animation and great force, and is suited to concision" (331); here the author of the *Ad Herennium* merely notices the immediate consequence of deleting connectives *(ad brevitatem adcommodatum)* but shows none of Aristotle's understanding of how the formal device carries the specific ideational function of making the one many.

The notion that figuration is an iconic matching of form to meaning, or the perfect formal expression of a function, is suggested at several other places in Book 3. Even metaphor has to reflect a substitution made to some functional end as it is described in the *Rhetoric*. The speaker should avoid far-fetched metaphors (3.3.4) and select those that bring about learning in an audience (3.10.2). "Urbanities," he writes, "in most cases come through metaphor and from an added surprise; for it becomes clearer [to the listener] that he learned something different from what he believed, and his mind seems to say, 'How true, and I was wrong'" (3.11.6). In other words, rhetorical metaphors, and indeed any rhetorical substitutions, are not chosen simply because they are strange or vivid, but because they express perfectly, efficiently, and unobtrusively the precise notion the speaker is trying to convey. Depending on whether the speaker's purpose is blame or praise, to use Aristotle's famous example, mules are half-asses or the daughters of storm-footed mares (3.2.14).

What is true of metaphor and asyndeton is true of the other two sources of urbane expression; each accesses conviction or creates insight in a uniquely efficient way. Hence Aristotle's frequent emphasis on "learning" as the result of the effective presentation of ideas and arguments, in turn the result of making the best possible verbal choices (3.9.8; 3.10.2; 3.10.4; 3.11.6). This emphasis on learning has to be puzzling from the later perspective that sets the figures apart as merely ornamental and that leads to a division of the levels of style based in part on the extent of such ornamentation. Aristotle has no theory of the levels of prose style (like three fixed dial settings—low, middle, and high) because he has a theory of continuously tunable appropriateness based on functionally selected forms suitable to the subject, speaker, and occasion. There is, to reestablish the implicit connection between this theory of functional verbal devices and the opening of the *Rhetoric*, a best available means or choice of *lexis* in every particular case (see also 3.2.13). Further evidence that Aristotle has a theory of functionally efficient verbal forms comes from his acknowledgment that such forms are potentially dangerous, something difficult for mere ornament to be. For if, as Aristotle explains, the "proper *lexis* also makes the matter credible," it is also possible to fake the credible with the proper *lexis*. The speaker who can master this art, particularly to convey the appropriate emotions, can lead the listener "to draw a false inference of the truth" (3.7.4) merely because of the successful manner of presentation.

Antithesis

Aristotle's reconstructed theory of figuration, the recognition of the ideational functions of certain verbal constructions, has consequences for our understanding of the relationship between language and thought. And indeed the first of Aristotle's sources of *asteia*, metaphor, has recently been reassessed as fundamental to human cognitive processes by, among others, the linguist George Lakoff and the philosopher Mark Johnson (1980). In their explication of how metaphors structure conceptual domains, they have in a sense returned to the Aristotelian understanding of metaphor as a mechanism for learning something new. Far less attention has been paid to the second of Aristotle's sources of *asteia*, the antithesis, which, in as potentially rich a way, provides an example of how a form of expression can epitomize a particular form of reasoning. Understanding the Aristotelian antithesis requires, first of all, unpacking Aristotle's brief characterization of this device in Book 3 and examining the intersection of this characterization in the *Rhetoric* with passages concerning the same form and line of reasoning in his dialectical treatises. This analysis will illustrate what it means to talk about the potential function of a verbal form.

Aristotle's account of the antithesis occurs in the context of his discussion of prose style in general in Book 3, for in fact the device is introduced before it is elevated to one of the especially effective three. Aristotle begins by distinguishing two kinds of prose style: prose that is "strung-on" or paratactic, loping along without closure from connective to connective, and prose that comes to points of completion or is periodic (3.9.1–3). Aristotle believes that the period, the unit of this second style, is an inherently satisfying syntactic unit because it has a perceivable beginning and end (3.9.3), and because such perceivable limits are always more pleasurable to the human mind than the unlimited (3.8.2).

Aristotle next takes this satisfying period apart, claiming that some periods can be built from two subunits called *cola* (3.9.5). Not just any two *cola*, however, produce an artistic period that both invites the audience to anticipate its completion and leaves a memorable impression because of its "number" or prosody. First, Aristotle claims, the length of the *cola* making up a period is critical. Excessively short ones disappoint listeners by closing too abruptly, and long ones frustrate them by postponing the expected completion (3.9.6). He prefers balanced *cola* of equal length, not too long and not too short (the usual Aristotelian middle way), and he believes that a first colon of temperate length will create the expectation of a second colon of equal length, causing listeners (or readers) to feel a certain satisfaction when the pattern is completed and the expectation fulfilled.

Second, the wording of the *cola* making up a period is critical. Since periods can be built from shorter *cola*, Aristotle explains that the *lexis*, the wording of these *cola*, can be either "divided" *(diêiremenê)* or "contrasted" *(antikeimenê)* (3.9.7). The example he offers suggests that a period with divided *lexis* is simply a period with parallel *cola:* "Often have I admired those organizing panegyric festivals and those instituting athletic games" (3.9.7). But in *cola* containing contrasted *lexis*, Aristotle stipulates, in words that echo a similar discussion in the *Topics*, "opposite lies with opposite or the same is yoked with opposites" (3.9.7).[5] This definition is immediately followed by several examples, including the following: "It happens often in these circumstances that the wise fail and the foolish succeed" and "Either while living to hold it; or when dead to lose it" (3.9.7).

Based then on Aristotle's commentary and examples, an antithesis can be defined as a verbal structure that places contrasted or opposed terms in parallel or balanced *cola* or phrases. Parallel phrasing without opposed terms does not produce an antithesis, nor do opposed terms alone without strategic positioning in symmetrical phrasing. Instead, the figure antithesis, according to Aristotle, must meet both syntactic and semantic requirements. It is shaped language, shaped into the form that best delivers a contrast (3.10.5), for, as Aristotle twice points out, as a commonplace about perception, "opposites are most knowable and more knowable when put beside each other" (3.9.8; see also 3.2.9).

Aristotle's original stipulation, that opposite lies with opposite or the same with opposites, further suggests two types of antithesis. The first kind has only one pair of opposed terms, as in Pascal's aphorism, "A trifle consoles us because a trifle upsets us" (1966, 38). This saying only makes sense if "trifleness," though applied to different things, is taken to mean the same thing in the two *cola*. But many antitheses, like Gorgias's "the stronger leads, the weaker follows," in his defense of Helen (Kennedy, 1991, 285), have two pairs of opposites; they constitute a second type—double antitheses. Both single and double antitheses can offer the predictability that Aristotle requires. Three-quarters of the way through the figure, most listeners familiar with the language used can finish an antithetical predication themselves (e.g., "The night is long and the day is ———."). Double antitheses, however, are the more familiar or "default" mode of the figure, more artificial yet more expected. But either kind qualifies as the device that Aristotle promotes as at once pleasing and powerful.

Aristotle makes several claims about what an antithesis can achieve. It pleases because it teaches, and it teaches, or causes a sudden realization, because opposites are "most knowable and more knowable when put beside each other," and they are "like a syllogism, for refutation *[elenkos]* is a bringing together of contraries" (3.9.8). In order to understand the persuasive power being attributed to the antithesis here, it is necessary to see the verbal device as the epitome of a line of reasoning. For though the term *antithesis* itself first appears in Book 3 (Kennedy, 1991, 242), other terms used in its definition appear elsewhere in the *Rhetoric*. Most significantly the definition of the figure in Book 3 strongly recalls the characterization of the first of the twenty-eight lines of argument in Book 2, chapter 23: "One *topos* of demonstrative [enthymemes] is that from opposites *[ek tìn enantiôn]*; for one should look to see if the opposite [predicate] is true of the opposite [subject], [thus] refuting the argument if it is not, confirming it if it is" (2.23.1; notably this last piece of aphoristic advice is expressed in an antithesis). Book 3, again, defines the antithesis as *cola* with contrasted *lexis*, when "opposite lies with opposite or the same is yoked with its opposites" (3.9.7). Clearly the figure and the topic are related, a relationship suggesting a qualification to Jonathan Barnes's observation that the three subjects taken up in the three books of the *Rhetoric* (logic, moral psychology, and language and composition) have "no common axioms, no common concepts, no common structures" (Barnes, 1995a, 263).[6] But a thorough analysis of how the verbal device epitomizes a topic requires reference to Aristotle's much fuller discussion of opposition and of this particular line of reasoning in his treatises on demonstration and dialectic (see Grimaldi, 1972, 115, 119).

The term that Aristotle uses in the *Rhetoric* in his definition of the figure, the word *opposite (enantièn)*, is for Aristotle a genus term divisible into four species. In the *Categories,* Aristotle explains that terms can be opposed in four ways: as contraries (hot and cold); as privation/possession pairs (blindness and sight); as relatives (double and half); and as affirmation and negation pairs (being and not being) (11b). In *De Interpretatione*, affirmation and negation pairs are identified as contradictory opposites (17a).[7] Aristotle did not distinguish among the four types of opposed *lexis* in his discussion of antithesis as a verbal device in Book 3 of the *Rhetoric*. But he did include examples using the three major kinds—contraries, contradictories, and correlatives—so it is likely he believed that any of these types could produce the figure. These semantic distinctions are, however, crucial to the anatomy of dialectical arguments in the *Topics*.

In the *Topics*, Aristotle explains in detail how arguers can build on the "reputable" opinions that are held, in his frequently repeated formula, by all, or most, or the most notable people. In Book 1, chapter 10, he explains how contrasted *lexis* can be used to construct plausible premise/conclusion pairs that, not coincidentally, take the form of antitheses:

> Likewise, also, propositions contradicting the contraries of reputable opinions will pass as reputable; for if it is a reputable opinion that *one ought to do good to one's friends*, it will also be a reputable opinion that *one ought not to do them harm*. Here, that one ought to do harm to one's friends is the contrary, and that one ought not to do them harm is the contradictory of that contrary. Likewise also, if *one ought to do good to one's friends, one ought not to do good to one's enemies:* this too is the contradictory of the contrary—the contrary being that one ought to do good to one's enemies. Likewise, also, in other cases. Also, on comparison, it will look like a reputable opinion that the contrary predicate belongs to the contrary subject: e.g., *if one ought to do good to one's friends, one ought also to do evil to one's enemies*. (104a; emphasis added; for a restatement of these points in terms of properties, see 135b–136a, and in terms of definitions, see 153a–153b.)

What Aristotle explicates here are the still-relevant commonsense correlates of propositions that contain terms with opposites. Quite simply, if you believe something, you don't believe its opposite, and if you don't believe its opposite, you will agree with a statement that contradicts or negates that opposite. Given the widely recognized contraries offered in Aristotle's examples—"friend" and "enemy," "doing good" and "doing harm"—the self-evidence of these patterns seems inescapable and the reasoning based on them compelling. Furthermore, these various inversions, as the italicized passages demonstrate, fall naturally into tight antitheses as their verbal epitomes.

Essentially then, in the *Topics*, Aristotle recognizes the combinatorial potential of pairs of semantic opposites to create either single or double antitheses. Putting four terms, that is two pairs of opposites, into play produces six possible combinations and hence six potential antitheses, two double and four single (112b–113a):

1. good to friends and evil to enemies (double)
2. evil to friends and good to enemies (double)
3. good to friends and evil to friends (single)
4. good to enemies and evil to enemies (single)
5. good to friends and good to enemies (single)
6. evil to friends and evil to enemies (single)

Aristotle acknowledges that the two *cola* in the first two of these antitheses can be maintained simultaneously: If it is right to help or to do good to one's friends, it seems plausible that it is also right to hurt one's enemies. Here opposite (help/hurt) lies with opposite (friend/enemy) and therefore either of these statements can be used in support of the other. Of course the support here will not be compelling from a Christian perspective,[8] and whenever such specific examples are involved, the temporal boundaries of plausibility begin to show. But the general point remains. The *cola* of double antitheses are potential sources of positive premises; arguers who can construct a statement plausible for their intended audience with the opposite of each of the terms in their claim have support for their arguments.

But the remaining four in the list above, the single antitheses with only one pair of contraries each, presumably cannot be held simultaneously. An arguer bent on refutation, even self-refutation, will try to construct one of these single antitheses to test a position. If contraries can be plausibly predicated of the same subject (at the same time and in the same relation and respect), an arguer has a problem; here is that refutation by bringing together of contraries, as they are brought together in single antitheses, that Aristotle mentions in his discussion of the verbal device in Book 3. Thus double antitheses support and single antitheses refute, or, again in the words of the first of the twenty-eight lines in the *Rhetoric*, "look to see if the opposite [predicate] is true of the opposite [subject], [thus] refuting the argument if it is not, confirming it if it is" (2.23.1).

Once the verbal form, the figure antithesis, is recognized as the epitome of an underlying topical reasoning, it becomes possible to use the figure itself as a stylistic prompt or syntactic frame for invention, though nothing perhaps illustrates the difference between the classical and Renaissance versus the contemporary mind-set more than the discomfort that any such notion of purely verbal invention produces. Yet that Aristotle intended this gimmick seriously has been supported by Robin Smith in a recent article on the very different goals of the *Topics* and the *Prior* and *Posterior Analytics*, the latter two a theoretically satisfying account of inference and the former a how-to manual for dialectical sparring (Smith, 1994, 140). The stand-up arguer needs easily retrievable premise patterns, "definite in outline but indefinite as regards the particulars," as Smith points out, quoting Alexander quoting Theophrastus. The figure antithesis is one such durable pattern as the general formula suggests: "If the contrary belongs to the contrary, then to the contrary the contrary" (Smith, 1994, 145–46). A constraint on this automatic premise generation is, of course, that the resulting antithesis be believable by some reference group, either the all, or the most, or the most learned, frequently specified in the *Topics*.

The antithesis of the *Topics*, then, is a syntactic frame for opposites that are already acknowledged as opposites. But as a rhetorical device, the figure is potentially more powerful depending on the status of the terms it deploys. An antithesis can certainly be built from what might be called "natural" opposites in the vocabularies of all languages—"up" versus "down" and "bitter" versus "sweet." Calling these antonyms "natural" merely means that pairs of words can have wide currency as opposites among users of a language outside any particular context of use. Word association tests give ample evidence of the consistent linking of opposites in verbal memory when subjects given one of a pair of antonyms most often respond with the other—"hot" triggering "cold" and "long" retrieving "short," as George Miller has shown (1991, 196). An antithesis as a figure of speech at the sentence level builds on those powerful natural pairs, the use of one in the first half of the figure creating the expectation of its verbal partner in the second half. Consider the defeat of such expectation and the consequent loss of force if instead of using the widely recognized opposites "succeed" and "fail," Kennedy had chosen to translate Aristotle's example as, "In these circumstances the wise fail and the foolish do much better."

In addition to pairs of opposites that have wide currency among the users of a language over centuries, there are also "local" opposites, specific to communities more narrowly definable in time and place. In the early Christian church, for example, *homoousian* and *homoiousian* were one such pair of local opposites; in the late twentieth-century United States, pairs like the "Odd Couple" Oscar and Felix or the political categories "Reaganite" and "Clintonite" are other examples of local opposites, not likely to survive their contexts. But there can also be temporary or "nonce" opposites constructed for a particular argument, a pair of terms not recognized as opposites beforehand by an intended audience, as the topical advice requires, but put into opposition in the course of an argument. All these degrees of opposition in terms of audience, stable to occasional, can form the semantic base of the figure.

The argumentative use of the antithesis in any particular case will then depend on the rhetorical status of the opposed *lexis* used to fill the syntactic frame of the figure. Given terms that are already accepted by an audience as contraries, whether local or more enduring, the form becomes an inventional prompt, the first colon determining the choice of terms and the form of the second, as in Theophrastus and Alexander's advice. Thus in a sense, the figure writes itself by drawing on known contrasts, and its effect with a particular audience depends on their prior recognition of those contrasts. The illustration for the first of the twenty-eight lines of argument in the *Rhetoric* gives an apt example as the second colon, "for to lack self-control is harmful," is formed from available terms that are the widely accepted opposites of terms in the first half: "that to be temperate is a good thing" (2.23.1). A premise is constructed using these existing or already accepted oppositions, and common wisdom readily accepts, or at least it did in Aristotle's day, that temperance has good effects while lack of self-control has bad ones. In fact, so strong is the power of widely accepted antonyms to recall their opposites that it is even possible, given the right textual and contextual environment, for an arguer to use only the first half of an antithesis and expect the audience to fill in the other half. Thus the speaker who says simply "I am tired of words" inevitably calls for deeds without saying so in a culture that recognizes "words/deeds" and "giving up on one thing/turning to another" as opposites.

The argumentative effects of an antithesis need not depend, however, on two pairs of already accepted semantic contrasts. To turn now to the more important syntactic character of the figure, the ability to perceive the pattern in an antithesis, to fulfill its predictions and even to feel its force, is part of the competence of an experienced user of the language. It belongs in a "stylistic vocabulary," a repertoire of higher formalisms in a language. Once a language user is familiar with the form created by placing opposed words in parallel phrases, the form can in a sense take on a life of its own, and an arguer can use the form and only one set of opposed terms to in effect create another set of semantic opposites. In others words, it is possible to force or fake a double antithesis by placing one pair of words in the strategic slots that are not pairs of antonyms to begin with in the existing vocabulary or prior usage of an audience. The arguer thus creates nonce antonyms out of terms not opposed before the argument. Hence the antithesis is a primary stylistic tool for a whole host of arguments whose purpose is to force a pair of terms into opposition.

In the late seventeenth century, Pascal, who distrusted this potential in the figure, compared this process to architectural *trompe l'oiel*: "Those who make antitheses by forcing words are like those who make false windows for symmetry. Their rule is not to speak accurately, but to make apt figures of speech" (Pascal, 1952, 175). The false window added for the sake of symmetry to a façade corresponds to a place-holding word that completes the figure, even though it would not be recognized by an audience beforehand as the opposite of its partner. Aristotle also noticed these false antitheses *(pseudeis antitheseis)* briefly, giving as an example a line from the poet Epicharmus: "Sometimes I was in their house, sometimes I was with them" (3.9.10). To be in someone's house and to be with them are usually synonymous notions, but the syntactic shaping into paired *cola* here encourages a construal of these phrases as opposed or mutually exclusive. In the case of this example, the audience is invited to interpret the author's intention as humorous.

But what is humorous here is very deadly in the use of antitheses to construct other entities such as peoples or nations into opposition. In the *History of the Peloponnesian War*, Thucydides provides an example of this process in his reconstruction of the speech of the Corinthians that incited the Spartans to go to war with Athens. The Corinthians use existing semantic oppositions as wedges, hammered in by successive predications, to create opposites of terms that did not previously exist as opposites in the language:

> Then also we think we have as much right as anyone else to point out faults in our neighbours, especially when we consider the enormous difference between you [the Spartans] and the Athenians. To our minds, you are quite unaware of this difference; you have never yet tried to imagine what sort of people these Athenians are against whom you will have to fight—how much, indeed how completely different from you. An Athenian is always an innovator, quick to form a resolution and quick at carrying it out. You, on the other hand, are good at keeping things as they are; you never originate an idea, and your action tends to stop short of its aim. . . . Think of this, too; while

> you are hanging back, they never hesitate; while you stay at home, they are always abroad; for they think that the further they go the more they will get, while you think that any movement may endanger what you have already. (Thucydides, 1954, 75–76)

Following this passage of immediate contrasts between Athenian and Spartan qualities, Thucydides places a long passage on the Athenians and then a long contradictory passage on the Spartans, the contrast continued though without the figure. When the Corinthians were done, they succeeded in sparking ethnic hatred and thirty years of war, and the two cities, Athens and Sparta, remain fixed in historical commonplace as opposites. As Aristotle warned, efficient formal presentation can lead an audience to draw false or at least dangerous inferences.

The Opposite Fates of Antithesis and Metaphor

Considering Aristotle's three sources of *asteia* as a group, focusing on what they have in common helps to reveal their function, their nature as devices that produce quick learning. Indeed the functional nature of energeia is impossible to ignore, since it can only be defined by its effect, bringing before the eyes. Trying to keep antithesis and metaphor together would also suggest Aristotle's functional theory of forms, but of course these two have long since parted ways. Most students of language and literature are thoroughly familiar with metaphor, but they are not likely to be able to recognize let alone define an antithesis. Why, given their similar status in the *Rhetoric,* does metaphor survive and acquire extraordinary conceptual dominance in the twentieth century, as John Kirby (1997) amply demonstrates, becoming for some scholars, especially the French and Belgian structuralists, nothing less than the single locus of all "rhetorical" activity? And why has antithesis been eclipsed? These questions could be treated separately by tracing the separate histories of these devices in rhetorical manuals across the centuries, but they can also be treated as two versions of the same question.

To treat them as versions of the same question requires remembering that the *Rhetoric,* where we find them nominated together as sources of *asteia,* is in many ways a balancing act between the advice on constructing arguments offered in the *Topics* and the observations on emotionally effective language in the *Poetics*. Metaphor, of course, is discussed extensively in the *Poetics*, and Aristotle even refers to this discussion in his treatment of metaphor in the *Rhetoric*. As metaphor is crucial to the *Poetics,* antithesis—the verbal epitome of a topical device—is crucial to the *Topics*, Aristotle's manual for arguers. Metaphor, however, is specifically banished from the *Topics* for interfering with correct dialectical procedure. In Book 6, concerning ways to demolish definitions, Aristotle cites the incorrectness of obscure language of which metaphor is one source:

> Another rule is to see if he has used a metaphorical expression [in constructing a definition], as, for instance, if he has defined knowl-

> edge as unsupplantable, or the earth as a nurse, or temperance as a harmony. For a metaphorical expression is always obscure. It is possible, also, to argue captiously against the user of a metaphorical expression as though he had used it in its literal sense; for the definition stated will not apply. (139b)

In Book 4 of the *Topics,* he points to the fallibility of a metaphorical genus, using the same example of classifying temperance as harmony, "for a genus is always predicated of its species in its literal sense, whereas harmony is predicated of temperance not in a literal sense but metaphorically; for a harmony always consists in notes" (123a; see also 154a).

While the detection of metaphor can be a point of attack in a dialectical contest, there is a reciprocal tradition of excluding antithesis from texts whose purpose is communicating emotion. In Book 9 of the *Institutio Oratoria,* when Quintilian concludes his discussion of the figures of speech (which would currently be called schemes) with advice about choosing figures appropriate to the time, place, and character of each occasion for speaking, he warns: "When terror, hatred and pity are the weapons called for in the fray, who will endure the orator who expresses his anger, his sorrow or his entreaties in neat antitheses [contrapositis], balanced cadences and exact correspondences? Too much care for our words under such circumstances weakens the impression of emotional sincerity, and wherever the orator displays his art unveiled, the hearer says, 'The truth is not in him'" (3:505–7). This caution against the coldness and impression of calculation in a too-balanced style has a long life in the rhetorical tradition.[9] Demetrius gives the same admonition in *On Style*, pointing out the dangers of overdetermined figures before the rhetorically trained audiences of antiquity. When speakers use too many predictable periods, Demetrius warns that listeners are apt to ". . . loudly declaim the endings of the periods which they foresee and forestall" (Demetrius, 1927, 309). Sixteen hundred years later, George Campbell repeats this same stricture, and exaggerates it almost to the point of absurdity: "The antithesis, it is thought, is particularly unfavorable to persuasion, and therefore quite unfit for the more vehement and argumentative parts of a discourse" (Campbell, 1963, 377).[10] An orator like Frederick Douglass, who learned his figure-making power from a Ciceronian manual, *The Columbian Orator*, and who wrote in impassioned antitheses ("You are loosed from your moorings, and are free; I am fast in my chains, and am a slave!" [Douglass, 1988, 96]), would have been amazed by such an observation.

Given the scholarly attention that Aristotle's *Poetics* has received and, at least since the seventeenth century and until recently, the relative lack of interest in the *Topics*, it is not surprising that metaphor has been elevated and antithesis ignored. The presumption, long since institutionalized, of privileging so-called "literary" uses of language has also contributed to the fixation on metaphor and the obscurity of antithesis. Even logicians, preferring demonstration over probable argument, have ignored antithesis and the peculiarly "figural logic" of the *Topics*. Yet the brilliance of Aristotle's *Rhetoric* is that it has a place for both antithesis and metaphor, and indeed for any other functionally powerful form. Later commentators on the figures exaggerated the differences between these two as vehicles of opposite effects, one poetic, the other logical. But the *Rhetoric* banishes neither, since actual rhetorical discourse uses both. Thus rhetoric is, as Kennedy justly observes, "the more all-inclusive phenomenon . . . better regarded as the archdiscipline of which dialectic and poetics are smaller, more limited parts" (Kennedy, 1991, 312).

Notes

1. The term *prototype* is being used in the sense that contemporary cognitive linguists give it when explaining semantic categories as families of members that resemble, more or less, a prototypical or exemplary member. Thus the most birdlike of birds for most North Americans is the robin; other birds are relative approximations, and the set as a whole has a fuzzy boundary (see Sweetser, 1990, 16–17).

2. Modern linguistics is frequently divided into five subdisciplines: phonology, morphology, semantics, syntax, and pragmatics. It would be possible to push a division of the figures among these five, relegating onomatopoeia and perhaps other sound elevating devices to phonology and placing the metaplasms (involving letter morphing within a word) in a "morphological" category of figures. But no obvious insight would be gained from such compulsive partitioning. It is also worth remembering that the still dominant school in linguistics, Chomskyan generative linguistics, pays no attention to figurative language.

3. It is unlikely that Aristotle would have recognized a category of devices under the misleading designation "figures of thought" in contrast to a category based on words. In *Sophistical Refutations* he seems to reject, at least strategically, a word/thought dissociation. "It is no true distinction between arguments which some people draw when they say that some arguments are directed against the word, and others against the thought; for it is absurd to suppose that some arguments are directed against the word and others against the thought, and that they are not the same" (170b). Aristotle has in mind the problems that arise when two debaters are dealing with a word that has several possible meanings.

4. The vexed exception here is of course the case of catachresis (in one of its senses), where a word is not imported to replace a literal term because there is no literal term. In the nineteenth century, Pierre Fontanier solved the "problem" of catachresis by conceding that it was a trope but denying that it was a figure, since no substitution was involved. Fontanier thus fortified the grand division between the literal and the figurative.

5. The original Greek text printed in the Loeb Classics edition is as follows: *"enantiôi enantion sunkeitai à tauto epezeuktai tois enantiois"* (Freese, 1926, 390).

6. Barnes's phrasing here provides an excellent example of asyndeton (with ploche), accomplishing the goal of making one thing seem many.

7. Twentieth-century semanticists distinguish six types of antonymy or opposition: "1. Contradictory terms (perfect/imperfect); 2. Contrary terms (white/black); 3. Reverse terms (constructive/destructive); 4. Contrasted terms (rich/destitute); 5. Relative terms (brother/sister); 6. Complementary terms (question/answer)" (Miller, 1991, 197). The contrary, contrasted, and reverse terms in this list can all, from the perspective of dialectic, be treated as contraries. Furthermore, the kind of opposition that Aristotle terms possession and privation, like blindness and sight, seems indistinguishable from the kind of opposition we find between contraries, and indeed these pairs behave like contraries in premise formation.

8. For an ethical position based on paradoxically maintaining contrary single antitheses, see Matthew 5:43–44: "You have heard that it was said, 'You shall love your neighbor and hate your enemy.' But I say to you, Love your enemies and pray for those who persecute you."

9. See also Cicero's complaint in his *Brutus*, against the Atticist Hegesias: "But where will you find anything so broken, so minced, anything so puerile as that balance and antithesis which he cultivated?" (Cicero, 1988).

10. Campbell's dismissal of the ability of antithetical phrasing to convey passion comes in part from the fact that he has a somewhat different definition of the figure. For Campbell, an antithesis is any pair of balanced or parallel *cola,* with or without opposed *lexis* (see Campbell, 1963, 372–73).

11

Aristotle's *Rhetoric:* A Guide to the Scholarship

Arthur E. Walzer, Michael Tiffany, and Alan G. Gross

This guide to the scholarship is intended for students beginning a systematic study of Aristotle's *Rhetoric.* It divides the eighty-five books and articles reviewed into three broad groups: those dealing with the text of the *Rhetoric,* those concerned with its political and intellectual contexts, and those that discuss the meaning of important concepts within the treatise.

As our title states, this essay is a guide intended to help students beginning their systematic study of the *Rhetoric.* This guide is also a taxonomy, and taxonomies are never neutral. Our scheme seems to have favored articles over books, probably because articles, with singleness of purpose, fit more easily into the boxes and the boxes within boxes of our system. Certainly, George A. Kennedy's (1963) discussion of the *Rhetoric* and the book-length treatments of it by William M. A. Grimaldi (1972), Larry Arnhart (1981), Thomas Farrell (1993), and Eugene Garver (1994b) deserve more than the passing mention that they receive. We have also favored recent over older work. This seems reasonable, but perhaps it has given undue prominence to two recent collections of work by philosophers: *Aristotle's "Rhetoric": Philosophical Essays,* edited by David J. Furley and Alexander Nehamas (1994); and *Essays on Aristotle's "Rhetoric,"* edited by Amélie Oksenberg Rorty (1996).

Our scheme has three basic parts—text, context, and concepts—as well as a note on the uses of the *Rhetoric* in composition. The first part, "Text," reviews available editions, translations, and basic references and discusses the problem of the apparent lack of unity in the *Rhetoric.* The second section considers work on the rhetorical, political, theoretical, canonical, and intellectual contexts of the *Rhetoric.* The motivation for much of the work reviewed in this section is to address the alleged disunity discussed in the first section. The third part takes up work on key concepts: the proofs *(pisteis),* the enthymeme, the example *(paradeigma),* the topics *(topoi),* and style *(lexis),* especially metaphor.

Text: Editions, Translations, Basic References

The best edition of the Greek text is Rudolf Kassel, *Aristotelis "Ars Rhetorica"*

(1976). There are two recent English translations: George A. Kennedy, *Aristotle on Rhetoric: A Theory of Civic Discourse* (1991) and H. C. Lawson-Tancred, *The Art of Rhetoric* (1991). There is general agreement among the contributors to this volume that the Kennedy translation is to be preferred, in part because of its helpful notes, its appendices, and its Greek glossary. The Freese translation (Loeb Library edition, 1926) is satisfactory also and has the advantage of having the Greek on the facing page, though the edition relied on, the Bekker, is outdated. The Rhys Roberts is also reliable, especially as reprinted in Barnes (1984) with corrections. The popular anthology of Bizzell and Herzberg (1990) prints excerpts from Rhys Roberts in its original form.

Since the text is so problematic, it is important to know its history. This may be surveyed in the thorough, lavishly illustrated and readable *A History of Aristotle's "Rhetoric" with a Bibliography of Early Printings* (1989) by Paul Brandes. A very readable account of the transmission of Greek manuscripts is L. D. Reynolds and N. G. Wilson, *Scribes and Scholars: A Guide to the Transmission of Greek and Latin Literature* (1991). It is not usually realized that the earliest manuscript of the *Rhetoric* postdates its composition by well over a thousand years.

Citations of the *Rhetoric* and other works by Aristotle are conventionally referenced by "Bekker numbers," for example, the opening line of the *Rhetoric* is 1354a. As Brandes explains, Immanuel Bekker (1785–1871) selected from the four hundred or more manuscripts he examined, the one hundred he judged most reliable, and collated these into a two-volume Greek text that was published in 1831. In addition to numbering the pages of this text, Bekker divided each page into columns. Thus, 1354a refers to page 1354, left column, of Bekker's two-volume edition of Aristotle's works (Brandes, 162–63). The number that sometimes follows a reference, for example, 1354a10, refers to the line number within the column. Even though Bekker's text is no longer considered the most authoritative (it has been superseded by Kassel's), his referencing system remains the standard one.

For information on ancient Greek texts, students should refer to the *Thesaurus Linguae Graecae: Canon of Greek Authors and Works,* edited by Luci Berkowitz and Karl A. Squitier (1990). This is familiarly known as *"TLG."* The best Greek dictionary is Henry George Liddell, Robert Scott, and Henry Stuart Jones, *A Greek-English Lexicon* (1968). This is familiarly known as *"LSJ."*

The Greek text of all of Aristotle, as well as most of ancient Greek literature, is available on the World Wide Web, thanks to the efforts of the Perseus Project (http://medusa.perseus.tufts.edu/). This site contains a comprehensive digital library that, as stated on the home page, contains texts, art and archaeology, secondary sources, and searching tools. Texts may be read in the Greek or in English translations, and many Latin translations of the Greek are also available. In addition, the texts contain links to various text tools, including morphological analysis of any given word; direct access from any given word to its entry in the Liddell, Scott, and Jones lexicon; citations of the frequency of any given word in other authors, with links to these locations; and Greek word searches. English translations of Aristotle's works, as well as those of others, are also available from the

Internet Classics Archive (http://classics.mit.edu/index.html), the Library of Congress Greek and Latin Classics Texts (http://lcweb.loc.gov/global/classics/clastexts.html), and Liberty Online (http://libertyonline.hypermall.com/Aristotle/index.html).

There are two excellent commentaries in English on the *Rhetoric*, that of Cope and Sandys on all three books (1877) and that of Grimaldi on the first two (1980; 1988). A recent collection in the Landmark Series, edited by Richard Leo Enos and Lois Peters Agnew (1998), reprints important essays on the *Rhetoric*, and a collection edited by Keith V. Erickson (1974), though now dated, provides convenient access to essays that are still valuable.

Because Aristotle is a systematic philosopher, acquaintance with at least some of his other works is requisite to understanding the *Rhetoric*. Two excellent guides to his philosophy are *Aristotle* by David Ross (1923) and *The Cambridge Companion to Aristotle* (1995) edited by Jonathan Barnes. There is also an excellent series of collections edited by Jonathan Barnes, Malcolm Schofield, and Richard Sorabji, of which *Articles on Aristotle: 1. Science* (1975) is a representative example.

For secondary work done on the *Rhetoric* by scholars in rhetoric and speech communication, consult the *Communication Index*, which is available also on compact disk (as *Comm Search*). For work in classics, several sources are currently available on the Internet. "Tables of Contents of Journals of Interest to Classicists" (TOCS-IN), provides tables of contents to more than 150 journals in classics (http://www.chass.utoronto.ca:8080/amphoras/tocs.html). The archive is divided according to subject and is searchable by key word. Gnomon also provides a large database (http://www.gnomon.ku-eichstaett.de/Gnomon/note_e.html). The Bryn Mawr Classical Review, or BMCR, contains several hundred book reviews, beginning in 1990, that are also searchable by key word according to text, author, or title (http://www.hti.umich.edu/b/bmr/bmcr.html). Finally, the Penn Library is a useful site that provides links to important classics links and journals, including TAPA (Transactions of the American Philological Association), BMCR, TOCS-IN, SCHOLAR (a site that provides text analysis), and others. Another link in the Penn Library is to Project Muse, which contains a search engine for listings in journals besides classics, such as the social sciences and mathematics (http://www.library.upenn.edu/resources/ej/ej-classics.html). It also provides a link to *Arethusa,* a classics journal now available on line.

Contexts: Rhetorical and Political, Theoretical, Canonical, Intellectual

If the *Rhetoric* is informed by a single, unifying conception of rhetoric, scholars do not agree on what that is. In parts of the text, especially the first chapter, Aristotle seems intent on treating rhetoric philosophically as an alternative to a competing handbook tradition. But subsequent sections, especially Book 3, read like a handbook, and a handbook that does not scruple to censor deceptive persuasive tactics. As George Kennedy writes, "There is thus present in the text as a whole a kind of dialogue in Aristotle's mind between two views of rhetoric, one making strong moral and logical demands on the speaker, one looking more toward success in debate" (xi).

Contemporary scholars express impatience with the explanation an earlier generation offered for the disharmony in the text, efforts that are reviewed by William M. A. Grimaldi (1972, 28–35). Friedrich Solmsen (1929) attributed the fissures to the circumstances of the *Rhetoric*'s composition as lectures created and delivered over an extended period of time. According to this explanation, the idealistic sections were written earlier, while Aristotle was under the influence of the Academy; the tactical, amoral sections were written later. The text reflects the evolution of Aristotle's views. But, as Glenn Most asks, "If Aristotle changed his mind, why did he not change his text?" (1994, 188). Not all find the conditions of the text's composition a sufficient explanation. We read Aristotle to experience an intellect of the greatest integrity: Shouldn't we make every effort to find unity in the *Rhetoric*?

Studies that seek to identify a coherent, Aristotelian view of rhetoric often do so by placing the text within one of the following frames: the political and rhetorical frame provided by reflecting on the particular context in which the *Rhetoric* was written; the theoretical frame provided by Aristotle's taxonomy of knowledge; the canonical frame provided by Aristotle's other works; and the intellectual frame provided by seeing the *Rhetoric* in dialogue with Plato, the Sophists, and Isocrates.

Those who wish to read the studies we review with a more critical eye might consult Michael Leff and Carol Poster. Leff (1993) perceptively reviews work on the "meta-theoretical" issues that have occupied American scholarship on the *Rhetoric*. Poster (1997) faults Anglo-American interpreters generally for assuming an "unproblematic hermeneutic" (221) that results in their insufficiently foregrounding the interpretative issues that confront any interpreter of ancient texts.

Rhetorical and Political Contexts

Two important contexts in which the *Rhetoric* ought to be placed are the rhetorical and the political. Josiah Ober places it in a political context in his *Mass and Elite in Democratic Athens* (1989). George Kennedy places it in a rhetorical context in *The Art of Persuasion in Ancient Greece* (1963).

The *locus classicus* of the argument that the *Rhetoric* is unified if seen as a handbook, but a handbook for elite politicians, is Carnes Lord's "The Intention of Aristotle's 'Rhetoric'" (1981). Lord maintains that Aristotle, consistent with Plato, believes that rhetoric is not an autonomous art or science but is subordinate to the goals of the city-state, potentially an instrument of responsible and prudent statesmanship. The *Rhetoric*'s purpose is to provide motive and means for the political elite to communicate to the masses. Aristotle hopes to transform the concept of rhetoric for "political men," to make it clearly subordinate to a philosophical politics, and thus to offer an alternative to an Isocratean tradition that equates rhetoric and politics. Aristotle's intention is to make rhetoric a practical instrument for political idealism. Jürgen Sprute (1994) maintains similarly that the seeming discrepancies between the ideals of the first chapter and the amorality of

Book 3 result from Aristotle's recognition that to be successful in the political arena ideals would have to be compromised.

Finally, a similar approach is taken and similar conclusion reached by Glenn Most (1994). Most argues that Aristotle intends to produce a handbook for the philosophical-minded who were contemplating political careers. *Rhetoric* 1.1 seeks to make rhetoric respectable to this philosophically minded audience; Book 3 is an effort to provide them with the handbook of tactics they need to succeed in the political arena.

Bernard E. Jacob (1996) explains the seeming differences in the first two chapters by understanding them rhetorically—that is, as having a strategic, audience-centered purpose. Jacob argues that in chapter 1, Aristotle offers a polemic on behalf of an exaggeratedly austere view of rhetoric in order to expose the absurdity of this extreme. He hopes thus to make an audience resistant to rhetoric open to his own new, reasonable conception of the art, a view that occupied a middle ground between the excesses of austerity and the trickery of the handbooks. A different approach that also centers on Aristotle's audience is taken by James A. Berlin (1992), who, by focusing on the specific economic, political, and social conditions in which the *Rhetoric* was written, attempts to explain the fissures in the text as Aristotle's efforts to placate defenders both of oligarchy and democracy.

An older account, Jacqueline de Romilly's provocative *Magic and Rhetoric in Ancient Greece* (1975), offers an unusual rhetorical context as an explanation of Aristotle's intentions in the *Rhetoric*. De Romilly traces the history of rhetoric from Gorgias to Aristotle with respect to the Greek understanding of magic. According to de Romilly, Gorgias recognized magic and rhetoric as *tekhnai,* as rational activities, subject to intellectual manipulation. To Plato, this amalgamation and transformation represents a danger to the state, given the part played by rhetoric in politics during the last thirty years of the fifth century, and so he reduced rhetoric to a "knack." In contrast, Aristotle's aim is parallel to that of Gorgias: to elevate rhetoric to a *tekhnê* but his task is to rescue it by separating it once and for all from its sophistic commitments to magic and the irrational.

Theoretical Context

As Kennedy observes, Aristotle divides intellectual activity into three basic types: theoretical studies, which, like the sciences, eventuate in knowing; practical arts, that is, politics or ethics, which eventuate in acting well or choosing wisely; and productive arts, such as crafts or medicine, which bring some thing or state into being, such as a poem or health (*Rhet.* 12). Although there would appear to be value in defining rhetoric as a single type of intellectual activity, that it is a hybrid of two or three types receives support from formidable scholars, including not only Kennedy but also Richard McKeon (1971) and Michael Leff (1993).

The studies reviewed in this section assume that placing the *Rhetoric* within Aristotle's taxonomy of knowledge will help in identifying its intentions. But which type or combination of types is characteristic of rhetoric as a discipline as Aristotle understood it is itself a question of dispute. For those in rhetoric, Barbara

Warnick (1989) provides a good introduction to Aristotle's theory of knowledge. Warnick reviews Aristotle's philosophy of knowledge, identifying rhetoric as a productive art, a *tekhnê*. She maintains that as a *tekhnê*, rhetoric can lead to virtuous outcomes only under the guidance of another mode of judgment, *phronêsis.*

As does Warnick, others who emphasize Aristotle's classification of rhetoric as *tekhnê* tend to construe the *Rhetoric* narrowly, to see the *Rhetoric* as providing a set of morally neutral techniques available to speakers. To Forbes Hill (1981) and Troels Engberg-Pedersen (1996), the *Rhetoric* is a technical, not a substantive, work. The *Rhetoric* is a handbook, asserts Hill, in an essay that directly contests Lois Self's essay (discussed below). It is a methodological art, useful for generating arguments on either side of any question, but subordinate to the substantive art of politics. As such, the *Rhetoric* "must be morally neutral" (141). Engberg-Pedersen, while accepting the *Rhetoric* as intrinsically morally neutral, argues that Aristotle understood rhetoric as situated within contexts that make rhetoric an art with a bias toward "truth-discovery" (127).

Joseph Dunne provides a masterly discussion of the relationship of *phronêsis* and *tekhnê* in his *Back to the Rough Ground* (1993). That rhetoric is a *tekhnê*, not a *phronêsis*, is part of the burden of the book's eighth chapter, "Theory, *Technê*, and *Phronêsis.*" This view is consistent with Oded Balaban's (1986). Balaban maintains that as a *tekhnê*, rhetoric is a *poêsis*, a form of activity that is a means to an end, not a *praxis*, which is a form of activity that is an end in itself. Jan Edward Garrett (1987) explores the implications of the relationship between the *tekhnê* of rhetoric and the master art of statecraft. For Garrett, Aristotle's *tekhnê* is always a disposition linked to the truth and a cause of perfection in objects in which human effort is implicated. In *Rhetoric Reclaimed: Aristotle and the Liberal Arts Tradition* (1998), Janet M. Atwill maintains that Aristotle conceptualized rhetoric as a productive art (a *poêsis* and a *technê*). But she insists that in doing so, Aristotle did not intend to limit rhetoric to a managerial or instrumental role. She examines the connotations of *"technê"* in Greek mythology and in Protagoras and Isocrates to identify a tradition that understands rhetoric as a contingent art of invention and intervention, a tradition that she claims survives in the *Rhetoric.*

Other scholars have seen Aristotle's view of rhetoric as sharing much with his understanding of *phronêsis* or practical wisdom. These scholars tend to see the *Rhetoric* as an art intended to guide the city-state in rational and ethical directions. There is no question that Aristotle wanted to move the state in those directions; the question is only whether he saw rhetoric as a vehicle enabling that movement. The broader construal of Aristotelian rhetoric raises the status of the *Rhetoric* as a philosophical work in the Aristotelian corpus, one more nearly central to the achievement of Aristotle's political goals.

Lois Self (1979) sees the *Rhetoric* as necessarily fostering the ends of Aristotle's ethics. Self argues that the qualities of mind that the *Nicomachean Ethics* associates with practical wisdom share significant similarities with the qualities required of an effective rhetorician. Christopher Lyle Johnstone (1980) goes even further.

For him, Aristotle conceived of rhetoric as necessary for both the practice of virtue and for the type of deliberation that characterized the ideal state.

Two recent works that follow in this direction are Thomas B. Farrell, *Norms of Rhetorical Culture* (1993), and Eugene Garver, *Aristotle's "Rhetoric": An Art of Character* (1994b). The first links rhetoric closely to *praxis;* the second construes the *Rhetoric* as a philosophical work focused on *phronêsis.* Grimaldi's earlier reading along these lines, *Studies in the Philosophy of Aristotle's "Rhetoric"* (1972), has been influential; its interpretation has in part been challenged by James Kinneavy (1987).

Canonical Context

At various points in the *Rhetoric,* Aristotle compares rhetoric to other arts, most frequently and notably to dialectic and politics. The famous opening line of the rhetoric characterizes rhetoric as the "counterpart *[antistrophos]*" to dialectic; an equally famous comparison at 1.2.7 defines rhetoric as "a certain kind of offshoot *[paraphues]* of dialectic and of ethical studies (which it is just to call politics)." Exactly what Aristotle intends by these comparisons is not clear. The work reviewed in this section attempts to probe the relationship of rhetoric to other arts within the Aristotelian corpus in an effort to understand the nature of rhetoric as Aristotle understood it.

Discussions of the relationship between rhetoric and dialectic have a long history, one surveyed by Lawrence Green (1990). According to Green, by the Renaissance, all the basic positions were articulated so that scholarship since then "has done little more than choose sides" (6). Alexander of Aphrodisias, a philosopher of the Peripatetic school, maintained that in Book 1 Aristotle meant to draw attention to the following similarities between dialectic and rhetoric: Neither has a specific subject matter, and both deal in questions where probable truth is the highest standard. The arts differ in these ways: Dialectic proceeds by question and answer to a generalizable conclusion; rhetoric is often monologic and seeks answers to particular questions. Within the Arabic tradition, Averroes identified as the most salient difference that while both dialectic and rhetoric deal with contrary positions, the purpose of dialectic is to destroy one of them, while rhetoric tries to keep both in sight. Finally within the Scholastic tradition, Giles of Rome maintained that rhetoric appealed to the passions (as well as reason), and dealt with particular moral matters for unsophisticated audiences, while dialectic appealed only to reason and concerned itself with universal speculation among subtle auditors.

Two recent articles take the famous opening line as an invitation to compare Aristotle's *Rhetoric* with the *Topics.* Jacques Brunschwig (1996) emphasizes the difference in the methods of *Rhetoric* and the *Topics.* Brunschwig identifies an historical method in the *Rhetoric,* where Aristotle corrects and exploits previous work, while in the *Topics* he approaches the subject theoretically and ahistorically (understandably since Aristotle claimed to be the originator of much of the art). By contrast, Robert Wardy (1996) emphasizes the similarity between rhetoric and dialectic in an essay that addresses the problem of the moral ambiguity of *Rhetoric*. If Aristotle's interest in truth in Book 1 of the *Rhetoric* seems to disappear behind an interest in tactics and victory in Book 3, a similar tension characterizes the *Topics*, according to Wardy, who offers a catalog of "fishy" eristic techniques from the *Topics* to match the questionable ones in the *Rhetoric*. Wardy insists that his intention is not to debase the *Topics* but to show a common inferential process in both works. To conclude from the presence of questionable tactics that the *Rhetoric* is either an inconsistent or amoral text is invalid, he claims.

Sally Raphael (1974) argues that we should read Aristotle's opening comparison rhetorically, that he meant only to evoke the *Gorgias*, where rhetoric is said to be the counterpart of cookery, not to make a profound point. Ultimately, Aristotle was victim to his own dramatic, rhetorical effort, for it led him to a detailed comparison between rhetoric and dialectic that will not stand up to philosophic scrutiny.

A number of studies compare the nature of knowledge in the *Rhetoric* and in the *Politics*, often to rehabilitate our understanding of rhetorical knowledge. From the point of view of the student of rhetoric, the studies are most valuable for their probing definitions of *endoxa*, the common beliefs of a culture that form the basis for rhetorical proofs. John M. Cooper (1994) claims that since *endoxa* are the basis for first principles in dialectic, rhetoric is a distinct and independent art; the rhetorician is in a position to see the truth. C. D. C. Reeve (1996) too would correct any view that limited *endoxa* to the uncontested half-truths that characterize a general "knowledge" of a subject. *Endoxa* include, he insists, those philosophical views that contest unexamined ones, including Socrates' and Plato's. Finally, Stephen Halliwell (1996) offers a nuanced description of a middle ground between Isocrates and Plato's view of the relationship between first principles and *endoxa*, a middle ground on which he locates Aristotle.

Intellectual Context

Many have seen the opening comparison of rhetoric to dialectic less as a comment on the relationship of the two arts than as an effort to initiate a discussion with Plato, who had, in the *Gorgias*, contrasted rhetoric and dialectic. But even those who agree that Aristotle engages Plato in the treatise do not necessarily agree on the extent to which Aristotle follows or departs from the views of his teacher or how close or distant he is from the competing views of the Sophists and Isocrates. The studies reviewed in this section argue or assume that a distinctive, consistent Aristotelian position becomes visible when the *Rhetoric* is placed against the backdrop of the theories that it evokes.

On Aristotle's relationship to Plato, Everett Lee Hunt and William Grimaldi offer sharply contrasting assessments. Hunt's early "Plato and Aristotle on Rhetoric and Rhetoricians" (1961) argues that Aristotle is closer to the Sophists than to

Plato, while Grimaldi's *Studies in Aristotle's "Rhetoric"* (1972) holds that the *Rhetoric* fulfills the ideal Plato called for in the *Phaedrus*.

Among recent discussions, Eckart Schütrumpf (1994) reads the *Rhetoric* as a dialogue with Plato but places less emphasis on the *Phaedrus* and *Gorgias* than on the *Laws*, where he finds a frame of reference that explains the "austere view" of the first chapter. Carol Poster (1997) points out that in Antiquity, Aristotle's views were assumed to be much closer to Plato's than they are today, an assumption that she maintains should bear on our interpretations of the *Rhetoric*. Furthermore, from the little we know of Aristotle's views on rhetoric in his published work, for example, from *Gryllus* (which has not survived), his views seem consonant with Plato's. Reading the *Rhetoric* under the influence of this assumption, Poster argues that Aristotle's presentation in the *Rhetoric* is of an art made necessary by a political system that invests too much authority in people too ignorant to appreciate or to partake in dialectic. Mary Margaret McCabe (1994) depicts a less committed Aristotle, maintaining the *Rhetoric* is Aristotle's effort to establish a subtle line between the opposed views on rhetoric of Isocrates and Plato. This perspective, she claims, brings into focus the basic coherence of the Aristotelian view. Her detailed reading centers on her contentions that Aristotle holds, against Plato, that rhetoric is an art and, against Isocrates, that rhetoric is a limited, highly contextualized art. Her conclusions are not dissimilar from John T. Gage's earlier reading (1984) in the context of composition pedagogy.

Articles on "dialectical rhetoric" and "rhetorical rhetoric" seem, indirectly, to reflect the same tension between the "Sophistic" and "Platonic" Aristotles. The terms "dialectical rhetoric" and "rhetorical rhetoric" are Carl Holmberg's (1977). He contrasts a "dialectical rhetoric" descended from Plato with Aristotle's "rhetorical rhetoric." The goal of rhetorical rhetoric (i.e., Aristotle's) is not persuasion in the name of truth or, indeed, persuasion at all. According to Holmberg, the goal is to make the audience aware of the different views of reality that others hold and to bring the audience to see how these views are alike and viable. But Robert Gaines (1986) argues that Holmberg's interpretation depends on a mistranslation of crucial lines, that the radical discontinuity that Holmberg alleges is not in the text. Gaines argues that Holmberg ignores Aristotle's overt efforts to align rhetoric with dialectic. Scott Consigny (1989) maintains that both of these perspectives are limited, that Aristotle in fact presents a third view—a rhetoric that enables the rhetor to discern the persuasive elements, while remaining free of ontological commitments.

Concepts

Pisteis: The Modes of Persuasion or Proof

In Book 1, chapter 2, of the *Rhetoric,* Aristotle identifies three modes of "artistic" proof *(pistis): êthos* (character), "*pathos*" (emotion), *logos* (reason). His inclusion of *êthos* and *pathos* in this second chapter has been the cause of some consternation, since, in the previous chapter (1.1), Aristotle expressed suspicions toward appeals to the judge and proposed limiting rhetoric to logical argument. Subsequent sections seem consistent with 1.2: In most of the *Rhetoric,* Aristotle treats both *êthos* and *pathos* as legitimate parts of the art. While there is general agreement that appeals from character originate in the speaker, that appeals to emotion originate in the audience, and that appeals to logos originate in the argument itself, the seeming inconsistency in Aristotle's attitude has led scholars, in Kennedy's words, to "seek to force the point of view of chapter 1 into conformity with what follows by making very careful distinctions about what Aristotle is saying" (*Rhetoric* 27). Many of the studies reviewed in this section probe each of the three types of artistic proof, assuming that our understanding of the relationship among the three will benefit from a deeper understanding of each. The discussion operates largely in the realm of philosophical psychology, where, despite areas of overlap, inquiries into *êthos* tend to highlight the significance of *phronêsis*, those about *pathos* to concentrate on elements of cognition, while those on *logos* consider whether the centrality of the enthymeme may mean that Aristotle thought of it as the vehicle for all three appeals—emotional and ethical as well as logical.

Êthos. Aristotle describes *êthos* as a tripartite complex consisting of *phronêsis* (practical wisdom), *aretê* (moral virtue), and *eunoia* (good will). Scholarship about the nature of *êthos* relies on joint philological and philosophical analyses. Principal areas of disagreement surround not so much what *êthos* is as whether argument grounded in character, broadly conceived, was seen by Aristotle as moral or amoral. The specific areas of interest and sometimes of contention are whether Aristotle regards appeals from *êthos* as necessarily arising within the speech only and not as also a function of the audience's previous knowledge of the speaker's character. Aristotle does classify *êthos* as an artistic proof, which would suggest that the speaker has control of it. But if *êthos* is entirely an artistic proof, then does Aristotle understand *êthos* as a rhetorical construct, and, therefore, not necessarily grounded in the rhetor's actual character?

A good introduction to *êthos* is Alan Brinton's "Ēthotic Argument" (1986). Brinton claims that *êthos* is a morally charged term that refers to personal character. He cautions that some speech theorists have confused it with *ethos,* a morally neutral term denoting habit or custom. Arthur B. Miller (1974) presents a contrary view, arguing that Aristotle believes habits lead to character, and so the two terms share "basic consubstantiality" (309). Despite this disagreement, both Brinton and Miller present a related understanding that *êthos* and its three constituents have their origin in the orator, that they are action-oriented, and that *êthos* is applicable wherever arguments have moral importance. Furthermore, both Brinton and Miller identify *phronêsis* in the *Rhetoric* as that element of *êthos* that governs action by directing the selection of choices made voluntarily from one's habits or moral education. In other words, a person's actions testify to the presence or absence of *phronêsis* based upon cultural norms of good and bad.

W. W. Fortenbaugh (1992) pursues this aspect of *phronêsis*. He sees *phronêsis* as an intellectual virtue, as a means-oriented faculty and, because praiseworthy actions arise from it, as a proof of a person's moral virtue *(aretê)*. Fortenbaugh maintains that Aristotle offers an alternative to the handbooks' presentation of *êthos*. Aristotle's paradigmatic case presents an orator as disposing a judge toward a speaker who is virtuous, wise, and well intentioned. At least ideally, *êthos* functions as enabling reasoned judgment, not obstructing it. Fortenbaugh adds that this tripartite view of *êthos* is not original to Aristotle but extends back to Homer. Eckart Schütrumpf (1993) traces more closely the development of this concept in Aristotle's predecessors and finds that what is original with Aristotle is the idea that the orator needs merely to appear to have these qualities.

Schütrumpf's view seems to have more support among scholars: that the Aristotelian orator may present an apparent rather than necessarily real personal *êthos*, one reflecting the specific circumstances of an oration and adapted to them and to the auditors' views. This deliberate and variable "construction" of one's *êthos* has raised the question of whether rhetoric is a sham art, in which neither the message nor the messenger is reliable from one speech to the next. Others defend Aristotle's position by claiming that his presentation of *êthos* as *phronêsis* turns it into a rational principle of judgment in both orator and oratory, whereby past actions guide present deliberations toward the selection of actions good both for the individual and the community. See, for example, the essay by Robert C. Rowland and Deanna F. Womack (1985), as well as the essay by C. Jan Swearingen and the Introduction by James S. Baumlin and Tita French Baumlin, both in *Ethos: New Essays in Rhetorical and Critical Theory* (1994), edited by Baumlin and Baumlin. Articles that bear generally on the moral tenor of the *Rhetoric* that have implications for the understanding of *êthos* include those by Christopher Johnstone (1980), Forbes Hill (1981), and Troels Engberg-Pedersen (1996), discussed earlier.

Pathos. The greatest current area of interest among Aristotle's three artistic proofs is in *pathos*, in part because the discussion in Book 2 is Aristotle's most complete consideration of the emotions from the perspective of philosophical psychology. Scholarly attention has tended to focus on two areas. Those interested generally in Aristotle's philosophy have inquired into whether Aristotle provides a philosophical account of the emotions or whether he, in the *Rhetoric*, offers a popular discussion adequate to the purposes of the practicing rhetorician only. The second issue of importance to scholars is Aristotle's understanding of the nature of the emotions—the extent to which the emotions are linked to cognition, on the one hand, and appetite or desire, on the other. The latter question has implications for our understanding of the morality or amorality of Aristotle's view of rhetoric. For an excellent introduction to both issues, see Martha Craven Nussbaum's knowledgeable and readable "Aristotle on Emotions and Rational Persuasion" (1996).

An earlier tradition regarded Aristotle's presentation of the emotions in the *Rhetoric* as a popular account, based on generally accepted views. This tradition is criticized in W. W. Fortenbaugh's "Aristotle's *Rhetoric* on Emotions" (1970). Three articles in the recent collection edited by Amélie Oksenberg Rorty (1996) have tended to accept and extend Fortenbaugh's critique. John M. Cooper (1996) argues that while rhetoricians do not require a scientist's understanding of the emotions, they do need genuine knowledge in order to affect the emotions of the audience. For Gisela Striker (1996), the rhetorician, like the contemporary lawyer, does not need complete knowledge but does need command of "theory based results" (287). Striker argues that Aristotle turned to the best work produced at the Academy, including most prominently Plato's late dialogue, *Philebus*, for an acceptable account. But because Aristotle relied on existing analyses, his presentation lacks the unified theoretical framework we have come to expect from him. Dorothea Frede (1996) distinguishes between Aristotle's discussions of the emotions within the *Rhetoric*. At some points (e.g., 1.10–15), Aristotle addresses the rhetorician's need to discuss the plausibility of human motivation—the likelihood of a particular set of circumstances eventuating in a particular action. Here, popular knowledge would be sufficient, even preferable. At other points, Aristotle provides a discussion of the emotions in the context of the rhetorician's efforts to actually affect judgment. In these cases, only an accurate account would enable the rhetor to achieve this goal.

Even more attention has been paid to the cognitive aspects within Aristotle's understanding of the emotions. The impetus arose with Friedrich Solmsen's early "Aristotle and Cicero on the Orator's Playing Upon the Feelings" (1938). Solmsen observed that Aristotle broke with the rhetorical tradition by analyzing emotional appeals to the audience not as appropriate only to specific parts of a speech (the introduction and conclusion) but as appearing throughout. Such pervasiveness might indicate that emotional appeals are inherent in (not prior or antecedent to) the enthymemes that comprise the argument.

In *Aristotle on Emotion* (1975), W. W. Fortenbaugh delivers the most comprehensive analysis of *pathê* in Aristotle. Fortenbaugh's primary aim is to establish a cognitive element as the efficient cause in *pathê*, which he calls "practical" (e.g., anger, fear) or "non-practical" (pity, indignation) in proportion to their capacity to invite action and so become generative of moral virtue. Fortenbaugh further takes pains to distinguish emotions from appetites according to the criterion of efficient cause, where appetites are caused by physiological disturbances other than cognition. Much of the most recent scholarship works within the framework Fortenbaugh established. Stephen R. Leighton (1996) agrees with Fortenbaugh's conclusions but not entirely with his argument. His article is helpful for its probing of the different meanings we intend when we say that "emotions affect judgments"—whether, for instance, we mean emotions are prior to and disabling of judgments or constituent of them. Thomas Conley (1982) argues that *pathê* in 2.2–11 are to be understood as elements of a topological reasoning process that functions to generate or dissolve emotions in the audience or as the basis for an analysis of probable cause for a person's actions. Alan Brinton (1988) maintains that Aristotle's *Nicomachean Ethics* connects virtues with passions and actions, and so *pathê* in the *Rhetoric* have legitimate moral and rational significance relative to virtuous and justified action.

An important dissent from Fortenbaugh is Amélie Oksenberg Rorty's "Aristotle on the Metaphysical Status of *Pathê*" (1984). She places Aristotle's classification of temporary, accidental response on a continuum. Stimuli vary from an orator's words that produce an emotion to the hunger that results in a growling stomach. If the affective experience actualizes a potentiality that is part of the person's nature, *pathos* is not said to occur, since the experience is not the cause but only the occasion of a natural condition, she argues. Therefore, the definition and determination of *pathos* varies with the nature of the patient or agent. Rorty does agree with Fortenbaugh, though, that the moral significance of the *pathê* is determined according to the cognitive response of the person experiencing them.

In "The Outmoded Psychology of Aristotle's *Rhetoric*" (1990), Alan Brinton identifies the fundamental issues that divide positivistic detractors from those who have respectful interest in Aristotelian *êthos* and *pathos*. He faults some in speech communication who would dismiss Aristotle's analysis for its failure to meet contemporary, empirical tests. Aristotle's interest in *êthos* and *pathos* is neither metaphysical nor social-scientific, but practical and based on a cognitive view of the emotions, according to Brinton.

Logos. The interpretation of *pathos* as having a cognitive dimension has implications for our understanding of *logos*. Does Aristotle intend us to understand *logos* as manifest through the enthymeme, for instance, as the vehicle or container for appeals to the emotions, or does he intend enthymeme to apply only to subject-oriented argumentative appeals? Is *logos* an umbrella principle or a discreet form of proof? Grimaldi (1972) has urged that we think of *logos* as the whole speech, not as a source of one of the three artistic proofs, which he identifies as *êthos, pathos,* and *pragma* or subject matter (66). More recently, Antoine Braet (1992) provides a discussion of these issues, arguing that the enthymematic form includes appeals from *êthos, pathos,* and *logos.* Other studies helpful to an understanding of *logos* are those concerned with the enthymeme and the example to which we now turn.

Enthymeme and Paradigm: The Means of Persuasion

Aristotle's claim that his attention to the enthymeme differentiates his from rival approaches and his reference to it as the "body of persuasion" (1.3.1) ensured the enthymeme's importance to scholars. This attention has tended to focus on Aristotle's characterization of the enthymeme as a "rhetorical syllogism" (1.2.12–14), as scholars have discussed how the enthymeme differs from the syllogism, a discussion made more complicated with the realization that "syllogism" is itself a contested term.

Work by James A. McBurney (1936), Nancy Harper (1973), and Eugene E. Ryan (1984) are good places to begin work on the enthymeme. McBurney, who contextualizes the enthymeme within the Aristotelian *organon* (his works on logic and method), understands it to differ from the apodictic syllogism less in its length (syllogisms can also suppress a premise) than by the probability of its premises and conclusions. He also argues that Aristotle understands the enthymeme not as a type of logical appeal only but as capable of embodying all three artistic proofs. Ryan's purpose is to address the inadequacies of the discussion of the enthymeme in many standard commentaries, which he reviews. His distinctive method is to resolve the problems by attending especially to the many examples of enthymemes that Aristotle provides as illustrations. His conclusions are that Aristotle features the enthymeme as a way to address the limitations inherent in the rhetorical audience—that enthymemes are appropriate to rhetoric because they are short arguments, based on plausible or probable premises that are related to the concerns of the three types of rhetoric. Aristotle, Ryan maintains, expects that enthymemes would be evaluated on the basis of their persuasiveness, not their formal validity. Nancy Harper also proceeds inductively in comparing illustrative examples of the syllogism and the enthymeme in the *Prior Analytics* as well as the *Rhetoric.*

In an essay that has been most influential in speech communication and composition, Lloyd Bitzer (1959) maintains that the enthymeme can be differentiated from the syllogism neither by its probable nature nor by a truncated form, since Aristotle states that some enthymemes proceed from certain premises and that some syllogisms are truncated. Bitzer maintains that what distinguishes an enthymeme is its psychological effect: The enthymeme implies a premise that the orator has reason to expect the audience will affirm; thus audiences participate in their own persuasion. Though this analysis has been contested by Conley (1984), Bitzer's closing paragraph in which he states that the enthymeme is a joint creation of speaker and audience is often cited in work that argues for a dialogic or interactive interpretation of Aristotle's *Rhetoric*. J. Scenters-Zapico (1994) reflects on "enthymematic understanding" as a site of interactional rhetorical theory and social constructionist epistemology in the *Rhetoric* and elsewhere.

There are other views on the enthymeme. Arthur B. Miller and John D. Bee (1972) draw on etymological arguments and on *De anima* to support their view that the enthymeme has a strong affective element; they maintain that enthymemes are intended not only to convince readers but also to move them to action. Jeffrey Walker (1994) contends that the enthymeme draws its force from its dramatic presentation more than from an overt or implied syllogistic structure. Walker draws on references in other classical writers to support this stylistic interpretation, an interpretation that Conley (1984) had earlier found precedence for in Quintilian. Walker's view would appear to receive support from M. F. Burnyeat (1994), who maintains that *syllogismos* itself did not necessarily evoke for Aristotle the formal structure we today attribute to syllogisms, that our view rests on a corrupt line in the *Posterior Analytics,* and that, in fact, any deductive argument, no matter how brief or valid, is a *syllogismos.*

Carol Poster (1992) traces this history of "multiple incommensurable accounts" (8) of the enthymeme from its use in Homer to its description in modern textbooks. She counsels that we forego the effort to arrive at a consensus among commentators, much less a definitive meaning; instead, we should view "enthymeme" as a site of revelation of cultural attitudes toward rhetoric and language generally. Thomas Conley (1984) regards scholarly preoccupation with the enthymeme as not entirely salutary. The centrality of the enthymeme in the *Rhetoric* has, he maintains, resulted in our overvaluing the importance of argument and logic and in a commensurate neglect of the role that the literary resources of language play in persuasion.

The other method of proof under *logos* within the Aristotelian system is the example or paradigm *(paradeigma)*. It too is a contested concept. The nexus of the debate among scholars is Aristotle's statement that the paradigm "is reasoning neither from part to whole nor from whole to part but from part to part, like to like, when two things fall under the same genus but one is better known than the other" (1.2.19). Interpreters of the *Rhetoric* have not agreed on what Aristotle intends by this statement.

Gerald Hauser (1968; 1985) and Scott Consigny (1975) take Aristotle's insistence that paradigm reasons "from part to part" to mean that readers infer on the basis of two similar cases—in Hauser's terms, that paradigm functions as an "unmediated inference" between two particulars (1968, 88). There can be no implication or inference of a generalization about all or most cases without blurring the distinction between the paradigm and enthymeme (86). In articles responding to Hauser's and Consigny's, William L. Benoit (1980 and 1987) contests this view. Benoit understands Aristotle's reasoning from "part to part" as "shorthand" for from "part to whole to part" (1987, 264). He cites Aristotle's discussion of induction in the *Prior Analytics*, as well as his discussion of the paradigm in the *Rhetoric*, in support of his claim that a mediating generalization is necessary for the paradigm to function argumentatively. James C. Raymond (1984) does not directly enter the debate between Benoit and Hauser and Consigny, though his contribution to our understanding is not lessened for this. Raymond argues that Aristotle expected the hearer to experience a paradigm as an analogic, diachronic pattern. From a series of events of known consequence (examples), the reader infers a pattern that would probably apply to similar events of unknown consequence. Raymond argues that his interpretation helps us to understand Aristotle's (for some, puzzling) remark that paradigms are "most appropriate to deliberative oratory" (3.17.5) because deliberative oratory would often draw on patterns of events from a known past to predict future consequences (147).

The Topics: Rhetoric, Dialectic

There is general agreement that in the *Rhetoric* the topics are means of rhetorical invention and that Aristotle designates two sorts: common and special. Common topics apply to all genres of rhetorical discourse; special topics apply only to specific genres, such as epideictic, or to specific subject matters, such as physics. To use Aristotle's examples, the topic of the more and the less can apply indifferently to epideictic, deliberative, or forensic discourse: "'If not even the gods know everything, human beings can hardly do so.' For this is equivalent to saying, 'If something is not the fact in a case where it would be *more* expected, it is clear that it is not a fact where it would be *less* expected'" (2.23; emphasis added). On the other hand, the topic of justice applies specifically to forensic discourse, where justice is centrally at issue. Even this distinction is not without its confusions, however: Although the special topics of physics are inapplicable to *any* genre of rhetoric, justice *can* be a topic of deliberative or epideictic discourse. There is another problem: It is unclear whether the topics, special or common, are material or formal, that is, whether they belong to the realm of semantics or the realm of syntax, a realm to which formal logic also belongs.

Donovan Ochs (1969) makes a significant contribution to the debate when he argues that the topics in the *Rhetoric* do not constitute a logical *system* of invention, since they leave out such essentials of formal logic as identity and contradiction. This insight also suggests the haphazard nature of Aristotle's rambling lists and, perhaps, our inability to make coherent sense of them in the aggregate. This may be Michael Leff's point when he says that Aristotle's rhetorical *topos* is "a confused notion" (1983, 23).

Ochs is on less sure ground when he argues that the twenty-eight *topoi* in 2.23 are "formal patterns of relationships existing between classes of terms" (422–23). For example, the first of these twenty-eight is an argument from opposites: "If the war is the cause of the present evils, things should be set right by making peace." In this, the formal pattern does not determine the conclusion as it would in the case of a valid syllogism. One could also argue: "Even if the war is the cause of present evils, things cannot be set right by making peace." Clearly, persuasiveness depends on both the formal and the material: *this* war and *this* peace.

What is the difference between the common and special *topoi*? In an important article, Thomas Conley (1978) argues, using terminology from Stephen Toulmin's *The Uses of Argument,* that the difference "is not one of matter *vs.* form but of *relative* degrees of 'field dependence/field invariance'" (97). The difference is not one of kind, but one of emphasis. Carolyn Miller (1987) extends an insight of Michael Leff's concerning this conflict between the formal or inferential and the material; she suggests that the common topics, which emphasize the inferential, are a product of pedagogical need, while the special topics, which emphasize the material, are a product of oratorical practice.

Lexis or Style

Chapters 2 through 12 of Book 3 of the *Rhetoric* focus exclusively on *lexis,* and as such constitute the fullest treatment of the topic in the Aristotelian corpus. The term *"lexis"* has broad application in Aristotle, ranging from "style," its most general reference, to "phoneme" in *Poetics* 20, to which Aristotle refers us at 3.1.9. The Proto-Indo-European root of "lexis" is "leg-," exactly the same root as that of *logos,* while its suffix, "-sis," indicates a state, condition, quality, or process related to the same rich complex of ideas indicated by the virtually untranslatable *logos.* As a result of this range of meanings, the relationship between *lexis* and *logos* in the *Rhetoric* has proved a source of disagreement between philosophy and rhetoric. In the context of this discussion, a nascent Aristotelian philosophy of language has been identified. Aristotle's remarks on metaphor have been most fruitful in this regard.

The question of whether or not Aristotle understands *lexis* as subordinate to or potentially coextensive with *logos* has confronted readers for two millennia. Aristotle writes at 3.2.1 that the cardinal virtue *(aretê)* of *lexis*-as-style is "clarity." This statement implies that clarity is not the absence of "style" but its achievement, as Book 3 goes on to make clear. Does this statement imply, then, that Aristotle views language and thought as coextensive? On the other hand, at other places in Book 3 Aristotle seems to regard style as antecedent and accessory to thought. How Aristotle understands the relationship between language and thought motivates Stephen Halliwell's "Style and Sense in Aristotle's *Rhetoric*, Bk. 3" (1983). Halliwell concludes that while Aristotle's analytic vocabulary often suggests a style-sense split, the details of the presentation of *lexis* in Book 3 do not reflect a "radical separation of style from sense"; rather, Book 3 conveys an awareness of the many ways in which stylistic choices "can help to determine both the significance and the expressive force of what is conveyed by words" (66–67).

Concerning *lexis*, of all subjects none has received more scholarly attention of late than that of Aristotle's treatment of metaphor. Richard Moran's essay is a good starting point. Moran (1996) notes that Aristotle focuses on the notion of transfer inherent to metaphor and explicates the relationships (e.g., species to genus; genus to genus) at the heart of Aristotle's analysis. This explication is a prelude to his consideration of the psychological response that Aristotle envisions as responsible for the impact appropriately used metaphor has in persuasive contexts. According to Moran, the effect of metaphor depends for Aristotle on the listeners' experiencing a sense of discovery as they take pride in their realizing the intended likeness.

John T. Kirby's recent "Aristotle on Metaphor" (1997) is the most comprehensive treatment to date in English of Aristotle's views on metaphor. Kirby places Aristotle's remarks within relevant contexts: of twentieth-century theories, Ancient practice (in Homer), and contemporary discussion (in Plato and Isocrates). This background is a prelude to Kirby's treatment of Aristotle's remarks, most prominently (but not only) in the *Poetics* and the *Rhetoric.* Kirby's analysis, which is informed by a sophisticated philology, concludes that semiotics is the lens that best illuminates Aristotle's understanding and that for Aristotle effective metaphor adds sophistication to discourse and produces pleasure in the audience.

Many scholars begin their consideration of metaphor by comparing its literal meaning ("to carry across") with its definition in *Poetics* 21 (1457b6–7), where this idea of conveyance is given by the term "epiphora." Paul Gordon translates "epiphora" as "supplement" in his "The Enigma of Aristotelian Metaphor: A Deconstructive Analysis" (1990), an essay that finds elements of the irrational and intuitive in Aristotle's theory. In his "Cognitive Aspects of Aristotle's Theory of Metaphor" (1984), Pierre Swiggers contests scholars who have attributed to Aristotle a formalistic, ornamental view of metaphor as verbal substitution (42). Swiggers understands Aristotle's contribution as an analysis of how metaphor works at the cognitive level. Drawing upon the *Poetics* and the *Metaphysics*, Swiggers claims that for Aristotle metaphor functions as an organic and rational interaction between speaker and hearer that produces first recognition, then knowledge. In "Aristotle's Analogical Metaphor," Steve Nimis (1988) uses Marxist analysis to probe the social implications of Aristotle's theory of metaphor.

Composition and the Uses of the *Rhetoric*

While essays by rhetoricians in composition that consider one or another concept important in the *Rhetoric* have been considered in earlier sections of this essay, some work by compositionists on the *Rhetoric* has been more global, attempting to view Aristotle's theory from modernist or postmodernist perspectives. Interpretation of the *Rhetoric* is carried out within the context of an argument about the character and direction of composition as a discipline. Andrea A. Lunsford and Lisa S. Ede's essay, "On Distinctions Between Classical and Modern Rhetoric," in the influential anthology *Essays on Classical Rhetoric and Modern Discourse* (1984b), would make the *Rhetoric* the foundation stone of composition studies. The authors argue in their essay that the theory advanced in the *Rhetoric* is the most appropriate theory for a discipline that is committed to epistemic and dialogic views of rhetoric. That the *Rhetoric* presents a genuinely dialogic theory is contested by Walzer (1997), who argues that modern (mis)appropriations of this sort prevent us from hearing Aristotle's genuine response to the problems monologic rhetoric poses. In contrast to Lunsford and Ede, Jasper Neel's *Aristotle's Voice* (1994) attacks Aristotle, making him responsible for much that plagues composition as a discipline particularly and Western culture generally. According to Neel, Aristotle valorized a disinterested and objective scientism that has fostered dismissals of rhetoric as a discipline, has enervated our teaching and scholarship, and has enabled him and us to conceal an ideology that fosters racism and sexism. If Neel would not entirely eliminate the *Rhetoric* from composition, he would at least insist that scholars and teachers of composition take a critical stance toward it. While these uses of Aristotle are helpful for spurring the type of debate that keeps the *Rhetoric* alive, they may finally prove only that the work of genius does not lend itself easily to polemic. This lesson is among those that Kathleen Welch offers in *Contemporary Reception of Classical Rhetoric* (1990). Welch warns compositionists to be wary of monolithic, tendentious presentations of classical rhetoric that have made it an easy target for critics.

Three textbooks also deserve mention: Edward P. J. Corbett's *Classical Rhetoric and the Modern Student* (1965; 3rd ed., 1990), Winiford Horner's *Rhetoric in the Classical Tradition* (1988), and Sharon Crowley's *Ancient Rhetorics for Contem-*

porary Students (1994). It is true that each of these textbooks draws on concepts developed by classical authors prior to and following Aristotle. It is also true that each manifests a slightly different emphasis within the rich, classical tradition: Crowley's is more influenced by the Sophists for example. Nonetheless, each bears unmistakably the imprint of Aristotle, and all are successful modern appropriations of the *Rhetoric* and are useful for students and their teachers alike.

LITERATURE CITED

CONTRIBUTORS

INDEX

Literature Cited

Aden, Roger C. 1994. "The Enthymeme as Postmodern Argument Form: Condensed, Mediated Argument Then and Now." *Argumentation and Advocacy* 31: 54–63.

Aly, Bower. 1946. "Review of Sergeant S. Prentiss: Whig Orator of the Old South, by Dallas C. Dickey." *Quarterly Journal of Speech* 32: 253–54.

Aristotle. 1984. *Categories.* Trans. J. L. Ackrill. *The Complete Works of Aristotle: Revised Oxford Translation.* Vol. 1. Rev. and Ed. Jonathan Barnes. Princeton: Princeton UP.

———. 1984. *The Complete Works of Aristotle: Revised Oxford Translation.* 2 Vols. Rev. and Ed. Jonathan Barnes. Princeton: Princeton UP.

———. 1937. *Eudemian Ethics.* Trans. H. Rackham. Loeb Classical Library.

———. 1953. *Generation of Animals.* Trans. A. L. Peck. Loeb Classical Library.

———. 1933. *The Metaphysics.* 2 Vols. Trans. Hugh Tredennick. Loeb Classical Library.

———. 1937. *Movement of Animals.* Trans. E. S. Forster. Loeb Classical Library.

———. 1962. *Nicomachean Ethics.* Trans. Martin Ostwald. Indianapolis: Bobbs-Merrill.

———. 1975. *Nicomachean Ethics.* Trans. H. Rackham. Loeb Classical Library.

———. 1978. *On Coming-to-Be and Passing-Away.* Trans. E. S. Forster. Loeb Classical Library.

———. 1984. *On Interpretation.* Trans. J. L. Ackrill. *The Complete Works of Aristotle: Revised Oxford Translation.* Vol. 1. Rev. and Ed. Jonathan Barnes. Princeton: Princeton UP.

———. 1960. *On the Heavens.* Trans. W. K. C. Guthrie. Loeb Classical Library.

———. 1957. *On the Soul [De Anima]* Trans. W. S. Hett. Loeb Classical Library.

———. 1970. *The Physics.* Trans. Philip H. Wicksteed and Francis M. Cornford. Vol. 1. Loeb Classical Library.

———. 1973. *Poetics.* Trans. W. Hamilton Fyfe. Loeb Classical Library.

———. 1984. *Poetics.* Trans. I. Bywater. Vol. 2. *The Complete Works of Aristotle: Revised Oxford Translation.* Rev. and Ed. Jonathan Barnes. Princeton: Princeton UP.

———. 1967. *Politics.* Trans. H. Rackham. Loeb Classical Library.

———. 1960. *Posterior Analytics.* Trans. Hugh Tredennick. Loeb Classical Library.

———. 1975. *Posterior Analytics.* Trans. Jonathan Barnes. Oxford: Clarendon.

———. 1965. *Prior and Posterior Analytics.* Rev. ed. Trans. W. D. Ross. Oxford: Clarendon.

———. 1953–57. *Problems.* Trans. W. S. Hett. Loeb Classical Library.

———. 1926. *The "Art" of Rhetoric.* Trans. John Freese. Loeb Classical Library.

———. 1976. *Aristotelis "Ars Rhetorica."* Ed. Rudolf Kassel. Berlin: de Gruyter.

———. 1984. *Aristotle's Rhetoric.* Trans. W. Rhys Roberts. Vol. 2. *The Complete Works of Aristotle: Revised Oxford Translation.* Rev. and Ed. Jonathan Barnes. Princeton: Princeton UP.

———. 1991. *Aristotle on Rhetoric: A Theory of Civic Discourse.* Trans. George A. Kennedy. New York and Oxford: Oxford UP.

———. 1991. *The Art of Rhetoric.* Trans. H. C. Lawson-Tancred. London: Penguin.

———. 1960. *Topica.* Trans. E. S. Forster. Loeb Classical Library.

———. 1984. *Topics.* Trans. W. A. Pickard-Cambridge. Vol. 1. *The Complete Works of Aristotle: Revised Oxford Translation.* Rev. and Ed. Jonathan Barnes. Princeton: Princeton UP.

Arnhart, Larry. 1981. *Aristotle on Political Reasoning: A Commentary on the Rhetoric.* DeKalb: Northern Illinois UP.

Arnold, Carroll C. 1959. "Rhetoric in America since 1900." *Re-establishing the Speech Profession: The First Fifty Years.* Ed. Robert T. Oliver and Marvin G. Bauer. N.p.: Speech Association of the Eastern States. 3–7.

———. 1971. "'Classicisms' and Speech Criticism." Review of *Speech Criticism.* 2nd ed. Ed. Lester Thonssen, A. Craig Baird, and Waldo Braden. *Southern Speech Communication Journal* 37: 105–6.

Atwill, Janet Marie. 1992. "Refiguring Rhetoric as Art: Aristotle's Concept of Techne and the Humanistic Paradigm." Doctoral dissertation, Purdue University.

———. 1998. *Rhetoric Reclaimed: Aristotle and the Liberal Arts Tradition.* Ithaca, NY: Cornell UP.

Bacon, Francis. 1952. *Advancement of Learning.* Ed. Robert Maynard Hutchins. Vol. 30, *Great Books of the Western World.* 54 Vols. Chicago: Encyclopaedia Britannica.

Baird, A. Craig, and Lester Thonssen. 1947. "Methodology in the Criticism of Public Address." *Quarterly Journal of Speech* 33: 134–38.

Balaban, Oded. 1986. "Aristotle's Theory of Praxsis." *Hermes* 114: 163–72.

Baldwin, Charles Sears. 1916. "Graduate Work in the Teaching of English." Summary, 60–61. NCTE, *Proceedings of the 6th Annual Meeting,* November 30 and December 1–2. New York. Reprinted in 1917. *English Journal* 6: 40–68.

———. 1928. *Medieval Rhetoric and Poetic.* New York: Macmillan.

Barbaro, Daniele (Danielus Barbarus, 1514–70), and Ermolao Barbaro. 1545. *Aristotelis Rhetoricorum libri tres, Hermolao Barbaro interprete. Danielis Barbari* in *eosdem libros commentarii.* Basle.

Barbaro, Ermolao (Hermolaus Barbarus, 1454–93). See Barbaro, Daniele.

Barilli, Renato. 1986. "Eloquenza, tecnologia, scienza della cultura." *Le ragioni della retorica.* Atti del Convegno: "Retorica: verità, opinione, persuasione," Cattolica, 22.2-20.4.1985. Ed. Gabriella Fenocchio. Modena: Mucci Editore. 47–69.

Barker, Andrew. 1985. "Theophrastus on Pitch and Melody." *Theophrastus of Eresus: On His Life and Work.* Ed. William W. Fortenbaugh. Rutgers University Studies in Classical Humanities, Vol. 2. New Brunswick: Transaction.

Barnes, Jonathan. 1981. "Proof and the Syllogism." *Aristotle on Science: The Posterior Analytics. Proceedings of the 8th Symposium Aristotelicum.* Ed. Enrico Berti. Padua: Editrice Antenore. 17–59.

———, ed. 1995a. *Cambridge Companion to Aristotle.* Cambridge: Cambridge UP.

———. 1995b. "Life and Work." *Cambridge Companion to Aristotle.* Ed. Jonathan Barnes. Cambridge: Cambridge UP. 1–26.

Barnes, Jonathan, Malcolm Schofield, and Richard Sorabji. 1975. *Articles on Aristotle.* Vol. 1. Science. London: Duckworth.

Barwick, K. 1922. "Die Gliederung der rhetorischen Techne und die Horazische Epistula ad Pisones." *Hermes* 57: 1–62.

Bauer, Marvin G. 1927. "Persuasive Methods in the Lincoln-Douglas Debates." *Quarterly Journal of Speech* 13: 29–39.

Baumlin, James S., and Tita French Baumlin, eds. 1994. *Ethos: New Essays in Rhetorical and Critical Theory.* Dallas: Southern Methodist UP.

Beiner, Ronald. 1983. *Political Judgment.* Chicago: U of Chicago P.

Benci, Francesco (Franciscus Bencius, 1542–94). *In librum secundum rhetoricae Aristotelis.* Laurentian MS Redi. 13 (136).

Benoit, William, L. 1980. "Aristotle's Example: The Rhetorical Induction." *Quarterly Journal of Speech* 66: 182–92.

———. 1987. "On Aristotle's Example." *Philosophy and Rhetoric* 20: 261–67.

Bensel-Meyers, Linda. 1992. *Rhetoric for Academic Reasoning.* New York: Harper.

Berkowitz, Luci, and Karl A. Squitier. 1987. See *Thesaurus Linguae Graecae.*

Berlin, James A. 1987. *Rhetoric and Reality: Writing Instruction in American Colleges, 1900–1985.* Carbondale: Southern Illinois UP.

———. 1990. "Writing Instruction in School and College English, 1890–1985." *A Short History of Writing Instruction: From Ancient Greece to Twentieth-Century America.* Ed. James J. Murphy. Davis: Hermagoras P. 183–220.

———. 1992. "Aristotle's *Rhetoric* in Context: Interpreting Historically." *A Rhetoric of Doing: Essays on Written Discourse in Honor of James L. Kinneavy.* Ed. Stephen P. Witte, Neil Nakadate, and Roger D. Cherry. Carbondale: Southern Illinois UP. 55–64.

Berry, Mildred Freburg. 1931. "Lincoln-The Speaker (Part I)." *Quarterly Journal of Speech* 17: 25–40.

Berti, Enrico. 1984. "Retorica, dialettica, filosofia." *Linguaggio, persuasione, verità. Atti del XXVIII Congresso Nazionale di Filosofia, Verona 28.4-1.5.1983.* Ed. Societa filosofica italiana. Padova: Casa Editrice Dr. A. Milani. 19–36.

Betti, Emilio. 1954. *Zur Grundlegung einer allgemeine Auslegungslehre.* Tübingen: J. C. B. Mohr.

———. 1955. *Teoria generale della interpretazione.* Milan: Dott. A. Giuffre.

———. 1962. *Die Hermeneutik als allgemeine Methodik der Geisteswissenschaften.* Tübingen: J. C. B. Mohr.

Bird, Otto. 1961. "The Re-discovery of the Topics: Professor Toulmin's Inference-Warrants." *Mind* 70: 534–39.

———. 1962. "The Tradition of the Logical Topics: Aristotle to Ockham." *Journal of the History of Ideas* 23: 307–23.

Bitzer, Lloyd F. 1959. "Aristotle's Enthymeme Revisited." *Quarterly Journal of Speech* 45: 399–408.

———. 1968. "The Rhetorical Situation." *Philosophy and Rhetoric* 1: 1–14.

Bizzell, Patricia, and Bruce Herzberg, eds. 1990. *The Rhetorical Tradition: Readings from Classical Times to the Present.* Boston: St. Martin's.

Black, Edwin. 1965. *Rhetorical Criticism: A Study in Method.* New York: Macmillan.

———. 1970. "The Second Persona." *Quarterly Journal of Speech* 56: 109–19.

Blettner, Elizabeth. 1983. "One Made Many and Many Made One: The Role of Asyndeton in Aristotle's *Rhetoric.*" *Philosophy and Rhetoric* 16: 49–54.

Boeckh, August. 1886. *Encyklopädie und Methodologie der philologischen Wissenschaften.* 2nd ed. Ed. Ernst Brautscheck. Corr. Rudolf Klussmann. Leipzig: B. G. Teubner. Translated in part by John Paul Pritchard under the title *On Interpretation and Criticism.* Norman: U of Oklahoma P, 1968.

Bolinger, Dwight. 1975. *Aspects of Language.* 2nd ed. New York: Harcourt Brace Jovanovich.

Booth, Wayne C., and Marshall W. Gregory. 1991. *The Harper and Row Rhetoric: Writing as Thinking, Thinking as Writing.* 2nd ed. New York: Harper.

Borchers, Gladys L. 1967. "[Speech Education.] An Overview: Philosophy, Objectives, Content." *The Communicative Arts and Sciences of Speech.* Ed. Keith Brooks. Columbus: Charles E. Merrill. 512–21.

Braden, Waldo W. 1961. "Teaching Public Speaking." *Speech Methods and Resources: A Textbook for the Teacher of Speech.* Ed. Waldo W. Braden. New York: Harper and Brothers. 165–87.

Braet, Antoine C. 1988. "Ethos, pathos en logos in *de Rhetorica* van Aristoteles." *Tijdschrift voor Taalbeheersing* 10: 14–27.

———. 1992. "Ethos, Pathos, and Logos in Aristotle's *"Rhetoric"*: A Re-examination." *Argumentation* 6: 307–20.

Brandes, Paul D. 1989. *A History of Aristotle's Rhetoric with a Bibliography of Early Printings.* Metuchen: Scarecrow.

Brandt, William J., Robert Beloof, Leonard Nathan, and Carroll E. Selph. 1969. *The Craft of Writing.* Englewood Cliffs, NJ: Prentice Hall.

Brent, Doug. 1996. "Rogerian Rhetoric: Ethical Growth Through Alternative Forms of Composition." *Argument Revisited, Argument Redefined: Negotiating Meaning in the Composition Classroom.* Ed. Barbara Emmel, Paula Resch, and Deborah Tenny. Thousand Oaks, CA: Sage. 73–96.

Brigance, William Norwood. 1933. "Whither Research?" *Quarterly Journal of Speech* 19: 552–61.

———, ed. 1943–55. *A History and Criticism of American Public Address.* 3 Vols. New York: McGraw.

Brinton, Alan. 1986. "Ēthotic Argument." *History of Philosophy Quarterly* 3: 245–58.

———. 1988. "Pathos and the 'Appeal to Emotion': An Aristotelian Analysis." *History of Philosophy Quarterly* 5: 207–19.

———. 1990. "The Outmoded Psychology of Aristotle's *Rhetoric.*" *Western Journal of Speech Communication* 54: 204–18.

Brown, Jason O. 1982. "Hierarchy and Evolution in Neurolinguistics." *Neural Models of Language Processes.* Ed. Michael A. Arbib, David Caplan, and John C. Marshall. New York: Academic P. 447–67.

Brunschwig, Jacques. 1996. "Aristotle's Rhetoric as a 'Counterpart' to Dialectic." *Essays on Aristotle's "Rhetoric."* Ed. Amélie Oksenberg Rorty. Berkeley: U of California P. 34–55.

Bryant, Donald C. 1933. "Edmund Burke on Oratory." *Quarterly Journal of Speech* 19: 1–18.

———, ed. 1958. *The Rhetorical Idiom. Essays in Rhetoric, Oratory, Language, and Drama.* Ithaca, NY: Cornell UP.

———. 1973. *Rhetorical Dimensions in Criticism.* Baton Rouge: Louisiana State UP.

Bryn Mawr Classical Review. (http://www.hti.umich.edu/b/bmr/bmcr.html).

Burke, Kenneth. 1969. *A Rhetoric of Motives.* Berkeley: U of California P.

Burnyeat, M. F. 1994. "Enthymeme: Aristotle on the Logic of Persuasion." *Aristotle's "Rhetoric": Philosophical Essays.* Ed. David J. Furley and Alexander Nehamas. Princeton: Princeton UP. 3–55.

———. 1996. "Enthymeme: Aristotle on the Rationality of Rhetoric." *Essays on Aristotle's "Rhetoric."* Ed. Amélie Oksenberg Rorty. Berkeley: U of California P. 88–115.

Calhoun, Cheshire. 1984. "Cognitive Emotions?" *What Is an Emotion? Classic Readings in Philosophical Psychology.* New York: Oxford UP. 327–42.

Campbell, George. 1963. *The Philosophy of Rhetoric.* Ed. Lloyd F. Bitzer. Carbondale: Southern Illinois UP.

Campbell, Karlyn Kohrs. 1972. "'Conventional Wisdom-Traditional Form': A Rejoinder." *Quarterly Journal of Speech* 58: 451–54.

Carlson, W. Bernard, and Michael E. Gorman. 1992. "A Cognitive Framework to Understand Technological Creativity: Bell, Edison, and the Telephone." *Inventive Minds: Creativity in Technology.* Ed. Robert J. Weber and David N. Perkins. New York: Oxford UP. 48–79.

Carrino, Elnora D. 1959. "Psychological Influences on Rhetorical Theory." *Re-establishing the Speech Profession: The First Fifty Years.* Ed. Robert T. Oliver and Marvin G. Bauer. N.p.: Speech Association of the Eastern States. 19–23.

Chamberlain, Charles. 1984. "From 'Haunts' to 'Character': The Meaning of Êthos and Its Relation to Ethics." *Helios* 11(2): 97–108.

[Cicero]. 1954. *Rhetorica ad Herennium.* Trans. H. Caplan. Loeb Classical Library.

Cicero, Marcus Tullius. 1914. *De finibus bonorum et malorum.* Trans. H. Rackham. Loeb Classical Library.

———. 1988. *Brutus.* Trans. G. L. Hendrickson. Loeb Classical Library.

———. 1988. *Orator.* Trans. H. M. Hubbell. Loeb Classical Library.

Clark, Stephen R. L. 1975. *Aristotle's Man.* Oxford: Oxford UP.

Clinton, William. 1995 (April 23). "Remarks by the President During 'A Time of Healing' Prayer Service." Oklahoma State Fair Arena, Oklahoma City. (White House).

———. 1995 (November 3). *New York Times.*

Cogan, Marc. 1984. "Rodolphus Agricola and the Semantic Revolutions of the History of Invention." *Rhetorica* 2: 163–94.

Conley, Thomas M. 1978. "'Logical Hylomorphism' and Aristotles Koinoi Topoi." *Central States Speech Journal* 29: 92–7.

———. 1982. "Pathê and Pisteis: Aristotle 'Rhet.' II 2–11." *Hermes* 110: 300–15.

———. 1984. "The Enthymeme in Perspective." *Quarterly Journal of Speech* 70: 168–87.

Connors, Robert J., Lisa S. Ede, Andrea A. Lunsford, eds. 1984. *Essays on Classical Rhetoric and Modern Discourse.* Carbondale: Southern Illinois UP.

———. 1984. "The Revival of Rhetoric in America." *Essays on Classical Rhetoric and Modern Discourse.* Ed. Robert J. Connors, Lisa S. Ede, and Andrea A. Lunsford. Carbondale: Southern Illinois UP. 1–15.

Consigny, Scott. 1974. "Rhetoric and Its Situations." *Philosophy and Rhetoric* 7: 175–86.

———. 1975. "The Rhetorical Example." *Southern Speech Communication Journal* 41: 121–32.

———. 1989. "Dialectical, Rhetorical, and Aristotelian Rhetoric." *Philosophy and Rhetoric* 22: 281–87.

Continentur hoc volumine. Venice, 1523.

Cooper, John M. 1975. *Reason and Human Good in Aristotle.* Cambridge: Harvard UP.

———. 1988. "Some Remarks on Aristotle's Moral Psychology." *Southern Journal of Philosophy* 27: 25–42.

———. 1994. "Ethical-Political Theory in Aristotle's *Rhetoric.*" *Aristotle's "Rhetoric": Philosophical Essays.* Ed. David J. Furley and Alexander Nehamas. Princeton: Princeton UP. 193–210.

———. 1996. "An Aristotelian Theory of the Emotions." *Essays on Aristotle's "Rhetoric."* Ed. Amélie Oksenberg Rorty. Berkeley: U of California P. 238–57.

Cooper, Lane, trans. 1932. *The Rhetoric of Aristotle.* Englewood Cliffs, NJ: Prentice Hall.

Cope, Edward Meredith, ed. 1877. *The "Rhetoric" of Aristotle with a Commentary.* Rev. and Ed. John Edwin Sandys. 3 Vols. Cambridge: Cambridge UP.

Corbett, Edward P. J. 1965. *Classical Rhetoric for the Modern Student.* New York: Oxford UP.

Cronkhite, Gary L. 1966. "The Enthymeme as Deductive Rhetorical Argument." *Western Journal of Speech Communication* 30: 129–34.

Crowley, Sharon. 1994. *Ancient Rhetorics for Contemporary Students*. New York: Macmillan.

Cyllenius Angelus, Raphael. 1571. *Tabulae rhetoricae, quibus omnia, quae ab Aristotele de arte dicendi libris, et a Demetrio Phalereo suo de elocutione libello tradiata sunt, praecepta fidissime, et planissime explicantur.* Venice.

D'Angelo, Frank J. 1984. "The Evolution of the Analytic Topoi: A Speculative Inquiry." *Essays on Classical Rhetoric and Modern Discourse*. Ed. Robert J. Connors, Lisa S. Ede, and Andrea A. Lunsford. Carbondale: Southern Illinois UP. 50–68.

Delia, Jesse G. 1970. "The Logic Fallacy, Cognitive Theory, and the Enthymeme: A Search for the Foundations of Reasoned Discourse." *Quarterly Journal of Speech* 56: 140–48.

Demetrius. 1927. *On Style*. Trans. W. Rhys Roberts. Loeb Classical Library.

Demosthenes. 1930. *Olynthiacs, Philippics, Minor Public Speeches, Speech against Leptines.* Trans. J. H. Vince. Loeb Classical Library.

de Romilly, Jacqueline. 1975. *Magic and Rhetoric in Ancient Greece*. Cambridge: Harvard UP.

de Sousa, Ronald. 1987. *The Rationality of Emotion*. Cambridge: MIT P.

Detienne, Marcel, and Jean-Pierre Vernant. 1978. *Cunning Intelligence in Greek Culture and Society*. Trans. Janet Lloyd. Atlantic Highlands: Humanities P.

Diels, Hermann, and Walther Kranz. 1964. *Die Fragmente Der Vorsokratiker*. Zurich: Weidmannsche.

Diogenes Laertius. 1958/1959. *Lives of Eminent Philosophers*. 2 Vols. Loeb Classical Library.

Dionysius of Halicarnassus. 1974/1985. *Critical Essays*. 2 Vols. Loeb Classical Library.

Douglass, Frederick. 1988. *Narrative of the Life of Frederick Douglass, An American Slave. Written by Himself.* Ed. Benjamin Quarles. Cambridge: The Belknap P of Harvard UP.

Dover, K. J. 1974. *Greek Popular Morality in the Time of Plato and Aristotle*. Berkeley: U of California P.

Dufour, Médéric, and André Wartelle, eds. and trans. 1972. *Aristote: Rhétorique, tome troisième (livre III)*. L'Association Guillaume Budé. Paris: Les Belles Lettres.

Dunne, Joseph. 1993. *Back to the Rough Ground: "Phronêsis and Technê" in Modern Philosophy and in Aristotle*. Notre Dame, IN: U of Notre Dame P.

Eamon, William. 1994. *Science and the Secrets of Nature*. Princeton: Princeton UP.

Eco, Umberto. 1986. "Il messaggio persuasivo." *Le ragioni della retorica*. Atti del Convegno: "Retorica: verità, opinione, persuasione," Cattolica, 22.2 20.4.1985. Ed. Gabriella Fenocchio. Modena: Mucci Editore. 11–27.

Eden, Kathy. 1986. *Poetic and Legal Fiction in the Aristotelian Tradition*. Princeton: Princeton UP.

Eemeren, Frans H. Van, Rob Grootendorst, and Tjark Kruiger. 1987. *A Handbook of Argumentation Theory*. Dordrecht: Foris.

Emmel, Barbara A. 1994. "Toward a Pedagogy of the Enthymeme: The Roles of Dialogue, Intention, and Function in Shaping Argument." *Rhetoric Review* 13: 132–49.

Engberg-Pedersen, Troels. 1996. "Is There an Ethical Dimension to Aristotelian Rhetoric?" *Essays on Aristotle's "Rhetoric."* Ed. Amélie Oksenberg Rorty. Berkeley: U of California P. 116–41.

Enos, Richard, and Lois Peters Agnew, eds. 1998. *Landmark Essays on Aristotelian Rhetoric*. Mahwah: Lawrence Erlbaum.

Erickson, Keith V., ed. 1974. *Aristotle: The Classical Heritage of Rhetoric*. Metuchen: Scarecrow.

Everson, Stephen. 1995. "Psychology." *Cambridge Companion to Aristotle*. Ed. Jonathan Barnes. New York: Cambridge UP. 168–94.

Fantham, Elaine. 1972. *Comparative Studies in Republican Latin Imagery*. Toronto: U of Toronto P.

Farrell, Thomas B. 1977. "Validity and Rationality: The Rhetorical Constituents of Argumentative Form." *Journal of the American Forensics Association* 13: 142–49.

———. 1993. *Norms of Rhetorical Culture*. New Haven, CT: Yale UP.

Fenocchio, Gabriella. 1986. "Premessa." *Le ragioni della retorica*. Atti del Convegno: "Retorica: verità, opinione, persuasione," Cattolica, 22.2-20.4.1985. Ed. Gabriella Fenocchio. Modena: Mucci Editore. 7–8.

Fisher, Walter R. 1964. "Uses of the Enthymeme." *Speech Teacher* 13: 197–203.

Fontanier, Pierre. 1977. *Les Figures du Discours*. Intro. Gérard Genette. Paris: Flammarion.

Fortenbaugh, William W. 1970. "Aristotle's *Rhetoric* on Emotions: A Contribution to Philosophical Psychology, Rhetoric, Poetic, Politics, and Ethics." *Archiv für Geschichte der Philosophie* 52: 40–70. Reprinted in Erickson.

———. 1975. *Aristotle on Emotion*. London: Duckworth.

———. 1985. "Theophrastus on Emotion" and "Theophrastus on Delivery." *Theophrastus of Eresus: On His Life and Work*. Ed. William W. Fortenbaugh, together with Pamela M. Huby and Anthony A. Long. Rutgers University Studies in Classical Humanities, Vol. 2. New Brunswick: Transaction. 209–29, 269–88.

———. 1992. "Aristotle on Persuasion Through Character." *Rhetorica* 10: 207–44.

Fortenbaugh, William W., Pamela M. Huby, Robert W. Sharples, and Dimitri Gutas, eds. and trans. 1992. *Theophrastus of Eresus: Sources for His Life, Writings, Thought, and Influence*. 2 Vols. Leiden: Brill.

Frankfurt, Harry. 1982. "The Importance of What We Care About." *Synthese* 53: 257–72.

Frede, Dorothea. 1996. "Mixed Feelings in Aristotle's *Rhetoric*." *Essays on Aristotle's "Rhetoric."* Ed. Amélie Oksenberg Rorty. Berkeley: U of California P. 258–85.

Fulkerson, Richard. 1996. "The Toulmin Model of Argument and the Teaching of Composition." *Argument Revisited, Argument Redefined: Negotiating Meaning in the Composition Classroom*. Ed. Barbara Emmel, Paula Resch, and Deborah Tenny. Thousand Oaks, CA: Sage. 45–71.

Furley, David J., and Alexander Nehamas, eds. 1994. *Aristotle's "Rhetoric": Philosophical Essays*. Princeton: Princeton UP.

Gadamer, Hans-Georg. 1960. *Wahrheit und Methode; Grundzuge einer philosophischen Hermeneutik*. Tübingen: J. C. B. Mohr.

———. 1967. "Rhetorik, Hermeneutik, und Ideologiekritik." *Kleine Schriften*. Vol. 1. Reprinted in *Philosophie, Hermeneutik*. Tübingen: J. C. B. Mohr. 113–30.

Gage, John T. 1982a. "Freshman English: In Whose Service?" *College English* 44: 469–74.

———. 1982b. "Towards an Epistemology of Composition." *Journal of Advanced Composition* 2: 1–10.

———. 1983. "Teaching the Enthymeme: Invention and Arrangement." *Rhetoric Review* 2: 38–50.

———. 1984. "An Adequate Epistemology for Composition: Classical and Modern Perspectives." *Essays on Classical Rhetoric and Modern Discourse*. Ed. Robert J. Connors, Lisa S. Ede, and Andrea A. Lunsford. Carbondale: Southern Illinois UP. 152–69.

———. 1991a. "A General Theory of the Enthymeme for Advanced Composition." *Teaching Advanced Composition: Why and How*. Ed. Katherine H. Adams and John L. Adams. Portsmouth: Boynton/Cook. 161–78.

———. 1991b. *The Shape of Reason: Argumentative Writing in College*. 2nd ed. New York: Macmillan.

———. 1996. "The Reasoned Thesis: The E-Word and Argumentative Writing as a Process of Inquiry." *Argument Revisited, Argument Redefined: Negotiating Meaning in the Composition Classroom.* Ed. Barbara Emmel, Paula Resch, and Deborah Tenny. Thousand Oaks, CA: Sage. 3–17.

Gaines, Robert. 1986. "Aristotle's Rhetorical *Rhetoric*?" *Philosophy and Rhetoric* 19: 194–200.

———. Unpublished. "Aristotle's *Rhetoric* in Twentieth Century Scholarship: The Hollow Colossus."

Galen. 1916. *On the Natural Faculties.* Trans. Arthur John Brock. Loeb Classical Library.

Garner, Richard. 1987. *Law and Society in Classical Athens.* New York: St. Martin's.

Garrett, Jan Edward. 1987. "Aristotle's Nontechnical Conception of TECHNE." *The Modern Schoolman* 64: 283–94.

Garver, Eugene. 1984. "Aristotle's Genealogy of Morals." *Philosophy and Phenomenological Research* 44: 471–92.

———. 1986. "Aristotle's *Rhetoric* as a Work of Philosophy." *Philosophy and Rhetoric* 19: 1–22.

———. 1988. "Aristotle's *Rhetoric* on Unintentionally Hitting the Principles of the Sciences." *Rhetorica* 6: 381–93.

———. 1989a. "Aristotle's Metaphysics of Morals." *Journal of the History of Philosophy* 27: 7–28.

———. 1989b. "The Human Function and Aristotle's Art of Rhetoric." *History of Philosophy Quarterly* 6: 133–45.

———. 1989c. "The Moral Virtues and the Two Sides of *Energeia*." *Ancient Philosophy* 9: 293–312.

———. 1990a. "Making Discourse Ethical: The Lessons of Aristotle's Rhetoric." *Proceedings of the Boston Area Colloquium in Ancient Philosophy*. Vol. 5. Ed. John J. Cleary and Daniel C. Shartin. Lanham, MD: UP of America. 73–96.

———. 1990b. "Why Pluralism Now?" *Monist* 73: 388–410.

———. 1994a. "Aristotle's Natural Slaves: Incomplete Praxis and Incomplete Human Beings." *Journal of the History of Philosophy* 32: 1–22.

———. 1994b. *Aristotle's "Rhetoric": An Art of Character.* Chicago: U of Chicago P.

Genette, Gérard. 1982. *Figures of Literary Discourse.* Trans. Alan Sheridan. New York: Columbia UP.

George of Trebizond (Georgius Trapezuntius, 1395–1484). 1523a. *Comparationes phylosophorum Aristotelis et Platonis* [written 1455–57]. Venice.

———. 1523b. *In tres rhetoricorum Aristotelis libros ad Theodecten tralatio* [trans. 1443–45, *princeps* c. 1475]. *Continentur hoc volumine.* Venice.

———. 1523c. *Rhetoricorum libri V* [written 1433/1434, *princeps* 1472]. *Continentur hoc volumine.* Venice.

Giles of Rome (Aegidius Romanus; Egidio Colonna; c. 1243/47–1316). 1515. *Expositio super tribus libris rhetoricorum* [written c. 1290]. Venice.

Ginzburg, Carlo. 1989. *Clues, Myths, and the Historical Method.* Trans. John and Anne C. Tedeschi. Baltimore: Johns Hopkins UP.

Gnomon Online Bibliographische Datenbank. (http://www.gnomon.ku-eichstaett.de/Gnomon/note_e.html).

Gordon, Paul. 1990. "The Enigma of Aristotelian Metaphor: A Deconstructive Analysis." *Metaphor and Symbolic Activity* 5: 83–90.

Gorman, Michael E., and W. Bernard Carlson. 1992 . "Mapping Invention and Design." *Chemtech:* 584–91.

Goulston, Theodore (1572–1632). 1619. *Tekhnês rhêtorikês biblia tria. De rhetorica seu de arte dicendi libri tres graecolat . . . Exteriori, adposita Analyticê Methodo: cujus Tabulae Synopticae, in sua loca distributae.* London.

Gray, Giles Wilkeson. 1954. "Some Teachers and the Transition to Twentieth-Century Speech Education." *History of Speech Education in America: Background Studies.* Ed. Karl R. Wallace. New York: Appleton-Century-Crofts. 422–46.

Gray, Jeffrey A. 1991. "Neural Systems, Emotion, and Personality." *Neurobiology of Learning, Emotion, and Affect.* Ed. John Madden IV. New York: Raven. 273–306.

Green, Lawrence D. 1980. "Enthymematic Invention and Structural Prediction." *College English* 41: 623–34.

———, ed. and trans. 1986. *John Rainolds's Oxford Lectures on Aristotle's "Rhetoric."* Newark: U of Delaware P; London and Toronto: Associated UP.

———. 1990 (Winter). "Aristotelian Rhetoric, Dialectic, and the Traditions of *Antistrophos.*" *Rhetorica* 8: 5–27.

———. 1994a. "Aristotle's *Rhetoric* and Renaissance Views of the Emotions." *Renaissance Rhetoric.* Ed. Peter Mack. London: Macmillan.

———. 1994b. "The Reception of Aristotle's *Rhetoric* in the Renaissance." *Peripatetic Rhetoric after Aristotle.* Ed. William W. Fortenbaugh and David C. Mirhady. Rutgers University Studies in Classical Humanities, Vol. 6. New Brunswick: Transaction. 320–48.

———. 1995. "Aristotle's Enthymeme and the Imperfect Syllogism." *Rhetoric and Pedagogy: Its History, Philosophy, and Practice. Essays in Honor of James J. Murphy.* Ed. Winifred Bryan Horner and Michael Leff. Mahwah: Lawrence Erlbaum. 19–41.

———. 1997. "Making Aristotle's *Rhetoric* Methodical." *Autour de Ramus: texte, théorie, commentaire.* Ed. Kees Meerhoff and Jean-Claude Moisan. Quebec: Nuit Blanche.

———. 1998. "Aristotle's *Rhetoric* and Renaissance Conceptions of the Soul." *La "Rhetorique" d'Aristote, traditions et commentaires: de l'antiquité à la Renaissance.* Ed. Irène Rosier-Catach. Paris: Librairie Philosophique J. Vrin. 283–97.

Greenspan, Patricia S. 1988. *Emotions and Reasons: An Inquiry into Emotional Justification.* New York: Routledge.

Grimaldi, William M. A. 1972. *Studies in the Philosophy of Aristotle's Rhetoric.* Hermes Einzelschriften, 25. Wiesbaden: Franz Steiner Verlag.

———. 1974. "The Aristotelian Topics." *Aristotle: The Classical Heritage of Rhetoric.* Ed. Keith V. Erickson. Metuchen: Scarecrow. 173–96.

———. 1978. "Rhetoric and Truth: A Note on Aristotle. *Rhetoric* 1355a21–24." *Philosophy and Rhetoric* 11: 173–77.

———. 1980a. *Aristotle, "Rhetoric" I: A Commentary.* New York: Fordham UP.

———. 1980b. "Semeion, Tekmerion, Eikos in Aristotle's *Rhetoric.*" *American Journal of Philology* 101: 383–98.

———. 1988. *Aristotle, "Rhetoric" II: A Commentary.* New York: Fordham UP.

Hairston, Maxine C. 1986. "Bringing Aristotle's Enthymeme into the Composition Classroom." *Rhetoric and Praxis: The Contribution of Classical Rhetoric to Practical Reasoning.* Ed. Jean Dietz Moss. Washington, DC: Catholic U of America P. 59–77.

Halliwell, Stephen. 1983. "Style and Sense in Aristotle's *Rhetoric,* BK. 3." *Revue Internationale de Philosophie* 47: 50–69.

———. 1996. "The Challenge of Rhetoric to Political and Ethical Theory in Aristotle." *Essays on Aristotle's "Rhetoric."* Ed. Amélie Oksenberg Rorty. Berkeley: U of California P. 175–90.

Harper, Nancy. 1973. "An Analytical Description of Aristotle's Enthymeme." *Central States Speech Journal* 24: 304–9.

Hathaway, Baxter. 1962. *The Age of Criticism: The Late Renaissance in Italy.* Ithaca, NY: Cornell UP.

Hauser, Gerard A. 1968. "The Example in Aristotle's *Rhetoric:* Bifurcation or Contradiction?" *Philosophy and Rhetoric* 1: 78–90. Reprinted in Erickson.

———. 1985. "Aristotle's Example Revisited." *Philosophy and Rhetoric* 18: 171–80.

Heidegger, Martin. 1927. *Sein und Zeit. Jahrbuch für Phänomenologie und phänomenologische Forschung* 8: X–438.

———. 1977. "The Question Concerning Technology." *The Question Concerning Technology and Other Essays.* Trans. William Lovitt. New York: Harper. 5–35.

Hendrix, J. A. 1968. "In Defense of Neo-Aristotelian Rhetorical Criticism." *Western Speech* 32: 246–52.

Hesse, Douglas D. 1992. "Aristotle's *Poetics* and *Rhetoric:* Narrative as Rhetoric's Fourth Mode." *Rebirth of Rhetoric: Essays in Language, Culture, and Education.* Ed. Richard Andrews. London: Routledge. 19–38.

Hill, Forbes. 1972. "Conventional Wisdom—Traditional Form: The President's Message of November 3, 1969." *Quarterly Journal of Speech* 58: 373–86.

———. 1981. "The Amorality of Aristotle's *Rhetoric.*" *Greek, Roman and Byzantine Studies* 22: 133–47.

Hippocrates. 1931. *Aphorisms.* Vol. 4 (of 6). Loeb Classical Library.

Hirsch, E. D., Jr. 1967. *Validity in Interpretation.* New Haven, CT: Yale UP.

———. 1976. *The Aims of Interpretation.* Chicago: U of Chicago P.

Holmberg, Carl B. 1977. "Dialectical Rhetoric and Rhetorical Rhetoric." *Philosophy and Rhetoric* 10: 232–43.

Hood, Michael D. 1984. "The Enthymeme: A Brief Bibliography of Modern Sources." *Rhetoric Society Quarterly* 14: 159–62.

Horner, Winifred Bryan. 1988. *Rhetoric in the Classical Tradition.* New York: St. Martin's.

Hubbell, H. M., trans. 1920. "The Rhetorica of Philodemus: Translation and Commentary." *Transactions of the Connecticut Academy of Arts and Sciences* 23: 243–382.

Hudson, Hoyt H. 1929. "Philip Snowden: 'Speech at the Hague,' August 6, 1929." *Quarterly Journal of Speech* 15: 595–97.

Hughes, Richard E., and P. Albert Duhamel. 1962. *Rhetoric: Principles and Usage.* Englewood Cliffs, NJ: Prentice Hall.

Hunt, Everett Lee. 1920. "Plato and Aristotle on Rhetoric and Rhetoricians." *Quarterly Journal of Speech* 6(3): 33–53. Reprinted in 1961. *Historical Studies of Rhetoric and Rhetoricians.* Ed. A. M. Drummond. Ithaca, NY: Cornell UP. 3–60.

———. 1934. "Matthew Arnold: The Critic as Rhetorician." *Quarterly Journal of Speech* 20: 483–507.

Internet Classics Archive. (http://classics.mit.edu/index.html).

Isocrates. 1928. *Works.* Trans. George Norlin and Larue van Hook. 3 Vols. Loeb Classical Library.

Jackson, Sally, and Scott Jacobs. 1980. "Structure of Conversational Argument: Pragmatic Bases for the Enthymeme." *Quarterly Journal of Speech* 66: 251–65.

Jacob, Bernard E. 1996. "What If Aristotle Took Sophists Seriously? New Readings in Aristotle's *Rhetoric.*" *Rhetoric Review* 14: 237–52.

Jacobi, Martin J. 1987. "Using the Enthymeme as a Heuristic in Professional Writing Courses." *Journal of Advanced Composition* 7: 41–51.

Jaeger, Werner. 1944. *Paideia.* Trans. Gilbert Highet. New York: Oxford UP.

Jasinski, James. 1995. "The Forms and Limits of Prudence in Henry Clay's (1850) Defense of the Compromise Measures." *Quarterly Journal of Speech* 81: 454–78.

Johnstone, Christopher Lyle. 1980. "An Aristotelian Trilogy: Ethics, Rhetoric, Politics, and the Search for Moral Truth." *Philosophy and Rhetoric* 13: 1–24.

Johnstone, Henry W., Jr. 1987. "Response." *Philosophy and Rhetoric* 20: 129–34.

Jolliffe, David A. 1992. "Writers and Their Subjects: Ethnologic and Chinese Composition." *A Rhetoric of Doing*. Ed. Stephen P. Witte, Neil Nakadate, and Roger D. Cherry. Carbondale: Southern Illinois UP. 261–75.

Jones, J. Walter. 1956. *The Law and Legal Theory of the Greeks*. Oxford: Clarendon.

Kassel, Rudolf, ed. 1976. *Aristotelis Ars Rhetorica*. Berlin: De Gruyter.

Kastely, James L. 1997. *Rethinking the Rhetorical Tradition: From Plato to Postmodernism*. New Haven, CT: Yale UP.

Kennedy, George A. 1963. *The Art of Persuasion in Greece*. Princeton: Princeton UP.

———. 1980. *Classical Rhetoric and Its Christian and Secular Tradition from Ancient to Modern Times*. Chapel Hill: U of North Carolina P.

———, trans. 1991. *Aristotle on Rhetoric: A Theory of Civic Discourse*. New York and Oxford: Oxford UP.

Kenny, Anthony. 1979. *Aristotle's Theory of the Will*. New Haven, CT: Yale UP.

King, C. Harold. 1933. "George Whitefield: Dramatic Evangelist." *Quarterly Journal of Speech* 19: 165–75.

Kinneavy, James L. 1971. *A Theory of Discourse: The Aims of Discourse*. Englewood Cliffs, NJ: Prentice Hall.

———. 1984. "Translating Theory into Practice in Teaching Composition: A Historical View and a Contemporary View." *Essays on Classical Rhetoric and Modern Discourse*. Ed. Robert J. Connors, Lisa S. Ede, and Andrea A. Lunsford. Carbondale: Southern Illinois UP. 69–81.

———. 1987. "William Grimaldi-Reinterpreting Aristotle." *Philosophy and Rhetoric* 20: 183–200.

———. 1990. "Contemporary Rhetoric." *The Present State of Scholarship in Historical and Contemporary Rhetoric*. Rev. ed. Ed. Winifred Bryan Horner. Columbia: U of Missouri P. 186–246.

Kirby, John T. 1997. "Aristotle on Metaphor." *American Journal of Philology* 118: 517–54.

Kosman, L. A. 1980. "Being Properly Affected: Virtues and Feelings in Aristotle's Ethics." *Essays on Aristotle's "Ethics."* Ed. Amélie O. Rorty. Berkeley: U of California P. 103–16.

Kuhn, Thomas S. 1970. *The Structure of Scientific Revolutions*. 2nd ed. International Encyclopedia of Unified Science. Chicago: U of Chicago P.

Lakoff, George, and Mark Johnson. 1980. *Metaphors We Live By*. Chicago: U of Chicago P.

Langholf, Volker. 1990. *Medical Theories in Hippocrates: Early Texts and the "Epidemics."* New York: Walter de Gruyter.

Lanigan, Richard L. 1973–84. "Enthymeme: The Rhetorical Species of Aristotle's Syllogism." *Southern Speech Communication Journal* 39: 207–22.

Lausberg, Heinrich. 1960. *Handbuch der Literarischen Rhetorik*. München: Max Hueber Verlag.

Leff, Michael C. 1983. "The Topics of Argumentative Invention in Latin Rhetorical Theory from Cicero to Boethius." *Rhetorica* 1: 23–44.

———. 1990. "Decorum and Rhetorical Interpretation: The Latin Humanist Tradition and Contemporary Critical Theory." *Vichiana* 1 (3rd ser.): 107–26.

———. 1993. "The Uses of Aristotle's *Rhetoric* in Contemporary American Scholarship." *Argumentation* 7: 313–27.

Leff, Michael C., and Gerald P. Mohrmann. 1974. "Lincoln at Cooper Union: A Rhetorical Analysis of the Text." *Quarterly Journal of Speech* 60: 346–58.

Leighton, Stephen R. 1996. "Aristotle and the Emotions." *Essays on Aristotle's "Rhetoric."* Ed. Amélie Oksenberg Rorty. Berkeley: U of California P. 206–37.

Leonard, Sterling A. 1917. *English Composition as a Social Problem.* Boston: Houghton.

Liberty Online. "The Works of Aristotle on Liberty Online." (http://libertyonline.hypermall.com/Aristotle/index.html).

Library of Congress Greek and Latin Classics Texts. (http://lcweb.loc.gov/global/classics/clastexts.html).

Liddell, Henry George, Robert Scott, and Henry Stuart Jones. 1968. *A Greek-English Lexicon.* Oxford: Clarendon.

Lienhard, Joseph T. 1966. "A Note on the Meaning of Pistis in Aristotle's *Rhetoric.*" *American Journal of Philology* 87: 446–54.

Lord, Carnes. 1981. "The Intention of Artistotle's *Rhetoric.*" *Hermes* 109: 326–39.

Lossau, Manfred. 1971. "*Mokhthêria tìn politeiôn* und *hupokrisis*: Zu Arist. Rhet. 3, 1, 1403 b34 f." *Rheinisches Museum* 3(114): 146–58.

———. 1981. *Pros krisin tina politiken, Untersuchungen zur aristotelischen Rhetorik.* Wiesbaden: O. Harrasowitz.

Lunsford, Andrea A., and Lisa S. Ede. 1984a. "Classical Rhetoric, Modern Rhetoric, and Contemporary Discourse Studies." *Written Communication* 1: 78–100.

———. 1984b. "On Distinctions Between Classical and Modern Rhetoric." *Essays on Classical Rhetoric and Modern Discourse.* Ed. by Robert J. Connors, Lisa S. Ede, and Andrea A. Lunsford. Carbondale: Southern Illinois UP. 37–49.

MacDowell, Douglas M. 1978. *The Law in Classical Athens.* London: Thames and Hudson.

MacIntyre, Alasdair. 1981. *After Virtue: A Study in Moral Theory.* Notre Dame, IN: U of Notre Dame P.

———. 1982."How Moral Agents Became Ghosts, or, Why the History of Ethics Diverged from That of Philosophy of Mind." *Synthese* 53: 295–312.

MacLean, Paul B. 1980. "Sensory and Perceptive Factors in Emotional Functions of the Triune Brain." *Explaining Emotions.* Ed. Amélie O. Rorty. Berkeley: U of California P. 9–36.

Maioragio, Marcantonio (Marcus Antonius Maiorgius, Maria Antonio de' Conti, 1514–55), trans. 1562. *Aristotelis artis rhetoricae libri tres* [1550]. *Aristotelis de rhetorica, et poetica libri, cum Averrois in eosdem paraphrasibvs, fols.* 1r–68v. Venice.

Manchester, Frederick A., Frank W. Scott, and Joseph M. Thomas. 1918. "Preliminary Report of the Special Committee on Freshman English." *English Journal* 7: 592–99.

Mayer, M. 1991. "Aristote et les principles de la rhétorique contémporaine." *Aristote. Rhétorique,* tr. Ch-E. Ruelle, revue P. Vanhemelryck, comm. B. Timmermans, 5-70. Livre de poche, 12. Paris: Librarie Générale Francaise.

McBurney, James H. 1936. "The Place of the Enthymeme in Rhetorical Theory." *Speech Monographs* 3: 49–74.

McCabe, Mary Margaret. 1994. "Arguments in Context: Aristotle's Defense of Rhetoric." *Aristotle's "Rhetoric": Philosophical Essays.* Ed. David J. Furley and Alexander Nehamas. Princeton: Princeton UP. 129–65.

McCall, Marsh. 1969. *Ancient Rhetorical Theories of Simile and Comparison.* Cambridge: Harvard UP.

McKeon, Richard. 1965. "Rhetoric and Poetic in Aristotle." *Aristotle's Poetics and English Literature: A Collection of Critical Essays.* Ed. Elder Olson. Chicago: U of Chicago P. 201–36.

———. 1971. "The Uses of Rhetoric in a Technological Age: Architectonic Productive Arts." *The Prospect of Rhetoric: Report of the National Development Project.* Ed. Edwin Black and Lloyd Bitzer. Englewood Cliffs, NJ: Prentice Hall. 44–63.

———. 1987. *Rhetoric: Essays in Invention and Discovery.* Ed. Mark Backman. Woodbridge: Ox Bow.

McNaughton, Neil. 1989. *Biology and Emotion.* Cambridge: Cambridge UP.

Mendell, Henry. 1987. "Topoi on Topos: The Development of Aristotle's Concept of Place." *Phronesis* 32(2): 206–31.

Miletich, John J. 1981. *Public Speaking: A Bibliography of Books 1955–1980.* Public Administration Series, Bibliography P-874. Monticello: Vance Bibliographies.

Mill, J. S. 1957. *Utilitarianism.* Indianapolis: Bobbs-Merrill.

Miller, Arthur B. 1974. "Aristotle on Habit *[ethos]* and Character *[êthos]:* Implications for the *Rhetoric.*" *Speech Monographs* 41: 309–16.

Miller, Arthur B., and John D. Bee. 1972. "Enthymemes: Body and Soul." *Philosophy and Rhetoric* : 201–14.

Miller, Carolyn R. 1987. "Aristotle's 'Special Topics' in Rhetorical Practice and Pedagogy." *Rhetoric Society Quarterly* 17: 61–70.

———. 1995. "Novelty, Decorum, and the Commodification of Invention in the Renaissance." Paper presented at the International Society for the History of Rhetoric, Edinburgh.

Miller, George. 1991. *The Science of Words.* New York: Scientific American.

Milton, John. 1644. *Of Education. To Master Samuel Hartlib.* London.

Moerbeke. See William of Moerbeke.

Mohrmann, G. P., and Michael C. Leff. 1974. "Lincoln at Cooper Union: A Rationale for Neo-Classical Criticism." *Quarterly Journal of Speech* 60: 459–67.

Monfasani, John. 1976. *George of Trebizond: A Biography and a Study of His Rhetoric and Logic.* Leiden: Brill.

Monroe, Alan H. 1935. *Principles and Types of Speech.* New York: Scott, Foresman.

Moran, Richard. 1996. "Artifice and Persuasion: The Work of Metaphor in the *Rhetoric.*" *Essays on Aristotle's "Rhetoric."* Ed. Amélie Oksenberg Rorty. Berkeley: U of California P. 385–98.

Most, Glenn W. 1994. "The Uses of Endoxa: Philosophy and Rhetoric in the *Rhetoric.*" *Aristotle's "Rhetoric:" Philosophical Essays.* Ed. David J. Furley and Alexander Nehamas. Princeton: Princeton UP. 167–99.

Mudd, Charles S. 1959. "The Enthymeme and Logical Validity." *Quarterly Journal of Speech* 45: 409–14.

Muret, Marc Antoine (Marcus Antonius Muretus, 1526–85). 1580. "Conatus emendandi duos locos è tertio libro Aristotelis De arte dicendi." *Variarvm lectionvm libri XV.* Antwerp.

———, trans. 1585. *Aristotelis rhetoricorum libri duo.* Books 1 and 2. Rome.

———. 1751. "Cum Aristotelis libros de arte rhetorica interpretari inciperet." [1576]. *Orationes, et epistolae, quae extant in Jacobi Thomasii editionibus, nec non praefationes in usum scholarum selectae. Tomus* I. Venice.

Murphy, James J. 1969. "The Scholastic Condemnation of Rhetoric in the Commentary of Giles of Rome on the *Rhetoric* of Aristotle." *Arts libéraux et philosophie au moyen âge.* 4th Congrès International de Philosophie Médiévale, Montréal 1967, 833–41. Montréal: Institute D'études Médiévales; Paris: Librarie Philosophique J. Vrin.

———. 1982. "Rhetorical History as a Guide to the Salvation of American Reading and Writing: A Plea for Curricular Courage." *The Rhetorical Tradition and Modern Writing*. Ed. James J. Murphy. New York: MLA. 3–12.

Natali, Carlo. 1994. "La 'Retorica' di Aristotele negli studi europei più recenti." *Peripatetic Rhetoric after Aristotle*. Ed. William W. Fortenbaugh and David C. Mirhady. Rutgers University Studies in Classical Humanities, Vol. 6. New Brunswick: Transaction. 365–82.

Neel, Jasper. 1994. *Aristotle's Voice: Rhetoric, Theory, and Writing in America*. Carbondale: Southern Illinois UP.

Nehamas, Alexander. 1994. "Pity and Fear in the *Rhetoric* and the *Poetics*." *Aristotle's "Rhetoric": Philosophical Essays*. Ed. David J. Furley and Alexander Nehamas. Princeton: Princeton UP. 257–82.

Newell, Allen, and Herbert A. Simon. 1972. *Human Problem Solving*. Englewood Cliffs, NJ: Prentice Hall.

Nimis, Steve. 1988. "Aristotle's Analogical Metaphor." *Arethusa* 21: 215–26.

Nothstine, William L. 1988. "'Topics' as Ontological Metaphor in Contemporary Rhetorical Theory and Criticism." *Quarterly Journal of Speech* 74(2): 151–63.

Nussbaum, Martha Craven. 1996. "Aristotle on Emotions and Rational Persuasion." *Essays on Aristotle's "Rhetoric."* Ed. Amélie Oksenberg Rorty. Berkeley: U of California P. 303–23.

Ober, Josiah. 1989. *Mass and Elite in Democratic Athens: Rhetoric, Ideology, and the Power of the People*. Princeton: Princeton UP.

Ochs, Donovan J. 1969. "Aristotle's Concept of Formal Topics." *Speech Monographs* 36: 419–25. Reprinted in Erickson.

O'Donnell, J. R. 1969. "The Commentary of Giles of Rome on the *Rhetoric* of Aristotle." *Essays in Medieval History Presented to Bertie Wilkinson*. Ed. T. A. Sandquist and M. R. Powicke. Toronto: U of Toronto P. 139–56.

Olian, J. Robert. 1968. "The Intended Uses of Aristotle's *Rhetoric*." *Speech Monographs* 35: 137–48.

Ong, Walter J. 1983. *Ramus: Method, and the Decay of Dialogue*. Cambridge: Harvard UP.

O'Rourke, Sean Patrick. 1996. "Modes of Discourse." *Encyclopedia of Rhetoric and Composition: Communication from Ancient Times to the Information Age*. Ed. Theresa Enos. New York: Garland. 446–47.

Palmer, Georgiana Paine. 1932. "The Topoi of Aristotle's *Rhetoric* as Exemplified in the Orators." Doctoral dissertation, University of Chicago.

Papadimitriou, Euthymios. 1979. *Ethische und psychologische Grundlagen der aristotelischen Rhetorik*. Frankfurt am Main: P. Lang.

Parks, Katherine. 1988. "The Organic Soul." *Cambridge History of Renaissance Philosophy*. Ed. Charles B. Schmitt, Quentin Skinner, and Eckhard Kessler. Cambridge: Cambridge UP. 464–84.

Parrish, Wayland Maxfield. 1954. "The Study of Speeches." *American Speeches*. Ed. Wayland M. Parrish and Marie Hochmuth. New York: Longmans, Green. 1–20.

Pascal, Blaise. 1952. *Pensées*. Trans. W. F. Trotter. Vol. 33, *Great Books of the Western World*. Chicago: Encyclopedia Britannica. 169–352.

———. 1966. *Pensées*. Trans. A. J. Krailsheimer. London: Penguin.

Penn Library-Journals/Classical Studies. (http://www.library.upenn.edu/resources/ej/ej-classics.html).

Perelman, Chaim. 1963. *The Idea of Justice and the Problem of Argument*. Trans. John Petrie. London: Routledge.

———. 1982. *The Realm of Rhetoric.* Trans. W. Kluback. Notre Dame, IN: U of Notre Dame P.

———. 1990. "The New Rhetoric: A Theory of Practical Reasoning." 1970. *The Rhetorical Tradition.* Ed. Patricia Bizzell and Bruce Herzberg. Boston: St. Martin's. 1077–103.

Perelman, Chaim, and Lucie Olbrechts-Tyteca. 1950. "Logique et rhétorique." *Revue Philosophique de la France et de L'Étranger* 140: 1–35. Reprinted in 1952. *Rhétorique et Philosophie. Pour une Théorie de L'Argumentation en Philosophie.* Paris: Presses Universitaires de France. 1–43.

———. 1958. *Traité de l'argumentation. La nouvelle rhétorique.* 2 Vols. Paris: Presses Universitaires de France.

———. 1969. *The New Rhetoric: A Treatise on Argumentation.* Trans. John Wilkinson and Purcell Weaver. Notre Dame, IN: U of Notre Dame P.

Perseus Project Home Page. (http://medusa.perseus.tufts.edu/).

Peters, F. E. 1967. *Greek Philosophical Terms: A Historical Lexicon.* New York: New York UP.

Philippe, M. D. 1971. "Phantasia in the Philosophy of Aristotle." *Thomist* 35: 1–42.

Philodemus of Gadara. 1964. *Volumina Rhetorica.* 2 Vols. and Supp. Ed. Siegfried Sudhaus. Amsterdam: Hakkert.

Plato. 1914. *Phaedrus.* Loeb Classical Library.

———. 1961. *The Collected Dialogues.* Ed. Edith Hamilton and Huntington Cairns. Princeton: Princeton UP.

———. 1979. *Phaedrus.* Trans. R. Hackforth. Cambridge UP.

Plebe, Armando. 1988. *Manuale di retorica.* Universale Laterza, 27. Roma: Laterza.

Plett, Heinrich F. 1975. *Rhetorik der Affekte: Englische Wirkungsästhetik im Zeitalter der Renaissance.* Studien zur englishchen Philologie, NF, 18. Tübingen: Niemeyer.

Poster, Carol. 1992. "A Historicist Recontextualization of the Enthymeme." *Rhetoric Society Quarterly* 22 (2): 1–24.

———. 1996. "Being and Becoming: Rhetorical Ontology in Early Greek Thought." *Philosophy and Rhetoric* 29: 1–14.

———. 1997. "Aristotle's *Rhetoric* Against Rhetoric: Unitarian Reading and Esoteric Hermeneutics." *American Journal of Philology* 118: 219–49.

Poulakos, John. 1984. "Rhetoric, the Sophists, and the Possible." *Communication Monographs* 51: 215–26.

Project Muse. (http://muse.jhu.edu/muse.html).

Quandahl, Ellen. 1986. "Aristotle's *Rhetoric:* Reinterpreting Invention." *Rhetoric Review* 4: 128–37.

Quinn, Warren. 1992. "Rationality and the Human Good." *Social Philosophy and Policy* 9: 81–95.

Quintilian. 1920. *Institutio Oratoria.* Trans. H. E. Butler. 4 Vols. Loeb Classical Library.

Raimondi, E. 1984. "Retorica e linguaggio letterario." *Linguaggio, persuasione, verità.* Atti del XXVIII Congresso Nazionale di Filosofia, Verona 28.4-1.5.1983. Ed. Societa filosofica italiana. Padova: Casa Editrice Dr. A. Milani. 83–99.

Rainolds, John (Joannes Rainoldus, 1549–1607). *Aristotelis rhetorica.* See Green, Lawrence D., 1986.

Ramus, Petrus (Peter Ramus, 1515–72), and Audomarus Talaeus. 1599. *Collectaneae praefationes, epistolae, orationes.* Marburg.

Raphael, Sally. 1974. "Rhetoric, Dialectic, and Syllogistic Argument: Aristotle's Position in *Rhetoric* I.1." *Phronesis* 19: 153–67.

Rawls, John. 1971. *A Theory of Justice.* Cambridge: Harvard UP.

Raymond, James C. 1984. "Enthymemes, Examples, and Rhetorical Method." *Essays on Classical Rhetoric and Modern Discourse.* Ed. Robert J. Connors, Lisa S. Ede, and Andrea A. Lunsford. Carbondale: Southern Illinois UP. 140–51.

Reddy, Michael J. 1979. "The Conduit Metaphor—A Case of Frame Conflict in Our Language about Language." *Metaphor and Thought.* Ed. Andrew Ortony. Cambridge: Cambridge UP. 284–324.

Rees, D. A. 1971. "Aristotle's Treatment of *Phantasia.*" *Essays in Ancient Greek Philosophy.* Ed. John P. Anton, with George L. Kustas. Albany: State U of New York P. 491–504.

Reeve, C. D. C. 1996. "Philosophy, Politics, and Rhetoric in Aristotle." *Essays on Aristotle's "Rhetoric."* Ed. Amélie Oksenberg Rorty. Berkeley: U of California P. 191–205.

Reynolds, L. D., and N. G. Wilson. 1991. *Scribes and Scholars: A Guide to the Transmission of Greek and Latin Literature.* 3rd ed. Oxford: Clarendon.

Riccoboni, Antonio (Marcus Antonius Riccobonus, 154–99), ed. and trans. 1606a. *Aristotelis artis rhetoricae libri tres* [1579]. Hanau.

———. 1606b. *Paraphrasis in rhetoricam Aristotelis, interiecta rerum difficiliorum explicatione, & collata ipsius Riccoboni multis in locis conversione, cum Maioragii, Sigonii, Victorii, Mureti conversionibus* [1587]. Hanau.

Rich, Charles, Richard C. Waters, and Howard B. Reubenstein. 1987. "Toward a Requirements Apprentice." P*roceedings of the 4th International Workshop on Software Specification and Design,* April 3–4. Washington, DC: Computer Society Press of the IEEE. 79–86.

Ricoeur, Paul. 1969. *Le Conflit des interpretations.* Paris: Editions du Seuil.

———. 1981. *Hermeneutics and the Human Sciences: Essays on Language, Action, and Interpretation.* Cambridge: Cambridge UP; Paris: Editions de la Maison des sciences de l'homme.

Rist, John M. 1971. "Notes on Aristotle *De anima* 3.5." *Essays in Ancient Greek Philosophy.* Ed. John P. Anton with George L. Kustas. Albany: State U of New York P. 505–21.

———. 1989. *The Mind of Aristotle: A Study in Philosophical Growth.* Toronto: U of Toronto.

Robortello, Franceso (Franciscus Robortellus, 1516–67).1548. *In librum Aristoteis de arte poetica explicationes.* Florence.

Rorty, Amélie Oksenberg. 1980. "Explaining Emotions." *Explaining Emotions.* Ed. Amélie O. Rorty. Berkeley: U of California P. 103–26.

———. 1984. "Aristotle on the Metaphysical Status of Pathê." *Review of Metaphysics* 37: 521–46.

———, ed. 1996. *Essays on Aristotle's "Rhetoric".* Berkeley: U of California P.

Ross, David. 1964 [1923]. *Aristotle.* 5th ed. London: Methuen.

Rossi, Paolo. 1970. *Philosophy, Technology, and the Arts in the Early Modern Era.* Trans. Salvator Attanasio. New York: Harper Torchbooks.

Rowland, Robert C., and Deanna F. Womack. 1985. "Aristotle's View of Ethical Rhetoric." *Rhetoric Society Quarterly* 15: 13–31.

Ryan, Eugene E. 1984. *Aristotle's Theory of Rhetorical Argumentation.* Montreal: Les êditions Bellarmin.

Scenters-Zapico, J. 1994. "The Social Construct of Enthymematic Understanding." *Rhetoric Society Quarterly* 24: 71–87.

Schenkeveld, Dirk M. 1994. "*Ta asteia* in Aristotle's *Rhetoric:* The Disappearance of a

Category." *Peripatetic Rhetoric after Aristotle*. Ed. William W. Fortenbaugh and David C. Mirhady. Rutgers University Studies in Classical Humanities, Vol. 6. New Brunswick: Transaction. 1–14.

Schiappa, Edward. 1990. "Neo-Sophistic Rhetorical Criticism or the Historical Reconstruction of Sophistic Doctrines?" *Philosophy and Rhetoric* 23: 192–217.

———, ed. 1994. *Landmark Essays on Classical Greek Rhetoric*. Davis: Hermagoras.

Schleiermacher, Friedrich. 1838. *Hermeneutik und Kritik mit besonderer Beziehung auf das Neue Testament*. Friedrich Schleiermacher's sammtliche Werke, 1. Abt., 7. Bd. Berlin: Reimer. Reprinted in 1977. Ed. Heinz Kimmerle. Trans. James Duke and Jack Forstman. *Hermeneutics: The Handwritten Manuscripts, Texts and Translation Series*. American Academy of Religion, No. 1. Missoula: American Academy of Religion.

Schütrumpf, Eckart. 1993. "The Model for the Concept of Ethos in Aristotle's *Rhetoric*." *Philologus* 137: 12–17.

———. 1994. "Some Observations on the Introduction to Aristotle's *Rhetoric*." *Aristotle's "Rhetoric": Philosophical Essays*. Ed. David J. Furley and Alexander Nehamas. Princeton: Princeton UP. 99–116.

Scott, Robert L. 1967. "On Viewing Rhetoric as Epistemic." *Central States Speech Journal* 18: 9–17.

Scott, Robert L., James R. Andrews, Howard H. Martin, J. Richard McNally, William F. Nelson, Michael M. Osborn, Arthur L. Smith, and Harold Zyskind. 1971. "Report of the Committee on the Nature of Rhetorical Invention." *The Prospect of Rhetoric: Report of the National Developmental Project*. Ed. Lloyd F. Bitzer and Edwin Black. Englewood Cliffs, NJ: Prentice Hall. 228–36.

Searle, John R. 1969. *Speech Acts: An Essay in the Philosophy of Language*. London: Cambridge UP.

———. 1983. *Intentionality: An Essay in the Philosophy of Mind*. Cambridge: Cambridge UP.

———. 1992. *The Rediscovery of the Mind*. Cambridge: MIT P.

Self, Lois. 1979. "Rhetoric and Phronesis: The Aristotelian Ideal." *Philosophy and Rhetoric* 12: 130–45.

Shklar, Judith. 1984. *Ordinary Vices*. Cambridge: Harvard UP.

Sigonio, Carlo (Carolus Sigonius, 1524–84), trans. 1565. *De arte rhetorica libri tres*. Bologna.

Simrell, V. E. 1927. "H. L. Mencken the Rhetorician." *Quarterly Journal of Speech* 13: 399–412.

Skinner, Quentin. 1988. "Language and Social Change." *Meaning and Context: Quentin Skinner and His Critics* Ed. James Tully. Princeton: Princeton UP. 119–32.

Smith, Robert W. 1974. *The Art of Rhetoric in Alexandria: Its Theory and Practice in the Ancient World*. The Hague: Martinus Nijhoff.

Smith, Robin. 1994. "Dialectic and Syllogism." *Ancient Philosophy* (Special Issue) 14: 133–51.

Solmsen, Friedrich. 1929. *Die Enwicklung der aristotelischen Logik und Rhetorik*. Berlin: Weidmann.

———. 1938. "Aristotle and Cicero on the Orator's Playing Upon the Feelings." *Classical Philology* 33: 390–404.

———. 1941. "The Aristotelian Tradition in Ancient Rhetoric." *American Journal of Philology* 62: 35–50, 165–90.

Solomon, Robert C. 1976. *The Passions*. Garden City: Anchor/Doubleday.

Sprute, Jürgen. 1994. "Aristotle and the Legitimacy of Rhetoric." *Aristotle's "Rhetoric": Philosophical Essays*. Ed. David J. Furley and Alexander Nehamas. Princeton: Princeton UP. 117–28.

Stewart, Charles J. 1973. "Historical Survey: Rhetorical Criticism in Twentieth Century America." *Explorations in Rhetorical Criticism*. Ed. G. P. Mohrmann, Charles J. Stewart, and Donovan J. Ochs. University Park: Pennsylvania State UP. 1–31.

Stocker, Michael. 1983. "Affectivity and Self-Concern: The Assumed Psychology of Aristotle's Ethics." *Pacific Philosophical Quarterly* 64: 211–29.

Striker, Gisela. 1996. "Emotions in Context: Aristotle's Treatment of the Passions in the *Rhetoric* and His Moral Psychology." *Essays on Aristotle's "Rhetoric."* Ed. Amélie Oksenberg Rorty. Berkeley: U of California P. 286–302.

Sturm, Johann (Joannes Sturmius, 1507–89), ed. and trans. 1570a. *Aristotelis rhetoricorum libri III. Latinvm sermonem conuersi, & scholis breuioribus explicati à Ioanne Sturmio* Strasbourg.

———, ed. and trans. 1570b. *Hermogenis Tarsensis rhetoris acvtissimi Partitionum rhetoricum liber vnus, qui vulgï De statibus inscribitur*. Strasbourg.

———, ed. and trans. 1571. *Hermogenis Tarsensis rhetoris acvtissimi De dicendi generibvs siue formis orationum libri II*. Strasbourg.

———. 1574. *De universa ratione elocutionis rhetoricae libri IIII*. Ed. Christophorus Thretius. Strasbourg.

Suarez, Cipriano (Cyprianus Soarius, 1524–93). 1569. *De arte rhetorica libri tres, ex Aristotele, Cicerone, et Quinctiliane praecipue deprompti*. Venice.

Sutton, Jane. 1986. "The Death of Rhetoric and Its Rebirth in Philosophy." *Rhetorica* 4: 203–26.

———. 1991. "Rereading Sophistical Arguments: A Political Intervention." *Argumentation* 5: 141–57.

Swearingen, C. Jan. 1994. "Ethos: Imitation, Impersonation, and Voice." *Ethos: New Essays in Rhetorical and Critical Theory*. Ed. James S. Baumlin and Tita French Baumlin. Dallas: Southern Methodist UP.

Sweetser, Eve. 1990. *From Etymology to Pragmatics: Metaphorical and Cultural Aspects of Semantic Structure*. Cambridge: Cambridge UP.

Swiggers, Pierre. 1984. "Cognitive Aspects of Aristotle's Theory of Metaphor." *Glotta* 62: 40–45.

Tables of Contents of Journals of Interest to Classicists. (http://www.chass.utoronto.ca:8080/amphoras/tocs.html).

Talaeus, Audomarus (Omer Talon, 1510–62). See Ramus, Petrus.

Thesaurus Linguae Graecae: Canon of Greek Authors and Works . 1990. Ed. Luci Berkowitz and Karl A. Squitier. New York: Oxford UP.

Thonssen, Lester, and A. Craig Baird. 1948. *Speech Criticism: The Development of Standards for Rhetorical Appraisal*. New York: Ronald.

Thucydides. 1954. *History of the Peloponnesian War*. Trans. Rex. Warner. London: Penguin.

Timmerman, David M. 1993. "Ancient Greek Origins of Argumentation Theory: Plato's Transformation of Dialegesthai to Dialectic." *Argumentation and Advocacy* 29: 116–123.

Tomkins, Silvan. 1995. *Exploring Affect: The Selected Writings of Silvan Tomkins*. Ed. E. Virginia Demos. Cambridge: Cambridge UP.

Too, Yun Lee. 1995. *The Rhetoric of Identity in Isocrates: Text, Power, Pedagogy*. Cambridge: Cambridge UP.

Toulmin, Stephen Edelston. 1958. *The Uses of Argument.* Cambridge: Cambridge UP.
Trebizond. See George of Trebizond.
Vancil, David L. 1979. "Historical Barriers to a Modern System of Topoi." *Western Journal of Speech Communication* 43: 26–37.
van Eemeren. See Eemeren, Frans H. van.
Vattimo, G. "Verità e retorica." *Linguaggio, persuasione, verità.* Atti del XXVIII Congresso Nazionale di Filosofia, Verona 28.4-1.5.1983. Ed. Societa filosofica italiana. Padova: Casa Editrice Dr. A. Milani. 145–56.
Vettori, Piero (Petrus Victorius, 1499–1585). 1548. *Commentarii in tres libros Aristotelis de arte dicendi.* Florence.
Vickers, Brian. 1988. *In Defence of Rhetoric.* Oxford: Clarendon.
Vincent, Jean-Didier. 1990. *The Biology of Emotions.* Trans. John Hughes. Oxford: Basil Blackwell.
Vincenti, Walter G. 1990. *What Engineers Know and How They Know It: Analytical Studies from Aeronautical History.* Baltimore: Johns Hopkins UP.
Vitanza, Victor. 1987–88. "Critical Sub/Versions of the History of Philosophical Rhetoric." *Rhetoric Review* 6: 41–66.
Vives, Juan Luis (Joannes Lodovicus Vives, 1492–1540). 1531. "De corrupta rhetorica." *De causis corruptibus artium. De disciplinis libri XX.* Antwerp.
Walbank, F. W. 1981. *The Hellenistic World.* Oxford: Oxford UP.
Walker, Jeffrey. 1990. "Of Brains and Rhetorics." *College English* 52(3): 301–22.
———. 1992."Enthymemes of Anger in Cicero and Thomas Paine." *Constructing Rhetorical Education.* Ed. Marie Secor and Davida Charney. Carbondale: Southern Illinois UP. 357–81.
———. 1994. "The Body of Persuasion: A Theory of the Enthymeme." *College English* 56(1): 46–65.
Wallace, Karl R. 1953. "On the Criticism of the MacArthur Speech." *Quarterly Journal of Speech* 39: 69–74.
———. 1954. "The Field of Speech, 1953: An Overview." *Quarterly Journal of Speech* 40: 117–29.
Wallace, William A. 1986. "Aitia: Causal Reasoning in Composition and Rhetoric." *Rhetoric and Praxis: The Contribution of Classical Rhetoric to Practical Reasoning.* Ed. Jean Dietz Moss. Washington, DC: Catholic U of America P. 107–33.
Walzer, Arthur. 1997. "Aristotle's *Rhetoric,* Dialogism, and Contemporary Research in Composition." *Rhetoric Review* 16: 45–57.
Wardy, Robert. 1996. "Mighty Is the Truth and It Shall Prevail?" *Essays on Aristotle's "Rhetoric."* Ed. Amélie Oksenberg Rorty. Berkeley: U of California P. 56–87.
Warnick, Barbara. 1989. "Judgment, Probability, and Aristotle's *Rhetoric.*" *Quarterly Journal of Speech* 75: 299–311.
———. 1996. "Argument Schemes and the Construction of Social Reality: John F. Kennedy's Address to the Houston Ministerial Association." *Communication Quarterly* 44: 183–96.
Warnick, Barbara, and Susan L. Kline. 1992. "The New Rhetoric's Argument Schemes: A Rhetorical View of Practical Reasoning." *Argumentation and Advocacy* 29: 1–15.
Wartelle, André. 1982. *Lexique de la "Rhétorique" d'Aristote.* L'Association Guillaume Budé. Paris: Les Belles Lettres.
Watson, Gerard. 1982. "*Phantasia* in Aristotle, *De anima* 3.3." *Classical Quarterly* 32: 100–113.

Weaver, Andrew Thomas. 1942. *Speech: Forms and Principles.* New York: Longmans, Green.

Weber, Robert J., and David N. Perkins. 1989. "How to Invent Artifacts and Ideas." *New Ideas in Psychology* 7(1): 49–72.

Wehrli, Fritz. 1968. *Die Schule Des Aristoteles.* Vol. 4. Demetrios von Phaleron. Basel: Schwabe.

Welch, Kathleen E. 1990. *The Contemporary Reception of Classical Rhetoric: Appropriations of Ancient Discourse.* Hillsdale, NJ: Lawrence Erlbaum.

Wellek, René. 1986. *American Criticism, 1900–1950.* Vol. 6, *A History of Modern Criticism: 1750–1950.* New Haven, CT: Yale UP.

White, Eric Charles. 1987. *Kaironomia: On the Will to Invent.* Ithaca, NY: Cornell UP.

Wichelns, Herbert A. 1925. "The Literary Criticism of Oratory." *Studies in Rhetoric and Public Speaking in Honor of James Albert Winans.* Ed. A. M. Drummond. New York: Century. 181–216.

Wiley, Earl W. 1956. "The Enthymeme: Idiom of Persuasion." *Quarterly Journal of Speech* 42: 19–24.

William of Moerbeke, trans. 1978. *Translatio Guillelmi de Moerbeka* [13th C]. Ed. Bernd Schneider. *Rhetorica: Translatio sive Vetus et Translatio Guillelmi de Moerbeka.* Aristoteles Latinus, Vol. XXXI 1–2. Leiden: Brill.

Williams, Bernard. 1979. "Internal and External Reasons." *Rational Action.* Ed. Ross Harrison. Cambridge: Cambridge UP. 17–28.

———. 1985. *Ethics and the Limits of Philosophy.* Cambridge: Harvard UP.

Wisse, Jakob. 1989. *Ethos and Pathos from Aristotle to Cicero.* Amsterdam: Hakkert.

Woolbert, Charles Henry. 1920. *The Fundamentals of Speech, A Behavioral Study of the Underlying Principles of Speaking and Reading, A Text Book of Delivery.* New York: Harper and Brothers.

Wôrner, Markus H. 1981. "'Pathos' als Überzeugungsmittel in der Rhetorik des Aristoteles." *Pathos, Affekt, Gefühl.* Ed. Ingrid Craemer-Ruegenberg. Freiberg/München: Verlag Karl Alber GmbH. 53–78.

———. 1990. *Das Ethische in der Rhetorik des Aristoteles.* Alber-Reihe praktische Philosophie 33. Freiburg/München: Verlag Karl Alber GmbH.

Worthington, Katharine Stewart. 1916. "The Classical Loss in Modern English Democratic Rhetoric." *English Journal* 5: 525–29.

Wu, Hiu. 1997. "The Enthymeme Examined from the Chinese Value System." *Making and Unmaking the Prospects for Rhetoric: Selected Papers from the 1996 Rhetoric Society of America Conference.* Ed. Theresa Enos. Mahwah: Lawrence Erlbaum. 115–22.

Young, Richard. 1976. "Invention: A Topographical Survey." *Teaching Composition: 10 Bibliographical Essays.* Ed. Gary Tate. Fort Worth: Texas Christian UP. 1–43.

Young, Richard, Alton L. Becker, and Kenneth L. Pike. 1970. *Rhetoric: Discovery and Change.* New York: Harcourt, Brace and World.

Zulick, Margaret D. 1997. "Generative Rhetoric and Public Argument: A Classical Approach." *Argumentation and Advocacy* 33: 109–119.

Contributors

Jeanne Fahnestock is a professor in the Department of English at the University of Maryland, where she has served as the director of Professional Writing and of the writing programs. She has published articles and chapters on Victorian fiction, argumentation, stasis theory, coherence, and the rhetoric of science and, with Marie Secor, has coauthored a text, *A Rhetoric of Argument.* Her study of key figures of speech in scientific argument, *Rhetorical Figures in Science*, was published in 1999.

Thomas B. Farrell is a professor of rhetoric and political communication at Northwestern University. He has published over seventy articles and monographs dealing with rhetoric and public culture. In 1990, Farrell received the Charles H. Woolbert Award for scholarship of exceptional originality and influence. His study of modernity and the rhetorical tradition, *Norms of Rhetorical Culture*, won the 1994 Winans-Wichelns Award for distinguished scholarship in rhetoric and public address. Farrell's collection, *Landmarks in Contemporary Rhetorical Theory*, appeared in 1998. Farrell is interested in the ways public symbols, images, and figures channel our participation toward partisan ends and collective projects.

Robert N. Gaines is an associate professor of communication at the University of Maryland. His research is principally concerned with the individuals and intellectual forces that shaped rhetorical theory in ancient times. He has published a number of essays that touch upon Hellenic rhetoric, especially in Isocrates, Plato, and Aristotle, but his most recent research has addressed the relation of rhetoric to philosophy in the Hellenistic era—particularly in the works of Cicero and Philodemus. He is currently at work on a critical edition and translation of Philodemus's *On Rhetoric*, Book 4.

Eugene Garver is Regents Professor of Philosophy at Saint John's University. He is the author of *Machiavelli and the History of Prudence* and *Aristotle's "Rhetoric": An Art of Character*. His work is designed to contribute to the history of prudence, that is, the history of good uses of practical reason, with special attention to the place of rhetoric in arguments about those good uses. His writings center on the relation between argument and character, and so among logic, rhetoric, and ethics and politics. Among his works in progress are explorations of the implications of his reading of Aristotle's *Rhetoric* for Aristotle's ethics and politics and the implications of all of them for contemporary practice.

Lawrence D. Green is a professor of English at the University of Southern California, where he teaches history of rhetoric, Renaissance literature, and Renaissance philosophy. He is the author of *John Rainolds's Oxford Lectures on Aristotle's "Rhetoric"* and *Rhetoric 1500–1700* in the *Cambridge Bibliography of English Literature* and has published many articles in Europe and North America on Renaissance understandings of Aristotle, Cicero, and rhetoric, including most recently "Making Aristotle's *Rhetoric* Methodical," "Aristotle's *Rhetoric* and Renaissance Conceptions of the Soul," and "Aristotle's Enthymeme and the Imperfect Syllogism." He is a frequent speaker at conferences and has received numerous awards, including fellowships from the National Endowment for the Humanities and the American Council of Learned Societies.

Alan G. Gross is a professor of rhetoric at the University of Minnesota–Twin Cities. He is the author of *The Rhetoric of Science* and of *Starring the Text: The Place of Rhetoric in Science Studies*. He is a coauthor of *Communication Science: The Scientific Article from the 17th Century to the Present* and of *Chaim Perelman*. He is a coeditor of *Rhetorical Hermeneutics: Invention and Interpretation in the Age of Science* and of *The Scientific Literature: A Guided Tour*. An article about Aristotle, "The Conceptual Unity of Artistotle's *Rhetoric*," which he wrote with Marcelo Dascal, appeared in *Philosophy and Rhetoric* in 2001.

Carolyn R. Miller is a professor of English at North Carolina State University. Her primary interests are rhetorical theory and rhetorical analysis, particularly as applied to scientific and technical discourse. She has published essays in the *Quarterly Journal of Speech*, *Rhetoric Society Quarterly*, *Argumentation*, and *Rhetorica*, as well as in several edited volumes, and has received an NEH Fellowship to work on a book about the rhetoric of high technology. She was the 1996–98 president of the Rhetoric Society of America.

Michael Tiffany is currently a doctoral candidate in classics at the University of Minnesota. His dissertation in progress is "*Energeia* and Aristotle's *Rhetoric:* Visual Imaging in the Theory and Practice of Ancient Rhetoric."

Jeffrey Walker is an associate professor of English at Pennsylvania State University and will be moving to Emory University in Fall of 2000. His scholarly interests include rhetoric and poetics (both ancient and modern), the history of rhetoric, and American literature; his publications include *Bardic Ethos and the American Epic Poem*, "Aristotle's Lyric: Re-Imagining the Rhetoric of Epideictic Song," "Enthymemes of Anger in Cicero and Thomas Paine," "The Body of Persuasion: A Theory of the Enthymeme," "Before the Beginnings of 'Poetry' and 'Rhetoric': Hesiod on Eloquence," and other articles and reviews. Walker recently was a Fulbright lecturer at the University of Athens. His most recent book is *Rhetoric and Poetics in Antiquity*.

Arthur E. Walzer is a professor in writing studies at the University of Minnesota. He is the author of *George Campbell: Rhetoric in the Age of Enlightenment* and a coeditor, with Richard Graff and Janet Atwill, of *The Viability of the Rhetorical Tradition*. His essays have appeared in *Rhetorica, Rhetoric Society Quarterly, Quarterly Journal of Speech, Rhetoric Review*, and other journals.

Barbara Warnick is a professor of speech communication and chairs that department at the University of Washington. She has also taught at Tulane University. Her areas of teaching and research interest are the history of rhetorical theory and argumentation theory. Her current interest is in how narrative and argument structures in texts operate rhetorically. Her book, *The Sixth Canon: Belletristic Rhetorical Theory and Its French Antecedents,* examines the metamorphosis of invention in seventeenth- and eighteenth-century rhetorical theories. She has served as editor of the *Quarterly Journal of Speech.*

Index

Rhetorical Terms

Writers